# CHANGING PARADIGMS IN HISTORICAL
# AND SYSTEMATIC THEOLOGY

*General Editors*
*Sarah Coakley    Richard Cross*

This series sets out to reconsider the modern distinction between "historical" and "systematic" theology. The scholarship represented in the series is marked by attention to the way in which historiographic and theological presumptions ("paradigms") necessarily inform the work of historians of Christian thought, and thus affect their application to contemporary concerns. At certain key junctures such paradigms are recast, causing a reconsideration of the methods, hermeneutics, geographical boundaries, or chronological caesuras which have previously guided the theological narrative. The beginning of the twenty-first century marks a period of such notable reassessment of the Christian doctrinal heritage, and involves a questioning of the paradigms that have sustained the classic "history-of-ideas" textbook accounts of the modern era. Each of the volumes in this series brings such contemporary methodological and historiographical concerns to conscious consideration. Each tackles a period or key figure whose significance is ripe for reconsideration, and each analyses the implicit historiography that has sustained existing scholarship on the topic. A variety of fresh methodological concerns are considered, without reducing the theological to other categories. The emphasis is on an awareness of the history of "reception": the possibilities for contemporary theology are bound up with a careful rewriting of the historical narrative. In this sense, "historical" and "systematic" theology are necessarily conjoined, yet also closely connected to a discerning interdisciplinary engagement.

This monograph series accompanies the project of *The Oxford Handbook of the Reception of Christian Theology* (Oxford University Press, in progress), also edited by Sarah Coakley and Richard Cross.

# CHANGING PARADIGMS IN HISTORICAL AND SYSTEMATIC THEOLOGY

*General Editors: Sarah Coakley (Norris-Hulse Professor of Divinity, University of Cambridge) and Richard Cross (John A. O'Brien Professor of Philosophy, University of Notre Dame)*

RECENT SERIES TITLES

Newman and the Alexandrian Fathers
*Shaping Doctrine in Nineteenth-Century England*
**Benjamin J. King**

Orthodox Readings of Aquinas
**Marcus Plested**

Kant and the Creation of Freedom
*A Theological Problem*
**Christopher J. Insole**

Blaise Pascal on Duplicity, Sin, and the Fall
*The Secret Instinct*
**William Wood**

Theology as Science in Nineteenth-Century Germany
*From F. C. Baur to Ernst Troeltsch*
**Johannes Zachhuber**

Georges Florovsky and the Russian Religious Renaissance
**Paul L. Gavrilyuk**

Knowledge, Love, and Ecstasy in the Theology of Thomas Gallus
**Boyd Taylor Coolman**

# God Visible

*Patristic Christology Reconsidered*

BRIAN E. DALEY, SJ

**OXFORD**
UNIVERSITY PRESS

# OXFORD
### UNIVERSITY PRESS

Great Clarendon Street, Oxford, OX2 6DP,
United Kingdom

Oxford University Press is a department of the University of Oxford.
It furthers the University's objective of excellence in research, scholarship,
and education by publishing worldwide. Oxford is a registered trade mark of
Oxford University Press in the UK and in certain other countries

© Brian E. Daley, SJ 2018

Published in the United States of America by Oxford University Press
198 Madison Avenue, New York, NY 10016, United States of America

British Library Cataloguing in Publication Data
Data available

Library of Congress Control Number: 2017940828

ISBN 978-0-19-928133-6

Printed and bound by
CPI Group (UK) Ltd, Croydon, CR0 4YY

*For my Brothers in the Company of Jesus*

# Preface

This book has been developing for a long time. My own early interest in the Church Fathers, which began during my days as an undergraduate at Fordham University in the late 1950s and early 1960s and was then shaped further as an Oxford undergraduate, finally was given direction and focus ten years later, when I studied theology, as a Jesuit scholastic preparing for ordination, at the Hochschule Sankt Georgen in Frankfurt-am-Main. There, in a richly designed curriculum, with an outstanding faculty teaching us, I had the good fortune of studying the Fathers with Aloys Grillmeier, S.J., whose great, unfinished survey of Patristic Christology, *Christ in Christian Tradition* (1975– ), remains the foundation of modern theological understanding of how early Christians interpreted the person of Jesus. After five fruitful years at Skt. Georgen, I happily went back to Oxford to do a doctorate, and at the suggestion of Fr. Grillmeier and the Abbé Marcel Richard—whom I first met in an Oxford pub during the Patristic Conference of 1971—critically edited, as my doctoral thesis, the works of the sixth-century apologist for the Christology of Chalcedon, Leontius of Byzantium. All of this focused my attention increasingly on the central doctrinal tradition of the early Church: the understanding of Christ, Son of God and Savior, as it was continually refined by theologians and councils, from the beginnings of Christian theological reflection, in the decades after the completion of the New Testament writings, until at least the great controversy over devotion to images that gripped many of the Eastern Churches in the eighth and ninth centuries.

After finishing doctoral studies in 1978, I began teaching Patristic theology at the Weston Jesuit School of Theology in Cambridge, MA, and more and more came to see, through my teaching and scholarly work, the dominant importance, in the development of doctrine and spirituality, of that early Christian reflection on who and what Christ is. The courses and seminars I offered, the talks and scholarly papers I was asked to give, seemed largely to circle around the subject of how Christians have understood—and might understand today—the Mystery of Christ's person. At the same time, it became clearer and clearer to me that the definition of Christ's identity forged at the Council of Chalcedon in 451, crucially important as it has been for the Orthodox and Western Churches' growing understanding of Christ, cannot be intelligibly seen as separate from the theological works of the great Patristic theologians in which it was embedded, or simply seen by itself as the summit of this process of what we have come to call Christological reflection.

The content of the definition of Chalcedon, if not its background and history, is well known to most Western and Eastern Orthodox Christians:

> "Following the holy Fathers," the bishops there declare, "we all, with one voice, teach [the faithful] to confess that our Lord Jesus Christ is one and the same Son— the same one perfect in divinity and perfect in humanity;... one and the same Christ, Son, Lord, Only-begotten, recognized in two natures without confusion, without change, without division, without separation, such that the difference of [his] natures is not at all destroyed by the union, but rather the distinctive character of each nature is preserved and comes together into one *persona* and one concrete individual: [we teach that] he is not split or divided up into two *personas*, but is one and the same Only-begotten Son, God the Word, our Lord Jesus Christ.

Christ is a single "person," a single acting individual or subject, whom we call at once Son of God and son of Mary; the difference of being, of definition and of ability to perform, involved in each of those sonships, remains intact, Chalcedonian Christians affirm, even while they in no way make him two acting persons, two subjects. The one Jesus Christ is, we say, both God and human at one and the same time. Many Christians of both East and West regard such an understanding of Christ's identity as foundational; theologians in recent centuries generally take this as the starting-point of any orthodox reflection on the Christ of faith, even as they continue to wrestle with its paradoxes. Yet to see the Chalcedonian definition, by itself, as the summation or climax of early Christian attempts to make sense of the Apostolic preaching of the crucified Savior is—by itself—surely too simple, too formulaic, too much open to the kind of schematic, theoretical reading that some philosophical traditions delight in, but that can lack the theological urgency of devotion, liturgy, and preaching. The significance of the definition of Chalcedon for Christian faith, it seems to me, is that it was a bold but, in the end, not entirely successful attempt to reconcile divergent historical voices attempting to articulate the Mystery of Christ's person and actions. More had been said and more needed to be said. The Chalcedonian formula's very importance for later Christian faith, I would argue, is distorted and unintelligible if it is detached from its place in a much longer, more complex narrative.

In the winter term of 2001, by now a faculty member at the University of Notre Dame, I was invited to deliver the annual Martin D'Arcy Lectures in Oxford, sponsored by the Jesuit community there, Campion Hall. It seemed obvious by then that I should choose as a subject the development of Patristic Christology, and that I should attempt to sketch out in these lectures a somewhat revised, though not revolutionary, narrative of how this aspect of theological reflection on the Gospels first developed. Although Patristic Christology is a familiar subject for anyone who studies the early Church, even cursorily, my lectures seemed at the time to meet with great interest and an encouraging reception: despite the familiarity of much of the subject, friends and hearers in Oxford seemed to be interested in reflecting further, along with me, on the wider theological context of our classical Christian understanding of Christ.

This book is a revised and much-expanded version of those Oxford lectures. The whole of chapter 2, on the second century, as well as chapter 9, on the iconoclastic controversy, and chapter 10, which looks summarily at the content of classical Christology and at the first seven councils received as "ecumenical," have been added, as well as the treatment of Eusebius of Caesaraea in chapter 4; all of the rest has been rethought, filled out, more fully documented, and thoroughly rewritten.

Despite this process of development, though, I am very much aware that the work remains an incomplete version of the full story of early Christology. To be a comprehensive history, much more would have to be said, particularly of the early development of an understanding of Christ in the Latin, Syriac, and Armenian traditions of the Church. Tertullian deserves significant treatment, certainly, as an early, terminologically and conceptually creative third-century critic of Gnostic views of the person and role of Jesus, particularly in his works *Adversus Praxean* and *De Carne Christi*. Hilary of Poitiers, especially in his so-called *De Trinitate*, from the late 350s, and Ambrose, in his *De Fide* and *De Incarnationis Dominicae Sacramento* from the 370s, both present compelling and learned defenses of the Nicene understanding of Christ and of God, heavily influenced by their reading of contemporary Greek sources but addressed to specific polemical challenges to Nicene Christology in the Latin Church of their day. Ephrem, writing in his own Syriac language and literary forms at roughly the same time, independently presents an orthodox and centrally biblical portrait of Jesus that serves as an important, still powerful complement to the more analytical approach of his Greek and Latin contemporaries. The fifth-century Armenian summary of orthodox Christian catechesis, the *Teaching of St. Gregory*, by the self-styled "Agathangelos"—apparently a disciple of the Katholikos Mashtotz (d. 440)—which is one of the earliest theological works we possess in Armenian, offers there a brief, centrally biblical summary of Christian doctrine that also reflects fourth- and fifth-century Greek theology, based on a Nicene understanding of Christ.

In the time after Chalcedon, important developments in Christological reflection continued. Sixth-century Latin theologians—writers like John Maxentius, active in Rome before 520, the Italian philosopher-bureaucrat Boethius (d. 524), and the African Fulgentius of Ruspe (d. January 1, 533), all promoters of a strongly unitive portrait of Jesus as divine Son, as well as the North African bishop Facundus of Hermiane, writing a few decades later, an outspoken defender of the three Antiochene theologians condemned at the council of 553—offered post-Chalcedonian refinements to the increasingly dominant portrait of Christ sketched by that council, which combined it with the Augustinian understanding of grace and freedom, of the divine initiative in the salvation of individuals and the world, that by then dominated the spirituality and theology of the West. My only reason for not including discussions of these important writers in this narrative of the growth of classic Christology—besides limitations of time and space—is that they were, as far as I can see, less directly representative of this longer tradition, or less influential on its future, than the authors I have dealt with here.

This book, then, is concerned with the early development and reception of what is today the most widely professed Christian conception of Christ. Clearly, the development of this doctrine admits of wide variations in expression and understanding, varying emphases in interpretation that are as striking in authors of the first millennium as they are among modern writers. Just as clearly, the evolving dogmatic consensus on the person of Christ that I speak of does not, by any means, include all Christians. The so-called "pre-Chalcedonian" Churches of the Armenian tradition, and the "non-Chalcedonian" Churches of present-day Coptic, Ethiopic, West Syrian, East Syrian or Assyrian, and South Indian Christianity, are major Christian bodies today, whose faith is identified clearly with certain streams in the debates on the person of Christ I have narrated here, but not with the synthetic dogmatic decisions of all the early councils that Eastern Orthodox, Roman Catholic, and Protestant Christians consider as normative for faith.

The seven early ecumenical councils and their dogmatic formulations, then, are crucial way stations in defining the shape of the journey I have attempted to narrate. But I have tried to present the work of these ancient councils as the outcomes of lively and intense theological argument and scriptural interpretation, as expressions of speculations and debates that were themselves embedded in older, more widespread traditions of faith, devotion, and ecclesial self-understanding and practice, and that led to the recognition by the whole Christian body—or at least by a large part of it!—of *some* episcopal gatherings and their formulations, but not of others, as authentically representing the long, continually developing apostolic tradition. And my argument here is that if a modern Christian believer—or catechist, or preacher, or theologian—wants to carry on his or her reflections on the Mystery of Christ within this long mainstream of Christian faith, he or she must begin with an awareness of more than the bare, familiar, paradoxical framework of the Chalcedonian definition. One needs to be aware, surely, of the zigzag, yet (in retrospect, at least) astonishingly continuous message of all seven of the major councils of the first millennium that we have come to call "ecumenical"—different as they were in organization, membership, and purpose—and also of the theologians whose work set the stage, and provided the language, for what those councils discussed and decided.

In writing a book like this, whose final production has taken more than ten years, I am aware of an enormous number of debts to the people who have helped and supported me. I will always be deeply indebted to my professors and mentors at Frankfurt and Oxford—especially to Father (later Cardinal) Aloys Grillmeier, S.J., to Frs. Heinrich Bacht, S.J., and Hermann-Josef Sieben, S.J., in Frankfurt; as well as to Nigel Wilson, J. N. D. Kelly, Bishop Kallistos Ware, and Prof. Henry Chadwick, in Oxford—for leading me along the path of deeper engagement with the Fathers, and also to the late Abbé Marcel Richard, of Paris, for his early advice and a great deal of expert help. I am grateful to the Master and community of Campion Hall, Oxford, for inviting me to give the D'Arcy Lectures in 2002, which led me to a first attempt at producing this narrative. I am also deeply grateful to the Center of Theological Inquiry in Princeton, NJ, for so graciously and generously supporting me in two sabbaticals devoted to working on this book, and to Ms. Kate Skrebutenas, of the Princeton Theological Seminary Library, for her gracious and cheerful help in the more truly *recherché* aspects of my research for it. I sincerely thank the Henry Luce III Foundation, for a generous fellowship in 2005–6, supporting me financially in one of those sabbaticals. And I am very grateful to my friend and colleague from "another Cambridge," Prof. Sarah Coakley, for her gracious willingness to include this book in the present series of monographs with the Oxford University Press.

I am deeply grateful, too, to many students through the years, at the Weston Jesuit School of Theology and later here at the University of Notre Dame, for their continuing interest in early Christology and their penetrating questions about it, as we have read these classic texts together many times, over many years. And I am particularly grateful to two of those former students and friends—Prof. Peter Martens, of St. Louis University, and Prof. Khaled Anatolios, my colleague here at Notre Dame—for reading through the manuscript of this book and correcting its more egregious inaccuracies.

Finally, I want to thank my superiors and brothers in the Society of Jesus— the Jesuits—for so patiently helping me discover what it is not only to think about Jesus, but to try to be his companion and disciple. That, after all, is what Christian faith is really about, and what moves me to dedicate this book to them.

University of Notre Dame
Feast of St. Ignatius Loyola, 2016

# Contents

*List of Abbreviations*                                                                          xv

1. The Christology of Chalcedon: Neither End nor Beginning                                        1
2. Second-Century Christology: The Word With Us                                                  28
3. Irenaeus and Origen: A Christology of Manifestation                                           65
4. The Early Arian Controversy: Christology in Search of a Mediator                              94
5. Apollinarius, Gregory of Nazianzus, and Gregory of Nyssa:
   Towards a Christology of Transformation                                                       126
6. Augustine of Hippo: Christology as the "Way"                                                  150
7. Antioch and Alexandria: Christology as Reflection on God's
   Presence in History                                                                           174
8. After Chalcedon: A Christology of Relationship                                                200
9. The Iconoclastic Controversy: Christology and Images                                          232
10. Epilogue: Christology and the Councils                                                       266

*Bibliography*                                                                                   281
*Index*                                                                                          291

# List of Abbreviations

| | |
|---|---|
| ACO | *Acta conciliorum oecumenicorum* |
| AH | Irenaeus, *Adversus Haereses* |
| AI | *The Ascension of Isaiah* |
| Alberigo/Tanner | Giuseppe Alberigo et al. (eds), *Decrees of the Ecumenical Councils*, I, trans. Norman P. Tanner et al. (London: Sheed and Ward; Washington, DC: Georgetown University Press, 1990) |
| *Anal. Boll.* | *Analecta Bollandiana* |
| ANF | Ante-Nicene Fathers |
| *Apol.* | Justin, *Apology* |
| CA | Athanasius, *Orotiones contra Arianos* |
| CAph | Leontius of Byzantium, *Contra Aphthartodocetas* |
| *Cat. Hom.* | Theodore of Mopsuestia, *Catechetical Homily* |
| CCG | Corpus Christianorum Series Graeca |
| CCL | Corpus Christianorum Series Graeca Latina |
| CCSA | Corpus Christianorum Series Apocryphorum |
| CCSG | Corpus Christianorum Series Graeca |
| CG | Athanasius, *Contra Gentes* |
| CH | Eusebius, *Church History* |
| CNE | Leontius of Byzantium, *Contra Nestorianos et Eutychianos* |
| *Conf.* | Augustine, *Confessions* |
| CSCO | Corpus Scriptorum Christianorum Orientalium |
| *De civ. Dei* | Augustine, *De civitate Dei* |
| *De praed. sanct.* | Augustine, *De praedestinatione sanctorum* |
| DI | Athanasius, *De Incarnatione* |
| *Dial.* | Justin, *Dialogues* |
| DTN | Leontius of Byzantium, *Deprenhensio et Triumphus super Nestorianos* |
| *Enarr. in Ps.* | Augustine, *Enarrationes in Psalmos* |
| *Epap* | Leontius of Byzantium, *Epaporemata* |
| *Epil* | Leontius of Byzantium, *Epilyseis* |
| *Exp. Fid.* | John of Damascus, *Expositio Fidei* |
| GCS | *Die Griechischen Christlichen Schriftsteller* |
| GNO | Gregorii Nysseni Opera |
| *JTS NS* | *Journal of Theological Studies*, New Series |

| | |
|---|---|
| *LThK* | *Lexikon für Theologie und Kirche* |
| *Magn.* | Ignatius of Antioch, *Letter to the Magnesians* |
| Mansi | G. D. Mansi, *Sacrorum Conciliorum nova et amplissima collectio* |
| MGH | Monumenta Germaniae Historica |
| NPNF | Nicene and Post-Nicene Fathers |
| *Opusc.* | Maximus the Confessor, *Opuscula theological et polemica* |
| PG | J.-P. Migne (ed.), *Patrologia: Series Graeca* |
| PL | J.-P. Migne (ed.), *Patrologia: Series Latina* |
| *RSPhTh* | *Revue des Sciences Philosophiques et Théologiques* |
| SChr. | Sources Chrétiennes |
| *Smyrn.* | Ignatius of Antioch, *Letter to the Smyrnaeans* |
| *Spic.Sol.* | J. B. Pitra (ed.), *Spicilegium solesmense complectens sanctorum patium scriptorumque ecclesiasticorum anecdota* (Paris: Firmin Didot, 1852) |
| *Trall.* | Ignatius, *Letter to the Trallians* |
| VA | Athanasius of Antioch, *Vita Antonii* |
| ZKG | *Zeitschrift für Kirchengeschichte* |
| ZNTW | *Zeitschrift für die neutestamentliche Wissenschaft* |

*Invisibile etenim Filii Pater,*
*Visibile autem Patris Filius.*

"*For the Father is the Invisible of the Son, but the Son is the Visible of the Father*"

(Irenaeus, *Adversus Haereses* IV, 6.6)

# 1

## The Christology of Chalcedon

### Neither End nor Beginning

#### CHALCEDON SCHOLARSHIP IN THE POST-WAR YEARS

Several decades ago, in the spring of 1952, an event occurred which, while not great on the stage of history, was surely remarkable within the more intimate theatre of theological scholarship: the appearance of the first volume of a collection of essays on the historical background and the theological consequences of the Council of Chalcedon. The collection, entitled *Das Konzil von Chalkedon: Geschichte und Gegenwart*,[1] took three years to be fully published, and eventually ran to three sizeable tomes. Its editors, Aloys Grillmeier and Heinrich Bacht, were two relatively young German Jesuit professors of theology at the Hochschule Sankt Georgen in Frankfurt-am-Main. The contributors, all Roman Catholic authors, were mainly Germans also, but also included Austrians, Belgians, French, and even an American. Their essays were, for the most part, serious examples of the high scholarship that had flourished in Europe in the first half of the twentieth century: learned, amply argued, fully and meticulously documented, and edited with an accuracy that, in the words of an admiring Oxford reviewer, Canon F. L. Cross, "cannot but command the admiration of all, and we suspect, the astonishment of many, of its readers."[2]

Dr. Cross's astonishment was probably due, first of all, to the hard circumstances in which scholarly work of such quality, at that time, had to be done. All of Europe was still in the grip of the shortages and suspicions that followed the Second World War. Germany was still divided and occupied; academic life was only slowly getting back to its ordinary pace; libraries were often understaffed, sometimes even inaccessible; paper for printing was scarce. Planning such an ambitious scholarly undertaking in the late 1940s took courage and

---

[1] Aloys Grillmeier, S.J., and Heinrich Bacht, S.J., (eds), *Das Konzil von Chalkedon: Geschichte und Gegenwart*, I (Würzburg: Echter Verlag, 1951 [1952]); II (1952); III (1954).

[2] *JTS* NS 4 (1953), 264.

vision, and bringing it to reality took a resourcefulness that often went beyond the library walls. While the ever-enterprising Fr. Bacht badgered bishops and benefactors across Germany for financial help for the project, in the years preceding its publication, the gentle Fr. Grillmeier travelled to Leuven, Brussels, and Paris to encourage contributors to take part—making himself as silent and inconspicuous as possible in railway carriages, because his travelling status in those years, as a German national, was never entirely clear. The goal of the project was more than simply an elaborate scholarly *Festschrift* celebrating the fifteenth centenary of the Council of Chalcedon in 451, more than just a learned echo of Pius XII's encyclical on Chalcedon and Christology, *Sempiternus Rex*, produced for the same occasion; the goal was also to celebrate the re-establishment of a German Jesuit theological faculty, now settled in Frankfurt after fifty years of exile in the Netherlands and the total disruption of the war years, and to get the wheels of Catholic theological scholarship turning again.

That anniversary of Chalcedon must also have seemed full of ecumenical promise in a Europe recovering from war and yearning for reconciliation. In September, 1951—the actual centenary, to the month, of the beginning of the council—F. L. Cross had assembled an International Conference on Patristic Studies in Oxford: the first of a distinguished series of meetings that still continues, and which quickly became a mirror and an important driving force for the modern study of the Church Fathers.[3] Cross was particularly eager to include German scholars in the meeting, as a step towards healing the war's cultural wounds, and hoped that the Conference would encourage collaboration and dialogue among theologians of all the Christian Churches. Fr. Grillmeier, invited to give a paper because of the collection he was editing on the council, was one of only two Jesuits who actually managed to attend that first Oxford Conference, even though nine were scheduled to participate;[4] theological contact with Protestants was still considered dangerous for Catholics in 1951, a year after the publication of Pius XII's encyclical *Humani Generis*,[5] and Jesuit

---

[3] Although Cross had hoped to publish the papers given at the 1951 Conference as a single collection, it proved impossible to interest a publisher in the project; since the second Conference, in 1955, however, proceedings of these meetings have appeared as the series *Studia Patristica*.

[4] In the conference program—*First International Conference in Patristic Studies, Oxford, September 24-28, 1951*—the following Jesuit Patristic scholars are listed as presenting papers: Frs. Thomas Corbishley, John Crehan, Cuthbert Lattey, and Bernard Leeming, from England; Fr. Peter Smulders from the Netherlands; Fr. Claude Mondésert from France; Frs. Aloys Grillmeier and Heinrich Bacht from Germany; and Fr. Engelbert Kirschbaum, a German archaeologist and art historian, from Rome. At the behest of authorities in Rome, all cancelled their presentations, except for Grillmeier and Mondésert, for whom news of the prohibition arrived too late. (I am grateful to Dr. Elizabeth Livingstone for details of these events.)

[5] Among other dangerous new trends in Catholic theology after the Second World War, the encyclical condemned an "eirenism," which, "under the mask of virtue," hopes to put an end to long-standing dogmatic controversies among Christians by abandoning Catholic apologetics

superiors in Rome had decided, at the eleventh hour, to forbid members of the Society to attend this "crypto-ecumenical" gathering—a prohibition that was communicated by mail only after Fr. Grillmeier and Fr. Claude Mondésert, the editor of *Sources chrétiennes*, had left home for the Conference. In Oxford, Grillmeier began a long friendship with Dr. Cross which eventually led, thanks to Cross's influence, to the publication of a much-expanded version of his own essay in the first volume of *Das Konzil von Chalkedon*, on the prehistory of the council's Christological formula, as an English book.[6] Christian dialogue and collaboration often begins in the rediscovery of common roots.

Besides the academic and ecumenical effects that the editors seem to have hoped for from their three Chalcedon volumes, there was clearly a theological agenda, as well. What has been called the *ressourcement*—the rediscovery of the living relevance of the Scriptures and of early Christian tradition for the Church's theology, not simply as footnotes or proof-texts but as actual *sources*, actual witnesses to contemporary faith and its reasoned understanding—had begun to give new life to the Roman Catholic Church in the 1930s.[7] Young scholars, such as the Jesuits Henri de Lubac, Jean Daniélou, Hugo and Karl Rahner, and Hans Urs von Balthasar, or the Dominicans Marie-Dominique Chenu and Yves Congar, among many others, had found in the Church

and traditional scholastic dogmas (11). Some, the Encyclical went on to suggest, link such reconciliation with the revived interest in Patristic studies then under way, and would like to "return in the explanation of Catholic doctrine to the way of speaking used in Holy Scripture and by the Fathers of the Church. They cherish the hope that when dogma is stripped of the elements which they hold to be extrinsic to divine revelation, it will compare advantageously with the dogmatic opinions of those who are separated from the unity of the Church" (14). Doubtless such a hope had been entertained by both Grillmeier and Cross!

[6] Aloys Grillmeier, *Christ in Christian Tradition*, trans. John Bowden (Oxford: Mowbray, 1965). In his review of *Chalkedon* I (*JTS* NS 4 [1953], 268, n.1), Cross had hinted that Grillmeier's essay in the volume, at least, deserved to be translated into English. A further expanded second edition, in 1975, was published as *Christ in Christian Tradition*, I: *From the Apostolic Age to Chalcedon (451)*, since Grillmeier had by then resolved to continue his history of early Christology, now in German and English, with other translations and volumes hoped for, at least to the end of the Patristic period. Volume I, expanded still further, appeared first in German in 1979. Volume II, conceived in five parts, was to extend the narrative from Chalcedon to the year 600: a period on which, for many authors, little previous scholarship existed. To date volumes II/1 (on the sources for the study of post-Chalcedonian Christology: German 1986; English 1987), II/2 (on the Christology of the imperial Church of Constantinople: German 1989; English 1995), II/3 (on the Christology of the Churches of Jerusalem and Antioch: German 2002) and II/4 (on the Christology of the Church non-Chalcedonian Egypt and Nubia: German 1990; English 1996) have been published, with increasing help from Dr. Theresia Heinthaler. (Volume II/3, begun by Grillmeier before his final illness, was completed by a number of authors and edited by Dr. Heinthaler.) Volume II/5, on the Christology of the sixth-century Latin West, is a more distant possibility. Although Grillmeier had originally hoped to take his history of Christology down to modern times, it seems unlikely that the project will continue past 600. Fr. Grillmeier retired from active scholarship because of ill health in 1993, and was created a cardinal in November of the following year. He died, at the age of 88, on September 13, 1998.

[7] See my essay, "*La nouvelle théologie* and the Patristic Revival: Sources, Symbols, and the Science of Theology," *International Journal of Systematic Theology* 7 (2005), 362–82.

Fathers and their medieval heirs a richness of theological vision and biblical interpretation that seemed to offer intellectual and spiritual liberation from the abstract, dogmatic rationalism of the officially recognized scholastic manuals used in seminaries. The study of major Church doctrines as inevitably embodying a continuous historical development in the articulation of faith—what the Germans called *Dogmengeschichte*—had been mainly the preserve of liberal Protestants, especially since the days of Ritschl and Harnack in the late nineteenth and early twentieth century; in their hands it often led to historicism and a relativizing of the abiding worth of doctrine for religious faith. Now, for Catholic theologians, that same historical approach seemed to offer possibilities for a new understanding of long-held truths, for a sense of their lasting validity in new contexts, and for the raising of questions and sketching of perspectives that had found no place in the manualist tradition. Chenu and de Lubac had argued, since the 1930s, for the particular necessity of this historical perspective in the articulation of a faith based on the historically incarnate Word of God;[8] but the reaction of Roman theologians and Church authorities had been cautious, at times hostile. Now, in the years after the Second World War, seemed the time to propose the importance of history once again.

In one of the most important essays in the third volume of Grillmeier and Bacht's collection on Chalcedon, published only in 1954, Karl Rahner makes this very point, cautiously but tellingly:

> Anyone who takes seriously the "historicity" of human truth (in which God's truth too has become incarnate in Revelation) must see that neither the abandonment of a formula nor its preservation in a petrified form does justice to human understanding. For history is precisely *not* an atomized beginning-ever-anew; it is rather (the more spiritual it is) a becoming-new which preserves the old, and preserves it all the more *as* old, the more spiritual this history is. But this preservation, which recognizes the true uniqueness of something which has taken place once and for all, is only historical preservation when the history goes on, and the movement of reflexion departs from the formula which has been reached in order to discover it (just this old formula itself) again.[9]

[8] See especially Chenu, "Position de Théologie," *RSPhTh* 25 (1935), 232–57, trans. Denis Hickey, "What is Theology?" *Faith and Theology* (New York: Macmillan, 1968), 15–35; *Une École de Théologie: le Saulchoir* (privately published, 1937; repr., with accompanying essays by Giuseppe Alberigo et al.: Paris: Éditions du Cerf, 1985); de Lubac, *Catholicism* [orig. publ. as *Catholicisme: Les Aspects sociaux du dogme* (Paris: Éditions du Cerf, 1937)], Eng. trans. *Catholicism: Christ and the Common Destiny of Man* (San Francisco: Ignatius Press, 1988), esp. chap. 6; see also his posthumously published essay, "La doctrine du Père Lebreton sur la Révélation et le dogme d'après ses écrits antimodernistes," in *Théologie dans l'histoire* 2 (Paris: Desclée de Brouwer, 1990), 108–56.
[9] Karl Rahner, "Chalkedon: Ende oder Anfang?" *Das Konzil von Chalkedon* 3 (Würzburg: Echter Verlag, 1954), 4 (whole article: 3–49); English trans. Cornelius Ernst, "Current Problems in Christology," *Theological Investigations*, I: *God, Christ, Mary and Grace* (London: Darton, Longman and Todd; Baltimore, MD: Helicon, 1961), 150.

Rahner goes on to make the point—which to us may seem a little startling—that most theologians in Europe in the 1950s, as well as most of the faithful, simply assumed that in Christology—reflection in faith on the person of Jesus Christ—all the real problems had been solved by the formula of the Council of Chalcedon in 451; raising further questions seemed unnecessary. For Rahner, such complacency, in fact, weakened Christology:

> One has only to consider how few really living and passionate controversies there are in Catholic Christology today which engage the existential concern of the faithful (is there a single one?). Unless someone is inclined to regard this fact simply as a mark of superiority, a proof of unruffled orthodoxy and crystal-clear theology, he will listen with patience and good will to the most modest attempt, undertaken with the most inadequate means, to depart from the Chalcedonian formula in order to find the way back to it in truth.[10]

For Rahner, quite clearly, the value of careful historical study of the origins and early consequences of the formula of Chalcedon was to loosen the Church's understanding of Christ from a rigid metaphysical focus on "nature" and "person" that, in his view, had led to serious distortions in the way both theology and popular devotion understood the person of the Savior—especially Jesus' humanity. It is significant, in fact, that this essay first bore the title, in the Grillmeier-Bacht collection, "Chalkedon: Ende oder Anfang?"—"Chalcedon: End or Beginning?"[11] When it appeared in the first volume of Rahner's collected essays that same year, 1954, the article bore a new, perhaps less challenging, title, "Probleme der Christologie von heute"—in Cornelius Ernst's English translation, "Current Problems in Christology."[12] To show that the Chalcedonian formula was not simply the end of an ancient controversy, but a starting-point for new and deeper questions about the identity and role of Christ, as Rahner felt serious historical analysis clearly did, was to show that Christology could indeed raise "current problems" and become the center of intense contemporary debate: a prophecy that most of us would probably consider amply fulfilled in the years since 1954!

For Grillmeier and Bacht, too, and for many of the contributors to these three volumes on Chalcedon, more was at stake than simply historical detail: a whole understanding of theology, especially of the theology of Christ's person, rested on "getting Chalcedon right." Grillmeier himself was particularly concerned, in this work and throughout his later writings, to underline two conclusions he felt we can draw from a study of early Christology. One was the indispensable service philosophical analysis and technical philosophical vocabulary had always offered to the preservation and clarification of the

---

[10] Rahner, "Chalkedon", trans. Ernst, 152–3.   [11] See n. 9.
[12] Rahner, *Schriften zur Theologie*, I (Einsiedeln: Benziger, 1954), 169–222, trans. Ernst, *Theological Investigations*, I, 149–200.

apostolic message that "Jesus is Lord" (I Cor. 12.3); this was articulated expressly in contrast to Harnack's theory of a gradual alienation of the original, simple, wholly ethical message of Jesus through the introduction of Greek concepts and practices, a "Hellenization," that Harnack saw as coming to an apex in the Chalcedonian formula. Unlike the lines of Christian interpretation which the Church eventually came to reject as "heresies," as Grillmeier continually tries to show in his writings, the mainstream or orthodox use of secular philosophical language is not a syncretistic compromise or an intellectualizing of Gospel faith, but is "intended to preserve the Christ of the gospels and the apostolic age for the faith of posterity."[13] It is this ability of the Church to use new, often secular concepts as a service to the maintenance of a living tradition, Grillmeier believes, which allows for continuity amidst genuine change.[14]

Second, Grillmeier is very much concerned to emphasize the "balance," in the Chalcedonian understanding of the person of Christ, between his complete divinity and his complete humanity, both of which are proper to him as a single, unique subject, a single divine agent or "person." Behind this concern, undoubtedly, was a conviction shared by many Catholic theologians of the late 1940s and early 1950s, including several of the contributors to the *Chalkedon* volumes, that modern scholastic theology had not taken the completeness of the humanity of Christ with full seriousness, and that the picture of Christ then presented in popular preaching and devotional manuals steered very close to the mythic caricature of "God in a human costume," "God who has put on a body."[15] It was in the 1950s, significantly, that a number of Catholic scholars engaged in controversy over the full meaning of the human consciousness and human freedom of Christ: over the limitations of knowledge

---

[13] Grillmeier, *Christ in Christian Tradition* (2nd edn; Oxford: Mowbray, 1975), 555. All subsequent citations of this work, unless otherwise noted, will be taken from this second edition. Cf. Grillmeier's article, "Hellenisierung—Judaisierung des Christentums als Deuteprinzipien der Geschichte des kirchlichen Dogmas," in *Mit Ihm und in Ihm: Christologische Forschungen und Perspektiven* (Freiburg: Herder, 1973), 423–88.

[14] See the review of Robert L. Wilken of the first English edition of *Christ in Christian Tradition* (1965), which makes just this point: "In Grillmeier's view the philosophical categories of the fathers and the terms from Greek philosophy actually aided the Church in interpreting and expressing its faith. Grillmeier also wishes to take change, development and diversity with utter seriousness, but he believes one can talk about a developing unity which is more than an arbitrary choosing of one tradition from among many. What emerges as Catholic Christianity in the later Church stands in continuity with the primitive Church" (*Church History* 35 [1966], 362).

[15] Karl Rahner makes this point in the article quoted above: "Looked at from this point of view a single basic conception runs through the Christian heresies from Apollinarism to Monothelitism, sustained by the same basic mythical feeling. The persistence of this idea even in theoretical formulations ought to make us realize that although it may have given up announcing itself in such a theoretical fashion today, the idea probably still lives on in the picture which countless Christians have of the 'Incarnation,' whether they give it their faith—or reject it" ("Current Problems in Christology", 156).

inherent in Jesus' human intellect, over his need to be born in a human way, and over the need for him to come to a free human decision to obey his Father's (and his own) divine will.[16] Against this background, one understands better Grillmeier's (and his contemporaries') elaborate efforts to argue that theologians of the Antiochene school, even the hapless Nestorius, were above all concerned to defend the full humanity of Christ, even if they often used somewhat novel biblical and philosophical arguments to do so.[17]

Grillmeier tends to read the whole early history of Christology as an evolution from what he calls a "word-flesh" (*logos-sarx*) model of understanding the person of Jesus, inspired by a literal understanding of John 1.14, towards what he calls the "word-human being" (*logos-anthropos*) model, first fully developed by the school of Antioch and decisively affirmed and nuanced in the mid fifth century by Pope Leo and the Council of Chalcedon. In a word-flesh Christology, Jesus' humanity is implicitly conceived as the physical, sensible, bodily human form in which the Word of God has lived among us; in a word-human being Christology, that "form" is understood as a fully developed human being with a soul—with all the interior faculties and qualities that characterize and make possible human knowledge, human freedom, and human love. The question of whether a particular author did or did not take the *soul of Christ* seriously, as a "theological factor," in his reflection on the Savior, is indeed one of the driving questions of Grillmeier's whole investigation of pre-Chalcedonian Christology; and the reason for his

---

[16] For the Catholic scholastic Christology of the late nineteenth and early twentieth century, it was considered most likely, although not dogmatically certain, that Jesus possessed, for the full length of his human existence, not only the immediate awareness of God proper to the beatific vision, but also "infused knowledge"—knowledge not acquired by the normal empirical process—of all that is humanly knowable. See, for example Joseph Pohle and Arthur Preuss, *Dogmatic Theology* IV: *Christology* (St. Louis, MO: B. Herder, 1925): "The human knowledge of Christ is relatively infinite in extent, i.e., it is the highest and most complete knowledge which it is possible for any creature to have in the present economy, and consequently, both with regard to natural and supernatural things, it is the ideal of all knowledge" (267). This became the subject of vigorous debate among Catholic theologians in the *ressourcement* movement that began in the 1930s and was revived after the war. See, for example: Paul Galtier, *L'unité du Christ: Être... Personne... Conscience* (Paris: Beauchesne, 1939), esp. 237–371; "La conscience humaine du Christ," *Gregorianum* 32 (1951), 525–68; 35 (1954), 225–46; Joseph Ternus, "Das Seelen- und Bewusstseinsleben Jesu," *Das Konzil von Chalkedon* III, 81–237; Aloys Grillmeier, "Das Christusbild der heutigen katholischen Theologie," in Johannes Feiner, Josef Trutsch, and Franz Böckle, *Fragen der Theologie heute* (Einsiedeln: Benziger, 1957), 265–300, esp. 286–96; Bernard Lonergan, *The Ontological and Psychological Constitution of Christ* (Toronto: University of Toronto Press, 2002); Karl Rahner, "Dogmatic Reflections on the Knowledge and Self-Consciousness of Christ," *Theological Investigations*, V (Baltimore, MD: Helicon; London: Darton, Longman and Todd, 1966), 193–215 (bibliography on the discussion, pp. 193–4, 196–7); Jean Galot, "La psychologie du Christ," *Nouvelle revue théologique* 90 (1958), 337–58; *La conscience de Jésus* (Gembloux: Duculot; Paris: Lethielleux, 1971); *Who is Christ? A Theology of the Incarnation* (Chicago: Franciscan Herald Press, 1981), 319–92.

[17] See, for example, Paul Galtier, "Un monument au concile de Chalcédoine—Nestorius mal compris, mal traduit," *Gregorianum* 34 (1953), 427–33.

concern seems to have been his desire to show that the developed portrait of Christ presented by Christian orthodoxy since Chalcedon cannot dispense with a serious treatment of his inner life as "a human being like us in all things but sin."[18]

Since the first reviewers of *Das Konzil von Chalkedon*, Grillmeier's history of the development of early Christology—in that work and in his later elaborations of its history—has been recognized by scholars as surpassing anything else available in the field in thoroughness, learning, and theological depth.[19] Yet there have been serious criticisms of Grillmeier's Christological narrative, too, as he developed it then and throughout his works. Albert Outler, for instance, pointed out the Western and Roman Catholic stereotypes that occasionally show themselves in *Christ in Christian Tradition* ("the volatile East, the subtle West; the East brought to impasse at Ephesus and then Leo's *Tome* to the rescue"),[20] as well as the unevenness of Grillmeier's treatment of certain ancient periods and authors.[21]

But it was Robert Wilken who first pointed to what is, in my view, the most serious and abiding flaw in Grillmeier's approach to the early history of Christology: it is really Western scholastic dogma, Protestant and Catholic, rather than the early Christian sources themselves, which supplies his narrative with its guiding thread, the lens through which ancient writers and their ideas are interpreted and arranged.[22] This is evident in Grillmeier's organizing focus on the Christological definition of the Council of Chalcedon, as "the formula which, like a hidden entelechy, had accompanied the wearisome struggles of centuries to interpret the *mysterium Christi*."[23] For Grillmeier, as for virtually all his contemporaries trained in the tradition of scholastic dogmatics, Christology was the "tract" within the discipline of theology which deals with the ontological structure of the person of Christ: with the "Mystery" by which the single, divine person of the Son or Word of God now "subsists," within created history, in two complete yet unconfused natures. Christology, as a branch of theology,[24] had come to be understood essentially as the

---

[18] Eucharistic Prayer IV, *Roman Sacramentary* (1970), alluding to Heb. 4.15: Jesus, our high priest, is "one who in every respect has been tested as we are, yet without sin."

[19] F. L. Cross said simply of *Chalkedon* I, "It is a book which everyone must have" (Review, *JTS* NS 4 [1953], 268); Albert Outler praised *Christ in Christian Tradition* I for "the immense erudition," "the insight and wisdom," the "excitement" of its narrative of ancient theology (Review, *Theology Today* 23 [1966], 451); Raniero Cantalamessa for the way in which it "demonstrates the seriousness and the profundity of the Christological problems debated in primitive Christianity" (Review, *Rivista di storia e di letteratura religiosa* 2 [1966], 529).

[20] Review (*Theology Today* 23 [1966]), 451–2.

[21] Review (*Theology Today* 23 [1966]), 452.

[22] Review (*Church History* 35 [1966]), 363.

[23] Grillmeier, *Christ in Christian Tradition*, 548.

[24] The word "Christology" itself, like most modern terms for the subject-divisions in theological reflection, is not of early Christian origin, but comes from the "scholastic" world of the post-Reformation university. It is first attested in English in 1673, in Barnabas Oley's preface to

explication of the final paragraph of the dogmatic formula of Chalcedon, which was the first official Church document to present this picture of Christ concisely, in so many words.

For Grillmeier and most theologians since at least Thomas Aquinas, the Chalcedonian formulation of Christ's "one person in two natures" expressed in a quintessential way what the Church's faith in Jesus Christ had always held, and what the four centuries of preaching, teaching, and controversy before it had continually been struggling to clarify. Grillmeier's first effort, his long chapter on the history of Christology before Chalcedon in the 1952 volume, begins by making this clear:

> The Mystery of the Incarnation of the Son of God found at the Council of Chalcedon that formulation that would dominate and influence the entire subsequent history of the dogma of the personality of Jesus Christ. If we look backwards from the year 451, the definition of the Council doubtless appears as the culmination of the development that had gone before it. If we look ahead to the centuries of Christological controversies which followed, the understanding of the Church's faith in Christ, as expressed in 451, constitutes the firm norm, as well as the great source of discord, which occupied and divided spirits. In any case, it was at Chalcedon that the decisive formulation of the Church's faith in the person of Jesus was forged.[25]

Here lies the real difficulty: to see this formula, pregnant with meaning as it is, as in itself the culmination of four centuries of Christian reflection on the person of Christ and the central norm of Christological orthodoxy ever since, is to say at once too little and too much—to force ancient reflection into a seriously distorting frame, by omitting those other themes and details that often seem to have little to do with the council's dense structural analysis of Christ's person, and by focusing simply on what did or did not anticipate the central elements of this definition. As Robert Wilken observed as early as 1965,

> Few will be convinced that Chalcedon is really a terminal point in the history of Christology, solely on historical grounds... Too many "accidents" precede Chalcedon, such as the two Ephesine councils in 431, the local councils of 448, 449, and the death of Theodosius and accession of Marcian. The violent reaction after Chalcedon, as well as the growing split in the empire, and the futile attempts at compromise in the century following—all these factors make it difficult to view Chalcedon as the end of a period. Are not the grounds for this view rather more dogmatic than historical?[26]

the Oxford Arminian Thomas Jackson's commentary on the creed (see *Oxford English Dictionary*, 2nd edn [Oxford: Oxford University Press, 1989], 3.183bc). It does not seem to have come into wide use, either among Protestant or Catholic theologians, until the nineteenth century.

[25] "Die theologische und sprachliche Vorbereitung der christologischen Formel von Chalkedon," *Das Konzil von Chalkedon*, I, 5.

[26] Review (*Church History* 35 [1966]), 363.

Grillmeier and his collaborators of the 1950s, as I have said, were not unusual in their view of the crowning importance of the Chalcedonian formula in the history of early Christian theology; textbooks on Christology were organized around it, histories of early Christianity tended to make it their final chapter, theological curricula in universities tended to require students to study the history and thought of the Fathers only as far as what was euphemistically— and misleadingly—called "the Chalcedonian settlement." As he continued his project in the decades after 1951, Grillmeier himself became increasingly aware that Chalcedon's way of formulating the ontological structure of the person of Christ was not an exhaustive summary of the New Testament witness to Jesus. So at the end of his revised history of pre-Chalcedonian Christology, *Christ in Christian Tradition* I (1975), he quotes with approval a sentence of Karl Rahner's from the beginning of his essay on problems in modern Christology. Every formal dogmatic statement is a necessary part of the Church's witness to its own tradition, Rahner had written, to "mark the boundary of error...Yet while this formula is an end, an acquisition and a victory, which allows us to enjoy clarity and security as well as ease in instruction, if this victory is to be a true one the end must also be a beginning."[27] Formulas that authoritatively sum up a tradition must always, in other words, be open to further reflection, raise further questions, lead us further into an understanding of the single, inexhaustible Mystery of God's saving presence in history. The question one must ask today, as Wilken asked in 1965, is whether a thorough reading of early Christian witnesses to faith in Christ really allows us to call the Council of Chalcedon, on its own, the end or the beginning of any identifiable period in the history of Christian faith, and so whether its formulation really ought to be taken, even with caution, as the summation of ancient thought about Jesus.

## THE ACHIEVEMENT OF CHALCEDON

What was, one may well ask, the real achievement of this gathering of Eastern bishops, called by the new emperor Marcian and his long-influential spouse, the Empress Pulcheria, in a suburb across the Bosporus from Constantinople, in the autumn of 451? On the level of Church politics, it was an effort to restore a balance between major centers of influence and the theological traditions with which they had become associated: a balance precariously achieved in 433, after the bitter controversy over Nestorius's views on how to conceive the person of Christ and the abortive attempt to hold a council at

---

[27] Rahner, "Current Problems in Christology," 149.

Ephesus in 431. The so-called "Formula of Reunion," sketching the outlines of traditional faith in the Savior—a formula apparently drafted by Theodoret of Cyrus and proposed by the Church of Antioch—was warmly embraced, as an expression of common faith for the moment, at least, by Nestorius's main opponent, Cyril of Alexandria.[28] Cyril had to labor hard, later in the 430s, to persuade his own sympathizers—bishops like the Armenian Acacius of Melitene, and Succensus of Diocaesaraea in southern Asia Minor, an old admirer of Athanasius—that in agreeing to the carefully balanced phrases in which the Antiochene draft of 433 had expressed its understanding of the person of Christ, specifically in confessing an "unconfused union" "of two natures," by which "the same one is coessential with the Father as to his deity and coessential with us as to his humanity," he had not abandoned Athanasius's vision of Jesus as the divine Savior who was God's own Son.

The principal agents of the peace of 433, however, were dead by the mid-440s: John of Antioch in 442, Cyril himself in 444, Proclus of Constantinople in 446. Tensions rose again in the imperial capital, as rival groups—doubtless driven both by political ambition and by religious traditionalism—accused each other of treachery and extremism. The story of the conflict between the archimandrite Eutyches, well supported at court and encouraged from afar by Cyril's successor, Dioscorus of Alexandria, on one side, and leading clerical figures of the capital, such as Eusebius of Dorylaeum, on the other, is well known. Although the motives for tension and rivalry between Constantinople, Antioch, and Alexandria seem to have been a complex mix of politics and religious commitment, according to ancient witnesses, the religious reasons given for choosing sides in the conflict all had to do with how one conceived the person of Christ. Eutyches, drawing on the older Alexandrian and Apollinarian tradition that emphasized the organic, dynamic unity of action and consciousness in the divine Savior of humanity, refused to accept any formula that spoke of two abiding "natures," or operative substantial realities, forming the "person" of the incarnate Word. Eusebius of Dorylaeum and most of the Constantinopolitan establishment, by contrast, held tenaciously to the "two unconfused natures" and "double consubstantiality" language of the Formula of 433. In response to his aggressive promotion of his highly unitive, God-centered picture of Christ, Eutyches was eventually deposed by the Patriarch and resident bishops in Constantinople—the standing committee known as the "Home Synod"—late in 448.

An outcry ensued. In the summer of 449, a council of Greek bishops met at Ephesus, with imperial support, to take up the conflict. Chaired, apparently in a highly dictatorial manner, by Archbishop Dioscorus of Alexandria, and

---

[28] For the text of this crucial letter, addressed in the spring of 433 by Cyril to Bishop John of Antioch—which Grillmeier has characterized as the real expression of "the faith of Ephesus"— see the *Acta* of Chalcedon, Session 1.246 (ACO II/1, 107–11).

sharply resistant to the reservations expressed by bishops from both Antioch and the Latin West, the assembled bishops reinstated Eutyches to his clerical rank, from which two subsequent patriarchal "home synods" in the capital had deposed him, and in turn deposed Eusebius of Dorylaeum and excommunicated the leading spokesmen of the Antiochene Church. Supporters of a more "symmetrical" picture of Christ felt that now *they* had been the victims of violence. Hence when the Emperor Theodosius II, who had permitted this radicalization to occur, himself died in the summer of 450, it was an obvious time for his successors, Marcian and Pulcheria, to take conciliatory steps, for the unity of both Church and society.

The Council of Chalcedon, convened in September and October of 451, was intended to be that step. In inviting and seating delegates, the court carefully assured a more balanced representation of voices than had been achieved at Ephesus in 449, and guaranteed a leading role in the conduct of business not only to the main Eastern sees but to Pope Leo's chief legate, the Greek-speaking Sicilian bishop Paschasius of Lilybaeum. It was easy enough for this new council to reverse the depositions enacted at Ephesus two years earlier, and even to depose Dioscorus of Alexandria, notably for the contempt he had shown there towards Leo of Rome. The *Acta* make it clear, however, that most of the bishops present at Chalcecdon were very hesitant to go further, and to propose a new "formula of union" expressing the Church's understanding of the person of Christ. They were content to reaffirm "the faith of Nicaea," regarded since the 370s as the touchstone of biblical orthodoxy, as expressed in its creed (i.e. the reformulated Nicene Creed produced by the Council of Constantinople of 381), and to take as also normative a few now-classic letters of Cyril and Leo on the Christological issue. It was the emperors, at the urging of Leo's representatives, who finally prevailed on the bishops to go beyond this, and to allow a drafting commission to finish and propose a new statement of common faith; this was driven largely by the Emperor's threat to adjourn, and to call a new council in the West to deal with the issue, if the Eastern delegations continued to resist making any additions to Nicaea. The resultant statement of the Church's central understanding of Christ's person, reluctantly agreed to ahead of time, enthusiastically acclaimed in the event, is what we know as the Chalcedonian definition.

It is important to look closely at the whole of the Council's statement of faith if one is to realize its intent and its real value. Grillmeier rightly stressed its "dogmatic," rather than speculative character:[29] it is a formal agreement on the boundaries of orthodox Christian faith concerning the person of Christ, but clearly not intended to break new theological ground, to solve age-old problems of understanding in creatively crafted new terms, nor even to give

---

[29] Grillmeier, *Christ in Christian Tradition*, 545.

unambiguous clarifications of the terms it does use. Probably most of the bishops present would have been hard put to define what "substance" and "nature," "hypostasis" and "prosōpon" actually meant, when applied to the reality of Christ; as Grillmeier puts it:

> Even if abstract concepts find their way in, the theological method here consists only in "listening to" the proven witnesses of the Christian faith. True, the formulas are carefully developed, but only in connection with an already formed tradition.[30]

The purpose of the statement, quite clearly, is rather to reaffirm what was generally understood to be the mainstream tradition of Christian orthodoxy, and to rule out the kind of language and thinking about Christ that seemed most seriously to present a danger of veering away from that tradition. To the degree that it offers a positive delineation of Christ's person, it sets out to piece together a patchwork of terms and phrases, culled from representative thinkers on both sides of the previous two decades of controversy, in the hope that the appearance, at least, of a seamless conceptual whole might in time become the basis of real concord in faith, worship and polity.

The statement begins, accordingly, with a description of the Council's understanding of its mission: to resist the discord sowed in the Church by the Evil One, to build peace by removing falsehood and reaffirming tradition.[31] Significantly, the weight is on liturgically and synodically formulated tradition, rather than on Scripture—perhaps because scriptural texts were capable of so many conflicting interpretations. Expressly following the precedent of the Alexandrian synod that had met at Ephesus in 431, the Council insists that the Creed of Nicaea (325) shall "shine in first place" (προλάμπειν)—an acknowledged primacy that now becomes commonplace in ancient conciliar efforts to deal with doctrinal controversy—and that the Creed of Constantinople (381), a reformulation of the Nicene symbol, aimed at ruling out heresies that had become evident after 325, shall also "maintain its force" (κρατεῖν). After quoting both creedal formulas in full—our first documentary evidence, in fact, for the text of the Creed of Constantinople—the formula goes on to assert that these "should have been sufficient for the knowledge and support of true religion,"[32] but that new views of the person of Jesus, obviously deviant from the Apostolic tradition, now call for new responses consistent with this Nicene understanding. Accordingly, the Council declares that it has "received, as in agreement [with Nicaea's faith], the synodical letters of the blessed Cyril, then

---

[30] Grillmeier, *Christ in Christian Tradition*, 545.
[31] Complete Greek and Latin texts of the decree, with an English translation, can be found in Giuseppe Alberigo et al. (eds), *Decrees of the Ecumenical Councils*, I, trans. Norman P. Tanner et al. (London: Sheed and Ward; Washington, DC: Georgetown University Press, 1990) [Alberigo/Tanner], 83-7.
[32] Alberigo/Tanner, 157.

shepherd of the Alexandrian church, to Nestorius and the Orientals"[33]—by which it seems to mean only Cyril's "second" letter to Nestorius, not his more challenging "third," along with his affirmation of the formula of agreement from 433[34]—and also "has appropriately included, as a support of right teaching," Pope Leo's letter to bishop Flavian of Constantinople,[35] the famous *Tome* in which Leo enunciates, in polished but somewhat ambiguous Latin phrases, the more "symmetrical" picture of Christ advocated in the Greek world by Theodoret and the Antiochenes. "Classic" texts, representative of different schools of thought, are here cited, in other words, as normatively echoing the two "Nicene" creeds.

Only then, in third place, does the statement of the Council move on to enunciate its own synthetic position, which, like what has gone before, is carefully drafted to be both traditional and even-handed. First, the statement *excludes* what it regards as extreme and unacceptable positions on the person of Christ: those who "split up the mystery of the dispensation"[36] into *two sons*; those who say that the *divinity can suffer*; those who conceive of a "*confusion or mixture*" of two natures in him;[37] those—presumably Apollinarian sectaries—who think of his human form as coming itself from heaven; those—like the now-discredited Eutyches—who insist that the two natures that together constitute the person of Jesus have become, at the moment of their union, only one ontological reality. Only then, in last place, does the statement proceed to express the Council's understanding of the person of Jesus in positive, declaratory terms.

As Grillmeier has observed, this positive Chalcedonian statement itself is a mixture of plain language—"one and the same Son, who is our Lord Jesus Christ"[38]—and technical language borrowed from the philosophical traditions of Hellenism and the theological writings of the Cappadocians, Cyril, Proclus of Constantinople, Basil of Seleucia, even Nestorius. So—as we have quoted already in the preface—this "one and the same Christ" is here

> acknowledged to be unconfusedly, unalterably, undividedly, inseparably [four adverbs with a considerable philosophical and theological history][39] *in two natures*, since [now borrowing two phrases from Leo's *Tome*] the difference of

---

[33] Alberigo/Tanner, 158.

[34] For Cyril's "second" letter to Nestorius, see the *Acta* of Chalcedon, Session 1.240 (ACO II/1.104–6).

[35] Alberigo/Tanner, 158.     [36] Alberigo/Tanner, 158.

[37] It is interesting to note that while Gregory of Nazianzus and Gregory of Nyssa used the language of "mixture" more than once to express the mystery of the union of the divine and the human in Christ, by the time of the Chalcedonian statement such terminology is rejected as suggesting a "confusion" of two totally different realities.

[38] Alberigo/Tanner, 159.

[39] See Luise Abramowski, "συνάφεια und ἀσύγχυτος ἕνωσις als Bezeichnung für trinitarische und christologische Einheit," *Drei christologische Untersuchungen* (Berlin: De Gruyter, 1981), 63–109.

the natures is not destroyed because of the union, but, on the contrary, the character of each nature is preserved and comes together in *one person* [πρόσω-πον: *persona*, role, self-presentation] and *one hypostasis* [or concrete individual], not divided or torn into two persons but one and the same Son and only begotten God, Logos, Lord Jesus Christ...[40]

All of this is traditional, the statement adds, "just as in earlier times the prophets and also the Lord Jesus Christ himself taught us about him [the statement's only reference to Scripture], and as the symbol of our Fathers [i.e. the Nicene Creed] transmitted to us."[41] Finally, the decree concludes by prohibiting any Christian from writing, thinking or teaching anything that might contradict the faith witnessed to here.

Read as a whole, the Chalcedonian statement makes it clear that its famous final section is not meant to offer a theoretical explanation of the Mystery of the person of Jesus, but simply to establish agreed standards for remaining within the tradition of orthodoxy. The emphasis is on the original, binding formulation of that tradition in the creeds of Nicaea and Constantinople, with priority given to the former; one might even say that all of what follows the quoting of those creeds is really meant as a set of hermeneutical rules for reading the creed of Nicaea correctly, in the context of current fifth-century controversy. Those rules are both negative and positive: how one may *not* interpret Nicaea, and how one *may*, even *must* interpret it, in order to remain in the Church's communion of faith and sacrament. But in setting up these rules, in carefully fixing this boundary to exclude some positions and leave room for others, the bishops at Chalcedon take great care that the main fears and favorite phrases of both sides of the current controversy be explicitly respected. The five positions excluded, presumably, are meant to represent extremes, caricatures perhaps: lines that probably no credible, centrist member of either side of the discussion would want to follow. What positions might be included under the positive part of the statement is less clear, precisely because phrases from a variety of authors, with a variety of contrasting positions on the person of Christ, are here skillfully woven into a single, paradoxical paragraph that is designed to give the appearance of tranquil cohesion. Somewhere in that vision, the statement suggests, lies orthodoxy.


## REACTIONS TO CHALCEDON

The lasting value of Church documents and synodal statements—their meaning within the continuing life of the community—lies, as we have come to say,

---

[40] Alberigo/Tanner, 159.    [41] Alberigo/Tanner, 159.

in their *reception*: in the messy, unpredictable process by which the wider
Church—its bishops, its writers, its holy people, its "ordinary" faithful—judges
such statements and decides, implicitly or explicitly, whether or not to recognize them as expressions of normative faith, and to pray and live by them.[42]
The difficulty with regarding the Chalcedonian formula as representing the
quintessence of the Church's classical understanding of the person of Christ is
precisely that its reception was not unambiguous and by no means unanimous, and that—in contrast to the creed of Nicaea, which also took a good
fifty years to be widely accepted as a central norm of orthodox faith—its
reception at all by Eastern Christianity depended on further modifications in
terminology and nuanced qualifications in its Christological formula: on
additional, crucially important hermeneutical rules for interpreting both
Chalcedon's language and the broader salvation narrative summed up in the
earlier creeds. These are the rules enunciated in the decrees of what most
Christians today recognize as the fifth, sixth, and seventh ecumenical councils:
councils whose formulas of faith all begin by referring to, or quoting in full,
the confessions of faith promulgated at Nicaea in 325 and at Constantinople
in 381. Without the canons of Constantinople II, Constantinople III, and even
Nicaea II as supplements to its formulations and guides to its proper interpretation, the Chalcedonian formula would probably be regarded as fully
orthodox only by Western Christians and a minority of Eastern ones.

The full story of the reception of Chalcedon is, of course, too lengthy and
complicated to be told here, although we shall be dealing with important
aspects of it in later chapters. Attempts by the Emperor Marcian, and by his
successor Leo I, to install in Alexandria bishops favorable to the Council's
union formula, and soon afterwards even in Antioch, ended in violence and
schism. Increasingly, in the decades after Chalcedon, more and more monks
and pastors in the Greek-speaking world raised irate objections to its representation of the person of the Savior: it was a political solution, opponents
charged, rather than an authentic articulation of the tradition of faith in which
the Churches worshipped and preached; it was a victory for the humanistic,
overly analytical thinking of Nestorius and his Antiochene supporters; it was
also a Western solution, an expression of the dry, neatly balanced categories of
papal bureaucrats rather than of the intense devotion to the Savior, the sense
of human transformation by the dynamic personal presence of the divine in
Jesus, that was regarded as the core of Greek, Egyptian, and Syrian

---

[42] On the theological and canonical process of the "reception" of official dogma, see Yves
Congar, "La 'réception' comme réalité ecclésiologique," *RSPhTh* 56 (1972), 369–403; Aloys
Grillmeier, "Konzil und Rezeption. Methodische Bemerkungen zu einem Thema der
ökumenischen Diskussion der Gegenwart," in *Mit Ihm und in Ihm*, 303–34; "Die Rezeption
des Konzils von Chalkedon in der römisch-katholischen Kirche," in *Mit Ihm und in Ihm*,
335–70; Michael J. Himes, "The Ecclesiological Significance of the Reception of Doctrine,"
*Heythrop Journal* 33 (1992), 146–60.

spirituality.[43] For Eastern bishops who had attended the Council, the decision of whether or not to abandon its statement of faith and to call for a new gathering on the issue of Christ's personal unity was a difficult one; most of them were not schooled in the niceties of the disputed terminology, yet they realized the pastoral dangers lurking both in continuing to maintain the Council's position and language as normative, and in returning to the ideological conflicts of the 440s by simply abandoning it. One bishop from the mountains of Polemonian Pontus in northern Asia Minor, Euippius of Neocaesaraea, when canvassed for his advice by the Emperor Leo, wrote back that he and his local colleagues had come to the conclusion that they should not abandon the Chalcedonian position: because so many wise and holy bishops had been present there, and because (more importantly) those bishops who were at Chalcedon had so strenuously endorsed the faith of Nicaea. Borrowing a catchy phrase, however, from Gregory of Nazianzus, the rhetorical genius of the fourth-century Church, Euippius assured the Emperor that he and his colleagues were supporting Chalcedon from a pastoral rather than a dogmatic standpoint—"as fishermen, not as philosophers (ἁλιευτικῶς, οὐκ Ἀριστοτελικῶς)."[44] All the dialectical complexities of person and nature, "unconfused" and "inseparable," may have been a little beyond them.[45]

In 482, the Emperor Zeno attempted to distance the court officially from Chalcedon, and to provide an alternative formula of unity, without the help (and the possible divisiveness) of a new council: the so-called *Henotikon*, drafted by his patriarch Acacius originally as an expression of imperial Church policy for Egypt, and later proposed more generally for the whole Empire. This document decrees, for the sake of unity and peace, that only the creed of Nicaea, and its later interpretations at Constantinople and at the Cyrilline synod at Ephesus (431), along with Cyril's more polemical, still controversial "third" letter to Nestorius,[46] shall be considered normative expressions of

---

[43] For a detailed attempt to depict this Eastern attitude to the Chalcedonian formula, see W. H. C. Frend, *The Rise of the Monophysite Movement* (Cambridge: Cambridge University Press, 1972), esp. 137–42 (the attitude of Eastern monks towards the person of Christ); 148–9 (many in the East saw Chalcedon as a victory for Nestorianism): on the general sympathy for Antiochene thinking in the West at this period, and on the post-Chalcedonian tendency of Popes and Western theologians to identify the Chalcedonian statement with papal teaching authority, because of the influence of Leo's *Tome* on its formulation, see 131–5, 196–9.

[44] The phrase, which became a cliché in later Greek theology, was originally part of a deft apology Gregory offers, in his Third Oration "On the Peace" (Or 23.12), for setting out again his understanding of God as Trinity. Complicated and speculative as such reflections may seem, he suggests, they are really pastoral and spiritual in their implications.

[45] For this reply, appearing with a number of others in a collection known as the *Codex Encyclius*, see Eduard Schwartz (ed.), *Collectio Sangermanensis*, Ep. 40: ACO II/5, pp. 83–4; for a discussion of the collection and its importance for the reception of Chalcedon, see Grillmeier, "*Piscatorie - Aristotelice:*" in *Mit Ihm und in Ihm*, 283–300; Frend, *Rise of the Monophysite Movement*, 161–3.

[46] This is the first instance of an official imperial document designating Cyril's "Third" Letter to Nestorius, from the fall of 430, as enunciating normative doctrine. It is the clearest and fullest

Christian faith; "and everyone who has held or holds any other opinion, either at the present or another time, whether at Chalcedon or in any synod whatever, we anathematize."[47] The result was a new schism: this time a break in communion between the Church of Constantinople and the pro-Chalcedonian Latin West (the so-called "Acacian" schism), which was not healed until 519—when the elderly Latin-speaking Emperor Justin, at the urging of his nephew Justinian, the future emperor and architect of a renewed Mediterranean unity, gave in to the demands of Rome and affirmed Chalcedonian theology as the standard once again.

Justinian himself, a learned theologian as well as a masterly politician, spent the first decade after his own accession to the throne in 527 in trying to bring the opponents and the defenders of Chalcedon together by patient dialogue on the theological issues. By now, however, positions had hardened into immovable fronts, and the issues dividing the main parties were not so much substantial differences over how to understand the person of Christ as differences in what figures and themes from the theological tradition one emphasized and privileged. If Cyril of Alexandria was to be the touchstone of orthodoxy, as most sixth-century parties to the discussion now agreed, how was the Church to evaluate the contribution of Leo, and of Leo's Antiochene correspondents, such as Theodoret? Which of Cyril's writings best represented his normative position? Was Cyril's approach to Christ, read diachronically, fully compatible with the formula of Chalcedon, and with the Christology of those who accepted Chalcedon as orthodox?[48] Was Chalcedonian Christology, in fact, a disguised form of the very Nestorianism Cyril had opposed?

Two things seem to have become apparent to Justinian during his own early efforts at trying to broker a new settlement. One was that, as Emperor himself from 527, responsible for both the civil and the ecclesiastical peace, he could not simply abandon the Christological statement of Chalcedon, or leave it among documents whose orthodoxy remained undecided, as Zeno's *Henotikon* insinuatingly did. If the Empire did not continue to affirm the

---

statement of Cyril's understanding of the person of Christ from the early years of his dispute with Nestorius, and also makes clear, in its concluding twelve anathemas, what Cyril feels orthodox faith must exclude. Its very clarity leaves little room for compromise.

[47] See Frend, *Rise of the Monophysite Movement*, 174–83, 192; translation of the full text, 360–2.

[48] In the late fifth and early sixth centuries, representatives of both sides of the controversy over Chalcedon produced florilegia of excerpts from Cyril's voluminous works, designed to show the compatibility or incompatibility of the Chalcedonian formula with his thought. See Robert Hespel (ed.), *Florilegium Cyrillianum: le florilège cyrillien réfuté par Sévère d'Antioche* (Louvain: Publications universitaires, 1955), which reconstructs a sixth-century collection of passages from Cyril's works that support the Chalcedonian statement. Severus of Antioch, in response, composed a treatise, the *Philalethes*, attacking the reliability of such a pro-Chalcedonian florilegium of texts from Cyril (CSCO 133–4; Louvain, 1952). See also Marcel Richard, "Les florilèges diphysites du Ve et du VIe siècle," *Chalkedon* I, 721–48 (= *Opera Minora* I, No. 3).

Chalcedonian statement, formed under imperial leadership, as integral to its official vision of Christianity, the Latin West would be lost to the Empire, and important voices in the Greek cultural and political elite would be alienated, as well. Equally important, perhaps, was that a long-defended monument of imperial religious policy, a document with the status of public law, would now be abandoned.

Justinian's other realization, however, was that he also could not continue to promote Chalcedon in its original, theologically inclusive form, if he was to have any hope of regaining for the Church and the Empire large regions of Syria and Egypt which were now in schism. It was simply too open to what many regarded as a "Nestorian" reading. The only hope for a single policy on Christian orthodoxy that might be acceptable to sizeable portions of both the Chalcedonian and the non-Chalcedonian public lay in holding on to the language and concepts of Chalcedon, while subtly but thoroughly transforming the way it was understood, along lines that made clear its fundamental compatibility with the later Cyril's vision of Christ. Although resisted by some controversialists of the 530s and 540s—notably Leontius of Byzantium—Justinian's mildly revisionist "neo-Chalcedonian" Christology[49] (to use a disputed term coined by modern historians) was eventually canonized as binding Church doctrine at a synod of Greek bishops summoned by the Emperor in 553—the synod that has been received by the principal Churches of both East and West as the Second Council of Constantinople. It spells out the way mainstream orthodoxy has read Chalcedon since the sixth century.

After a lengthy introduction, condemning three celebrated representatives of the classic "school of Antioch"—Theodore of Mopsuestia, the principal Antiochene exegete and theoretician, from the fourth century; Theodoret of Cyrus, the most influential Antiochene voice at Chalcedon; and the fifth-century Syrian bishop Ibas of Edessa, writer of a well-known letter attacking Cyril—all precisely for their resistance to the form of Christology laid out in Cyril's uncompromising "third" letter to Nestorius, the fourteen canons of Constantinople II make it clear that the "one hypostasis or person" in Christ, mentioned at Chalcedon, *is* in fact none other than the eternal Word of God,[50] and that the Jesus "who was crucified in his human flesh *is* truly God and the

---

[49] On this term, see Charles Moeller, "Le chalcédonisme et le néo-chalcédonisme en orient de 451 à la fin du Vie siècle," *Chalkedon* I, 637–720; Siegfried Helmer, "Der Neuchalkedonismus: Geschichte, Berechtigung und Bedeutung eines dogmengeschichtlichen Begriffes," dissertation, University of Bonn, 1962; Aloys Grillmeier, "Der Neu-Chalkedonismus: Um die Berechtigung eines neuen Kapitels in der Dogmengeschichte," in *Festschrift B. Altaner: Historisches Jahrbuch* 77 (1957), 151–66 (= *Mit Ihm un in Ihm*, 371–85); Christian Lange, *Mia Energeia: Kirchenhistorische und dogmengeschichtliche Untersuchungen zur Einigungspolitik des Kaisers Heraclius und des Patriarchen Sergius von Constantinopel* (Tübingen: Mohr Siebeck, 2012), 398–415.

[50] Canons 2, 3, and 5: Alberigo/Tanner, 114–16. This seems to be expressed unambiguously in the concluding phrases of the Chalcedonian formula, but apparently was not unambiguous enough for Chalcedon's critics.

Lord of glory and one of the members of the holy Trinity."[51] It also suggests
that there are both orthodox and unorthodox ways of understanding traditional Cyrillian phrases about Christ's person—a union of the divine and the
human "*from* two natures;" "*one nature* of the Word of God, *made flesh*"—as
well as orthodox and unorthodox understandings of the "two-nature" language of Antioch and Chalcedon. Both sides of the controversy, in other
words, stood on equal footing; each had truth on its side, when properly
understood, but each stood in danger of heretical exaggeration.[52] After Constantinople II, in consequence, the Chalcedonian formula remained a central
part of the recognized tradition of imperially sponsored orthodoxy reaching
back to Nicaea, but was now qualified, in some degree: submitted to new
official norms, and ranged alongside other, non-conciliar Christological
formulas, precisely in order to be clearly recognized as part of that orthodox
tradition.

Even Justinian's efforts of 553, however, and of the two decades that
preceded it, did not succeed in mending the Christological breach. Later
attempts by the seventh-century emperors Heraclius and Constans II to
reconceive and re-express the "hypostatic unity" of Christ, articulated at
Chalcedon and Constantinople II, yet again, to present it as pointing towards
a single divine *energy* that bound the two ontologically distinct natures of
Christ into an organic, functioning whole—another attempt, clearly, to make
two-nature Christology palatable to those who sensed Nestorian divisiveness
behind it—only led to further controversy: this time over whether distinct
operational "energies" or, in more psychological terms, distinct operational
"wills," were inherent in Christ's two distinct natures. Thanks to the theological leadership of St. Maximus the Confessor, a Roman synod in 649,
presided over by Pope Martin I, rejected both the "monenergist" (one-energy)
and "monothelete" (one-will) positions, essentially as expressing a later form
of Apollinarian Christological monism. If two utterly distinct natural and
substantial realities are, in fact, yoked together in the concrete personal
existence of Jesus, the God-man, then both divine and human operations,
both divine and human wills, must somehow be part of his way of being, intact
but in mutual dialogue.[53]

When it had become clear to later emperors and Eastern patriarchs that
their seventh-century predecessors' attempts at reformulating Chalcedonian
Christology, in terms of an identified energy and will in Christ, had come to a
dead end, a synod meeting in Constantinople in 680 and 681—recognized

---

[51] Canon 10: Alberigo/Tanner, 118.        [52] Canons 8 and 9: Alberigo/Tanner, 117–18.

[53] For a study of the unfolding of the seventh-century attempt to move beyond the polarities
of the reception of Chalcedon by speaking of "one energy" or "one will" in Christ, and the
resistance to this policy by Maximus and his colleagues, see Christian Lange, *Mia Energeia*,
531–622.

subsequently by the Churches of East and West as the sixth ecumenical council, Constantinople III—officially "received" the canons of the Synod of 649 (which had probably been written by Maximus himself)[54] and formally condemned "monenergism" and "monothelitism." The dogmatic statement of Constantinople III is clearly modelled on that of Chalcedon, citing in full not only the Nicene and Constantinopolitan creeds, but the positive statement of Chalcedon. It then adds its own further qualifications, in similar style, citing Athanasius, Gregory of Nazianzus, Leo, and Cyril as authorities for proclaiming the existence of "two natural volitions or acts of will ($\delta\acute{v}o$ $\varphi v\sigma\iota\kappa\grave{a}s$ $\theta\epsilon\lambda\eta\sigma\epsilon\iota s$ $\eta\tau\omicron\iota$ $\theta\epsilon\lambda\acute{\eta}\mu\alpha\tau\alpha$)" in Christ, and "two natural principles of action ($\delta\acute{v}o$ $\varphi v\sigma\iota\kappa\grave{a}s$ $\acute{\epsilon}v\acute{\epsilon}\rho\gamma\epsilon\iota\alpha s$), which undergo no division, no change, no partition, no confusion, in accordance with the teaching of the holy fathers."[55] Unlike the theological intent of Constantinople II, perhaps, that of Constantinople III is clearly to amend and clarify the Chalcedonian Christology in a "friendly" or affirming, rather than in a restrictive way: but its definition of two energies and wills in Christ is still an amendment of Chalcedon, a clarification of precisely how seriously Chalcedon's two-nature language for Christ does need to be taken.

Even the seventh and last of the ancient ecumenical councils, as they have come to be received and numbered by the Churches of East and West—the Second Council of Nicaea, called by the regent-empress Irene in 786 and 787—attempted, as we shall see, to provide new clarification for the implications of this now-classical understanding of the person of the Savior. The main purpose of this imperial synod was to give the official approval of the whole Christian body to the veneration of religious icons, after several decades of simmering theological debate about their use, and of steady imperial attempts to suppress the practice.[56] The underlying issues were still largely Christological, as the literature of the controversy makes clear: could Christ, as a divine person, or the angels and saints as creatures divinized by his grace, be represented by a material image, in such a way that the image itself reveals something of the divine reality in sensible, earthly form, and so becomes an object worthy of Christian devotion? In a decree once again modelled on that

---

[54] See Richard Riedinger's collected articles on the controversy over Christ's two wills in the seventh century, particularly on Maximus's role at the Lateran Synod of 649, in *Kleine Schriften zu den Konzilsakten des 7. Jahrhunderts* (Turnhout: Brepols, 1998). In a monograph discussing at length Riedinger's hypothesis and the evidence he presents, papal historian Pietro Conte suggests the leading bishops mentioned in the *Acta* of 649 may actually have read their own translated speeches, as Maximus had composed them, at the October gathering, in a carefully scripted dramatization of Maximus's theological argument: *Il Sinodo Lateranense dell'ottobre 649* (Vatican City: Pontificia Accademia Teologica Romana, 1989), esp. 142–8.

[55] Alberigo/Tanner, 128; see also 129–30. Note the echo of Chalcedon in this addition.

[56] On the political and theological dimensions of the Iconoclastic Controversy, see chapter 9; also Christoph von Schönborn, *God's Human Face: the Christ-Icon* (San Francisco: Ignatius Press, 1994); Thomas F. X. Noble, *Images, Iconoclasm, and the Carolingians* (Philadelphia, PA: University of Pennsylvania Press, 2009).

of Chalcedon, citing the Nicene creed and the received conciliar decrees that followed it, the Second Council of Nicaea insisted that holy icons can and should be venerated, even though such devotion to sensible images of Christ or holy people must not be the same as the adoration (λατρεία) owed to the divine nature alone.[57] The first canon of Nicaea II brings home the Christological point concisely: "If anyone does not confess that Christ our God is circumscribed (περίγραπτον) in his humanity, let him be anathema."[58] To be circumscribed—limited in area and shape—in any way, Greek philosophy had long agreed, was foreign to the divine nature. That Christ is *both* personally God and humanly circumscribed, however, and therefore in some way circumscribable as the incarnate God—as a divine person—by human pen and brush, was a paradox before which even many of the bishops at Chalcedon might well have balked; now it, too, by logical development, had become part of mainstream Christian tradition. The eternal Son of God has a human face, and that face—even as represented in a painted image—is one before which we must bow in veneration, "in the name of the Lord."[59]

## RETHINKING CHALCEDON

My purpose in this somewhat lengthy narration has not been to give a general history of the early councils of the Church—later chapters will do that, to some extent—but simply to argue that, in terms of the growing formulation of Christian faith and theology, Chalcedon was neither an end nor a beginning, but a crucially important way station: one of several. From the point of view of the next three centuries, certainly, its statement of faith was not a "settlement" in any final sense, any more than the Union Agreement of 433, or even the creed of Nicaea, had been. Chalcedon had not caused controversy over Christ's person to abate, but in fact only inflamed it further, in many parts of the Christian world. It divided Christians, as well as uniting them. Its formula had not emerged as the hidden "entelechy" of earlier Christian attempts at articulating the Mystery of Christ, summarizing the tradition with a fullness that enabled all participants to recognize their chief religious concerns in its mosaic of hallowed phrases. Nor was it, by itself, the beginning of a discernible new level of certainty about the limits of orthodoxy, or the inspiration—except, perhaps, in the works of Leontius of Byzantium—for serious new theological penetration into the implications of that Mystery, until it had been further focused and qualified by the definitions of later councils. The great virtue of the Chalcedonian definition—its abiding value for theology,

---

[57] Alberigo/Tanner, 136.       [58] Alberigo/Tanner, 137.
[59] Nicaea II, canon 3: Alberigo/Tanner, 137.

and for the Churches today—is surely the breadth and balance with which it harnesses together phrases and ideas from competing traditions, to be the frame within which a theological picture of Christ, faithful to the biblical narrative and to the Nicene Creed that sums up that narrative, can continue to be developed. But that frame has always needed filling in; and in the Church of late antiquity, it also needed a number of added joints and braces, clarifications and definitions, if it was to hold together at all. It is one stage in a much longer process of staking out the course for orthodox Christology.

The real disadvantage for theology in taking the dogmatic statement of Chalcedon as a programmatic theological norm in its own right is that such a practice can narrow and distort reflection on the Mystery of Christ into an exercise in paradoxical metaphysics, an attempt simply to affirm that in Christ the infinite and the finite, the Creator and the creature, the Absolute and the contingent, are together a single individual—the wholly asymmetrical realms in and through which a single subject acts. Clearly this paradox is of inescapable importance; but it is not the whole of the Mystery. If Christology is the study in faith of the person of Jesus Christ, then it must concern itself in even broader terms with the one whom faith recognizes as Savior and Lord, who reveals to us in fully human terms the way the creating, saving God lives and acts to heal us and draw us to himself. The Mystery of Christ is the bridge between a transcendent, unimaginable God and a world of limited, visible things, forcing us to reconceive the relationship of eternity and time, Creator and created—and in the process, forcing us completely to reconceive the very being of the biblical God: as Trinity and indivisible Unity, as other and yet with us, including us, as Church and as individuals, within the very relationships that constitute the divine flow of life. The Mystery of Christ's identity is the mystery of one who transforms our life, even now in the community of faith and worship, teaching us to anticipate a final, endless transformation that exceeds all our power of imagination. As the First Letter of John says of the glorified Christ, "All we know is that when he is revealed we shall be like him, because we shall see him as he is" (I John 3.2).

The Mystery of Christ is also the mystery of Israel's relationship to the Church: the mystery by which those who call the rabbi Jesus of Nazareth "Lord" and "Savior" come to understand him, as a Jew, against the background of Israel's long history as the elect of a God who calls to them from darkness and from fire; it is the mystery by which non-Jews can call Jewish Scripture their own, and Jews and Gentiles alike find in the early witnesses to him written testimony to a "New Testament," forming with Israel's Scripture a larger canonical whole. The Mystery of Christ, then, is the key to Christian biblical interpretation, as well as to the Christian understanding of God and creation, of grace and the human potential. If one takes Christology to be, in the strict sense, only focused on the unity of his person in the duality of his natures, only the theological "tract" that reflects on the paradoxical formula of

Chalcedon, one runs the risk of leaving most of what Jesus means for Christian faith out of consideration altogether, or at least of impoverishing these other aspects of human thought about God—soteriology, theological anthropology, Trinitarian theology, biblical interpretation—by putting them at an unjustified distance from faith in him.

Karl Rahner, in the essay we referred to earlier, remarks that "the history of theology is by no means just the history of the progress of doctrine, but also a history of forgetting."[60] What I am arguing here is that an exclusive or exaggerated focus on the Chalcedonian formula can make us forget other themes and emphases in patristic thought about the person of Christ, which, for the writers of those early times, may have seemed more important than the human consciousness of Christ or the continuing balance between his human and divine natures. I certainly do not want to suggest that Chalcedon's approach to the person of Christ has been unimportant to the progress of normative Christian faith, or that it is not still a key definition of Christian boundaries, an indispensable guide to the full expression of what we understand Jesus Christ to be. But it was—and is—only part of the story: an ingenious but not entirely successful attempt to unify conflicting voices; a sign along the way, provoking further reflection and further, deeper penetration into the Mystery of our salvation in Jesus.

What I am suggesting, too, is that it is crucially important for us, in our post-scholastic and heavily secularized religious culture, to look at the development of the classical Christology of the early Church *apart* from the lens of the Chalcedonian definition, as well as *through* it: to attempt to identify what the major patristic writers themselves, from the second century on, thought most important about the person and identity of Christ, what they chose to emphasize rhetorically and conceptually—regardless of whether they conceived of him in a "word-flesh" or "word-human being" model, or of whether his human soul was a "theological factor" in their formulation. I do not mean, in any way, to cast shadows on the remarkable achievement of Cardinal Grillmeier and his colleagues in the early 1950s, or on the enormous contribution Grillmeier's later work on the history of Christology has made to patristic studies. But I think the best memorial we could erect to Grillmeier and his generation is simply to continue studying ancient Christology, asking some questions of it from the point of view of our increasingly complex intellectual and ecclesial world, that they, in their world, may have overlooked.

In doing this, I suggest it is especially important to look at the treatment of Christ by those Fathers whose work Grillmeier found to be either deficient or puzzling or uninteresting, by Chalcedonian standards: theologians who seemed to confuse or combine the two classic models of Christ in their

---

[60] "Current Problems in Christology", 151.

thinking, who showed little concern for the issues that erupted into controversy in the fifth century, or who responded to the issues of the structure of Christ's person in seemingly non-Chalcedonian ways. If one looks closely at Irenaeus, for instance, or at Origen or Athanasius—all thinkers whose theological agenda and styles differ substantially from each other—one finds that their approach to the person of Christ shares at least one central theme in common: the notion that it is in *understanding* Christ as the divine Son or Word physically present in history, manifesting the eternal glory and Wisdom of God, that human creatures are renewed—restored to a unity with God for which they were originally intended, and which gives them imperishable life. It is God's *epiphany* in Christ, as a source of transforming life for creatures, which constitutes for these three authors the core of what we today call their "Christology." As a result, Christology doubtless takes on a different shape in their hands from that of the Chalcedonian formula: less concerned with ontological analysis, surely, and less designed to emphasize the completeness and balance of Christ's human and divine realities, but also more explicitly focused on the long narrative of God's salvation, on Jesus' role as the fullness of divine revelation, and on the effect of right faith in Jesus on the Church and the believer. In its existential and spiritual urgency, as well as its hermeneutical implications for understanding the Christian biblical canon, the Christology of these three authors seems to me to offer the modern reader a healthy and challenging perspective quite different from that of our post-Enlightenment questions about God's action in history.

Similarly, if we look closely at the work of Augustine—one the most Christ-centered of ancient theologians, yet whose Christology Grillmeier found undeveloped, in places even self-contradictory, precisely because Augustine stood largely outside the debates of the later fifth century—we find an extraordinarily rich and sophisticated portrait of Christ, yet one that escapes the usual scholastic categories. For Augustine, the person of Christ is always best described, in fact, by paradox: a paradox that brings to rhetorical emphasis the irreducible Mystery of a "humble God," a God who has "emptied himself" to fill our material, historical mode of existence with his own, and to become "head" of the "body" which we are. It is by affirming this reality of Christ in faith, Augustine suggests in a number of places,[61] on the basis of contingent knowledge and the Church's proclamation, that the fallen human mind is ultimately able to be healed of the pride that aims to know God by its own unaided power of speculation, and so is enabled to move towards the participatory knowledge of Christ's godhead that is itself life-giving Wisdom. In this sense, "Christology" itself—the affirmation in intellectually humble faith of the paradox of Christ's person—becomes for Augustine the way to salvation.

---

[61] See, for example, *Confessions* 7.xvii.23–xviii.24; *De Trinitate* 4.1–4, 15–17; 13.10–15.

One might give similar characterizations of other ancient approaches to the person of Christ that seem to fall outside the Chalcedonian pattern: the language of "mixture," and the emphasis on the transformation or "divinization" of the human reality of Christ in the work of Gregory of Nazianzus and Gregory of Nyssa; the divergent views of the possibility of divine circumscription and of God's suffering that loom behind the fifth-century quarrel between the Antiochenes and Cyril of Alexandria; the fundamentally soteriological interpretation of the Chalcedonian formula itself, as the key to understanding God's saving plan, by some of Chalcedon's later defenders, such as Leontius of Byzantium, Maximus the Confessor and John of Damascus; the implications of Chalcedon, properly understood, for the devotion that prompts believers to erect images of Christ and his holy ones, and to honor those images with religious piety. For all of these writers and Church leaders, the Mystery of Christ is not simply about his personal identity or about his historical completeness as a human being; it is also about us and our salvation, about the future of *our* humanity; about the mode of God's involvement in nature and history; and about the unity and continuity of Scripture and its overall narrative, as the story of that involvement. Only if we see these broader implications of what we call ancient Christology can we come to see the richness of early struggles to understand the full significance of the person of Christ, and draw profit from them for our own faith.

Many modern theologians, Protestant and Catholic, question whether it is intellectually responsible for Christian believers, in an age characterized by an empirically grounded view of truth, a consciousness of the historical contingency of human events, and a suspicion of the mythic character of religious narrative, to continue to assert that Jesus *is* genuinely the eternal Son of God, who lived, died, and rose again in history as a complete human being. For others, including myself, the Christian faith relies, in the end, on affirming this paradox as literally true—as the truth that, of itself, necessarily reshapes our entire understanding of God, reality, history, and human welfare. But precisely because our understanding of Jesus—what Grillmeier called our *Christusbild*—has again become so uncertain, we need more than ever to return to the sources of our classical Christology in their entirety: to listen seriously to the wise and holy scholars and preachers of the pre-critical age, who struggled with equal energy to penetrate the Mystery of Jesus, but who often saw him with other eyes than we do. We need to keep in our sights the balanced, analytical picture Chalcedon drew of him, but we also need to recover much more from theology's "history of forgetting": the whole conciliar tradition, from Nicaea I to Nicaea II and beyond; and the whole theological and exegetical and homiletic and spiritual tradition of the first centuries of Christianity, which saw in Jesus the fullness of God's saving revelation of himself and of our human destiny: Emmanuel, "God with us"—"God visible."

At the end of his review of the first volume of *Chalkedon*, F. L. Cross observed of the essays in the book:

> If contemporary theological controversies occasionally peep out, it is arguable that a positive religious standpoint is necessary to the understanding of a period which thought in such very theological terms. And if there is a certain tendency to show that the early theologians were generally "right," it must also be granted that this is the view which has the *a priori* probabilities in its favour; for, however it happened, the growth of Christology necessarily converged on what was eventually canonized as "orthodox." While for those who believe in the Divine guidance of the Church, these inherent probabilities will have an additional basis.[62]

Generations from now, I hope the same can be said of what we do here ourselves, as we attempt to reconsider patristic Christology.

---

[62] Cross, review of *Chalkedon* I, *JTS* NS 4 (1953), 269.

# 2

---

# Second-Century Christology

## The Word With Us

Christians of the early second century seem to have been unanimous in seeing in Jesus the fulfillment of God's long history with Israel: a history of intervention in the world of men and women, to reveal himself as guide, patron, and source of saving Wisdom. The familiar opening verses of the *Letter to the Hebrews* are typical of the earliest Christian efforts to identify who Jesus really is, in terms of a faith that saw itself as both part of biblical tradition, and as glimpsing a new vision of history's ultimate goal: "In many and various ways God spoke of old to our ancestors, by the prophets; but in these last days he has spoken to us by a Son, whom he appointed the heir of all things."[1] The author goes on to present this "Son and heir" as the one obscurely promised in several passages of the Hebrew Bible, especially in the Psalms, and as the "great high priest,"[2] whose fidelity to the Father's will, in the face of persecution and death, has now brought the meaning of Israel's temple liturgy to final and permanent fulfillment.

As one reads the writings current in Christian communities in the second century—writings generally several decades younger than most of the works now included in the canonical New Testament—one sees a number of the details of this understanding of Jesus reappear, despite the variety of literary forms and styles in which these documents are presented.

(a) The context of early Christian thought is clearly and centrally *Jewish*: Jesus is portrayed not as a wonder-worker, king, or deified shaman, as in some popular Hellenistic religious traditions, but as an observant Jew whose life and death only can be given a religious interpretation in terms of the Hebrew Bible and the late Jewish traditions—including apocalyptic works, the Qumran writings, rabbinic midrash—in which biblical tradition was then received.

---

[1] Heb. 1.1–2.    [2] Heb. 4.14.

(b) Jesus is related to these writings as *fulfillment* is related to promise. If one understands him from the perspective of the Church's faith, many texts in the Hebrew scriptural canon can be read as pointing to him, finding its divinely intended meaning fully disclosed in him. His person, and the story of his life, are already interpreted as "contained" somehow beneath the surface meaning of ancient Israel's narratives, prophecies, and wisdom works.

(c) For this reason, Jesus' primary role in history, as understood in most second-century Christian works, is to be the *revealer* of what Israel's God intends to accomplish, for the welfare and restoration of creatures who have turned from him. God is presented in the Hebrew Bible as the only creator, the transcendent source of all that is; Jesus, for the first Christians, is frequently presented as God's "word" or *logos*: the expression, in humanly recognizable terms, of God's rational purpose in forming the world, the personal formulation of God's creative wisdom. For Justin, after mid-century, Jesus also embodies the divine *logos*, the intelligible structure of things, which the Greek philosophers—aided, Justin assumed, by their own forays into the tradition of Hebrew wisdom—had contemplated, and had used as a guide for building a good society and pursuing a happy life. This was the same Logos that Philo, the Jewish Middle Platonist of a century earlier, had seen as the mediator between God and the world.

(d) But the story of Jesus ended, as was well known, in failure, rejection, and an ignominious death as a criminal, at the hands of the Roman occupation. For second-century Christians writers, as implicitly also for the Gospels and Paul, the death of Jesus was a theological challenge, which had to be met in terms that presented it not so much as destructive of faith in him, but as faith's very heart. The *cross* that visibly represented the manner of Jesus' death, the isolation and finality of his suffering, had to be engaged head-on, and integrated into the central message of God's care for fallen humanity that Jesus' ministry had embodied. The cross had to be seen as bearing a religious meaning in clear continuity with the historic Jewish faith.

(e) Most Christian writings of the second century that reflect directly on Jesus and on his significance for disciples emphasize, without a great deal of further explanation, that the believer finds life and healing in him both through personal *faith* and devotion and through the liturgical actions of the Christian community—especially through baptism, which involves the disciple in Christ's life, and through the Eucharist. Both of these "mysteries" or sacraments (in modern terminology) flow from the person of Christ, are grounded in the events of his lifetime, and are intended to incorporate the believer into his "way." It is through these community actions that one becomes a sharer in both his death and his resurrection.

(f) The central call of faith in Jesus, as the crucified revealer of God's purposes, was seen, from the beginning of the second century, as a call to *unity*: unity in a single new community of believers with both Jewish and Gentile backgrounds; unity not simply with each other, but with the ultimate God, through Jesus as Lord and mediator, in the transforming power and charismatic vision given by the Spirit whom Jesus has sent. The message clearly enunciated in the *Letter to the Ephesians*, that "in Christ Jesus you (Gentiles) who once were far off (from faithful Israel) have been brought near in the blood of Christ,"[3]— that inclusion in the new community of Christian disciples meant a new reconciliation of religious traditions that once were rivals—seems always to have been taken as the first step to deeper union with God himself, a participation in the life and "fullness of God."[4]

## THE ODES OF SOLOMON

One of the earliest Christian documents not included in the Christian Bible is a set of Syriac hymns, discovered by chance in a previously unstudied and uncatalogued manuscript in Manchester, England, by the Biblical scholar J. Rendel Harris, early in 1909. Since that spectacular discovery—and since the identification and publication of a second, older but less complete Syriac manuscript of the *Odes* in the British Museum, three years later, by F. C. Burkitt— much has been written and conjectured about these ancient poems.[5] Their Jewish character, closely paralleling many of the canonical psalms in spirit and style, makes it clear that they come from a Semitic milieu. Parallels in mood and style with the *Hodayoth* from Qumran are also unmistakable.[6] It is generally

---

[3] Eph. 2.13.      [4] Eph. 3.19; see 14–19.

[5] For Harris's initial response to his discovery of the *Odes*, see "An Early Christian Hymn-Book," *Contemporary Review* 95 (1909) 414–28. His *editio princeps*, published along with the Jewish apocryphon *The Psalms of Solomon*, which is contained in the same manuscript, appeared later in 1909. The manuscript itself has been dated to somewhere between the thirteenth and fifteenth century. F. C. Burkitt's discovery of the text was announced in his short article, "A New MS of the Odes of Solomon," *JTS* 13 (1912), 372–85. This manuscript contains fewer Odes, but is older than Harris's—dating probably from the tenth century. There are a number of modern editions and translations of the *Odes*. The most accessible of these for English readers is James H. Charlesworth, *The Odes of Solomon* (Oxford: Oxford University Press, 1973); a revised version of Charlesworth's translation—which I use here—appears in his *The Old Testament Pseudepigrapha* 2 (New York: Doubleday, 1985), 725–71. Another translation, accompanied by an elaborate literary, historical and philological commentary, has appeared in the *Hermeneia* series, by Michael Lattke (trans. Marianne Ehrhardt): *The Odes of Solomon* (Minneapolis, MN: Fortress, 2009).

[6] See James H. Charlesworth, "Les Odes de Salomon et les manuscrits de la mer morte," *Revue Biblique* 77 (1970), 522–49.

accepted today that their original language was Syriac, even though several of them also exist in a Coptic Gnostic collection known as the *Pistis Sophia;*[7] a Greek translation of Ode 11, too, was discovered in 1955, in Bodmer Papyrus XI.[8] Yet for all their Jewish biblical echoes, the content of the *Odes* is dramatically Christian, and parallels in content and language with a number of New Testament writings—especially the Gospel of John—also abound.

Scholars today generally agree that the *Odes* were composed by a Christian author or authors in one of the Judaeo-Christian communities of eastern or western Syria, sometime around 100: close in time and place, in other words, both to the Gospel of John and to the letters of Ignatius. Spoken mainly in the person of a prophetic singer, who is inspired by the Spirit to receive the risen Christ's messages of guidance, and to celebrate his presence in the Church of Jesus' disciples,[9] these poems represent both the ecstatic joy and the deep moral earnestness of people who see themselves as sharing Christ's life by faith and the sacraments. As James Charlesworth remarks, "The *Odes* are a window through which we can occasionally glimpse the earliest Christians at worship; especially their apparent stress on baptism, their rejoicing over and experiencing of a resurrected and living Messiah, Lord, and Savior, and their frequent exhortations to live a life of the highest conceivable righteousness."[10] They are a celebration of Christian life, from the earliest decades of the Church; a life of God-given peace and unity, which the hymns often designate as "rest" (*nyāhā*), and which expresses itself, in turn, through ecstatic poetry.[11]

One of the main titles used for Jesus in the *Odes of Solomon* is "the Beloved," a name that was a favorite among Semitic Christians of the second century, and that suggested clear connections both with the Hebrew Bible and with the

---

[7] The original edition of this miscellaneous collection—also in a manuscript in the British Museum, dating from the fourth century—is that of Carl Schmidt, *Koptisch-Gnostische Schriften* (Leipzig: Hinrichs, 1905); an English translation of the collection was published by G. R. S. Mead, *Pistis Sophia: A Gnostic Miscellany* (London: Watkins, 1921). In chapters 58, 59, 65, 69, and 71, this collection contains a Coptic translation of Odes 5.1–11, 1, 6.8–18, 25, and 22.

[8] Thie was first published by M. Testuz, *Papyrus Bodmer X–XII* (Cologny-Genève: Bibliothèque Bodmer, 1959).

[9] See, for instance, *Ode* 6.1–2: "As the [wind] moves through the harp
And the strings speak,
So the Spirit of the Lord speaks through my members.
And I speak through his love." (trans. Charlesworth, *OT Pseudepigrapha*, 738)

Or *Ode* 16.1–2, 5: "My work is the psalm of the Lord in his praises.
My art and my service are in his praises,
Because his love has nourished my heart,
And his fruits he poured onto my lips...
I shall open my mouth,
And his spirit will speak through me
The praise of the Lord and his beauty." (trans. Charlesworth, *OT Pseudepigrapha*, 749)

[10] *OT Pseudepigrapha* 2.728.     [11] See, for example, *Odes* 36–7.

writings that would become the New Testament.[12] For the Odist, this title is an obvious way of expressing his own devotion to Christ, as the one centrally loved by both God and the Church. So he writes, in Ode 3:

> Who is able to distinguish love,
> Except him who is loved?
> I love the Beloved (*rḥimā*) and I myself love him,
> And where his rest is, there also am I.[13]

Ode 7, which narrates in enigmatic but recognizable terms the story of the Incarnation and its effect, begins by contrasting "the course of anger over wickedness" with "the course of joy over the Beloved"—something the Odist clearly shares. More frequently, the author speaks of Christ as "the Lord's Messiah"[14] or Christ (literally, "anointed one"), or even as "Lord Messiah."[15]

Ode 41, one of the most explicit affirmations of the author's understanding of Christ, begins with an invitation to "all the Lord's little ones"[16] to praise him and receive his truth, because they share in the "great day" of his grace.[17] After a brief section in which Christ himself seems to address the community, with an allusion to Isa. 52.14 ("All those who see me will be astonished"), the Odist, speaking with the community in the first person plural, returns to sum up his presentation of the passion and resurrection of Christ:

> And his word is with us in all our way,
> The Savior who gives life and does not reject ourselves;
> The Man who humbled himself,
> But was raised because of his own righteousness.
> The Son of the Most High appeared
> In the perfection of his Father,
> And light dawned from the Word.
> The Messiah in truth is one,
> And he was known before the foundations of the world,
> That he might give life to humans forever by the truth of his name.[18]

---

[12] See, for example, Deut. 33.12 (referring to Benjamin, the object of God's favor); Isa. 5.1 (beginning of parable of the vineyard of Israel, referring to Israel itself as "my beloved"); Matt. 3.17, Lk. 3.22 (voice from heaven at baptism of Jesus); Matt. 17.5 (voice from heaven at Transfiguration of Jesus); Eph. 1.6 (thanks to God "for the grace which he freely bestowed on us in the Beloved"). As a title of Jesus in second-century writings, see Ignatius, *Smyrn.* Prologue; *Ascension of Isaiah* 1.4; 1.6–7; 1.13; 3.13–18; 8.18; *Martyrdom of Polycarp* 14.1, 3; Irenaeus, *Adv. Haer.* 4.5.4. See also *Test. Levi* 17.3, which may be a second-century Christian work.

[13] Ode 3.4–5 (trans. Charlesworth, *OT Pseudepigrapha*, 735).

[14] Odes 9.36; 29.6; 36.6; cf. 41.3.

[15] Odes 17.16; 24.1; 39.11. For a discussion of the use of the title "Messiah" in the *Odes*, see Michael Lattke, "Die Messias-Stellen der Oden Salomos," in Cilliers Breytenbach and Henning Paulsen (eds), *Anfänge der Christologie: Festschrift für Ferdinand Hahn* (Göttingen: Vandenhoeck & Ruprecht, 1991), 429–45.

[16] Ode 41.1.     [17] Ode 41.4.

[18] Ode 41.11–15 (trans. Charlesworth, *OT Pseudepigrapha*, 770).

Combining allusions to a number of familiar New Testament texts—Phil. 2.7–8; Lk. 1.32; John 1.4–5, 9; John 17.24; Eph. 1.4—the writer presents the career of Jesus as beginning in God's eternity, where he is related to the Father as his eternal Word; it continues in time, through his humiliation and resurrection, in order to reveal "the perfection of his Father," and to give life to those who accept him as the revealer of God's way.

This conception of Jesus and his mission as a revelation of the triumphant love of God for all peoples, despite all the shocking details of his rejection that the Gospels provide, stands also behind the powerful, somewhat mysterious Ode 23. Here, after an opening promise of joy, grace and love for God's elect (vv. 1–3), the poet invites his hearers to "walk in the knowledge of the Lord, and you will know the grace of the Lord generously" (v. 4). For the rest of the Ode, the poet's dominant metaphor for divine revelation is that of a letter from God, shot into the world like an arrow, which no one in earlier times had been able to open (vv. 5–10). The letter is then bound to a wheel, "and with it was a sign of the Kingdom and of providence": a suggestion, perhaps, of the wheeled chariot, representing God's triumphant plan for Israel, described in Ezekiel 1, which would also be the basis of later Jewish mystical *merkabah* ("chariot") spirituality.[19] The conclusion of this majestic, if puzzling, scene is the final glorification of the Son, who is himself God's revealer, and the affirmation of the content of his revelation as professed in the Church's baptismal faith:

> The letter was one of command,
> And hence all regions were gathered together.
> And there appeared as its head, the Head which was revealed
> Even the Son of Truth from the Most High Father,
> And he inherited and possessed everything...
> And the letter became a large volume, which was entirely written
>     by the finger of God.
> And the name of the Father was upon it;
> And of the Son and of the Holy Spirit,
> To rule for ever and ever.[20]

For the Odist, the life-giving revelation of God's reality that is realized in the life of Jesus Christ clearly includes Jesus' humiliation and death—that central paradox and challenge to faith that is also a formative element in the composition of the four Gospels, and a central part of the New Testament message. In Ode 25, for example, Christ speaks of his rescue by God from human hostility and even from death itself, by God's faithful protection:

> I was rescued from my chains
> And I fled unto you, O my God,

---

[19] See Charlesworth, *The Odes of Solomon*, 96 n. 8; Lattke, *The Odes of Solomon*, 332–4.
[20] trans. Charlesworth, *OT Pseudepigrapha*, 756.

Because you are the right hand of salvation
And my helper...
Because your face was with me, which saved me by your grace.
But I was despised and rejected in the eyes of many,[21]
And I was in their eyes like lead...
And I was covered with the covering of your Spirit,
And I removed from me my garments of skin.[22]
Because your right hand raised me,
And caused sickness to pass from me,
And I became mighty in your truth
And holy in your righteousness...[23]

Here, as in several other passages in the *Odes* that reflect on Christ's passion, the implication is that these sufferings of the Messiah were, in reality, the beginning of a process of transformation that now extends to the whole community.

This transformation is even clearer in Ode 31, which celebrates the liberation from death offered by God through Christ to "those that had become sons through Him."[24] Here Christ addresses his own vulnerable followers:

Come forth, you who have been afflicted,
And receive joy.
And possess yourselves though grace,
And take unto you immortal life.
And they condemned me when I stood up,
Me who had not been condemned.
Then they divided my spoil
Though nothing was owed them.
But I endured and held my peace and was silent,[25]
That I might not be disturbed by them,
But I stood undisturbed like a solid rock...
And I bore their bitterness because of humility,
That I might redeem my nation and instruct it...[26]

The death of Jesus, in fact, and his entry into the depths of Sheol, death's stronghold, is not simply an expression of his self-emptying and concern for his people; it is a march to victory, in which Jesus leads to freedom and life all those who are similarly vulnerable and turn to him. So, in the final Ode—Ode 42—Christ again speaks to his followers:

I was not rejected although I was considered to be so,
And I did not perish, although they thought it of me.

[21] Another allusion to the "Suffering Servant" passage in Isaiah: here Isa. 53.3.
[22] An allusion to death in terms recalling Gen. 3.19–21, as well as a suggestion of Jesus' entry into glory.
[23] Ode 25.1–10 (trans. Charlesworth, *OT Pseudepigrapha*, 757–8).
[24] Ode 31.4 (trans. Charlesworth, *OT Pseudepigrapha*, 762).   [25] An echo of Ps. 22.18.
[26] Ode 31.6–12 (trans. Charlesworth, *OT Pseudepigrapha*, 762–3).

Sheol saw me and was shattered,
And death ejected me and many with me...
And those who had died ran towards me;
And they cried out and said, "Son of God, have pity on us.
And deal with us according to your kindness,
And bring us out from the bonds of darkness...
May we also be saved with you,
Because you are our Savior."
Then I heard their voice,
And placed their faith in my heart,
And I placed my name upon their head,
Because they are free,[27] and they are mine.[28]

The main purpose of the *Odes*, in fact, seems to be to celebrate with ecstatic praise the possibility now offered to the Christian liturgical community: to share in the freedom from death and corruption won by Christ through his faithful obedience. In many of them, this is expressed in imagery that clearly suggests the baptismal liturgy: allusions to drinking from springs of water,[29] to milk and honey,[30] to spiritual circumcision,[31] to feeding babies and to faces made shiny with oil[32]—all in the context of accepting the Truth of Christ in faith and of sharing in his risen life. A striking example of this is Ode 41:

Let all the Lord's little ones praise Him,
And let us receive the truth of his faith...
For a great day has shined upon us,
And wonderful is he who has given to us of his glory.
Let us, therefore, all of us, agree in the name of the Lord,
And let us honor him in his goodness.
And let our faces shine in his light,
And let our hearts meditate in his love
By night and by day...
And his word is with us in all our way,
The Savior who gives life and does not reject ourselves.
The man who humbled himself,
But was exalted because of his own righteousness...[33]

---

[27] Charlesworth observes here that the emphatic plural, *bnai hi're*, can also mean "nobles" or "princes." The dead, set free from Sheol by Christ, become the new aristocracy of his Kingdom.

[28] Ode 42.10-11, 15-16, 19-20 (trans. Charlesworth, *OT Pseudepigrapha*, 771). For similar evocations of the triumph of the crucified Christ over death, see Odes 22 and 28.

[29] See, for example, Ode 6.11-14; Ode 11.6-7; Ode 30.1-3; Ode 35.1; Ode 40.2.

[30] For example, Ode 8.14; Ode 19.1-3 (where milk from the Father becomes the image for the reality of the Incarnation); Ode 30.4; Ode 40.1.

[31] For example, Ode 11.2-3.     [32] For example, Ode 41.1-2, 6.

[33] Ode 41.1, 4-6, 11-12 (trans. Charlesworth, *OT Pseudepigrapha*, 769-79).

The cross of Christ, which is now also his sign of victory, becomes for the Odist also the mark of Christian prayer, the new interpretation of the traditional *orans* posture used by suppliants in many ancient religious traditions:

> I extended my hands
> And hallowed my Lord;
> For the expansion of my hands
> Is his sign,
> And my extension is the upright cross.[34]

The cross shapes the way Christians are to pray, because their life, as baptized believers, is to be nothing less than an identification with him in his death and resurrection. And the goal of this identification with Christ, in the view of the Odist, is nothing less than eschatological transformation of the human person, in body and spirit. In this life, it means even bodily renewal and strength:

> My heart was raised and enriched in the love of the Most High,
> So that I might praise him with my name.[35]
> My members were strengthened,
> That they may not fall from his power.
> Infirmities fled from my body,
> And it stood firm for the Lord by his will...[36]

For the life to come, the promise is one of eternal vitality and joy: "immortal rest," a home in a blooming and verdant Paradise, a new bodily nature described as a garment of light, which will take the place of this present, coarse "garment of flesh."[37] As Jesus himself emphasizes, in the last supper discourse in John's Gospel, it is by continuing union with the dead and risen Christ, in knowledge and love—with the "redeemed Redeemer"—that the disciple himself finds a pledge of life. The Odist, too, urges the members of the community of faith to "stand and be established," and to "bring forth fruits to the Lord, a holy life":[38]

> Seek and increase,
> And abide in the love of the Lord;[39]
> And you who are loved in the Beloved;
> And you who are kept in him who lives;

---

[34] Ode 27 (complete) (trans. Charlesworth, *OT Pseudepigrapha*, 759).

[35] Does this refer to the common name of "Christian"—Pliny's *nomen Christianum* (Ep. 10.96)—which, according to Acts 11.26, was first used of the disciples of Jesus at Antioch?

[36] Ode 18.1–3.          [37] Ode 11.10–16. For "garments of flesh," cf. Ode. 8.9.

[38] Ode 8.3, 2.

[39] Cf. John 15.4–10; cf. John 6.56, where "abiding" in Jesus seems to suggest being nourished by him in the Eucharist.

And you who are saved in him who was saved.
And you shall be found incorrupted in all ages,
On account of the name of your Father.[40]

## IGNATIUS OF ANTIOCH

If the *Odes of Solomon* are a relatively recent discovery among the rich treasures of early Christian literature, the letters of St. Ignatius of Antioch have, for centuries, been much better known—even though both these collections may come from the same time and region, possibly from the same Church. Yet although Ignatius's letters, addressed to a variety of Christian communities in western Asia Minor, were read and admired even in Christian antiquity, the actual number of them, as well as their length, text and dating, have been a matter of dispute throughout the Christian tradition, and continue to be debated today. According to Eusebius's *Church History* (composed between 295 and 325), Ignatius was bishop of the Church in Antioch during the reign of Trajan (95–117)—although it is unclear just what the title "bishop (*episkopos*)" in Christian communities meant at that time or what a bishop's role was—and was "sent from Syria to Rome and became food for wild beasts, on account of his testimony to Christ."[41] Ignatius has been honored as a martyr since Christian antiquity, even though the *Acta* recounting his death are generally considered late and untrustworthy, and it is unclear what the charges might have been on which he was condemned.[42] In any case, Ignatius, on his way to Rome under guard, apparently urged Polycarp, bishop of Smyrna, to have his presbyteral council send an official delegate back to the church in Antioch with news of Ignatius's continuing fidelity in persecution, and Polycarp seems to have carried out this request.[43] What we do possess, in the opinion of most scholars, is a set of seven letters that have come down under the name of Ignatius: six to

---

[40] Ode 8.20–2 (trans. Charlesworth, *OT Pseudepigrapha*, 742).

[41] Eusebius, *Church History* 3.36, trans. A. C. McGiffert, in Philipp Schaff and Henry Wace (eds), *NPNF* II.1.167. Jerome, in his brief survey of earlier Christian writers from 392/3, *De viris illustribus*, simply repeats the information found in Eusebius's history (*De vir. ill.* 16).

[42] See J. B. Lightfoot, *The Apostolic Fathers: Ignatius and Polycarp* 1.31–3; 2.377–91. References in several of his letters to a restoration of peace in Antioch and the Church of Syria, as a result of the prayers of fellow Christians in Asia Minor (*Philadelphians* 10.1; *Smyrn.* 11.1–2; *Polycarp* 7.1) suggest that Ignatius may have been arrested by the Roman authorities because of the suspicion that he was responsible for some kind of factional disturbance. In *Smyrn.* 11.1, he also refers to having been "judged worthy" of martyrdom because of his "conscience." Ignatius himself emphasizes the importance of concord in the Christian community, based on "being in accord with the bishop's mind" (*Ephesians* 4.1–2). In the ecclesial vision of the letters ascribed to him, the presence of a single bishop, whose guidance is normative, at the heart of the local Christian body, is the source of the unity that draws the community, through Christ, to God.

[43] *To Polycarp* 7.2; Polycarp, *To the Philippians* 13.

small local Christian communities in western Asia Minor, urging unity in faith, Church structure, and liturgical practice; and a seventh personally addressed to Polycarp, bishop of Smyrna. From these letters—although their integrity, authenticity and dating continues to be discussed[44]—we can put together a plausible narrative of the context of their composition, and so of the difficult conditions under which Ignatius found himself, as he emphasized the fundamentals of Christian faith for communities not his own.

Ignatius and his Roman military escort apparently made their way across modern Turkey by the old Roman road, and chose the northern route from Laodicaea, in west central Asia Minor, to the coastal city of Smyrna. Delegations from the Christian communities at Ephesus, Magnesia and Tralles, which lay somewhat to the south, came to join him along his way. When they reached Smyrna, Ignatius had the time to write brief letters of spiritual encouragement to those delegations' home churches, urging them to be faithful to the Gospel and its way of life, as well as to their bishops and leaders. From Smyrna, Ignatius apparently also wrote ahead to the Church of Rome,

---

[44] Eusebius, in his account of Ignatius's life and work, lists seven letters written by him to local Asian Churches, with whom he had come into contact while being taken, under military guard, overland from Antioch to Rome. In the Middle Ages, the most common Greek text of his work included thirteen letters: these seven, plus six others to individuals and communities in more or less the same style. The medieval Latin translation of Robert Grosseteste, however, included only the seven listed by Eusebius, which led Archbishop James Ussher, in 1644, to publish an elaborate argument, based on text-critical grounds, for the authenticity of only those letters. In 1646, the Dutch philologist Isaac Voss published, from a manuscript in Florence, a Greek version of six of those "Eusebian" letters, several of them somewhat shorter than the Greek texts then known; Ignatius's letter to the Romans, which does not appear in that Florentine manuscript, had, in any case, a separate manuscript tradition. In the nineteenth century, the English Syriac scholar William Cureton published a Syriac translation of a collection of only three of Ignatius's letters—*Ephesians*, *Romans*, and *Polycarp*—in still briefer form, and argued that this was based on the original text of Ignatius's works. Since the late nineteenth century, it has been generally accepted by scholars that the corpus of seven letters, in the shorter form published by Voss, is Ignatius's authentic corpus; the longer version, with expanded texts and additional letters, seems to come from a non-Nicene circle in the Church of Antioch in the 370s, perhaps associated with Bishop Meletius, which also compiled the *Apostolic Constitutions*—both of these collections being intended as "documentation" for the Christology and liturgical practice of a "middle" party in the late years of the conflict over Nicene faith. (See my article, "The Enigma of Meletius of Antioch," in Ronnie J. Rombs and Alexander Y. Hwang (eds), *Tradition and the Rule of Faith in the Early Church: Essays in Honor of Joseph T. Lienhard, SJ* [Washington, DC: Catholic University of America Press, 2010], 128–50.)

In the last few decades, this standard view of the Ignatian corpus, as well as its dating, has been challenged again by several European scholars, mainly on the grounds that the seven accepted letters offer a portrait of Church leadership—a single bishop at the center of things, a small body of presbyters or "elders" who advise and support him, and a body of ministers or "deacons" who carry out the bishop's pastoral initiatives and facilitate the liturgy—which is otherwise not attested at such an early date. For a thoughtful and detailed survey of the debates about the Ignatian corpus, see Allen Brent, *Ignatius of Antioch. A Martyr Bishop and the Origin of Episcopacy* (London: Continuum, 2007), esp. 1–13 (determining the corpus), 14–43 (reconstruction of the charges on which Ignatius was condemned to death), 95–143 (modern attempts to date the Ignatian corpus in the late second or even the fourth century).

where his journey, and foreseeably his life, would end; the point of that famous letter, expressed with an intensity that may shock us still, is to urge the Christians in Rome not to make any effort to secure his release, since that would prevent him from giving final witness to his faith and love of Christ; they must allow him to perfect his discipleship by imitating Christ in self-sacrifice: "Let me imitate the passion of my God!"[45] As Ignatius and his escort moved on towards the Hellespont and the borders of continental Europe, he seems to have written three more letters from the town of Troas, once the launching-site for Paul's evangelistic travels in the Greek world: letters to two of the towns he had visited, Philadelphia and Smyrna, to thank the communities for their hospitality, and another to Bishop Polycarp of Smyrna, with whom he evidently shared a common pastoral and spiritual vision.[46] Taken together, these seven letters do not offer a body of developed theological arguments or structural directives for the emerging Church; rather, they are warm, intense letters of encouragement in Christ, written apparently under pressure of time and before the prospect of an almost certain violent death, revealing what a leader of one of the earliest Christian communities considered it most important to say to his brothers and sisters in other places. As a result, they show an earnestness that is almost unique in Christian literature.

Like the poet who speaks in the *Odes of Solomon*, Ignatius presents himself as a charismatic prophet. In the opening paragraphs of all seven letters, Ignatius claims the title or nickname *theophoros*, "carried by a god," which in classical Greek carries the suggestion of inspiration, even of divine frenzy.[47] In his letter to the Philadelphians, he insists that his exhortation to maintain Church unity through respectful deference to the bishop and his presbyters has been a kind of prophetic word, inspired not simply by human prudence:

> He for whose sake I am in chains is my witness that I did not come to know this on the basis of human flesh; but the Spirit proclaimed it, saying "Do nothing apart from the bishop!"[48]

And the content of Ignatius's vision extends, at least potentially, to "heavenly things, the arrangement of the angels," such as Paul also claims to have glimpsed.[49] So he urges his colleague Polycarp to pray, too, "that what is unseen may be revealed to you, that you may lack nothing and that you may

---

[45] *Romans* 6.3.

[46] For a helpful reconstruction of the steps of Ignatius's journey, see Brent 10–13; also the still eloquent book of Virginia Corwin, *St. Ignatius and Christianity in Antioch* (New Haven, CT: Yale University Press, 1960).

[47] See, for example, Aristophanes, *Agamemnon* 1150; Philodemus, *On the Gods* 1.

[48] *Phld.* 7.2. For thoughtful reflections on Ignatius's self-presentation as a prophetic figure, see Christine Trevett, *A Study of Ignatius of Antioch in Syria and Asia* (Lewiston, NY: Edwin Mellen Press, 1992) 131–8.

[49] *Tral.* 5.2; cf. 2 Cor. 12.1–5.

overflow with every spiritual gift."[50] Even the members of the community at
Ephesus are, Ignatius suggests—like a procession of devout religious initiates
in a Hellenistic city—all "fellow pilgrims, inspired by God (*theophoroi*)[51] and
carrying your shrine, carrying Christ and your holy things, decked out in every
way in the commandments of Jesus Christ."[52] The result of this prophetic gift
in the community, in Ignatius's view as in the Odist's, is an abiding joy and
faith that cannot be secured on the basis of human experience alone; so he
addresses the church at Philadelphia as a community that "rejoices without
hesitation in the suffering of our Lord and is convinced, completely by his
mercy, of his resurrection; I embrace you in the blood of Jesus Christ, which is
eternal and lasting joy—especially if you are one with your bishop."[53] Both
bishop and community, it seems, are able to understand the paradoxical "way"
of Jesus, crucified and risen, and to find joy in it, because they experience
together the power of his Spirit.

For Ignatius, too, as for the *Odes of Solomon*, the Christ of the Christian
Gospel is himself God's final word of revelation, "the mouth that does not
deceive, through which the Father has spoken truly."[54] So the community of
Jesus' disciples must resist the temptation to continue forming their daily lives
according to the Jewish law.

> For the divine prophets lived according to Christ Jesus. For that reason they were
> persecuted, since they were inspired by his grace in order to convince those who
> did not believe, that there is one God, who has revealed himself through Christ
> Jesus his Son, who is his Word coming forth from silence,[55] and who, in every
> way, was pleasing to the one who sent him. . . . How shall we be able to live apart
> from him, of whom the prophets, too, were disciples in the Spirit, and waited for
> him as their teacher?[56]

The Christian community, then, like the prophets of Israel, "all become wise
by receiving the personal knowledge (*gnōsis*) of God, which is Jesus Christ."[57]
The reason that the community now shares Israel's love for the "prophets"—a
term that probably includes the whole range of Israel's written witnesses—is
"because they, too, proclaimed a word directed towards the Gospel, and hoped

---

[50] *Pol.* 2.2.
[51] If one places the Greek accent differently, this could also be translated as "carrying your
god." This does not seem to coincide with Ignatius's other uses of this word, however, although it
does fit better linguistically with the rest of the sentence.
[52] *Eph.* 9.2.       [53] *Phld.* Inscr.       [54] *Rom.* 8.2.
[55] The one extant Greek manuscript of this letter, an eleventh-century codex now in Florence,
as well as the medieval Latin translation, reads here "his eternal Word who did not come forth
from silence." Most modern editors, however, follow the reading of the Armenian and Arabic
translations, as well as a quotation in a sixth-century Syriac version of a work by Severus of
Antioch, and accept the somewhat more puzzling reading that we have given here. It is a case of
the *lectio difficilior* being assumed to be right!
[56] *Magn.* 8.2, 9.2.       [57] *Eph.* 17.2.

in him and waited for him, and by believing in him were saved, as being part of the unity of Jesus Christ."[58] The faithful voices of Israel, who saw their own message as directed towards future fulfillment, were, in Ignatius's view, already part of the same community of faith in which he and his correspondents now lived and suffered in hope.

Ignatius uses some of the same traditional Semitic–Christian titles for Jesus that we find in the *Odes of Solomon* and other second-century works: he is "the Beloved,"[59] for instance, and may also be what Ignatius means when he refers simply to "the Name."[60] The reason, however, for Jesus' unique role as revealer of God's final word to humanity is that he is himself originally located within the saving divine Mystery. Ignatius does not, of course, develop a technical vocabulary in which this can be consistently articulated. He does, however, refer several times to Jesus simply as "our God;"[61] he is also "Son of the Father,"[62] who is "in the Father"[63] and eternally "with the Father,"[64] and who was always "subject" to the Father[65]—all phrases echoing, in a general way, the language of John's Gospel. Yet, as Ignatius insists—particularly in his letter to the Smyrnaeans—Jesus lived and suffered as a real human being, "and not, as some unbelievers say, in appearance only;"[66] in fact, Ignatius says, "I know and believe that he was in the flesh also after the resurrection.... And after the resurrection he ate and drank with [the disciples] as a fleshly person, even though he was spiritually united with the Father."[67] Even the charismatic preaching and courageous witness of Ignatius and his fellow apostles loses its meaning, if Jesus was not himself their human model; "For how does it benefit me, if someone praises me but blasphemes my Lord, by not confessing that he was clothed in flesh?"[68] So, when referring to Christ, Ignatius occasionally speaks in densely paradoxical terms that seem to reflect formulas his readers may already have known. He writes to the Ephesians, for instance:

There is one physician, fleshly and spiritual, begotten and unbegotten, God in a human being, true life in death, both from Mary and from God, first passible and then impassible: Jesus Christ, our Lord.[69]

---

[58] *Phld.* 5.2. See also *Trall.* 9.2.       [59] *Smyrn.* Inscr.

[60] *Eph.* 1.2: Ignatius is a prisoner "for the sake of our common Name and hope;" *Eph.* 20.2: "Come together, all of you together, in the grace that arises from the Name, in one faith and in one Jesus Christ."

[61] *Eph.* Inscr. and 18.2; *Rom.* Inscr. and 3.3; in the single Greek manuscript and in the Latin translations, also *Smyrn.* 10.1.

[62] *Rom.* Inscr. (twice).       [63] *Rom.* 3.3.       [64] *Magn.* 6.1, cf. 7.1.

[65] *Magn.* 13.2; cf. *Smyrn.* 8.1: the community is exhorted to "follow" the bishop as Jesus followed the Father.

[66] *Smyrn.* 2.1; cf. 4.2.       [67] *Smyrn.* 3.1–2.       [68] *Smyrn.* 5.2.

[69] *Eph.* 7.2. For "God in a human being," which is the reading of the short Syriac recension as well as of several Fathers who quote this text, the Greek manuscript and the Latin translation give "God who has become flesh." Is this latter reading an attempt to avoid the possibly "Nestorian" implications of the Syriac phrasing?

Or as he urges his fellow bishop Polycarp:

> Recognize the times. Look for him who is above time, the timeless one; the
> invisible one, who became visible for our sakes; the one who cannot be touched
> and cannot suffer, who became capable of suffering for our sakes; the one who
> endured in every way for our sakes.[70]

As a result, the events of Christ's life recounted in Gospel tradition all become
"shouted mysteries, which were worked in the silence of God"[71]—manifestations
in concrete actions of the power of God. His conception and birth from Mary
were the beginning of this transforming revelation;[72] he was revealed by a
star—presumably to the Magi—in order to put an end to "all magic and spells"
and bring star-worship to an end;[73] he was baptized "that by his passion he
might purify water;"[74] he was anointed with precious ointment by a woman at
the house of Simon the leper,[75] just before his passion, "so that he might
breathe incorruptibility on the Church."[76] Above all, it is the death of Jesus on
the cross that brings, to those who are united with him in faith, a share in his
risen life.[77] This comes about, it seems, on the one level, through the emblematic
revelation, in Jesus' resurrection, of his triumph over death;[78] but it also seems to
involve, for Ignatius, a voluntary choice on the part of the believer to give up
seeking his or her own will, and to share personally in Jesus' "obedience unto
death."[79] So he writes to the Trallians:

> When you are subject to the bishop as to Jesus Christ, you seem to me to be living
> not in the human fashion but according to the way of Jesus Christ, who died for
> our sakes so that, by believing in his death, you might escape death.[80]

For Ignatius, the cross fully embodies the paradox of faith. In his letter to the
Magnesians, he compares the world's style of living and God's as "two kinds of
coin (*nomismata*)," each with its own distinctive stamp:

> Unbelievers bear the mark of this world, but believers, in their love, [bear] the
> mark of God the Father through Jesus Christ, whose life is not in us unless we
> voluntarily choose to die into his suffering.[81]

Echoing Paul, he writes to the Ephesians, "My spirit is an offscouring of the
cross, which is a scandal to unbelievers, but to us salvation and eternal life."[82]
More boldly still, he addresses the Church at Philadelphia as

> receiving mercy and established in the harmony of God, and rejoicing in the
> suffering of our Lord without any hesitation, finding full reassurance in his
> resurrection, in all mercy; I embrace you in the blood of Jesus Christ, which is

---

[70] *Pol.* 3.2.          [71] *Eph.* 19.1.          [72] *Eph.* 19.1.          [73] *Eph.* 19.2–3.
[74] *Eph.* 18.2.          [75] Matt. 26.7.          [76] *Eph.* 17.1.          [77] So *Smyrn.* 5.3.
[78] *Smyrn.* 1.1–2.1.          [79] Phil. 2.8.          [80] *Trall.* 2.1.          [81] *Magn.* 5.2.
[82] *Eph.* 18.1; see 1 Cor 4.13; cf. 1.18.

eternal, unwavering joy—especially if your members are in unity with the bishop and his presbyters and deacons, who have been selected according to the mind of Jesus Christ...[83]

In fact, in Ignatius's view, union with the crucified Christ through faith and religious practice is the fundamental guarantee of eternal life, as God's promised gift. He writes to the Trallians:

> Flee, then, from the shoots of wickedness, which produce a deadly fruit; if anyone tastes of this, he will die immediately—for these are not the Father's planting. If they were, they would have been revealed as branches of the cross, and their fruit would be undying. Through the cross, in his passion, he calls you, since you are his members.[84]

The implications are institutional, as well as personal. To be united to God through Christ in this way involves not only external membership in the Christian community, but genuine faith and love, which lead to the union of believers both with God and with each other. To be in "blameless unity" is to "have a share in God always."[85] In the clearly articulated structure of the Church that Ignatius seems to presume, and in the "harmony of God" that results from the mutual respect and obedience of believers, Ignatius sees the roots of a social order that mirrors and anticipates the fullness of salvation, the "peace" of the *Odes*:

> Let everyone, then, seek personal agreement with God and show respect for each other, and let no one look at his or her neighbor in a fleshly way; rather, love one another always in Jesus Christ. Let there be nothing among you that can possibly divide you, but be united to the bishop, and to those who have authority among you, as an example and lesson in incorruptibility.[86]

Harmony within the community, like the harmony of a well-trained chorus, is an expression of love for Christ, and a lived hymn of praise for his Father.[87] It is the living, social form of faith.


## THE ASCENSION OF ISAIAH

A third early Christian document, which seems also to have originated in the rich religious culture of the eastern Mediterranean world, is the mysterious narrative, in apocalyptic style, that has come down under the title *The Ascension of Isaiah*. This puzzling but dramatically engaging work, most

---

[83] *Phld.* Inscr.

[84] *Trall.* 11.2. Cf. *Trall.* 9.2: apart from the risen Christ "we do not have true life;" *Magn.* 1.2: Christ is "our constant life."

[85] *Eph.* 4.2.      [86] *Magn.* 6.2 (altered).      [87] *Eph.* 4.1.

scholars today agree, is a combination of two parts. The first (chs 1–5) seems to be a redaction of an originally late-Jewish narrative of the final conflict and death of the prophet Isaiah, often referred to today as "the Martyrdom of Isaiah," and dates probably from the second or first century before Christ. It includes what is clearly an early Christian interpolation, sometimes called "the Testament of Hezekiah," (chs 1.2b–13; 3.13–4.22), which summarizes the longer narrative that will be unfolded in the second part of the work: a vision—put into Isaiah's mouth—of the coming life, death, and resurrection of Jesus Christ, of the corruption of the Christian community after his ascension, and of Christ's future coming to save his faithful ones. The second part of the work (chs 6–11) seems to be wholly a Christian composition, offering in greater detail the content of Isaiah's vision of Christ and his coming into the world; it is told in the classic Jewish–Christian form of an apocalyptic journey and vision. This second part, as well as the formation of the whole text, seems—on theological and literary grounds—to have been completed during the first decades of the second century, and most likely comes from Antioch or Western Syria: the same geographical milieu in which the *Odes of Solomon* and Ignatius, as well as the Gospels of Matthew and John, probably found their home. Although the complete text exists today only in an Ethiopic translation, fragments of ancient versions in Greek, Latin, Slavonic, and Coptic have also been published. The original language of the pre-Christian first section, if it existed independently, was probably Hebrew, but its expanded, Christian version, as well as the second half of the work, was more likely Greek.

The *Ascension of Isaiah*, then, as we now have it, is a classic instance of the complex hybridization of texts, religious traditions, and theological motifs that very much characterized Syrian Judaeo-Christianity at the turn of the second century. Enrico Norelli, the most recent translator of the full Ethiopic text, as well as the general editor and commentator in the volume containing all the ancient versions,[88] suggests that the work may represent the prophetic, charismatic Judaeo-Christian stream within that world that Ignatius himself criticizes as insidious, in his *Letter to the Philadelphians*, by being too Jewish, and that he attacks for its docetic Christology in his *Letter to the Smyrnaeans*.[89] Norelli concedes that any conjecture about the work's original context remains speculative, but writes:

> Recalling that Ignatius had to deal with charismatics who opposed him as bishop, and with people who did not believe in the reality of the flesh of Christ, one is led

[88] A. Giambelluca Kossava, C. Leonardi, L. Perrone, E. Norelli, and P. Bettiolo (eds), *Ascensio Isaiae: Textus*, CCSA 7 (Turnhout: Brepols, 1995); E. Norelli (ed.), *Ascensio Isaiae: Commentarius*, CCSA 8 (Turnhout: Brepols, 1995). Norelli has also published numerous articles on this work.
[89] See *Phld.* 6; 8.2; *Smyrn.* 1–3; 6.

to ask oneself if the group behind the *Ascension of Isaiah* did not have its own roots in the same theological and ecclesiastical ground.... It seems to me legitimate to propose that, although it is improbable Ignatius was struggling with the same group from whom the *Ascension* came, still the docetist opponents of Ignatius and the prophets of the *Ascension* could represent different branches within the same Hellenistic Judaeo-Christian ambience in Western Syria— charismatic Christian élites, which had developed an authoritative role in the Christian communities, even quietly working their way into the presbyteral and episcopal leadership.[90]

Whatever its origin, the purpose of the work is clearly not just to offer an account of the Jewish prophet's martyrdom, but to present him, in a still fuller form than the Book of Isaiah itself makes possible, as Israel's key prophetic witness to the career of Christ the Savior. In the clearly Christian redaction of the first part of the *AI*, King Hezekiah is depicted as handing on to his son Manasseh the contents of a vision that the prophet Isaiah had had, eleven years earlier, in his palace, "concerning the judgments of the angels and the destruction of this world, concerning the garments of the righteous, and concerning the going forth, the transformation, the persecution and ascension of the Beloved."[91] Even in this first chapter of the work, Isaiah is depicted as knowing that "the Beloved," who is Christ, will be led by the same prophetic spirit that is in Isaiah himself, and that is in control of the struggles swirling around the king. The prophet is also sure of his own vocation, and knows that "I must have my portion with the inheritance of the Beloved."[92] Later on in this first section of the work, after a description of the conflicts between various prophetic camps in Israel based on I Kgs 22.8–25, the text returns to Isaiah's vision of Christ. Through Isaiah,

> the coming forth of the Beloved from the seventh heaven had been revealed, and his transformation, his descent and the likeness into which he was to be transformed, namely the likeness of a man, and the persecution which he was to suffer..., and that he was to be crucified together with criminals, and that he would be buried in a sepulcher...; and that the angel of the Holy Spirit and Michael, the chief of the holy angels, would open his grave on the third day, and

[90] Norelli, *Ascensio Isaiae: Commentarius*, 54 (trans. mine). Norelli observes here (and n. 8) that the *Gospel of Peter*, which may well come also from West Syria in the early second century, shares some details of the vision of Christ's resurrection represented in *Ascension* 3.14–17, and could be a witness to "Petrine" traditions in that Church that opposed those in the Gospel of Matthew; Ignatius—with his strong insistence on episcopal authority—may have wanted to counteract them.
[91] *Ascension of Isaiah* 1.5; trans. Robert McLaren Wilson (based on the German trans. of J. Flemming and H. Duensing) in Edgar Hennecke and Wilhelm Schneemelcher (eds), *New Testament Apocrypha* 2 (London: Lutterworth, 1963–5), 644. A more recent English translation, with introduction and brief commentary, is that of M. A. Knibb, in James H. Charlesworth (ed.), *The Old Testament Apocrypha* 2 (New York: Doubleday, 1985), 143–76.
[92] *AI* 1.7, 1.13.

that the Beloved, sitting on their shoulders, will come forth and send out his twelve disciples, and that they will teach to all the nations and every tongue the resurrection of the Beloved, and that those who believe in his cross will be saved, and in his ascension to the seventh heaven, whence he came...[93]

After Jesus' ascension, according to Isaiah's vision, the church will fall into disorder and corruption, "and many elders will be lawless and violent shepherds to their sheep."[94] Prophets and their visions will be set aside,[95] and the world will be led by Beliar, the prince of darkness, and by the Antichrist, into its final apostasy.[96] At the end of a limited period, however, "the Lord will come with his angels and with the hosts of the saints from the seventh heaven," and will defeat the forces of Beliar; then "the saints will come with the Lord in their garments which are stored on high in the seventh heaven," and will descend to rule those still alive in the world.[97] After a time of peace for the just—the standard apocalyptic picture of a final millennium—the Beloved will rebuke Beliar and consume the wicked with fire.[98] Following this summary narrative of the end, the first part of the *Ascension* concludes with an account of the prophet's violent death, by being sawed in two at the order of King Manasseh, who was moved by evil spirits to hate the seer and his visions.

The second half of the document (chs 6–11) is a longer, more detailed account of this same purported vision of Isaiah. Here all the usual details framing a biblical apocalyptic narrative are spelled out in some detail: ascription to a well-known prophetic figure from Hebrew Scripture; a sense of the activity of the Holy Spirit among the narrator's prophetic colleagues; a trance, a summons, an angel to guide him towards a vision of the heavenly world.[99] Isaiah is then led upwards, through six heavens that arch, domelike, above the earth; in each of them he sees groups of angels ranked around an empty throne, in progressively greater degrees of splendor, singing praise "for him who is in the seventh heaven..., and for his Beloved."[100] When the prophet finally comes to the seventh and highest heaven, he glimpses previous prophets and saints, all robed in the "higher garments" that signify a transformed, spiritual body;[101] although thrones and crowns—the other signs of sharing in the Kingdom—are also standing ready for them, they cannot yet receive them, since "first the Beloved must descend...into the world."[102]

From his location in this heavenly world, in the glorious company of angels and saints, the seer is given a glimpse of "one standing, whose glory surpassed that of all, and his glory was great and wonderful."[103] He sees that the angels and

---

[93] *AI* 3.13, 16–18 (*New Testament Apocrypha* 2.647–8). The brief picture of Jesus' resurrection here, as he emerges from the tomb, carried on the shoulders of two angels, parallels that in the *Gospel of Peter* 39–40, which may come from the same milieu (see n. 89).

[94] *AI* 3.23. This portrait of a Christian Church in discord may be alluding to the same disturbances that seem to have prompted Ignatius's arrest and condemnation.

[95] *AI* 3.31.     [96] *AI* 4.2–13.     [97] *AI* 4.14–16.     [98] *AI* 4.18.

[99] *AI* 6.     [100] *AI* 7.17.     [101] *AI* 9.9.     [102] *AI* 9.12–13.     [103] *AI* 9.27.

righteous gathered there approach to worship this figure, and after being changed himself into angelic form, Isaiah is told to worship him also; his guide tells him, "This is the Lord of all glory, whom you have seen," Christ the Beloved.[104] Next to him, on the Lord's left, is "a second angel," who he hears is the Holy Spirit, and he is directed to worship him as well.[105] Both of them then invite him to join in their worship "of the glorious one, whose glory I could not see;" "and I saw how my Lord worshipped, and the angel of the Holy Spirit, and how both together praised God."[106] In this majestic setting, the prophet hears the voice of the Father, "the Most High of the High Ones," directing the Son to descend through the seven heavens, at each level becoming like those who live there, so that none of them will know his identity until he ascends again to hold judgment over the powers of evil.[107]

In what follows, the prophet then "sees the transformation of the Lord and his descent"[108] into our own world. According to the Father's plan, Christ's appearance changes as he enters each of the heavens: "he took the appearance of the angels there (i.e. in each heaven), and they did not praise him, for his appearance was like theirs."[109] Eventually he takes on human form, being conceived virginally by Mary; and he is born in extraordinary fashion, after only two months of being carried in Mary's womb, without disturbing her physical virginity.[110] Isaiah emphasizes that the human appearance and behavior of Jesus was also part of God's plan to keep his Son from being known in his true divine identity:

> And I saw...that this was hidden from all the heavens and all the princes and every god of this world. And I saw: in Nazareth he sucked the breast like a baby, as was customary, so that he would not be recognized.[111]

So he "performed great signs and wonders in Israel,"[112] but is crucified by the leaders of Israel, at the prompting of "the adversary," and descends into the realm of the dead.[113] Yet after three days in the tomb, Jesus is raised to life again, and his ascent to glory is very different from his descent: now he does not change his glorious form, or attempt to hide himself from the inhabitants of each of the heavens. So after passing triumphantly through the heavens, "he sat down on the right hand of that great glory, whose glory, as I told you, I was not able to behold. And also I saw the angel of the Holy Spirit sitting on the left."[114] Like Dante at the end of the *Divine Comedy*, Isaiah has now seen all that he needs to see—the foundation of his hope, and of the hope of Israel. "You must return unto your garment" on earth, he is told, "until the last days are fulfilled: then you will come here!"[115] The vision of Christ's future journey is enough.

---

[104] *AI* 9.32.    [105] *AI* 9.36.    [106] *AI* 10.2; 9.40.    [107] *AI* 10.6–12.
[108] *AI* 10.18.    [109] *AI* 10.20.    [110] *AI* 11.5–14.    [111] *AI* 11.16–17.
[112] *AI* 11.18.    [113] *AI* 11.19.    [114] *AI* 11.32–3.    [115] *AI* 11.35.

This remarkable story has enough similarities to other Jewish and Christian documents of the time to sound familiar: the elaborate apparatus of an apocalyptic journey and vision; the details of a layered cosmos, populated with various species of unseen spirits; the clear sense of conflict and competition within the Christian community itself; the compressed story of the birth, life, and death of Jesus, and of his resurrection and ascension to glory, as the central narrative promising redemption and glorious life for God's people. As with the other works from this same milieu we have already considered, this anonymous writing is deeply rooted in the prophetic tradition of Israel, and presents the person and life of Jesus, most notably his humiliation and glorification, as foreseen in detail by one of the Hebrew Bible's most important figures, several of whose other oracles had already been applied to Jesus' birth and career in the Synoptic Gospels. Jesus, for the author and his community, is the historic savior, the coming judge of the world; yet the point to be communicated here, it seems, is not simply the outline of his career, which all would have known, but the idea that his coming was glimpsed and its meaning grasped in faithful Israel, centuries before his birth, as rooted in the eternal design of God. The Holy Spirit is clearly an important figure in the story, too; it is his inner guidance, in the prophetic community, that "opens a door" to Isaiah's central vision of Christ.[116]

Theological details of the *Ascension of Isaiah* can strike us as odd, even deficient by the standards of later orthodoxy; some of them, as Enrico Norelli has suggested, may even have appeared heterodox to a contemporary figure such as Ignatius. God's mysterious being is presented in terms—no doubt drawn from biblical language and liturgical use—that strikingly anticipate positions in the Trinitarian debates of the fourth century. The Father, "the Beloved," and the Holy Spirit are together the object of angelic praise and worship, and are enthroned together at the center of the heavenly realm.[117] Yet they are also clearly ranked within that place of exaltation: the seer is told by is angel guide to worship "the Lord of glory," who is the Beloved, and then to worship the one standing beside him, "for this is the angel of the Holy Spirit";[118] both of them, in turn, instruct the seer to join them in worshipping God himself, "the glorious one, whose glory I could not see ... the most high of the high ones ..., who will be called by the Holy Spirit, through the mouth of the righteous, the Father of the Lord."[119] Further precision about the relationship between these three figures, and about the meaning of offering worship to them all, is understandably still wanting.

There are also hints in the *Ascension* that the human form the Beloved put on for his sojourn on earth—like all the forms he assumed on his journey there from the highest heaven—was simply a matter of appearance, and not a full

---

[116] *AI* 6.7–10.     [117] *AI* 8.18; 9.30–10.7.
[118] *AI* 09.31–6.     [119] *AI* 9.40; 10.6–7.

human reality. Jesus is born in a miraculous way, after two months of Mary's pregnancy; as a newborn, "he sucked the breast like a baby" to disguise his identity.[120] Still, there is no suggestion in the document that Jesus' suffering was also "in appearance only," as Ignatius suggests his Antiochene opponents held.[121] In the thought world of this apocalyptic work, one's "appearance," and even the "garments" one wears, suggest a genuine identification of a person with the community and the surroundings in which one is seen; for the Lord as he descends, and even as he lives on earth, such appearances may be a disguise of his real identity, but for those called to be saved, new "garments" are signs of a graced transformation.[122] In any case, the crucifixion of Jesus is presented as something "the Beloved," who is sent to earth as Savior from the heavenly realm, has personally undergone. So after Jesus' resurrection, the disciples will be sent out by him to

> teach to all the nations and every tongue the resurrection of the Beloved, and that those who believe in his cross will be saved, and in his ascension to the seventh heaven, from which he came.[123]

To accept the scandal of the cross, along with Jesus' glorification, is seen here as central to Christian faith.

The real mission of Jesus, however, in this work—as in the other second-century works we have discussed—is above all revelation (*apokalypsis*): he is the one who comes into the world from the highest level of reality, from the side of the invisible God, to show forth and to achieve God's plan for the human world. The real content of the Savior's story is that he "descended" into the midst of our cosmos unknown to all its inhabitants, but that, after going down into the depths of humiliation and defeat, he "ascended" again triumphantly to his own place, recognized now by all creatures as victorious over the forces of death. His whole career is the fulfillment of this prophetic vision, the apocalyptic reassurance that God rules in his world.

## MELITO OF SARDIS

A fourth figure from the mid second century Greek East, who, in his understanding of Christ and his work, shows both differences and similarities when compared to the authors we have been considering, is Melito of Sardis. Besides fragments handed down by a variety of ancient sources, only one complete work of Melito's survives: a treatise called *On Pascha*, written in elaborate, poetic prose, which seems to have been a homily delivered during a Christian

---

[120] *AI* 11.7, 17.   [121] *Smyrn.* 2–4.1.
[122] See, for example, *AI* 8.14–16.   [123] *AI* 3.18.

Paschal celebration in Asia Minor, probably in the 160s. This work itself remained unknown, except in name, until 1941, when Campbell Bonner published an edition of it, based on a fourth-century papyrus now partly preserved in Dublin and partly at the University of Michigan.[124] Michel Testuz discovered another third- or fourth-century copy among the Bodmer papyri in Switzerland, which he published in 1960;[125] early Latin translations have also been identified, as well as papyrus fragments, which allow scholars to fill in some gaps in the text, so that we now have this important early interpretation of the Christian Pasch in what seems to be its complete original form.[126] Melito himself seems to have been well known in his own time, although most of the information we have about him comes from several centuries later. Eusebius, in his *Church History* IV, 26, identifies him as bishop of Sardis in western Asia Minor, and lists a number of works attributed to him in early Christianity. In *CH* V, 26, Eusebius quotes a letter from Bishop Polycrates of Ephesus, a younger contemporary of Melito's, to Bishop Victor of Rome, probably in the 190s, arguing for the acceptability of the practice, still widespread in Asia Minor in the late second century, of celebrating the death of Jesus and the end of the Church's pre-Paschal fast on the 14th of the Jewish month Nisan—the same day local synagogues were celebrating the Passover. In the course of this letter, Polycrates appeals to the example, among others, of "Melito, the eunuch who lived altogether in the Holy Spirit, and who lies in Sardis, awaiting the episcopate from heaven, when he shall rise from the dead."[127] This suggests both that Melito was a celibate and that he was known in his time as a charismatic figure—a point confirmed in Jerome's later remark that Tertullian had criticized Melito for opposing the charismatic Montanist movement, even though "he is thought by most of our people to have been a prophet."[128]

---

[124] Campbell Bonner, *The Homily on the Passion by Melito Bishop of Sardis and some Fragments of the Apocryphal Ezekiel*, Studies and Documents 12 (London: Christophers; Philadelphia, PA: University of Pennsylvania Press, 1941).

[125] Michel Testuz, *Papyrus Bodmer XIII: Méliton de Sardes, Homélie sur la Pâque* (Geneva: Biblioteca Bodmeriana, 1960).

[126] Early translations exist in Coptic, Georgian, and Syriac, as well as in Latin. There are several modern critical editions; I am here using that of S. G. Hall, *Melito of Sardis: On Pascha and Fragments* (Oxford: Oxford University Press, 1979; rev. edn, 2012).

[127] Eusebius, *Church History* 5.24.5 (trans. McGiffert, 242). This may mean that Melito, now dead, had been a bishop already during his lifetime, and was awaiting the eschatological fulfillment of his ministry.

[128] Jerome, *De Viris Illustribus*, 24. Jerome also emphasizes Melito's rhetorical gifts: "Tertullian, in the seven books which he wrote against the Church on behalf of Montanus, belittles his elegant talent for declamation, saying that he is thought by most of our people to have been a prophet." Since the Montanists themselves claimed to be the Church of "the new prophecy," Tertullian—a sympathizer with the sect himself, from around 207 until his death in 212–14—would understandably have been unsympathetic towards anyone claiming to be a prophet who nonetheless opposed the Montanist movement.

Melito's treatise *On Pascha* clearly illustrates his interest in the celebration of the Paschal festival, as well as his rhetorical accomplishments. Although a number of theories have been advanced since its original publication about a possible context for the work, as part of a "Quartodeciman" Easter celebration,[129] a final consensus has still not been formed; in any case, Melito seems clearly to be speaking or writing within a liturgical setting that centrally engages the story of Israel's escape from Egypt in Exodus 12 as relating directly to the disciples of Jesus. As a Christian, Melito finds the divinely intended meaning of the Exodus of Israel in the death and resurrection of Jesus; as a result, the real emphasis of his sermon is not just on Jesus as savior, but on the relationship of Israel to the Church, as the community of the saved, and thus on the relationship of the writings that would later be referred to as the Old and the New Testaments. The urgency and power of the work, as a homily for the Paschal night, comes from its central focus on Jesus, and on the community of his disciples, as bringing Israel's faith and practice to its fulfillment.

The main category underlying Melito's interpretation of the Hebrew Bible and the Christian Gospel, as in the other second-century works we have considered, is the fulfillment of promise: what the patriarchs since Abraham hoped for, what the prophets had pointed to in their inspired oracles, has now been fulfilled in the coming of Jesus, especially in his death on the cross. "The Lord made prior arrangements for his own suffering," Melito argues in chapter 57 of his homily,

> For the thing which is to be new and great in its realization
> is arranged for well in advance (ἐκ μακροῦ),
> so that when it comes about, it may be believed in,
> having been foreseen well in advance...
> Just so the mystery of the Lord,
> having been prefigured well in advance
> and having been seen through a model,
> is today believed in now that it is fulfilled,
> though considered new by men and women.[130]

Melito has laid down the basic principle for this promise-fulfillment model of interpreting the Bible a few paragraphs earlier:

> The very salvation and reality (ἀλήθεια) of the Lord were prefigured in the [Jewish] people,

---

[129] i.e. his celebration of the Christian Pasch on the 14th Nisan. See, for instance, Cyril C. Richardson, "The Quartodecimans and the Synoptic Chronology," *Harvard Theological Review* 33 (1940), 177–90; Bernhard Lohse, *Das Passahfest der Quartodecimaner* (Gütersloh: Bertelsman, 1953); Anton Baumstark (rev. Bernard Botte), *Comparative Liturgy* (Westminster, MD: Newman, 1958); Hall, *Melito of Sardis*, xxiv–xxviii; Alistair Stewart Sykes, *The Lamb's High Feast: Melito, Peri Pascha, and the Quartodeciman Paschal Liturgy at Sardis* (Leiden: Brill, 1998).

[130] Melito, *On Pascha* 57–8, trans. Hall, 31 (altered).

And the decrees (δόγματα) of the Gospel were proclaimed in advance by the Law.
The people, then, was a model (τύπος), by way of preliminary sketch
(προκέντημα),
And the law was the writing of a parable;
The Gospel is the recounting (διήγημα) and fulfillment of the law,
And the Church is the repository (ἀποδοχεῖον) of the reality.[131]

It is only in the person of Jesus and in the narrative of his life and death, in
other words, that the biblical narrative of ancient Israel discloses its full
meaning—just as a parable's full meaning is only discovered in the real-life
events it illuminates. The importance of the Hebrew Scripture, on the other
hand, is for Melito its ability to point to that meaning by *foreshadowing* it;
apart from the correspondence that Christian faith sees between the "truth" of
Jesus' life and the "type" or "sketch" offered in Jewish history and celebrated in
the annual Jewish liturgy, neither Jesus himself nor the community formed by
his disciples could be seen as part of God's longer plan. And the failure of
Israel as a nation, in Melito's view—the grounds for the solemn and bitter
reproaches that occupy the last quarter of his homily (chs 72–100)—is precisely its collective failure to recognize that fulfillment during Jesus' lifetime:

> You did not turn out to be "Israel";
> You did not "see God,"
> You did not recognize the Lord.
> You did not know, Israel,
> That he is the firstborn of God...[132]

Israel's central, naming quality, in Melito's view, is its ability to "see God"
present and working in history; for him, this also implied the ability eventually
to recognize God in Jesus.

Jesus' identity, for Melito, is clearly divine. He is "the firstborn of God,
begotten before the morning star," the hidden agent of the six days of
creation.[133] The irony, as well as the central significance, of the story of
Jesus' passion turns on the fact that he is both human—and therefore
mortal—and God:

> For as a son [being] born,
> And as a lamb led,

---

[131] *On Pascha* 40–1, trans. Hall, 21.

[132] *On Pascha* 57–8, 81–2, trans. Hall, 45. Since Philo, *De mutatione nominum* 81, as Hall
points out here, the etymological meaning of the name "Israel" had widely been assumed to be
"the one who sees God." This is the generally accepted interpretation of the name among many
Fathers: see, for example, Clement of Alexandria, *Paedagogos* 1.9; Origen, *De principiis* 4.3.12;
Hippolytus, *Contra Noetum* 5; and see G. Delling, "The 'One who sees God' in Philo," in
F. E. Greenspahn, E. Hilgert, and B. L. Mack, *Nourished with Peace: Studies in Hellenistic
Judaism in Memory of Samuel Sandmel* (Chico, CA: Scholars' Press, 1984), 27–42.

[133] Melito, *On Pascha* 82, trans. Hall, 45, alluding to Genesis 1, Pss. 103 and 109 (LXX).

And as a sheep slain,
And as a human being buried,
He rose from the dead as God, being by nature God
and a human being.[134]

So the image of Jesus crucified embodies the supreme paradox of early Christian faith: violence done to God by God's own people:

He who hung the earth is hanging;
he who fixed the heavens has been fixed;
he who fastened the universe has been fastened to a tree;
the Sovereign has been insulted;
the God has been murdered;
the King of Israel has been put to death by an Israelite right hand.[135]

The reason for this tragic rejection of Jesus by Israel, however, in Melito's view, is not simply ignorance, but God's providential concern to involve himself in human ignorance, violence and suffering: it is in *response* to human suffering, seen as the direct result of the fall and the epidemic of violence that has grown out of it, that God the Son chooses to become involved in humanity's violent history and to take its force upon himself. So at the approximate midpoint of the homily, after telling the story of Israel's exodus from Egypt and the institution of the Paschal feast, Melito comes to the heart of his own soteriological message: God the Son has involved himself more broadly with suffering humanity, has allowed himself to be rejected and to suffer, in order to bring an end to all human suffering.

What is the Pascha? [he asks]
It gets its name from its characteristic:
From "suffer" ($\pi\alpha\theta\epsilon\hat{\iota}\nu$) comes "keeping the pasch" ($\pi\acute{\alpha}\sigma\chi\epsilon\iota\nu$).[136]
Learn therefore who is the suffering one,
and who shares the suffering of the suffering one,
and why the Lord is present on the earth
to clothe himself with the suffering one
and carry him off to the heights of heaven.[137]

As the homily goes on (chapters 47–56), it becomes clear that "the suffering one" whom the preacher is talking about here is humanity itself ($\acute{o}$ $\check{\alpha}\nu\theta\rho\omega\pi\sigma$), drawn ever deeper, throughout history, into the moral and physical destructiveness that

---

[134] *On Pascha* 8, trans. Hall, 5–7 [altered].  [135] *On Pascha* 96, trans. Hall, 55.
[136] Hall (23 n. 13) rejects this translation, preferring to render the Greek text as: "From *suffer* ($\pi\alpha\theta\epsilon\hat{\iota}\nu$) comes *suffering* ($\pi\acute{\alpha}\sigma\chi\epsilon\iota\nu$)." But it is hard to see how the text can be understood in this way, without being simply tautologous. Both Testuz and Perler, in earlier editions of the work, see the second verb, $\pi\acute{\alpha}\sigma\chi\epsilon\iota\nu$, as meaning "celebrate the Pasch," based on a false etymology of the Hebrew word *Pascha*.
[137] Melito, *On Pascha* 46, trans. Hall, 23–5.

began with the first sin.[138] And although Melito is not concerned with systematic, philosophical reflection on the ontological makeup of Jesus, he clearly wants to see Jesus' humanity—which enables him to take up the "suffering" of the whole human race, caused by sin[139]—as identified with the human flesh that the Son "put on" like clothing: the same image we have already met in the *Odes of Solomon* and the *Ascension of Isaiah*. So Melito writes:

> It is he [Jesus] who, coming from heaven to the earth because
>   of the suffering one,
> and clothing himself in that same one through a virgin's womb,
> and coming forth as a man,
> accepted the passions of the suffering one
> through the body which was able to suffer,
> and dissolved the passions of the flesh . . . [140]

Although Jesus is seen as fulfilling the typology of the Paschal lamb, his suffering and death are not presented as an expiatory sacrifice here, so much as an identification with human suffering that breaks its hold on the race by his very presence—a victory over death for all, grounded in Jesus' identity as Son and Word. So Melito continues in this same passage:

> And by the Spirit which could not die
> he killed death, the killer of men and women.[141]

In the final, summary section of the homily, Melito speaks again of Christ's victory over human suffering in similar terms, as the victory of divine life over inherited human death:

> The Lord, when he had clothed himself with humanity
>   (ἐνδυσάμενος τὸν ἄνθρωπον)
> and suffered because of him that was suffering
> and been bound because of him that was held fast
> and been judged because of him that was condemned
> and been buried because of him that was buried,
> arose from the dead . . . [142]

By identifying himself with all the victims of violence and envy in the long history of Israel, and so, implicitly, with those in all religious traditions who have suffered in similar ways since the start of humanity, the Lord realizes in his own Passion the divinely intended typological meaning of the Paschal lamb, and so brings about the final "exodus" of all humanity from suffering.

---

[138] See especially chs 48–9.      [139] See, for instance, *On Pascha* 54–5.
[140] *On Pascha* 66, trans. Hall, 35; see also *On Pascha* 100.
[141] *On Pascha* 66, trans. Hall, 35.
[142] *On Pascha* 100–1, trans. Hall, 57. See also 102: " 'I am the one,' says Christ, 'I am the one that destroyed death and triumphed over the enemy' " (trans. Hall, 57–9).

He is the Pascha of our salvation.
It is he who in many endured many things:
it is he that was in Abel murdered,
and in Isaac bound,
and in Jacob exiled...
It is he that was enfleshed in the Virgin,
that was hanged on a tree,
that was buried in the earth,
that was raised from the dead,
that was taken up to the heights of the heavens.[143]

The reproaches Melito makes against Israel in his own time—including those in his own city who are celebrating the Pasch simply in the traditional Jewish way—is that they have failed to see Jesus as the typological fulfillment of God's saving history in their midst. Yet the salvation worked by Jesus in his death, he is convinced, still includes them.

## JUSTIN

Justin, writing also in the mid second century, was the first Christian author to be generally styled, perhaps even in his own time, as "a philosopher" by profession. This title, however, doubtless carried a somewhat different connotation in late antiquity than it does today. One of the most influential recent achievements of Pierre Hadot, the distinguished French historian of later Greek philosophy, has been to remind us of the essentially practical, "pastoral" character of most of what we usually characterize as philosophical activity in the ancient world. Ancient philosophy—literally the "love of wisdom"—even in its earliest known stages, certainly focused on asking ultimate questions about the nature of reality, and about the values human individuals and society strive to realize. Most of its practitioners, however—from the Sophists and Socrates to the Peripatetics, the Stoics, and the Cynics—saw the relevance of their work mainly in more immediate terms, as a way of raising unsettling questions in the minds of their contemporaries: moving ordinary people, especially the young, to develop a critical, liberating understanding of their inherited cultural and religious and ethical assumptions, by suggesting strategies of reflective thought—"spiritual exercises," as Hadot calls them—designed to lead individuals to deeper awareness of the truth and to greater personal freedom.[144] So it was perfectly understandable that early Christian

---

[143] *On Pascha* 69–70, trans. Hall, 37–9.
[144] See, for example, Pierre Hadot, *What is Ancient Philosophy?*, trans. Michael Chase (Cambridge, MA: Harvard University Press, 2002), esp. pp. 2–4. Hadot writes (p. 3): "In the

ascetical practice, too, at least from the early fourth century, was often called the "philosophic life" (βίος φιλοσοφικός), even when those who practiced it had little formal education.[145] If one thoughtfully prayed over a selection of memorized Psalms and Gospel sayings, lived a life as free as possible from sensual distraction, and was under the guidance of an experienced spiritual director, all in the interest of seeking ultimate Wisdom and Truth, one was—in the ancient sense—living as a "philosopher."

For Justin, too, it seems, becoming a Christian and teaching the life of the Gospel to others, through careful reflection on biblical texts, was to practice, with the fullest authenticity, this classical "philosophical" commitment. Originally from Flavia Neapolis in Samaria (present-day Nablus), Justin spent the last few decades of his life as a teacher of the Christian way of life in Rome, and was put to death for it, with a few of his pupils, by a Roman magistrate around the year 165. The first eight chapters of his *Dialogue with Trypho* give us a glimpse—somewhat unusual in ancient documents—of his early intellectual formation, which he describes as a continuing, if circuitous search for the consistent vision of truth on which, most philosophers assumed, a "happy life" is founded.[146] "Philosophy," he says at the start of his narrative, "is in fact the greatest possession, and most honorable before God, to whom it leads us and who alone commends us; and they are truly holy men who have bestowed attention on philosophy."[147] So philosophy, as Justin understands it, is first of all a pursuit of holiness, a way to God; what disturbed him in his early years was not its secularity or the intensity of its gaze, but the variety of schools and theories by which, in his culture, it was characterized.

After brief but unsatisfying stints as a pupil of Stoic, Peripatetic, and Pythagorean teachers, Justin tells us that he made greater progress towards what he was seeking when he studied the works of Plato, in the systematized form of second-century textbooks now usually called "Middle" Platonism. This led him to discover the importance of contemplating immaterial reality as the ultimate place to find Truth.[148] Later on, however, he says, he encountered

---

first place, at least since the time of Socrates, the choice of a way of life has not been located at the end of the process of philosophical activity, like a kind of accessory or appendix. On the contrary, it stands at the beginning, in a complex interrelation with critical reaction to other existential attitudes, with global vision of a certain way of living and of seeing the world, and with voluntary decision itself. Thus, to some extent, this option determines the specific doctrine and the way this doctrine is taught. Philosophical discourse, then, originates in a choice of life and an existential option, not vice versa."

[145] See Hadot, *What is Ancient Philosophy?*, 237–52; also Anne-Marie Malingrey, *Philosophia: Étude d'un groupe des mots dans la literature grecque, des présocratiques au IVe siècle après J-C.* (Paris: Klincksieck, 1961).

[146] Justin, *Dialogue* 2, 8.

[147] Justin, *Dial.* 2, ed. Archibald Roberts and James Donaldson, *Ante-Nicene Fathers* 1 (repr. Grand Rapids, MI: Eerdmans, 1981), 195.

[148] *Dial.* 2.

a "venerable old man" while walking by the sea, who apparently was himself a Christian teacher. Justin recounts their conversation—stylized, probably, to reflect a living genre of philosophical conversion stories[149]—as itself a kind of Socratic dialogue. The old man leads him to clarify his conception of philosophy, as "the knowledge of that which really exists, and a clear perception of the truth," knowledge which leads to happiness and is rooted in the conviction that there *is* a transcendent God.[150] Further, Justin and his teacher agree that this God can be known by the human mind, which has an affinity with God because it is itself "divine and immortal."[151] They also agree that living a just life is the prerequisite for the happy survival of the human soul. But Justin's companion leads him to reject Plato's theory of reincarnation as the soul's mode of survival, and to affirm that our hope for everlasting life is founded not on living through a cycle of rebirths, or on some primordial identification of the conscious soul with life itself, as an impersonal force (as Plato's *Phaedo* suggests), but rather on the soul's eternal participation in the radically personal life of God, for which our present life prepares us.[152] Gradually, their conversation leads Justin to ask where one might turn to find a reliable teacher in the art of living well, and his partner points to the Christian Bible as the source of a philosophy which "alone is safe and profitable":

There existed, long ago, certain men more ancient than all those who are thought of as philosophers, blessed and righteous and beloved by God, who spoke by the Divine Spirit and foretold events which would take place, and which are now happening. They are called prophets.... They did not use demonstration in their treatises back then, seeing that they were trustworthy witnesses to the truth that is above all demonstration... They both glorified the Creator, the God and Father of all things, and proclaimed his Son, the Christ sent by him.[153]

It is the Hebrew prophets, in their Spirit-led witness to the Christ who was to come, who emerge here in the dialogue as the real teachers of a philosophy that can be relied on—the purveyors of a wisdom that alone leads its practitioners to the happy life, and is therefore alone worth living.

Behind Justin's identification of the biblical prophets as the most trustworthy teachers of the "truth that makes us free" lies the story, found in a variety of ancient pagan and Christian sources, that Plato, the most religious of Hellenic teachers, had once traveled to Egypt on his own quest for wisdom, and had learned there how to find it from sources more ancient and more venerable than his own Greek contemporaries.[154] Philo and other Hellenistic

---

[149] See Arthur J. Droge, "Justin Martyr and the Restoration of Philosophy," *Church History* 56 (1987), 304.
[150] *Dial.* 3 (ANF, 196).    [151] *Dial.* 4.
[152] *Dial.* 5–6.    [153] *Dial.* 7 (ANF 198; trans. altered).
[154] For the idea, suggested by Poseidonius, Numenius, and others, that Plato had made contact with an *Urphilosophie* among the Egyptians, see Droge, "Justin Martyr", 311, 317.

Jewish thinkers identified this source of classical Greek wisdom with the Hebrew Bible, especially the books of Moses—by Plato's time, they assumed, already available in Egypt in Greek translation. Early Christian writers readily picked up the story. For Justin, the central point is not simply that Plato borrowed from Moses, but that the fullness of the divine wisdom, guiding the world and offering itself to us as a norm for right living, is to be found in the one to whom Moses and the Prophets all pointed in the Scriptures: Jesus Christ.[155] In Jesus, in fact, God's providential wisdom, offered to the human race in many forms, has finally taken human shape, lived a human life, and died a human death.

So for Justin, as for most Christian thinkers of the second century, Christ is first of all the key to discovering the full prophetic and philosophical sense of the Hebrew Scriptures. Interpreting a long series of passages from the Hebrew Bible as prophecies of Christ, Justin points both to his eternal existence in the divine Mystery, and to his incarnation in time: "he was 'before the morning star' (Ps. 109.3) and the moon, and, when he was made flesh, submitted to be born of this virgin, of the family of David."[156] "The first-begotten of God, before all creatures," Christ is also "the son of the patriarchs, since he assumed flesh by the Virgin, from their family."[157]

> He said then that he was the Son of Man, either because of his birth from the Virgin, who was, as I have said, of the family of David and Jacob and Isaac and Abraham; or because Adam was the father both of him and of those who have been first mentioned, from whom Mary derives her descent.[158]

Mary and Eve, then, play parallel roles as ancestors of a race. Both "received the Word (λόγος)" about God from an angelic source; Eve, however, received it from the serpent, an evil angel, and "brought forth disobedience and death," while Mary "received faith and joy, when the angel Gabriel announced the good tidings to her."[159] So, too, the details of human distress and abandonment mentioned in Psalm 22 must be assigned, as their central reference, to Jesus in his passion.[160] Jesus' life, in other words, as known from the Gospels, is embedded in the continuity of common images and historical references that the Hebrew Bible lays before us; as a result, they can be seen in their full biblical contours only in the context of the whole Christian narrative. Justin identifies Jesus, in fact, as "the unique offspring of the Father of all things, being begotten from him in a distinctive manner as Word and Power, and afterwards becoming man through the Virgin."[161] That "Word and Power," for Justin, is not simply the divine Word that formed the world in the

---

[155] See, for instance, *Apol.* 1.47–53; *Dial.* 13–14, 28–30, 32–34, 36–38, 43–45, 49, 53, 66, 68, 77–78, 98, 125.

[156] *Dial.* 45 (trans. altered). See also 48, 63, 68, 75.

[157] *Dial.* 100 (ANF 249; trans. altered).          [158] *Dial.* 100 (trans. altered).

[159] *Dial.* 100.          [160] *Dial.* 100.          [161] *Dial.* 105 (ANF 251; trans. altered).

beginning and inspired the Bible, but the saving and life-giving Word of sacred history and prophecy, expressing and carrying out God's sovereignty; it is directed to all people, and signifies the rational (λογικός) presence of God in creation.[162]

Behind this Logos-centered pattern of Christian biblical interpretation, which we have seen in earlier second-century writers and which will become the standard pattern from now on, Basil Studer has pointed out a genuine theology of history, an interpretation of "the course of human events" that gives definitive shape to early Christian understandings of the role of Christ.[163] The purpose of such a theological scheme is not so much speculative, Studer argues, as it is apologetic—not so much to represent Jesus as an eternal divine person, the embodiment of God's eternal Wisdom, as to answer the educated pagans' question of how he could be seen as savior of *all* people, bringing true religion to the *whole* of humanity (as the Christians were—disturbingly— beginning to claim), when he had lived so recently, and was the heir to such a restricted religious tradition as that of Israel. To counter such objections, as we have seen, Justin takes up again a theme already familiar from Philo, and echoed by his own contemporary Tatian:[164] that Plato and the other great philosophers had borrowed some of their main theories from the Pentateuch, which they had come to know through Greek translations in Egypt, and that in their quest for truth and wisdom they had encountered the ultimate form of both in God's eternal Logos, immanent in the very order of things and accessible to all people of moral integrity.[165]

Justin's boldest, most famous statement of this eternal identity of Christ as the reason or Logos of God occurs in his *First Apology*, where the Christian philosopher affirms:

We have been taught that Christ is the first-begotten of God, and have previously testified that he is the reason (λόγος) of which every race of humanity partakes. Those who lived in accordance with reason are Christians, even though they were called atheists—such as, among the Greeks, Socrates and Heraclitus and others like them; among the barbarians, Abraham, Ananiah, Azariah, and Misael,[166] and Elijah, and many others, whose deeds and names I forbear to list for now, knowing that this would be lengthy. So also those who lived without reason (λόγος) were ungracious,[167] enemies to Christ, and murderers of those who lived

---

[162] *Apol.* 1.10.

[163] Basil Studer, "Der apologetische Ansatz zur Logos-Christologie Justins des Märtyrers," Adolf Martin Ritter (ed.), *Kerygma und Logos*, Festschrift for Carl Andresen (Göttingen: Vandenhoeck & Ruprecht, 1979), 435–48, here 435.

[164] See, for example, Tatian, *Oratio ad Graecos* 31–2.

[165] See Studer, "Der apologetische Ansatz", 438–43.

[166] These last three names refer to the "three young men" thrown in the furnace by Nebuchadnezzar, in Daniel 1.7 (LXX).

[167] Greek: ἄχρηστοι. Justin is playing on the title "Christ (Χριστός)," "anointed one," which, though unrelated, is similar in sound to the Greek word χρηστός: "good," "honest," "upright."

by reason; and those who live by reason (λόγος) now are Christians, fearless and unperturbed.[168]

In a single stroke, Justin here identifies the Jesus of the Gospels both with the object of Old Testament prophecy and the referent of Old Testament types, on the one hand, and with the divine reason guiding the cosmos, on the other—a divine mind, in whose activities and knowledge the searching human mind, at its best, is able to share. The implications, though hardly worked out here in detail, are nonetheless enormous: serious philosophical ethics are essentially the same as biblical teaching, for Justin, and are summed up most perfectly in the moral teachings and parables of Jesus; the divine Wisdom, by which God shaped and still guides the world,[169] is a universal presence, which has become embodied, personified, in the carpenter of Nazareth. Christ has implicitly become, for Justin, the norm for an adequate philosophical quest for truth, the implied content of the philosopher's attempts to lead others to freedom and personal integration. On the other hand, the language and concepts of Platonism and Stoicism—the terms we would call "philosophical" in the more usual sense—are now available to Justin and his colleagues not as religious alternatives, but as tools for deepening their own grasp of biblical images and narratives, and for making them intelligible as religious teachings of universal significance.

In this light, Justin shows no hesitation in identifying the Jesus of the Gospels, and of Christian devotion, with the God of the Hebrew Scriptures. Larry Hurtado has pointed out that Justin here echoes the practice already discernible in other first- and second-century Judaeo-Christian documents, of recognizing in the name "Jesus" a form of the unprounceable and sacred name of God.[170] It is not only a name powerful enough to exorcise demons, as Justin suggests in the *Dialogue*;[171] but even "the name of God himself."[172] In Exodus 23.20–1, God says to Moses, "Behold, I send an angel before you, to guard you on the way and to bring you to the place which I have prepared. Give heed to him and listen to his voice . . . , for my name is in him." As Justin explains this and similar passages in the Pentateuch, this "name of God," which was "not revealed to Abraham or to Jacob," is the name of Jesus, first shared by Moses'

---

[168] *Apol.* 1.46, trans. Edward R. Hardy, in Cyril C. Richardson (ed.), *Early Christian Fathers*, Library of Christian Classics 1 (Philadelphia, PA: Westminster, 1953), 272 (trans. altered).

[169] See, for example, Prov. 8.22–36; Ps. 104.24.

[170] See Larry W. Hurtado, *Lord Jesus Christ: Devotion to Jesus in Early Christianity* (Grand Rapids, MI: Eerdmans, 2003), 640–8; "'Jesus' as God's Name, and Jesus as God's Embodied Name in Justin Martyr," in Sara Parvis and Paul Foster (eds), *Justin Martyr and his Worlds* (Minneapolis, MN: Fortress, 2007), 128–36. Hurtado writes: "I propose that the writings of Justin Martyr give us the earliest extant example of a proto-orthodox Christian seriously attempting to articulate an understanding of Jesus as divine in terms he hoped to make comprehensible and even persuasive both to Jewish interlocutors and the wider culture" (*Lord Jesus Christ*, 641).

[171] *Dial.* 30.3; 76.6–7.    [172] *Dial.* 75.

assistant Joshua, the "messenger" (ἄγγελος) whom God provided to lead the people Israel into the promised land.[173] So in *Dial.* 111, Justin sees in the story of Israel's battle with the Amalekites in Ex 17.8–13 a prophetic type of Jesus' eschatological defeat of God's enemies on the cross:

> In what Moses and Joshua did, the same thing [i.e. Jesus' purifying sacrifice] was symbolically announced and told beforehand. For the one of them, stretching out his hands, remained till evening on the hill, his hands being supported; and this reveals a type of no other thing than of the cross. And the other, whose name was altered to Jesus, led the fight, and Israel conquered. Now this took place in the case of both those holy men and prophets of God, that you may perceive how one of them [= Moses] could not bear up both the mysteries: I mean, the type of the cross and the type of the name. For this is, was, and shall be the strength of him alone, whose name every power dreads, being very much tormented because they shall be destroyed by him.[174]

In Jesus' name, God's power is invested in a way that both demonstrates Jesus' divine identity and points to his providential role in history, as the one who fulfilled God's plan to form a people of his own. Like God's Wisdom and Logos, the very name of Jesus has a power that is both distinct from that of Israel's God, and an embodiment of God's irresistible purposes.[175]

In both his *Apologies* and in his *Dialogue with Trypho*, Justin the apologist is mainly concerned to demonstrate to his Jewish and Christian readers—especially to those who sought religious meaning in philosophy, including the Emperor Marcus Aurelius and his heirs—that the faith and practice of the Christian community, by the mid-second century, realized all the deepest aspirations of the human heart, in its quest for the transcendent Mystery. So in the *First Apology*, after arguing that the central motifs of both the Hebrew Bible, in its prophetic passages, and of pagan religion and philosophy, were hidden messages of the same "prophetic spirit," and pointed ultimately to Jesus as Savior, Justin explains the Christian liturgical rites of baptism and the Eucharist as mysteries that bring the worship of both the Jewish and pagan traditions to fulfillment.[176] Drawing on—and slightly altering—Jesus' saying in Matthew 11.27, "No one knows the Father except the Son, and no one knows the Son except the Father, and those to whom the Son will reveal it," Justin insists that the revelation of Jesus now makes possible a full understanding of key incidents in Israel's history, such as Moses' encounter with God's saving word at the burning bush. Referring to the undiscriminating

---

[173] For this same identification, see *Dial.* 89.1; 90.4; 91.3; 106.2–3; 128.1. Moses had changed Joshua's name from "Hoshea," according to Num. 13.16; his new name, in the Greek of the Septuagint, is *Iēsous*.

[174] *Dial.* 111.    [175] See Hurtado, "'Jesus' as God's Name", 133–6.

[176] *Apol.* 1.61–7.

monotheism he sees in Jewish worship, and probably in some forms of philosophical religion, Justin adds, addressing the Emperor:

> For those who identify the Son and the Father are condemned, as neither knowing the Father nor recognizing that the Father of the universe has a Son, who, being the Word and First-begotten of God, is also divine. Formerly he appeared in the form of fire and the image of a bodiless being to Moses and the other prophets. But now in the time of your dominion, he was, as I have said, made man of a virgin according to the will of the Father, for the salvation of those who believe in him, and endured contempt and suffering, so that by dying and rising again he might conquer death.[177]

It is faith in the crucified and risen Christ, expressed not only by "philosophers" like Justin, but also by the simple Christians who gather each Sunday for worship, that in Justin's view enables the disciples of Jesus to find fulfilment for the central inner longings of human religion.

For Harnack and other liberal Protestant scholars, at the end of the nineteenth century, this identification of philosophical insight and cosmic speculation, as well as of the Word of God revealed in the Hebrew Bible, with the historical kerygma of Jesus was the first major step in the alienation of the Christian message from its original importance: the distancing of the simple, essentially ethical Christian message Jesus preached from the person of the rabbi of Nazareth, and the beginning of a clerical "intellectualism" that even the Reformation—with its presumed emphasis on salvation *sola Scriptura*—had not completely purged from Christian faith.[178] For the longer orthodox tradition, on the other hand, Justin's intellectual interests marked the beginning of theology in the full sense, as the engagement of faith by reason and the transformation of reason by faith. The *logos* of the philosophers had become flesh for the Church, tangible and immediately nourishing, because it was embodied in the Church's Lord.

---

[177] *Apol.* 1.63, trans. Hardy, 284–5.

[178] Harnack writes wistfully, in the fourth chapter of Book II of his *History of Dogma*: "In the dogmas of the Apologists . . . , we find nothing more than traces of the fusion of the philosophical and historical elements; in the main, both exist separately side by side. It was not till long after this that intellectualism gained the victory in a Christianity represented by the clergy. What we here chiefly understand by 'intellectualism' is the placing of the scientific conception of the world behind the commandments of Christian morality and behind the hopes and faith of the Christian religion, and the connecting of the two things in such a way that this conception appeared as the foundation of these commandments and hopes. Thus was created the future dogmatic in the form which still prevails in the churches and which presupposes the Platonic and Stoic conception of the world long ago overthrown by science. The attempt made at the beginning of the Reformation to free the Christian faith from this amalgamation remained at first without success" (*History of Dogma* II, trans. Neil Buchanan (London: Constable, 1900), 229. For Harnack, it would only be in the less institutional, non-clerical form of liberal Protestantism in the late nineteenth and early twentieth centuries, presumably, that dogma and Hellenistic "intellectualism" would finally come to an end, being replaced by a dogma-free Christianity of high-minded, middle-class ethical sentiment.

## CONCLUSION

The five second-century authors we have discussed are clearly quite different from each other, in the literary character of the works they have left us, and in the theological and pastoral concerns those works express. A number of features, though, seem to reappear in all of them, as reflections of how Jesus was most widely understood by Christians in the century immediately following the composition of the works that have come to be called the New Testament.

(1) Jesus is clearly and unequivocally understood as the divine Savior of humanity. The Gospel accounts of his birth from the Virgin Mary, of his miracles and teaching, of his abandonment and death, and of his resurrection into glory, are the central elements that reveal his identity. He is not simply a rabbi or a village sage, for second-century Christians; he is God's Son and Word, who has taken on our human flesh in all its vulnerability. And this coming in flesh means that his human brothers and sisters now share, through him, in an unprecedented new access to the God beyond all things.

(2) All these second-century authors, in a variety of ways, understand Jesus as fulfilling the prophetic promise implied in the canonical Hebrew Bible. Biblical themes and images, biblical texts and personalities, help them to locate him in the story Israel told of God's work in history, and to enunciate better how and why his disciples belong to, yet occupy a distinct place in, the longer history of God's chosen people. Implied in these second-century works, then, is a theology of history: an understanding of the traditional story of Israel, the "nations," and Greco-Roman civilization that takes its shape and meaning from their confessed understanding of Jesus. Implied, too, is a growing sense of the importance of defining Christian identity through the community's complex relationship to Israel and its faith and practice.

(3) Also central to these early testimonies of Christian faith and practice is a strong emphasis on the activity of the "prophetic Spirit" within the community. The singer of the *Odes* presents himself as an inspired voice, witnessing to the story of Jesus and to its origins in the divine Mystery. Ignatius, too, is "inspired (θεόφορος)," and assumes an authoritative role in encouraging communities distant from his own, as he sees himself bearing personal witness to Christ. The prophetic author of the *Ascension of Isaiah* enters the world of late Jewish apocalyptic hagiography to construct his own vision of Christ's role as cosmic savior and victor. Justin emphasizes the importance of the fulfillment of Hebrew prophecy, and appeals to the community's devotion to "the prophetic Spirit," along with the God of Israel and Jesus his Son, as defining marks of religious

authenticity.[179] Charismatic experience was clearly one of the accepted pointers to the second-century's understanding of Jesus as "Lord," as it had been decades earlier for Paul (see I Cor. 12.3).

(4) All of these writers, in different ways, emphasize the centrality of Jesus' cross and passion to his work of human transformation. For the seer of the *Odes*, as for the narrator of the *Ascension of Isaiah*, Christ's death is an inescapable part of his journey to victory and glorification. By embedding his vision of the future career of Christ in the story of Isaiah's betrayal and martyrdom, the *Ascension* even suggests that Christ's descent into the material world is part of a wider valorization of martyrdom. Ignatius not only emphasizes the human reality of Jesus' suffering and death (e.g. *Smyrnaeans* 1–2), but insists that for him, to "imitate the passion of my God" is the only way to fulfill his vocation (Romans 6). Melito's homily on the Paschal narrative and celebration is focused on seeing its fulfillment in Jesus' death, as God's way of healing the human suffering that is rooted in sin (e.g., *On Pascha* 66–71). Justin sees the suffering of Christ as proof that Christ is the one spoken of by Israel's prophets (e.g. *Dialogue* 89–91, 95–7, 104–5).

(5) All of these works, too—except the *Ascension of Isaiah*—witness to a shared conviction that the present believer, whatever his or her religious background, shares in the saving effects of Jesus' life, death, and resurrection by sharing in the Church's sacramental signs: notably in baptism and the Eucharist. To be a disciple of Jesus, to be transformed by his coming and his work, means not simply accepting the Apostles' witness to his identity as Savior, but becoming an initiate in the community that continues his work in the world. Jesus the Lord lives on, in the view of these ancient authors, in the faith and worship of the Church that bears witness to him.

---

[179] See *Apol.* 1.6, 13, 61, and the long section appealing to the fulfillment of biblical prophecy as authenticating Jesus in *Apol.* 1.30–60, and well as virtually the whole *Dialogue with Trypho*. Only Melito's *On Pascha*, of the works we have considered, shows little explicit interest in the role of the Holy Spirit in the community, despite the author's reputation as an inspired prophet; other fragments, however, which seem likely to be from lost works of Melito, place more emphasis on the community's charismatic side. See especially Stuart Hall's translation of the "new" Georgian fragments attributed to Melito by Michel van Esbroeck, in *Melito, On Pascha and Fragments* (Oxford: Oxford University Press, 1979) 94–5 ("new fragments" 2.20; 3.1).

# 3

## Irenaeus and Origen

### A Christology of Manifestation

In one of the more disturbing passages of the Gospel of Matthew—disturbing, one assumes, also for its original hearers—Jesus asks the Pharisees, "What do you think about the Christ?" His question introduces the final episode in chapter 22, a series of intense arguments about the Kingdom of God between Jesus and his challengers from the Jerusalem, which has already begun in chapter 21 of the Gospel. Jesus has told two parables—the parable of the vinedressers, and the parable of the wedding banquet—which present his understanding of God's plan to overturn traditional expectations for the salvation of Israel, and to gather together a new people, formed from both Jews and Gentiles, as his own. In the process, Jesus raises what seems to be his, and Matthew's, real question: what kind of figure do they expect the coming Messiah to be? What will be his origin, his roots, his identity? Whose *son* will he be? And when they offer the expected answer, "A son of David," a king from Israel's ancient line, Jesus disturbs their certainty (and implicitly ours) by suggesting that the origin and identity of the Christ, when he finally comes, may be much more mysterious, more divine, than anyone in Israel had guessed (see Matt. 22.41–46).

This Gospel incident reminds us that our "Christology"—what *we* think of the Christ—is always more than simply a question of analyzing philosophically the personal identity, the ontological structure, of one unique figure in history whom Christians call by that title, Jesus of Nazareth. It includes our understanding of God, of the entire biblical narrative of God's creation of human beings and his plan to reclaim and save them when they turn away. It includes, too, the presuppositions with which we interpret particular passages within that narrative, especially the way we read the Scripture of Israel, as it is brought to a crisis of interpretation by the words and the person of Jesus. It even includes our way of understanding our moral duties, the *practice* of biblical faith, and the ultimate account for that practice which all human beings will have to give, to a God who remains present in history. "What we think about the Christ" implies what we think about all of these things, because it is an interpretation of how we think God will save his world.

In the present chapter, I want to consider the work of two major patristic figures from the late second and early third centuries, who took on these broad questions: Irenaeus of Lyons and Origen of Alexandria. Their ways of understanding the person of Christ may seem, for different reasons, somewhat deficient by later Chalcedonian and modern standards; nevertheless, their work forms a continuum, spanning almost a century, that was to leave an indelible imprint on Christian theology—including what we call Christology—down to our own time. Different as they are in many features of their thought about the Mystery of Christ, both Irenaeus and Origen develop in surprisingly similar ways what one might call a "Christology of divine epiphany"—or, put more clumsily but perhaps more clearly, a "Christology of the saving self-manifestation of God the Word." For both of them, the path to understanding Christ is not mainly through ontological analysis of the person of the Incarnate Word, but is embedded in their interpretation of the whole biblical narrative—the drama of the creation, fall and redemption of human beings. The Word of God is always identified, by both of them, in terms of his relationship to intelligent creatures, as the form or archetype of which all creatures are images. His full divinity, his unique relationship to God the Father and to God's sanctifying Spirit, is the crucial identifying characteristic of who the Son always is, and a hint of what intelligent creatures, through him, might reach for, by growing in his likeness. His human career, his enfleshment or humanization, is also complete, in the eyes of both authors, involving his full entry into this material world and its history. But in coming to be human among humans, the Son brings to the rest of humanity the stability, incorruptibility, and unchanging vitality which belong to God, as a reconstitution and a fulfillment of what intellectual creation was originally intended to be. In the view of Irenaeus and Origen, Christ does this fundamentally by revealing—in his person, his birth from a Virgin, his words and miracles, his death on the cross and bodily resurrection—the glorious, vital, incorruptible reality of God, in terms now accessible to human minds and even human senses. Christ reveals God by being with us, and saves us by letting us share in a transforming, life-giving vision of who and what God is.

## IRENAEUS OF LYONS

The main concern of Christian writers in the early and mid second century, for all the variety of themes and images that occur in their works, was really to express a sense of Jesus as universal, eschatological savior: the human figure, sent by God and embodying in his own person God's universal Logos or reason. Jesus, as we have seen, for Ignatius and the *Odes of Solomon*, for Melito and for the philosopher Justin, and even for *The Ascension of Isaiah*, is the hidden key to the meaning of the Hebrew Bible: God's Beloved, ready to be sent into the world and to fulfill his will; the one who has realized the "plan" God had in mind when calling his people from Egypt to the land of promise. God the Logos is the principle of rationality and order, latent in the functioning of the cosmos, increasingly present to all people of good will who use their reason to make moral judgments, and to search for Truth revealed in biblical history. Now he has become flesh, has spoken to us of God, has revealed God's way in his own words and actions. Second-century writers tried in various ways to point to Jesus as the answer to humanity's ancient questions, the fulfillment of universal promise: for Jews, who still waited for the hope offered to Abraham to be fulfilled; for Hellenistic philosophers, seeking universal order but critical of the practices and beliefs of any new religious group; and for their pagan neighbors, consumed by suspicious ignorance of what Christians thought and did.

By the mid second century, however, Christian reflection on the person of Christ had begun to encounter an additional, different kind of challenge: the challenge from groups of believers, who accepted the news that Jesus is Savior and Lord, and who also read most of the basic documents mainstream Christianity would come to recognize as Scripture, but who understood Jesus' work as one of unprecedented, world-defining *new* revelation, which had suddenly broken into human consciousness without intelligible continuity with the past. For this early form of Christianity, Jesus offers those willing to accept enlightenment a wholly new understanding of the world, of materiality and the body, of human institutions and practices: a new way of reading the present, burdensome human situation, which promised believers release from anxiety and pain by questioning their lasting reality. This was the Christianity of religious groups known by their contemporary critics as "Gnostic,"[1] because they shared the assumption that secret, revisionist *knowledge* itself—learning to read the human situation and the Christian Gospel with their group's new

---

[1] For a recent criticism of the validity of this term to designate a variety of second-century religious groups, see Michael Allen Williams, *Rethinking "Gnosticism": an Argument for Dismantling a Dubious Category* (Princeton, NJ: Princeton University Press, 1996). Assuming that this ancient term, first used by early Christian authors, is still a useful way of designating a pattern of ancient religious phenomena, the best general surveys of "Gnostic" teachings are Kurt Rudolph, *Gnosis: the Nature and History of Gnosticism*, trans. Robert McLaren Wilson (San Francisco: Harper and Row, 1983) and Giovanni Filoramo, *A History of Gnosticism*, trans. Anthony Alcock (Oxford: Basil Blackwell, 1990). Bentley Layton has published a useful annotated translation, with informative introductions, of the "Gnostic" works found in 1947 at Nag Hammadi in Egypt—the collection that remains our main source for first-hand documentation of this ancient movement: *The Gnostic Scriptures* (Garden City, NY: Doubleday, 1987): see 5–22 for a description of "Gnostic" religion, which readily makes use of the term.

eyes—was the key to liberation, the purpose of religious practice, and the source of salvation.

Gnostic religion, in antiquity and in its constantly recurring modern mutations, was certainly not a uniform system of thought. Groups that understood and practiced such religious ideals could be found in ancient and medieval Judaism and in philosophical paganism, as well as in Christian circles; they shared many features with modern "new age" groups, curious to find hidden paths to religious enlightenment and moral liberation. Despite its wide and somewhat erratic variations, Gnostic thought was (and still is) characterized by the driving tendency to "deconstruct" the accepted continuities of mainstream religious faith: to argue that the present world, in its regular functioning and even in its materiality, is the work of a lesser creator, a "god" of limited goodness and intelligence, who is responsible for our bodily existence and our traditional religious institutions, but cannot offer us real freedom or life. This world, Gnostic teachers tended to argue, is not part of the ultimate story of cosmic purpose and well-being. Redemption from its pressures—available only to those who know how to reinterpret this world and our presence in it on the basis of secretly transmitted knowledge—is, rather, release from materiality and time, from the burden of the body, and from the narrow literalness of biblical dogma. Such liberating secret knowledge, in the early Christian Gnostic scheme, was understood to have been communicated to a small number of privileged people by the Savior Jesus, who had been sent into the darkness of creation by a God who is the ultimate source of all reality and goodness, but who had hitherto remained unknown. Initiates into this new, redeeming knowledge were often urged to keep it secret, sharing it only with the worthy.

Although, for most ancient Gnostic Christians, Jesus himself was thought to be made of higher substance than ordinary materiality, in the Valentinian Gnostic narrative he took on a "dispensational" body of some kind—a bodily form to use as a tool for his saving work—and with it "passed through Mary" into our world. At his baptism, he was empowered for his mission by a still higher agent, from the realm above matter: united with the aeon or super-terrestrial agent "Christ," who was the actual Savior and who descended upon him to direct his activity. This higher figure, as mainstream Christian sources of the time recount the Valentinian story, returned to the *Plēroma*—the realm where heavenly qualities exist forever, personified and gathered in a collective fullness—when Jesus suffered and died.[2] The Gnostic believer, who has learned from other "insiders" who Jesus really is and what his message really means, can eventually follow in this same path that Jesus took: he or she can learn to escape death, shake off the burdens of embodiment, of day-to-day

---

[2] For this version of the Valentinian narrative, see Irenaeus, *Adversus Haereses* (AH) 3.16.1.

meaninglessness and even of the restrictive, traditional moral teaching of the Church, by realizing that these are part of a world made by a lesser creator, and by turning through Christ to the ultimate source of being and truth.

One of the most precociously original and synthetic thinkers in the history of Christian theology, Irenaeus of Lyons wrote his *magnum opus*, usually known as the five books *Against the Sects* or *Adversus Haereses*, at the end of the second century.[3] A trained rhetorician, Irenaeus was born in Smyrna in the early second century and formed in the Apostolic tradition of faith by Smyrna's bishop, the venerable martyr Polycarp. Irenaeus is said to have traveled west as a mature man, to have spent some time visiting Rome, and finally to have settled in Lyons, in the Rhone valley, where he became bishop around 185, after the martyrdom of his elderly predecessor, Pothinus.[4] *Adversus Haereses* is intended as a comprehensive, rhetorically explosive "examination and refutation" (ἔλεγχος καὶ ἀνατροπή) of the theories of contemporary Gnostic Christians, most notably the Valentinians—the most theologically sophisticated of the "sects," and probably the closest to mainstream Christianity in thought and practice. Irenaeus's central concern, throughout all five books of his *Refutation*, is to argue for the unity, continuity, and reliability of the assumptions "ordinary Christians" accept as true, on the basis of the Scriptures and the Church's public teaching.

Irenaeus is, one could say, a theologian of *unities*. The continuing theme of his work is the unity of *God*, a title which includes—in a way Irenaeus never fully articulates—both the unknown Father of Jesus, who is the God of the Old Testament, and God's two "hands," who work his will in history: his Son, or Word, and his Holy Spirit, or Wisdom. Irenaeus also emphasizes the unity of the *biblical narrative*, as set out in both Old and New Testaments, and of its history of the creation, divine instruction, and ultimate redemption of humanity. He argues also for the unity of the *human person*, as a creature of body, mind, and spirit—the last of these being the divine gift of the Holy Spirit, whose presence in each of us brings our existence here in time to its intended completion and enables us to share the life of God; for the unity of the *Church* throughout the world, as the community of faith, which receives and hands on the authentic traditions of Jesus' companions; and for the unity of God's promised *salvation*, which will ultimately be the gift of life to the whole human person—flesh, soul, and spirit—in a transformed material world, a life centered on a contemplative vision of God. Fundamental to this whole

---

[3] This work, presumably written in Greek in the late 180s, survives complete only in a Latin translation, which seems to have been made in Spain or North Africa in the mid fourth century. Sizeable fragments of the original Greek survive, which show that the Latin translation is generally careful and consistent. There are also large fragments of early Armenian and Syriac translations.

[4] For the traditional details of Irenaeus's life, see Eusebius, *Church History* 3.3; 5.24; see also Irenaeus's own preface to Book 1 of *Against the Heresies*.

comprehensive vision is Irenaeus's constant affirmation of the complex personal unity of *Jesus Christ*, the Savior. As God the Word, whose role in history
has always been that of mediator and revealer of the unknown Father, the agent
of the Father's will, Christ is able to bring to completion the original plan of
God's creation. By becoming fully human, by taking on our full human, post-
Adamic reality from Mary his mother, God the Son "recapitulates"—for
Irenaeus, a characteristic term, meaning both "unify" and "transform," "bring
to completion" and "set right"—all human history since Adam, and indeed all
creation.

Irenaeus begins this anti-Gnostic narrative of salvation, in Book 3 of
*Adversus Haererses*, by considering the person of Christ:

> There is, therefore, as I have pointed out, one God the Father, and one Christ
> Jesus, who came by means of all the dispensational arrangements [that pointed to
> him], and gathered together all things in himself (see John 12.32; Eph. 1.10). But
> in every respect, too, he is a human being, the formation (*plasmatio*; probably
> Greek πλάσμα) of God; and thus he took up humanity into himself, the invisible
> becoming visible, the incomprehensible being made comprehensible, the impass-
> ible becoming capable of suffering, and the Word being made human—thus
> summing up all things in himself; so that as in super-celestial, spiritual and
> invisible things the Word of God is supreme, so also in things visible and
> corporeal he might possess the supremacy, and taking to himself the pre-
> eminence, as well as constituting himself head of the Church, he might draw all
> things to himself at the proper time.[5]

Let us consider this conception of Christ as savior of humanity in more detail.

## God's Saving Work in History

In his grand, unified view of history as the work of a single, wise, beneficent,
yet unknowable God, Irenaeus puts particular emphasis on the unity of the
incarnate person of Christ, as achieving in himself the gift of creaturely
participation in God's life, the *communio* or κοινωνία that is the original
goal for which God created the human race. Christ, the Son of God, was
genuinely human, Irenaeus insists in the same section of Book 3; he genuinely
suffered as we do, and by his obedience to the Father's will reversed our
disobedience. It is the fullness of Christ's divine and human qualities, including his growth and even his weakness as a human—here laid out not in the
style of a Chalcedonian analysis, but by means of a narrative—which makes
him Mediator and Savior. Irenaeus writes about the purpose of the Incarnation, in terms uncannily anticipating Anselm's argument in *Cur Deus Homo*:

---

[5] *AH* 3.16.6, trans. W. H. Rambaut, in Alexander Roberts and James Donaldson (eds), ANF 1,
442–3 (altered).

[Christ] caused humanity to cleave to and to become one with God. For unless a human being had overcome the enemy of humanity, the enemy would not have been legitimately vanquished. And again, unless it had been God who had freely given salvation, we could never have possessed it securely. And unless the human race had been joined to God, we could never have become partakers of incorruptibility. For it was incumbent upon the Mediator between God and humanity, by his relationship to both, to bring both to friendship and concord, and present humanity to God, while he revealed God to humanity. For how could we be partakers of adoption as [God's] sons and daughters, unless we had received from him, through the Son, that fellowship (*communio*) which refers to himself— unless his Word, having been made flesh, had entered into communion with us? So he passed through every stage of life, restoring to all communion with God.[6]

Irenaeus conceives of the salvation of the human race from the dangers that constantly surround it—from oppression, from spiritual and material poverty, from disease and mortality, and from the interior alienation from God caused by sin—as all being fully accomplished, at least in principle, through the unification of God and humanity in the single person of Jesus. His vision of the human race is expressed in his narrative of origins and ends—much like the Valentinian retelling of the origin of creation and of our present human predicament, in documents like the *Apocryphon of John*.[7] Each of us lives out in our own experience both the alienation of the fallen Adam and Eve from God, and—if we are ready to accept the news of redemption—the rescue from that alienation realized in the person and work of Jesus. So, for Irenaeus, the core of the news of redemption is precisely the full self-identification of the eternal, creative, life-giving Word of God with a complete human being, who is a descendant and counterpart of Adam. The Word's coming in human form resumes, reverses, and heals—"recapitulates," in Irenaeus's term—the old story of Adam's fall, and so brings the biblical narrative to a positive conclusion, which unexpectedly fulfills God's ancient promises to Abraham.

In another passage from the same section of Book 3, filled with biblical allusions, Irenaeus sums up his vision of this overarching narrative of salvation:

For as [the Son] was human in order to undergo temptation, so also was he the Word that he might be glorified; the Word remaining quiescent, that he might be capable of being tempted, dishonored, crucified, and of suffering death, but the human nature being swallowed up in it [i.e. the Word] when it conquered, took death on itself, rose and ascended. He therefore, the Son of God, our Lord, coming forth as the Word of the Father, and as the Son of man (since he had the generation of his human nature from Mary, who was descended from the human race, and who was herself a human being) had a human birth and [so] became the Son of man. Therefore also "the Lord himself gave us a sign, in the

---

[6] *AH* 3.18.7 (altered; emphasis mine).    [7] See Layton, *The Gnostic Scriptures*, 28–51.

depth below and in the height above," which no human being asked for, because we never expected that a virgin, who was truly a virgin, could "conceive and bear a son," and that what was thus born should be "God with us."[8] ... [God's purpose was] that, as the head rose from the dead, so also the remaining part of the body—that of everyone who is found in life—when the time is fulfilled of that condemnation which existed by reason of disobedience, may rise, "blended together and strengthened in every ligament"[9] by the increase of God, each of the members having its own proper and fit position in the body.[10]

God redeems humanity, in other words, by uniting both its story—told in Isaiah and the Gospels—and its physical reality with himself, through the Son's incarnation. That unity is what gives it new, indestructible life.

For Irenaeus, in fact, throughout the last three books of *Adversus Haereses*, the ultimate goal of Christ's mission is to draw humanity into a "fellowship with God": a new relationship involving peaceful, obedient service from our side, and the sharing of God's own transcendent being—which Irenaeus calls simply God's "glory"—from his. "Salvation," in our way of speaking, is shorthand for the finding of human fulfillment, validity, permanence, continued well-being, the satisfaction of needs; in Irenaeus's view, it is above all the result of a permanent, growing, vital relationship with God, who is the source of life.

In Book 4, where he develops this theme of salvation at greater length, in the context of an extended reflection on the diachronic unity of God's saving history—first in the story of Israel, now in that of the Church—Irenaeus points out that human beings are actually *saved* not by escaping, as fallen souls, from their unfortunate exile in a misconceived creation, as the Valentinians suggested, nor by being liberated from the oppressive demands of a jealous, inferior creator and lawgiver, as the Marcionites taught, but by serving the one gracious God in freedom, "following" Jesus on his way, doing the Father's will:

> To follow the Savior is to be a partaker of salvation, and to follow light is to receive light. But those who are in light do not themselves illumine the light, but are illumined and revealed by it; they certainly contribute nothing to it, but, receiving the benefit, they are illumined by the light.... For this reason God demands service from the human race, in order that, since he is good and merciful, he may benefit those who continue in his service. For God is in need of nothing, but we ourselves stand in need of communion with God. For this is the glory of the human race: to continue and remain permanently in God's service. Therefore also the Lord said to his disciples, "You have not chosen me, but I have chosen you," indicating that they did not glorify *him* when they followed him, but that, in following the Son of God, they were glorified *by*

---

[8] Isa. 7.11–14.        [9] Eph. 4.16.
[10] *AH* 3.19.3, trans. W. H. Rambaut, NPNF 1.449 (altered).

him.... [So] we participate in the glory of the Lord, who has both formed us and prepared us for this purpose, that, when we are with him, we may partake of his glory.[11]

The one who communicates this divine glory in fullness to willing human receivers is, of course, Christ: a human being who is also God the Word, and who "recapitulates" in himself, as we have already seen, both our human history of weakness and God's history of promise. But the vehicle of this communication, it seems, in Irenaeus's scheme of salvation, is the Holy Spirit—the other "hand" doing the God the Father's work in history. The one who descended on the human Jesus at his baptism and rested on him, in order to "accustom" all Jesus' fellow men and women to recognize and imitate him, is now bestowed by Jesus on them as well, "renewing them, from their old habits, into the newness of Christ."[12] Irenaeus, in fact, sees the descent of the Spirit on Jesus as the beginning of the Spirit's presence in the Church, which now bears authentic witness from within itself to Jesus and to the beginning of a new era of salvation.[13] Like God's breath in the nostrils of Adam in Genesis 2, the Spirit has been given to the Church

> for this purpose, that all the members receiving it may be vivified; and the [means of] communion has been distributed throughout the Church, that is, the Holy Spirit, the pledge of incorruption, the means of confirming our faith, and the ladder of ascent to God.... For where the Church is, there is the Spirit of God, and where the Spirit of God is, there is the Church, and every kind of grace...[14]

The Church, formed from the disciples of Jesus and those who receive their witness, is for Irenaeus the locus of transformation and participation in his life, which God has intended for humanity from its very origin; it is the place where humans, gathered by the action of the Spirit of Jesus, find both God and themselves.

God's strategy in dealing with humanity, then, in Irenaeus's view, has not been a sudden irruption of the ultimate source of being into an alien, dysfunctional realm, but a long process of self-revelation and self-communication, gradually "accustoming the human race to bear his Spirit, and to have communion with God" in the community of believers.[15] It began with Israel, and has come to final clarity and force in the Church. In Irenaeus's theological scheme, it is unequivocally the Son, the Word of God, who stands at the center of this growing communion of grace. As the Word, who was the instrument of creation and who is now flesh, he has been the instrument of this

---

[11] *AH* 4.14.1 (altered).   [12] *AH* 3.17.1.

[13] See, for example, *AH* 3.17.2–4, where Irenaeus invokes the biblical story of Gideon's fleece and Jesus' parable of the Good Samaritan as support for his view of the Spirit's role in saving humanity from destruction. This theme of the bestowal of the Spirit, as we shall see, will reappear in an important way in the Christology of Athanasius, and later in that of Cyril of Alexandria.

[14] *AH* 3.24.1 (altered).   [15] *AH* 4.14.2 (altered).

communication through history, the increasingly active bestower of the Spirit; he now plays that role in fullness. Building on an exegesis of Matthew 11.27, "No one knows the Son except the Father, and no one knows the Father except the Son, and anyone to whom the Son chooses to reveal him," Irenaeus argues:

> The manifestation of the Son is the knowledge of the Father; for all things are manifested through the Word.... For the Lord taught us that no one is capable of knowing God, unless he be taught of God—that is, that God cannot be known without God—but that this is the express will of the Father, that God *should* be known.... For by means of the creation itself, the Word reveals God the Creator; and by means of the world, the Lord as maker of the world; and by means of the formation [of the human creature] the craftsman who formed him, and by the Son, that Father who begot the Son.[16]

Irenaeus seems to think of the biblical narrative, in fact, reaching from the creation account in Genesis 1, through the Gospels, to the vision of the triumphant Christ in Revelation 19, as an increasingly intense process of divine self-revelation, as God moves from the manifestation of his presence in creation, to the verbal manifestation of his Word in "the law and the prophets" of ancient Israel, and finally to his personal, visible presence in the incarnation:

> And through the Word himself who had been made visible and palpable, the Father was shown forth; and although all did not equally believe in him, still all did see the Father in the Son: for the Father is the invisible of the Son, but the Son is the visible of the Father. And for that reason everyone called him "the Christ" while he was present [on earth], and named him "God."[17]

Christ saves humanity, communicates renewed and triumphant life, simply by *being* "God visible"!

Irenaeus identifies this revelation of God through the Word, which has reached its climax in the Word made flesh, as the fulfillment of every human creature's deepest need and desire. To "see" the Father in his Word, as well to know the glorified Christ as the same Word who was born and suffered, will be the cause of unending final joy for believers, "perfect salvation."[18] The relationship of God's knowing us to our knowing God, Irenaeus emphasizes, is not a symmetrical one. For God is unchanging, while we—simply by being creatures—are constantly changing, constantly reaching out for a deeper knowledge of God and ourselves, for fuller communion—constantly either growing towards God or away from him. God remains, we develop; and the key to our development towards life and fulfillment is precisely that we recognize our dependence on him, as our source and goal.

---

[16] *AH* 4.6.3, 4, 6 (altered; emphasis mine).

[17] *AH* 4.6.6 (translation altered, based on Greek fragment).      [18] *AH* 4.9.2–3.

For as God is always the same, so also the human creature, when found in God, shall always go on towards God. For neither does God at any time cease to confer benefits upon, or to enrich the human creature; nor does the creature ever cease from receiving those benefits, and from being enriched by God. For the receptacle of God's goodness and the instrument of his glorification is the creature who is grateful to the one who made him.[19]

Our gratitude, which is grounded in our sense of God's Mystery and power, as well as in our recognition of his blessings to us and his nearness to us in Christ, is, for Irenaeus, an indispensable part of faith, the creature's reverent recognition of the Creator.

So while God remains incomprehensible in his "greatness"—in his own infinite essence—he has made himself known and even visible in his "love"— in his condescension, his self-communication to us in human history: to this statement Irenaeus adds, "now *this is his Word*, our Lord Jesus Christ, who in the last times was made human among humans."[20] In fact, it is the very hiddenness of God's own being, the necessity that he reach out to us from his unknowable Mystery and show us his glory, if we are to realize even the extent of our own dependence and need, which determines the structure of saving revelation. For Irenaeus, to recognize this is real *Gnosis*, the knowledge that changes everything for the good. This is the rhythm of grace in history: God freely reminds us of our total dependence on him, even to know him, but also assures us that this knowledge, carefully "dispensed" in historic, communally remembered events, is what gives us the fullness of life. So he writes:

> For this reason the Word became the dispenser of his Father's grace for the benefit of men and women, for whom he shown such great expressions of care, revealing God indeed to human beings, but also presenting human beings to God, and preserving at the same time the invisibility of the Father, lest humans should at any time become despisers of God, and that they might always possess something towards which they might advance; but, on the other hand, revealing God to human beings through many such expressions of care, lest humans, falling away from God altogether, should cease to exist.[21]

In a celebrated passage that immediately follows this text, in Book 4, Irenaeus explains in memorable language why God's revelation of himself in the incarnate Word is of such importance for the human race: the simple vision of God's glory—the grateful, direct knowledge of God through Jesus and his Spirit, which forms "communion" and friendship between creatures and the Creator—is alone the source of everlasting life for them. The revelation of God's glory in Christ is both salvation from death and a promise of everlasting

---

[19] *AH* 4.11.2 (altered).     [20] *AH* 4.20.4 (altered); cf. 4.20.5.
[21] *AH* 4.20.7 (altered). What we have translated here as "expressions of care" is *dispensationes* in the ancient Latin translation, and presumably οἰκονομίας in Greek. It refers to God's merciful ways of "managing" history: his plan and his particular interventions to achieve it. See n. 32.

renewal, because God is himself the source of life. To become what humans were created to be, to "live" authentically, we need no further gift of redemption than knowledge of God in Jesus Christ, through the teaching and practice of his Church, in the power of his Spirit:

> For as those who see the light are within the light, and partake of its brilliancy, so those who see God are in God, and receive of his splendor. But his splendor vivifies them; those, therefore, who see God do receive life. And for this reason, He, although beyond comprehension and boundless and invisible, rendered himself visible and comprehensible and within the capacity of those who believe, that he might vivify those who receive and behold him through faith.... It is not possible to live apart from life, and the means of life is found in fellowship with God; but fellowship with God is to know God, and to enjoy his goodness.
>
> Human creatures therefore shall see God, that they may live, being made immortal by that sight, and attaining even unto God... For the glory of God is a living human being;[22] and the life of the human person consists in beholding God. For if the manifestation of God, which is made through the creation, affords life to all living on earth, much more does that revelation of the Father, which comes through the Word, give life to those who see God.[23]

The logic of Irenaeus's anti-Gnostic argument is clear: the God proclaimed by the Christian community is not a remote, unknown God who seeks to rescue us from the isolating ignorance of our creaturehood by sending us a Savior who will teach us how to escape: how to reinterpret this world as largely irrelevant, the product of malice or deception. The God of the Church is a transcendent Mystery, surely, but is also well known: he is the world's Creator, who has always been at work in the world, through his Word and his Spirit, to reveal himself to creatures, to disclose the glory at the core of his being, so that creatures, in the very act of knowing his goodness and giving him thanks, might find communion with him, and in that communion find for themselves incorruptible life. By taking on real human flesh, by becoming human among humans, the Word of God saves humanity, with its flesh and even its material surroundings, from darkness and annihilation; he does this, above all, by revealing God to us in unmistakably human terms, becoming humanity's full and most perfect exemplar—becoming what God has intended each of us to be, the *vivens homo*. The incarnate Word "sums up" human nature and

---

[22] The "living human being" Irenaeus mentions here is clearly not just any person whose natural human potential has been developed to the full—"man fully alive," as it is sometimes translated today, with an implied emphasis on "fully." It is rather the person formed by faith and the life of the sacraments to know and share fully in *God's* life, in the image of the incarnate Word. First of all, the "living human being" who embodies the glory of God is the God-man, Christ himself! For a similar passage, see 3.20.2. See also Ysabel De Andia, *Homo Vivens: incorruptibilité et divinisation de l'homme selon Irénée de Lyon* (Paris: Études Augustiniennes, 1986).

[23] *AH* 4.20.5–7 (altered).

history in himself, and in that very summation reveals in his own person the glory of God, which communicates indestructible vitality. In our encounter with Christ, we find both God and ourselves, and so find real Gnosis: real, experiential knowledge of the world's central Mystery, as it involves us in its own endless life.

## The Human Creature

Irenaeus's understanding of the identity and role of Christ the Savior, forged from a detailed reading of the emergent Christian Scriptures in the face of the challenges raised by "Gnostic" forms of Christianity, presupposes a vision of the human person and the human future that is also not shared by the Gnostic sects. Let us consider at least a few of the main features of that wider understanding of humanity distinctive to Irenaeus.

(a) *Historicity.* Valentinian and other Gnostic interpretations of the biblical narrative of salvation through Christ drew a great deal of their power from appealing to the present negative features of human life: ignorance, moral impotence, physical frailty and temporal limitation. Through elaborate cosmogonies, these Christian groups contrasted the present state of the human race in history with the affirmation that the transcendent source of all things must be above change and weakness, and that the salvation of those humans who are capable of being rescued must come ultimately from that unknown, fundamentally unknowable God. Existing beyond the limits of the present world, the ultimate God must communicate to them knowledge of an origin and a goal that are now only masked by the realities of history, which are the work of a lesser creator. Irenaeus, by contrast—radically committed to affirming the unity of God as both creator and savior, and to pointing out a continuity and an organic meaning in history—explains the negative aspects of our present human life by insisting on the fundamental importance for creatures of change and growth: humans are made in God's image, we read in Genesis (Gen. 1.27), but that image implies a perfection that must be achieved in us over time, precisely because, as creatures, we are radically historical.

So, explaining the human creation narrative in Genesis 1, Irenaeus writes:

> For [God] formed [the human person] for growth and increase, as the Scripture says: "Increase and multiply." And in this respect God differs from humans, that God indeed makes, but the human person is made; and truly, he who makes is always the same, but that which is made must receive both beginning, and middle, and addition, and increase. And God does indeed create in a skillful way, while the human person is created skillfully. God is also truly perfect in all things, himself equal and similar to himself, as he is all light and all mind and all substance, and the fount of all good; but the human creature receives

advancement and increase towards God. For as God is always the same, so also the human creature, when situated in God, shall always go on towards God.[24]

Implied in our very mutability, which is fundamental to humanity's created status, in Irenaeus's view, is the requirement that rational creatures—angelic and human—must freely choose for themselves whether or not to make progress towards their intended goal of union with God. Only if knowledge of God and communion with him require from creatures deliberate choice and struggle, will creatures recognize their supreme value.[25] "And indeed," he writes, "the harder we strive, so much the more valuable [our goal] is; while the more valuable it is, so much more should we esteem it. And indeed, those things that come spontaneously are not esteemed so highly as are those that are reached by much anxious care."[26] So the question raised by the critics of the canonical Christian narrative of fall and redemption, "Why could not God have made the human creature perfect from the beginning?" loses its force, when seen in the context of a world created to grow. God is unlimited in his own power, Irenaeus argues, but imperfection and a capacity for improvement is always characteristic of what is limited by space and time; what perfection they do achieve, if it is to last, must involve choice, training, and gradual change.

Irenaeus sums up his understanding of this process of human growth towards perfection near the end of Book 4:

> By this arrangement, therefore, and these harmonies, and by a sequence of this kind, the human person—a created and organized being—is formed after the image and likeness of the uncreated God: the Father planning everything well and giving his commands, the Son carrying these into execution and performing the work of creating, and the Spirit nourishing and increasing what is made, but the human person making progress day by day, and ascending towards the perfect— that is, approximating to the uncreated One. For the Uncreated—that is, God—is perfect...For God is the one who is yet to be seen, and the beholding of God is productive of immortality, but immortality renders one near to God.[27]

By undergoing growth towards knowledge and union with God, by experiencing the work of both the Son and the Holy Spirit in biblical history and in the present life of the Church, the human creature discovers by experience both what he is not yet and what God is.[28] The full vision of God is always something to be hoped for.

---

[24] *AH* 4.11.1–2 (altered).    [25] *AH* 4.37.    [26] *AH* 4.37.7.    [27] *AH* 4.38.3.

[28] Irenaeus makes a similar point about the importance of our experience of human weakness, as necessary to our discovery of the sole power of God, in *AH* 5.3.1: "'Strength is made perfect in weakness' (II Cor. 12.9), rendering us better human beings who, by means of our infirmity, become acquainted with the power of God. For how could anyone have learned that he is himself an infirm being, mortal by nature, or that God is immortal and powerful, unless he had learned

(b) *Capacity for God.* Irenaeus's conviction, then, is that the human person, created in God's image from the beginning, is intended to belong to "the earthly kingdom which is the beginning of incorruption"—the community of the Church and the future millennial Kingdom to which it points—and in that context "gradually to grasp hold of God."[29] Earlier, in Book 3, he makes this same point in broad terms, as a summary of the biblical narrative, of which Christ's coming forms the climax:

> This, therefore, was the object of the long-suffering of God, that the human race, passing through all things, and acquiring the knowledge of death, then attaining to the resurrection from the dead [i.e. in Christ's resurrection], and learning by experience what is the source of his deliverance [i.e. the work of Christ], may always live in a state of gratitude to the Lord, having obtained from him the gift of incorruptibility, that he might love [Christ] the more ... For [Christ], too, was "made in the likeness of sinful flesh" (Rom. 8.3) to condemn sin, and to cast it away, as now a condemned thing, beyond the flesh, only that he might call the human creature forth into his own likeness, assigning him to be an imitator of God, and imposing on him his Father's law, in order that he [i.e. the human subject] may see God, and granting him power to receive the Father—being the Word of God who dwelt in a human being. So he became the Son of man, that he might accustom humans to receive God, and God to dwell in them, according to the good pleasure of the Father.[30]

Central to this vision of the human future is Irenaeus's paradoxical, even scandalous insistence that the "flesh"—the material, world-centered dimension of human life—is an integral part of the creature destined for union with God. Gnostic Christian writers had followed the classical philosophical practice of speaking of every human person as a composite of flesh, soul, and spirit, and divided society at large into three corresponding classes, depending on which element was dominant in any individual. Only the "spiritual" were thought to be capable of putting into effect the call of Jesus to leave the present world behind, and to be united with the primordial, pre-cosmic "pleroma" of beings, the full assembly of the living, intelligible abstractions on which the present world is modelled, and whom the Gnostics often referred to as "aeons." Paul had adopted the same tripartite terminology for the human person, in a more casual way, in I Thess. 5.23. Irenaeus generally adopts it, too, but welds it into his own distinctive anthropological vision, in which each human person is composed of material flesh, an intellectual soul made in the image of the eternal Word or divine Mind, and the dynamic, sanctifying gift of the Holy Spirit, whose presence is necessary—along with the other two elements—for

---

by experience what lies in both.... But the experience of both confers upon the human creature true knowledge of God and of humanity, and increases his love towards God" (trans. altered).

[29] *AH* 5.32.1. Irenaeus's striking phrase here, in the ancient Latin translation, is *capere Deum.*
[30] *AH* 3.20.2. The manuscripts of the Latin version of *AH* read "moral discipline" here, instead of "death."

the human person to be complete as he was made to be, and to move towards perfection.

Irenaeus makes this clear in Book 5:

> God shall be glorified in his handiwork,[31] fitting it so as to be conformable to, and modeled after, his own Son. For by the hands of the Father—that is, by the Son and the Holy Spirit—the human person, and not merely a part of the human person, was made in the likeness of God. Now the soul and the spirit can certainly be *parts* of the human person, but not *the* human person; for the perfect human being consists in the commingling and union of a soul, receiving the Spirit of the Father, and its combination with that fleshly nature, which was molded after the image of God.... If anyone should take away the substance of flesh—that is, of God's handiwork—and understand that which is purely spiritual, such would not be a spiritual human being, but would be the spirit of a human being, or the Spirit of God. But when the spirit, here blended with the soul, is united to God's handiwork, the human being is rendered spiritual and perfect, because of the outpouring of the Spirit; and this is he who was made in the image and likeness of God.[32]

In this understanding of the human person, the gift of the Holy Spirit is not simply a blessed addition; it is necessary to our attainment of the full, living, God-centered humanity for which we were originally created. Having the intellectual capacities of a mind or a soul is not enough.

This completion of our humanity only comes about through the Incarnation of God's Word in a human soul and body:

> For it was necessary that, in the first place, a human being should be fashioned, and that what was fashioned should receive the soul, and afterwards, that it should receive the communion of the Spirit. Wherefore also "the first Adam was made" by the Lord "a living soul, but the second Adam a life-giving spirit" (I Cor. 15.45). As, then, he who was made a living soul forfeited life, when he turned aside to what was evil, so, on the other hand, the same individual, when he reverts to what is good and receives the life-giving Spirit, shall find life.[33]

Irenaeus reads the biblical accounts of creation and redemption, in Genesis and in the writings of the New Testament, as having meaning only in light of each other. Made by the Father, through the complementary activity of the Son and the Spirit, the human person grows towards the full realization of his own identity, despite his original fall, only by being conformed to Christ and enlivened with his Spirit, in Christ's "recapitulation" of God's original design.

---

[31] The original Greek term here, again, is probably πλάσμα, which suggests a figure made of pliable matter, such as clay. Irenaeus seems to be thinking here of Genesis 2.7, where God is represented as creating Adam by forming the clay of the earth and breathing life into what he has shaped.

[32] *AH* 5.6.1 (trans. altered; emphasis mine).      [33] *AH* 5.12.2 (trans. altered).

(3) *Eschatology*. Because he connects the original, divinely planned creation of the human person, as a synthesis of material flesh, intellectual soul, and divine Spirit, with the restoration and final confirmation of God's design through Christ's redeeming work, Irenaeus insists—in contrast to his Gnostic opponents— that *bodily resurrection* is central to human salvation. Clear proof that our bodies will be saved along with our minds is, for him, contained both in creed and in sacrament: the Christian confession that Christ has redeemed us by shedding the human blood that gave life to his flesh, and also the practice of the Christian Eucharist, which seems already to be commonly understood—presumably by both mainstream and Gnostic Christians—as the opportunity for believers to eat and drink Christ's flesh and blood in the liturgical "Mystery." He writes:

> Vain in every respect are they who despise the entire dispensation of God,[34] and deny the salvation of the flesh, and treat with contempt its regeneration, saying that it is not capable of incorruption. But if this [flesh] cannot achieve salvation, then clearly neither did the Lord redeem us with his blood, nor is the cup of the Eucharist communion in his blood, nor the bread which we break communion in his body. For blood can only come from veins and flesh, and whatever else makes up the substance of the human person; the Word of God was actually made this. He redeemed us by his own blood . . . When, therefore, the mingled cup and the manufactured bread receive the Word of God, and the Eucharistic meal of the blood and the body of Christ takes place, from which things the substance of our flesh is increased and supported, how can they affirm that the flesh is incapable of receiving the gift of God, which is life eternal . . . ?[35]

Human flesh, integral to each human person as it was to Christ, is both the means and the object of God's saving action in history. Salvation is not simply God's intervention on the level of ideas.

Tied in with his conviction that the whole human person, including one's material nature, is called to salvation in Christ and the Spirit, and that this promise is clearly intimated in the Church's present practice of the Eucharist, is another eschatological detail we have already mentioned in passing: Irenaeus's belief that the first stage of realizing this divine promise will be a *millennium*, a thousand-year Kingdom of peace and prosperity for Jesus' faithful disciples—a stage of history hinted at in Revelation 20.1–6.[36] Commenting, for instance, on Jesus' promise at the Last Supper that he would not "drink henceforth of the fruit of this vine, until that day when I will drink it new with you in my Father's Kingdom," (Matt. 26.27), Irenaeus insists that this amounts to the assurance that Jesus' final Kingdom begins in a full-fledged human community on earth; so at the Last Supper Jesus is

---

[34] *Dispensatio*: see n. 21.    [35] *AH* 5.2.2–3 (trans. altered).

[36] For a discussion of just how widespread this Christian millennial expectation was in the second century, see especially Charles E. Hill, *Regnum Caelorum* (Oxford: Oxford University Press, 1992; Grand Rapids, MI: Eerdmans, 2001).

indicating both these points: the inheritance of the earth, in which this new fruit of the vine is drunk, and the resurrection of his disciples in the flesh. For the new flesh, which rises again, is the same that also receives the new cup. And he cannot by any means be understood as drinking of the fruit of the vine when he is settled down with his disciples above in some super-celestial place; nor are those who drink it devoid of flesh, for to drink what flows from the vine pertains to flesh, and not spirit.[37]

The millennial Kingdom, as Irenaeus imagines it, is painted largely in colors borrowed from Isaiah, Ezekiel, and the Book of Revelation. It will begin with the resurrection of the just from the dead, and will be a time of peace, of astounding fertility and plenty on the earth, and of boundless life in a landscape of extraordinary beauty—all centered on Jerusalem. The assurance that this period of earthly revival will come is part of the promise that the whole human person, not just a fleshless mind, is destined for salvation through Christ. And the purpose of such an age is not to be itself the final state of salvation, but a penultimate stage of growth and maturation, preparing those who have followed Christ for a still greater final transformation afterwards.

In the times of the resurrection, the righteous shall reign in the earth, growing stronger by seeing the Lord: and through him they shall become accustomed to partake in the glory of God the Father, and shall enjoy in the Kingdom intercourse and communion with the holy angels, and union with spiritual beings.[38]

The final stage of human existence, which will follow—life in the presence of God the Father through the redeeming work of the Son and the power of the Spirit—clearly exceeds our present ability to know or imagine. So Irenaeus writes, at the conclusion of his great work of apologetics:

When this present form of things passes away, and the human person has been renewed and flourishes in an incorruptible state, so as to preclude the possibility of becoming old, then "there shall be the new heaven and the new earth,"[39] in which the new person shall remain, always holding fresh communication with God....And in all these things, and by them all, the same God the Father is manifested, who fashioned the human person and gave a promise of inheriting the earth to our ancestors, who brings them forth from bondage at the resurrection of the just, and who fulfils the promises for the Kingdom of his Son, subsequently bestowing in a paternal manner those things which "neither the eye has seen nor the ear has heard, nor has the thought of them arisen within the human heart..."[40]

---

[37] *AH* 5.33.1 (trans. altered).     [38] *AH* 5.35.1 (trans. altered).     [39] Rev. 21.1.
[40] *AH* 5.36.1, 3 (trans. altered), referring at the end to I Cor. 2.9. The final phrase is taken from Rom. 8.19–21.

Our present existence, for all its rich history of fall and renewal, as summed up and healed in the single, historical person of Christ, is only a preparation for an eternal life and joy, beyond all history and beyond all imagining.

## ORIGEN

Although he was Irenaeus's junior by at least a generation, and lived at the other end of the Mediterranean world, Origen faced many of the same challenges that the bishop of Lyons did in interpreting the Christian Gospel, if in a significantly different way. Alexandria, Origen's first home, was in the late second and early third centuries the intellectual stronghold of Gnostic Christianity, as well as the world's leading center of Hellenistic literary criticism, philosophical study, and what we would call today natural science. In this rich cultural setting, the sophisticated members of Origen's Church, like their fellow Christians on the frontier of Gaul, faced the powerful attraction of a revisionist Christian narrative, apparently more spiritual than that increasingly accepted by the major Churches: one that built on a widespread late antique restlessness at the limitations that embodiment and its vulnerabilities place on our knowledge and freedom. Biblical Christians in Alexandria, too, like most Gnostic groups, were inclined to preach a Gospel that separated the creation of this world from its redemption. They usually assumed, however, that the origins of our present woes lie in some human guilt or misfortune, long before our present existence, rather than in the ignorance or malice of superhuman agents: and they saw in Christ, the Savior, one who would release us from both sin and the burden of materiality, as well as from all the mundane concerns that come in their wake. Origen, like Irenaeus, sought to present the narrative of the whole Christian Bible—Old Testament and New—in an integrated way that was explicitly rooted in the Church's traditional "rule of faith"—its creedal summary of the biblical story of creation and salvation. Origen's peculiar genius, as the first professional Christian Scripture scholar we know of, was to do this mainly through direct biblical interpretation, in a way carefully anchored in the text, but also making use of the philosophical suppositions, the techniques of literary criticism, and even the Gnostic love for esoteric contextual narratives, that so engaged Alexandrian intellectuals.[41]

---

[41] For discussions of Origen's Christology, see especially Henri Crouzel, *La Théologie de l'image de Dieu chez Origène* (Paris: Aubier, 1956); *Origène et la "connaissance mystique"* (Paris: Desclée de Brouwer, 1961); Marguerite Harl, *Origène et la fonction révélatrice du Verbe incarné* (Paris: Éditions du Seuil, 1958). See also J. Nigel Rowe, *Origen's Doctrine of Subordination* (Bern: Peter Lang, 1987), for much useful material on Origen's Christology. On Origen's overall approach to biblical interpretation, see Peter W. Martens, *Origen and Scripture: The Contours of the Exegetical Life* (Oxford: Oxford University Press, 2012).

In the preface to his celebrated treatise *On First Principles*, probably written about 230—a comprehensive interpretation of the Christian biblical story in anti-Gnostic and anti-Marcionite terms, which is meant to provide the supportive context for the Christian interpretation of puzzling biblical texts— Origen begins by identifying all Christian faith as rooted in the Johannine conviction that "grace and truth have come through Jesus Christ" (John 1.17).[42] This holds true, he believes, for graced humanity throughout the whole of history: Moses and the prophets of Israel, too, were nourished by "the words and teaching of Christ," in his continuing revelatory role as God's Word and the giver of God's Spirit.[43] The problem for faith, then, is not so much its source; Origen, like Justin, assumed the Logos or communicating mind of God is always active in history, even before the Incarnation, revealing God's truth to those created minds open to receive it. Rather, the problem for faith is simply that believers now understand the teaching of Christ the Word in a variety of ways, which at times conflict. Just as secular philosophers, as Justin complained, all professing to pursue the truth, can offer radically different prescriptions for how to live well, biblical Christians tend to hear different messages within the Logos's single revelation, and Christian groups may claim the same apostolic authority for very different interpretations of God, the world, and salvation in Christ. As a result, Origen suggests, Christian thinkers need first to "lay down a sure line and a clear rule for those details" that are central to Christian faith, before speculating on more conjectural matters.[44] He finds this in the Church's traditional "rule of faith" or formulated baptismal creed, and dedicates the first three books of his treatise *On First Principles* to not one, but two expansive and biblically well-documented expositions of the meaning of that creed.[45]

In the summary of the Rule of Faith, with which Origen prefaces his treatise, he lays out what he understands to be core of the Church's conception of Christ the Word:

> [He was] begotten of the Father before all creation. And when he had assisted the Father in the creation of all things—for "through him all things were made" (John 1.3)—in these last times he emptied himself and was made human, became flesh although he was God, and as a human being remained what he was: God. He took

---

[42] Origen, *De Principiis* Preface 1. John 1.14–17, in turn, seems to be a deliberate echo of the narrative of God's self-disclosure to Moses on the top of Mt Sinai in Exodus 34, where—though intrinsically invisible—he identifies himself as "the Lord . . . , rich in mercy and truth (*rav ḥesed w'emeth*)." In Jesus, that gracious and truthful but invisible God has now shown himself as "dwelling among us."

[43] Origen, *De Principiis* Preface 1.       [44] *De Principiis* Preface 2.

[45] For a discussion of the original purpose and structure of this treatise, see my article, "Origen's *De Principiis*: A Guide to the 'Principles' of Christian Scriptural Interpretation," in John Petruccione (ed.), *Nova et Vetera: Patristic Studies in Honor of Thomas Patrick Halton* (Washington, DC: Catholic University of America Press, 1998), 3–21.

up a body like our body, differing only in the respect that it was born from a virgin and from the Holy Spirit. And because this Jesus Christ was born and suffered truly, not merely in appearance, he truly died our common death; for he truly rose from the dead, and having had contact with his disciples after his resurrection, he was taken up.[46]

As Origen goes on to develop his understanding of the Church's faith, he stresses that although Father, Son, and Holy Spirit—unlike all other beings in the universe—exist together always, "transcending all time and all ages and all eternity;"[47] and although the generation of the Son is not to be understood as a material division or multiplication of the divine substance, or even as production from nothing, but as the eternal sharing, within God, of a single "reality and substance;"[48] still the Son differs from the Father not only by being generated, but by being, in a certain sense, *multiple*. While God the Father remains "incomprehensible and immeasurable,"[49] "a simple intellectual nature,"[50] the Son, who in his incarnate being is Christ, contains within himself from the beginning, as the Father's eternal, creative Wisdom, the intelligible "forms and descriptions" of what would, in time, populate the created cosmos; "there was never a moment when the prefiguration of what was to be was not already present in Wisdom."[51] In this sense, Origen saw the intelligible shape of creation itself, with all its myriad details, as co-eternal with God, potentially and intelligibly contained in the eternal Mind, which *is* the Logos, even though the actual existence of created intellects and bodies, all of which are historical and contingent, clearly began at some point in time.[52]

But the divine Wisdom, which is the most proper and "original" identity of God the Son, contains in itself, as the "beginning" or ἀρχή of creation, not only the core ideas of particular creatures, but a host of other titles or intelligible attributes particularly applicable to the Son alone—what Origen calls his ἐπίνοιαι—that express his work of mediation, as he realizes the eternal plan of God in both creation and redemption. As is well known, the first book of Origen's *Commentary on John* is a listing and an explanation of the significance of those ἐπίνοιαι or titles, as they are given in the various books of the New Testament; all of them together are intended to convey to created minds, in kaleidoscopic fashion, the nature and work, the intelligible identity, of this

---

[46] *De Principiis* Preface 4.   [47] *De Principiis* 4.4.1.   [48] *De Principiis* 4.4.1.
[49] *De Principiis* 1.1.5.   [50] *De Principiis* 1.1.6.
[51] *De Principiis* 1.4.4. Cf. 1.2.2; *Commentary on John* 1.22.
[52] *De Principiis* 2.9.2: Because created intellects are subject to change, and do not exist simply by their own nature, "whatever that power of subsisting is that is in them is neither their own nor eternal, but is produced by the beneficence of the Creator. What they are, then, is not their own nor is it eternal, but is given by God. For it did not always exist, and everything that is given can also be withdrawn and taken away." Individual intellects, as well as the material world they now inhabit, must be called out of nothingness by God to realize, as many images, the various possible aspects of God's one eternal design.

divine Wisdom: Word, Christ, Shepherd, Door, Way, Vine, and many others. All, to Origen, provide together the exegesis of the first phrase of John's Gospel, "In the beginning—in the divine Wisdom—was the Word," and with that creative and revealing Word all the other names (thirty-seven, by my count) are included that the New Testament applies to Jesus, and that reveal to us the fullness of who and what he is.[53]

This way of conceiving the Word of God, who becomes flesh in Christ, is not simply an echo of the Middle Platonic notion of a world mind, a cosmic *nous* that knows the identity of all possible things, and in knowing them contains the forms or ideas that underlie their intelligible identity. It is also, for Origen, a way of asserting that Christ, the divine Wisdom expressed in flesh, is himself the source of the creative and redemptive process, the heart and climax of the biblical narrative. So Christ himself is the inner meaning of the objects and images associated in Scripture with God's work of salvation. Although Peter is given the name "Rock" by Jesus in Matthew 16.18, for instance, Origen suggests that this is only because Christ himself, as God's Word, is identified by Paul as the "spiritual rock" from which the people Israel spiritually drank in the desert (I Cor. 10.4). As a result, in Origen's view, "all those who imitate Christ are given the name 'Rock'; he is the spiritual rock who accompanies those who are being saved."[54]

Because of this multiple identity, Jesus is also the real fulfillment of the images he himself uses for the Kingdom of God in his parables. So, for instance,

> The "pearl of great price" is the Christ of God, the Word who stands above the precious writings and thoughts of the Law and the prophets. Where it is found, all the others are easily acquired along with it.[55]

Christ is the "master of the household," who "brings out of his treasury things new and old" (Matt. 13.52), reaffirming the teachings of the Old Law while beginning the radically new Kingdom of God in himself and in his disciples.[56]

---

[53] For another example of Origen's approach to describing who God the Son is by exploring his New Testament titles, see *De Principiis* 1.2. This method of discovering the distinctive identity of the Son lived on in the Origenist tradition: see Gregory of Nyssa, *On Perfection*, which is an exposition of the shape of our Christian perfection in the image of Christ, based on a listing and interpretation of the titles by which Paul speaks of him; see also Gregory of Nazianzus, Or. 29.17; 30.20–21.

[54] *Commentary on Matthew* 12.11 (GCS Orig. 10.88; PG 13.1004).

[55] *Commentary on Matthew* 10.8 (GCS Orig. 10.9; PG 13.853–6).

[56] *Commentary on Matthew* 10.15 (GCS Orig. 10.19; PG 13.872): "Is not, then, the householder Jesus himself? He brings forth from his treasury, at the proper time, new and spiritual things, things always being renewed by him in the 'inner man' of the just person, and 'renewed always day after day' (II Cor. 4.16), but also old things, inscribed on stones and the stony heart of the old person, so that by joining the letter and the Spirit which he gives he might enrich 'the scribe learned in the Kingdom of God,' and might make him like himself, so that the disciple might become like the master. . . ."

In fact, he is, in his own person, himself the Kingdom of God (ἡ αὐτοβασι-λεία)."[57] As the one divine Word who inspires the Scriptures and speaks in them, Jesus is also the model and source of all genuine prophecy for his disciples. So Origen, characteristically, applies to Christ the declaration God makes to the prophet in Jeremiah 1.5: "I have made you a prophet among the nations." He continues:

> If this refers to the Savior, what else is there to say? He is truly the one who prophesied to all the nations. For as he is countless other things, so he is also a prophet. As he is high priest, as he is savior, as he is physician, so he is a prophet. Moses, after all, prophesied about him and said not only that he was a prophet, but that he was so in the most distinctive way, when he said, "The Lord your God will raise up a prophet for you from among your brothers. Listen to him as you do to me."[58]

Origen's way of unifying and defending the Christian narrative of creation and redemption in his *De Principiis*—more specifically, his way of dealing with the problems of believing in the providence and saving goodness of the Creator, in a world that constantly scandalizes us with the tragic inequalities and hardships of the human lot—is to contextualize the biblical story in a speculative "meta-narrative" of his own, which in its general outline is not unlike the more complex cosmogonic myths of the Valentinians.[59] There is no need for us to rehearse all the details of his proposed story here. Briefly, Origen suggests, at least as a hypothesis, that all intelligent creatures were originally brought into being as simple intellects, created to find their bliss in knowing and loving God through union with his Wisdom, ultimately to be sanctified by the gift of his Spirit. By a mysterious and perverse impulse, however, intellects began to turn away from God, Origen speculates, at some point of their primal existence before the creation of this material world, and began to pursue their own will instead of his. God then formed the present material cosmos to "receive" them, in a kind of therapeutic exile, and allowed their "intellectual" bodies—their identifying and limiting forms—each to take on a material character, of different kinds and capabilities, situating them in different circumstances corresponding to the gravity of their fall. The purpose of this "second stage" of creation was to produce a context for conversion: to insure that eventually *all* fallen minds might discover their loneliness and need, and turn back to God.

---

[57] *Commentary on Matthew* 14.7 (GCS Orig. 10.289; PG 13.1197).
[58] *Homily on Jeremiah* 1.12 (GCS Orig. 3.10; PG 13.268).
[59] See *De Principiis* 1.4–2.3, 2.8–2.11. For supposed structural correspondences between the Valentinian "system" and Origen's *De Principiis*, see Holger Strutwolf, *Gnosis als System: Zur Rezeption der Valentinianischen Gnosis* (Göttingen: Vandenhoeck & Ruprecht, 1993); for a strong rejection of this position, see Mark Edwards, *Catholicity and Heresy in the Early Church* (Farnham: Ashgate, 2009), 79–108.

One created intellect did *not* fall, in the hypothesis Origen proposes in *On First Principles*, because it was so intensely united with the Wisdom and Word of God that it had already become, in its dynamic qualities and behavior, utterly one with him despite its creaturehood—unified with the Word like a lump of iron glowing with fire.[60] It was this created soul, inseparably joined with the Word by the identity of contemplative love, who eventually was sent by God to take on its own fleshly human body, as Jesus of Nazareth, in order to be among the other fallen souls in their exile and to reveal to them, in his words and actions, the obedience to the Father for which all were created.[61] That work of revelation, by which the Word calls all intelligent creatures, one by one, to a new conversion—to learn the truth about themselves and to live in accordance with God's creative will—has in fact gone on throughout all of history; its details are first expressed in written form in the canon of Scripture—a kind of "incarnation" of the Word in the letter, which precedes and points to his incarnation in flesh.[62] And the goal of revelation will be realized, in the phrase of I Corinthians 15.28, when, after Christ's role as teacher and healer of all humanity is fully accomplished, "God will be all in all."[63] Origen interprets that state of fulfillment in a characteristically intellectual, contemplative way, based on his reading of Paul's text:

> He will be all things for each person in this way, that everything which the rational mind, purged of all the filth of vices and thoroughly cleansed from every shadow of wickedness, can feel or understand or think, will all be God; nor will it feel anything other than God from that time on, but it will think God, will see God, will hold on to God, and all its movements will be God. And "God will be everything to it," for it will no longer be able to distinguish between evil and good, because evil will be no longer—God will be all to it, and no evil is present in God! Nor will one who then exists always in the Good, for whom God now is all, desire any more to eat from the tree of knowledge of good and evil.[64]

In that final state of union with God in knowledge and desire, all intellectual creatures will also be united with each other, by sharing as one in God's incorruptible and eternal light, which enables them to contemplate both God and each other. Even though there may, at first, be some differences in the degree to which they will participate in his light, the ability of the created mind to keep growing suggests that it will continue to progress towards "an increasingly perfect understanding," and so to share God's uniquely spiritual

---

[60] *De Principiis* 2.6.5–6.      [61] *De Principiis* 2.6.7.

[62] See *Homily on Leviticus* 1.1 (SChr. 286.66); *Comm. Ser. in Matt.* 27 (GCS Orig. 11.45).

[63] *De Principiis* 3.6.8.

[64] *De Principiis* 3.6.3. Origen suggests here that "eating from the tree of the knowledge of good and evil," in the Genesis account, refers to the created intellect's perverse desire to determine the difference between good and evil for itself, rather than to accept God's determination of good and evil in his commandments.

way of being.[65] This state of unity, in which creatures will reflect all the many forms of perfection that exist eternally in the divine Wisdom, will be the final realization in every creature of the "image of God,"[66] which already exists in its perfection in God the Son.[67]

Because salvation, in Origen's theology, comes to fulfillment in a union, both affective and cognitive, between created minds and God's own Word or Wisdom, the saving, active presence of the Word in history, and his climactic "appearance, which he manifested in a body"[68]—his Incarnation, in other words—are for Origen the key to both an authentic understanding of Christian doctrine and correct biblical interpretation. So, despite his deep interest in the spiritual interpretation of Scriptural texts and in intellectual speculation, Origen is, in fact, one of the most strongly incarnational thinkers of the early Church. Since the Word has taken on a human mind as well as a human body, for instance, Jesus necessarily must *grow*, during his lifetime, from ignorance to full knowledge, at least as far as concerns the future of God's saving work. So, in one of his commentaries on Matthew's Gospel, Origen wonders out loud how Jesus, who is the Son of God and asserts that he alone knows and reveals the Father (Matt. 11.27), can still admit to being unaware of the "day and hour" of the end of things (Matt. 24.36). His answer is to point to the necessarily temporal nature of Jesus' humanity and to his knowledge as a man:

> One may, perhaps, dare to say that a man who, like the Savior, is understood to "grow in wisdom, age and grace before God and human beings" (Lk. 2.52), who makes real progress, beyond all others, in knowledge and wisdom, still might not know that what had been fully accomplished had come, before he had fulfilled the plan (*dispensatio*) of his own life. It is no wonder, then, if he is unaware of this thing alone: the day and hour of the end. But perhaps, too, when he says that he does not know the day and hour of the end, he is speaking of the time before the plan of his own life (*dispensatio sua*) is complete, which "no one knows, neither the angels nor the Son, but only the Father." After that plan is complete, however, he no longer says this—after "God highly exalted him, and gave him the name above every name" (Phil. 2.9). For after this, the Son also knows, receiving his knowledge from the Father—even concerning the day and hour of the end, so that not only the Father knows these things, but the Son does as well.[69]

---

[65] *De Principiis* 4.4.10. See also my article, "Incorporeality and 'Divine Sensibility': the Importance of *De Principiis* 4.4 for Origen's Theology," *Studia Patristica* 41 (2006), 139–44.

[66] *De Principiis* 4.4.10; see also 3.6.1, where Origen develops the idea, familiar from other early Christian writers, that "the human race received the honor of [being] God's *image* in their first creation, whereas the perfection of God's *likeness* was reserved for them at the consummation." Origen understands "likeness" here, presumably, as a state of freely chosen moral perfection, resembling the goodness of God. See Irenaeus, *AH* 5.6; Clement of Alexandria, *Stromateis* 2.38.5; 2.131; also Origen, *Contra Celsum* 4.30; *Commentary on Romans* 4.5; *On Prayer* 27.2; etc.

[67] *De Principiis* 1.2.6; 2.6.3.      [68] *De Principiis* 2.6.1.

[69] *Commentariorum series in Matthaeum* 55 (GCS Orig. 11.124–125; PG 13.1086).

This pattern of Jesus' own growth towards a full understanding of what is being achieved, by God's plan, in and through his own life, becomes the pattern of growth for those who come to share his life through faith—those with whom the Word has identified himself in the Incarnation. Like Augustine, Origen sees Christ as personally one with those who make up his body, and even recognizes Christ's passion as being re-enacted in the persecution of his fellow Christians:

> My Lord Jesus himself says, "I gave my back to the whips, my cheeks to the blows; I did not turn my face away from the shame of spitting" (Isa. 50.6). The foolish think this only applies to that time in the past, when Pilate had him scourged, when the Jews plotted against him. But I see Jesus giving his back to the smiters day after day... Think of the Word of God being held in contempt, maligned, hated by unbelievers; recognize that he gave his cheeks to buffeting; and when he taught us, "If someone strikes you on the cheek, turn to him also the other" (Lk. 6.29), that he does this himself.[70]

Jesus' human struggles, in fact—his need to grow towards the fullness of knowledge of God's plan and of his own future, and the suffering he undergoes along with this growth, as part of our human world—are, for Origen, precisely Jesus' means of leading his disciples to God, his way of revealing to the human race the "steps" by which each of us, as fallen souls, must ascend to God's presence again. In the nineteenth book of his *Commentary on John*, Origen insists that the only way for a created intelligence to come to a knowledge of God is to be led to God gradually, through God's Wisdom, who is Christ.

> And perhaps, just as there were steps in the Temple, by which a person went up into the Holy of Holies, so all our steps are [contemplated in] the Only One of God. As he is the lowest step, he is also the one above it, and so in order, up to the highest step. The Savior, then, *is* all the steps: the lowest one is his humanity, by which we make our way upwards; and all the rest are his as well, since he is the whole staircase, so that one ascends through him—he is also an angel, and each of the other powers. And according to the meanings contained in him (κατὰ τὰς ἐπινοίας δὲ αὐτοῦ)—since the *way* is one thing and the *door* another[71]—one must first begin with the way, that after that one might so arrive at the door, and come under his rule, insofar as he is *shepherd*,[72] so that one might also enjoy him also as *king*; and one must benefit from him first as *lamb*, that he might first take away our sins,[73] so that after this, in a purified state, we might eat his flesh, our true *food*.[74]

---

[70] *Homily on Jeremiah* 18 (19).12 (GCS Orig. 3.167–168; PG 13.488).
[71] See John 14.6, "I am the way," and John 10.7, 9, "I am the door."
[72] See John 10.11.      [73] See John 1.29.
[74] Origen, *Commentary on John* 19.6.38–9 (SChr. 290.66–8; PG 14.536). For the reference to Jesus' flesh as "true food," see John 6.55. In this passage of his commentary, focused on John 8.19 ("If you knew me, you would know my Father also"), Origen is skillfully mingling the various

In a way consonant with this sense of the paramount importance of Jesus the human being, as the *beginning* of the path by which fallen creatures return to God, Origen shows a constant theological and devotional interest in the physical and psychological humanity of Jesus.[75] In some texts, for instance, Origen's deep personal conviction of the importance of a direct, spiritual contact between believers and the Savior appears as a prayer—as in the famous petition, echoing the thirteenth chapter of John's Gospel, that is suddenly addressed to Jesus in his Fifth Homily on Isaiah:

> Who will make me clean? Who will wash my feet? Jesus, come; I have dirty feet. Become a servant for my sake. Pour your water into your basin. Come, wash my feet. I know what I say is brash, but I fear the threat you uttered: "If I do not wash your feet, you will have no part in me." Therefore, wash my feet, so that I may have a part in you.[76]

In his Fifteenth Homily on the Gospel of Luke, too, where he is interpreting the scene of Jesus' presentation in the Temple as an infant, Origen emphasizes that close personal contact with him, such as Symeon had with Jesus as a child, is the presupposition for any believer's experiencing his healing and liberating power.

> And therefore [Symeon] says to [Jesus], "'Now, Lord, let your servant go in peace.' For as long as I did not hold Christ, as long as I did not embrace him in my arms, I was locked up, and could not escape my chains." But this is not only to be understood of Symeon, but of the whole human race. If anyone would come forth from the world, if anyone would be released from prison and from being confined among those who live in chains, so that he might go forward and reign, let him take Jesus in his hands, and embrace him with his arms, let him hold Jesus tightly against his breast; and then he will be able to go forth, exulting, in whatever direction he will.[77]

To know deeply and personally who Jesus is, to grasp something of the mystery of his presence in the world, is for Origen a contact that goes beyond merely theoretical understanding. In his chapter reflecting on the Incarnation of the Word, for instance, in the second book of *On First Principles*, Origen dwells at some length on the astonishment this event stirs up in him:

> When, therefore, we see some things in him that are so human that they seem to stand at no distance from our common mortal frailty, and other things so divine that they only befit that primordial, ineffable nature of the Godhead, the

biblical images used for Christ's salvific role into a coherent outline of the way a human person may "ascend" to know God.

[75] See Frédéric Bertrand, *Le Mystère de Jésus chez Origène* (Paris: Aubier, 1951).

[76] Origen, *Homilies on Isaiah* 5.2 (GCS Orig. 8.264); trans. Angela Russell Christman, in Mark C. Kiley (ed.), *Prayer from Alexander to Constantine* (London: Routledge, 1997), 306 (altered).

[77] Origen, *Homilies on Luke* 15.2 (SChr. 87 [Paris: Cerf, 1962]), 232–4.

narrowness of our human intellect constricts us, and the mind is struck dumb
with such amazement that it does not know where it should turn, what it should
hold on to, where it should go. If it understands him as God, it sees him as mortal;
if it thinks of him as human, it recognizes him returning from the dead, having
despoiled the conquered kingdom of death. Therefore we must contemplate him
with all fear and reverence, so that the truth of both natures might be revealed, on
one side and on the other...[78]

The language here, even two centuries before Chalcedon, is already that of
complementarity and paradox; but the purpose of it is not simply to enunciate
correct, balanced doctrine, but to arouse wonder at how it is that Christ, the
everlasting Word of God who united a created intellect to himself, and who
eventually took on a fleshly human body, has "cast his shadow" across all of
history;[79] and at how this same incarnate Christ provides the key for an
understanding of Scriptural texts that finds in *all* of them, rightly understood,
not simply flesh but spirit, not simply promise but fulfillment, not simply law
but grace.

The result of such a discovery of Christ in Scripture, for Origen, is joy and
exultation, as well as redeeming knowledge. In a famous passage in the
introduction to his commentary on the Gospel of John, Origen meditates on
what a "gospel" really is. He defines it as promise already known to be fulfilled:
"a promise of things which naturally, and because of the benefits they bring,
give joy to the hearer as soon as the promise is heard and believed."[80] In this
sense, as the fulfillment of what all the Scriptures promise, as the enfleshed
divine Word who speaks throughout the Bible, Jesus Christ is in his person the
whole Gospel: "the good things the Apostles announce in the Gospel are
simply Jesus."[81] To interpret the Scriptures not only in their plain meaning
but "spiritually" (as Origen always labors to do, with great ingenuity), by
seeing both Testaments as a single narrative of creation and redemption,
enables the reader to grasp the *whole* of the biblical canon as *Gospel*, as good
news: a promise that already gives us joy, because we know it has now been
substantially accomplished, in the fullness of God's self-revelation as the Word
made flesh.

Before that Gospel (he writes), therefore, which came into being by the sojourn-
ing of Christ, none of the older works [in the Bible] was a Gospel. But the Gospel,
which is the new covenant, having delivered us from the oldness of the letter,
lights up for us, by the light of knowledge ($\gamma\nu\tilde{\omega}\sigma\iota\varsigma$), the newness of the spirit, a

---

[78] *De Principiis* 2.6.2.
[79] See *De Principiis* 2.6.7, where Origen, reflecting on the Septuagint text of Lamentations 4.20—
"The breath of our countenance is the Christ, the Lord, of whom we said that we shall live under
his shadow among the nations"—interprets this "shadow" to be both the created soul of Christ,
which is "inseparably attached" to the Word before the Incarnation, and the murky beginnings
of revelation in history, which will only be fully disclosed at the end of time.
[80] *Commentary on John* 1.7.        [81] *Commentary on John* 1.10.

thing which never grows old; which has its home in the New Testament, but is also present in all the Scriptures. It is fitting, therefore, that that Gospel, which enables us to find the Gospel present even in the Old Testament, should itself receive, in a special sense, the name of Gospel.[82]

Because Origen, like Irenaeus, sees the fullness of human salvation as the intimate knowledge of God, given to us through his self-revealing Word—a revelation that unites us to him in love, and enables us to participate in his unending life—the real identity of Christ, divine Word and enfleshed human soul acting as one in human history, is to be for us the key to all of Scripture, and to make intelligible the continuous story Scripture tells of our human destiny. For both Origen and Irenaeus, to realize this is true Gnosis. Christ is the heart of that Gnosis—of that unitive knowledge of God and our own identity, which alone saves us from death.

---

[82] *Commentary on John* 1.8 (trans. Allan Menzies, *The Ante-Nicene Fathers* 10.301, altered). By "that Gospel," of course, Origen specifically means the Gospel of John, with its identification of Christ as the eternal Word of God, who is now made flesh.

# 4

---

# The Early Arian Controversy

## Christology in Search of a Mediator

Struggles to understand the identity of Jesus in fourth-century Christian circles were focused mainly on his role as mediator. Since the beginnings of Christian literature, it was generally assumed by Christian believers that Jesus is the Savior of the world, the one who has restored a sinful, wounded humanity to a vital relationship with the God at the heart of all things. As the Savior, Jesus was also thought to be, in the language of John's Gospel, God's "Word made flesh": the active, intelligent presence of God in the world, revealing and guiding humanity on its path to union with the Father, showing humanity who God is, and whose children we are all called to be. Beyond this, Jesus was confessed to be genuinely God's "only Son, our Lord," in the words of the Old Roman Creed: a figure uniquely related to the God of both Israel and the philosophers by an utterly intimate, "family" relationship, sent by God as part of his provident plan to reclaim the human world and make it part of that family, too. Most importantly, perhaps, this Son and Word of God, personally encountered in Jesus, was confessed by virtually all the Christian faithful to be himself, in some sense, *divine*: to be a part of the ultimate Mystery of being and well-being we speak of and adore as God.

Ancient religious thought, both Jewish and Greek, by the end of the pre-Christian era largely agreed that the God human beings are ultimately drawn to worship is an absolute, transcendent reality: beyond human language and concepts, lying at the root of all reality and acting constantly through history as reality's source, more real than all other reality, yet for that very reason not fully identifiable or imaginable in terms of the realities we daily measure and record with our senses. The *Apocryphon of John*, for instance, a second-century Valentinian treatise that offers a revised interpretation of the familiar narrative of cosmic and human origins in the first three chapters of Genesis, echoes some of these broader late-antique convictions in its meditation on the Monad who is the source of all things:

The Monad [is a] monarchy with nothing above it. [It is he who exists] as [God] and Father of everything, [the invisible] One who is above everything... He [is the] invisible [Spirit] of whom it is not right [to think] of him as a god, or something similar. For he is more than a god... He is [immeasurable light] which is pure, holy [and immaculate]. He is ineffable [being perfect in] incorruptibility. (He is) [not] in perfection, nor in blessedness, nor in divinity, but he is far superior. He is not corporeal [nor] is he incorporeal. He is neither large nor is he small. [There is no] way to say, "What is his quantity?" or "What [is his quality?"], for no one can [know him]. He is not someone among (other) [beings, rather he is] far superior.[1]

So, too, the second-century Syrian Neo-Pythagorean philosopher, Numenius of Apamaea, who saw the roots of the classic Platonic cosmological tradition in the more contemplative and mystical philosophy of the Pythagoreans, insisted that the origin of all reality is a single, incomprehensible and transcendent Good; but since this source is, by definition, totally impervious to contact with limited creatures, its involvement in the world—beginning with the act of creation, and including a constant presence within creation to hold it in order—is only achieved through a Demiurge or Creator, a "second god," who is produced out of him and who discovers in him, by contemplation, the ideas and principles he then uses as models for shaping worldly realities. Eusebius of Caesaraea, in his *Preparation for the Gospel*, preserves fragments of Numenius's treatise *Of the Good*, for instance, where the philosopher writes:

The First God, remaining in himself, is simple, because, being completely united with himself, he can never be divided. The Second and Third God, however, is one; but by being associated with matter, which is duality, He makes it one but is Himself divided by it, since it possesses the attitude of sensual desire and is in flux.[2]

Numenius goes on to observe that "it is not at all necessary that the First God should be the Creator; but the First God must be regarded as the father of the God who is Creator of the world,"[3] then adds:

Now the modes of life of the First God and of the Second are these: evidently the First God will be at rest, while the Second, on the contrary, is in motion. So then the First is concerned with intelligible things, and the Second with both intelligibles and sensibles. But do not be surprised if I say this: for you will hear something still more amazing! I say that in the place of the motion that is appropriate to the Second God, the appropriate motionlessness of the First God

---

[1] *Apocryphon of John* 2.27–3.28, trans. Frederik Wisse; in James M. Robinson (ed.), *The Nag Hammadi Library in English* (San Francisco: Harper, 1990), 106). See also Bentley Layton, *The Gnostic Scriptures* (Garden City, NY: Doubleday, 1987), 29.
[2] Numenius, Fragment 11, ed. Edouard des Places (Paris: Belles Lettres, 1973), 53.
[3] Frag. 12 (des Places, 54).

is itself an innate motion, from which the order of the world, and its eternal
steadiness and well-being, are poured forth on all things.[4]

It is always difficult to trace out lines of influence between Greek philosophical, Hebrew biblical, and early Christian traditions in the second and third
centuries, especially in their cosmology. Perhaps all that can be said with
certainty is that a certain approach was widely shared by several religious
and philosophical traditions which, in the first three centuries of the Christian
era, flourished side by side in Greek-speaking Eastern Mediterranean culture:
the assumption that the source of all reality is a transcendent, simple being
who cannot be conceptualized or approached directly, but who contains in
himself the qualities and values that are embodied in the world we live in. This
style of thought is radically monotheistic, and gives rise to a way of conceiving
human history—including the narrative told in the Hebrew and Christian
Bible—that is just as radically theocentric. Yet there is clearly room here for a
limited number of other divine agents. A "second God," produced from the
first by a kind of generation, must act as creator and guide of the cosmos and
all intelligent beings; as the creative "mind" ($\nu o \hat{\upsilon} s$) or "word" ($\lambda \acute{o} \gamma o s$) of the
transcendent God, he forms limited realities to share in the perfections of the
first God's qualities and values, shaping "images" of what he understands to
characterize his own Father. How the relationships of these two divine agents
are understood in detail varies greatly from one writer to another; yet this
general pattern of transcendent source, creative and preservative mediation,
and a limited, dependent, vulnerable world of material creatures, can be found
in Philo and late Jewish Wisdom literature, in Middle Platonist Greek philosophy, in Gnostic Christianity, and in many mainstream Christian theologians up to the last quarter of the fourth century. It is simply a common way in
which people conceived the relationship of this world of multiplicity and
limited intelligibility to its source and intelligible standard in another, transcendent world of eternal absolutes.

## THE CONTROVERSY OVER ARIUS

The controversy over the ontological status and identity of the Savior, which
occupied so much of the Christian Church's political and theological energies

---

[4] Frag. 15 (des Places, 56). All three of these fragments are quoted in Eusebius, *Preparation for
the Gospel* 11.18. A devout religious Platonist, who emphasized Platonism's links with other
ancient religions as well as its Pythagorean origins, Numenius was apparently critical of later
forms of Greek philosophical cosmology. His thought was clearly influential on Plotinus and
what we call Neoplatonism, as well as on the Christian Fathers of the second, third, and fourth
centuries.

in the fourth century, has to be understood against this intellectual background, if it is to be understood at all. It is really a controversy about *mediation*: about the way in which the Scriptural God, as the supreme and infinite being, the source of all, is related to the world Christians confess he has created and redeemed through Christ. The celebrated "Arian controversy," which began probably in the early 320s as a dispute over Christ's role and identity as mediator of creation and salvation, between Alexander, the bishop of Alexandria, and one of his presbyters, Arius, enveloped most of the Church, East and West, at least until 381 and in places until much later. The first, haltingly successful attempt to heal the controversy was the worldwide synod of bishops the Emperor Constantine summoned at Nicaea in the summer of 325. This council, and its creedal formula, eventually became, for the later dogmatic tradition of early Christianity, the paradigm for how to formulate the traditional faith of the Church concerning Christ's person in binding, technical terms that were understood to summarize and embody biblical teaching, without themselves being taken directly from the Bible.[5]

Arius himself was the energetic pastor of a large community of working-class Christians near the docks in Alexandria, an enterprising and well-connected promoter of some long-accepted themes in the tradition we have been describing. His preaching and popular outreach unleashed a conflict which—through several phases, and with variations of terminology and theological nuance—inevitably came to clash with the wider, classical tradition of the Church. The initial clash was with his local bishop, Alexander. Although our sources are less than clear about what Arius's actual positions and intentions were, his approach to proclaiming the Church's faith in Jesus as divine Savior seems to have been filtered through Middle Platonism's traditional understanding that the transcendent deity needed a "second God," a mediator whom God himself had produced, in order to create, order, and redeem the world of limited beings.

---

[5] A great deal has been written, in the twentieth and twenty-first centuries, on Arius, his intentions, and his achievement, as well as on the repercussions of the controversy later in the fourth century. Perhaps the best summary of earlier scholarship on Arius and his aims, as well as the most convincing attempt to explain him in his intellectual and religious context, is Rowan Williams, *Arius: Heresy and Tradition* (2nd edn, Grand Rapids, MI: Eerdmans, 2002). For modern attempts to trace and evaluate the progress of the fourth-century controversies over the person and status of the Savior, see especially R. P. C. Hanson, *The Search for the Christian Doctrine of God: The Arian Controversy, 318–381* (Edinburgh: T. and T. Clark, 1988); Lewis Ayres, *Nicaea and its Legacy: An Approach to Fourth-Century Trinitarian Controversy* (Oxford: Oxford University Press, 2004); John Behr, *The Nicene Faith* (Crestwood, NY: St. Vladimir's, 2004); Khaled Anatolios, *Retrieving Nicaea: The Development and Meaning of Trinitarian Theology* (Grand Rapids, MI: Baker Academic, 2011); and Christopher A. Beeley, *The Unity of Christ: Continuity and Conflict in Patristic Tradition* (New Haven, CT: Yale University Press, 2012). The debate continues.

Our most reliable ancient evidence for understanding Arius's position are two letters preserved from the period of his main controversy with Bishop Alexander, early in the 320s: one a letter from Arius himself to a sympathetic bishop in Asia Minor, Eusebius of Nicomedia, soliciting understanding and support; the other a manifesto sent by Arius and fourteen of his Egyptian clerical colleagues to Alexander, attempting to make their position clear. From these documents, at least, it is clear that Arius was above all concerned to emphasize the strict, exclusive monotheism of the biblical and philosophical traditions. So in their confession of faith, Arius and his colleagues insist:

> We know there is one God, the only unbegotten, only eternal, only without beginning, only true, who only has immortality, only wise, only good, the only potentate, judge of all, governor, arranger (οἰκόνομον), unalterable and unchangeable, righteous and good, God of the Law and the Prophets and the New Covenant.[6]

Against the background of such a conception of God, it is clear to Arius that God the Son—attested in the traditional Rule of Faith, and in the Gospels and letters of Paul, as identical with Jesus of Nazareth—must himself have been brought into being for a saving purpose by the God whom he would address as "Father": must have been *produced*, by the Father's inscrutable and transcendent will, to be the actual agent of creation and redemption. So he continues:

> Before everlasting ages he [= God] begot his unique Son, through whom he made the ages and all things. He begot him not in appearance, but in truth, constituting[7] him by his own will, unalterable and unchangeable, a perfect creature of God, but not as one of the creatures—an offspring, but not as one of things begotten.[8]

Jesus, Arius seems to be saying, is presented by the Church's confession as playing a unique historical role in bringing about the reconciliation of fallen humanity with God; if there is one transcendent God at the source of all things, that God must have *created* the Son, Jesus, to do this.

In presenting the Son in this way, Arius and his colleagues in Alexandria seem to want to insist on several things they consider essential to right faith in the Savior, if it is to represent Scripture and still be philosophically acceptable: he *existed alone with God*, as Son, before the material and temporal realms were created, since in fact he is also presented by Scripture as the agent of *their* creation; he *cannot be a part* of the one transcendent God, who is unique and has no parts; he is *brought forth* from God, not by some kind of material

---

[6] *Confession of Faith to Alexander*, in Athanasius, *De Synodis* 16.2 (*Athanasius Werke* 2.243), trans. Edward R. Hardy, *The Christology of the Later Fathers*, Library of Christian Classics 3 (Philadelphia: Westminster, 1954), 332–3 (altered).

[7] Arius uses the Greek word ὑποστήσαντα, related to the noun *hypostasis*, which suggests God's act of producing a concrete, individual being who exists within creation.

[8] *De Synodis* 16.3 (*Athanasius Werke* 2.244), trans. Hardy, 333.

subdivision, or by emanation or "projection" (which was understood to be the model by which the "aeons" came into being in Valentinian and Manichean cosmogonies); but rather "by the *will* of God [the Son was] *created before times and before ages and received life and being and glories from the Father*."[9] Thus while the Son's generation is different from that of the creatures who constitute the historical universe—while he is "begotten timelessly before all things"[10]—still he must also be "after" the Father in terms of both historical and causal sequence: "He is neither eternal nor co-eternal nor co-unbegotten with the Father... But as Monad and cause of all, God is thus before all. Therefore he is also prior to the Son."[11]

In his letter to Eusebius of Nicomedia, his influential supporter, Arius expresses his notion of the Son's generation somewhat more clearly:

> What is it that we say and think...? That the Son is not unbegotten, nor a part of the unbegotten in any way, nor [formed out] of any substratum, but that he was constituted[12] by [God's] will and counsel, before times and before ages, fully divine, unique, unchangeable. And before he was begotten or created or ordained or founded, he was not. For he was not unbegotten.[13]

For Arius, in other words, a proper understanding of who and what the Son is flows not simply from the biblical narratives, that present him as creator and savior, sent into the world by his Father, but from a clear commitment to the uniqueness, the *monarchia* or sole originality, of the God of Israel. Only this God is absolute, eternal, unchanging. The Son is himself necessarily contingent, Arius assumes, because he is begotten or produced; he depends on the will of his Father in order to exist. Yet he is certainly also "divine," generated to play the unique and divine role of being the creator and savior of all else that is, besides the God who sent him on his mission.

Other texts of Arius, reported in a hostile context by Athanasius, suggest that the Alexandrian presbyter even argued that the Son himself—despite Jesus' words in Matthew 11.27—could not fully know the Father, because the Father infinitely surpasses him in perfection. Still other quotations suggest that he believed the Son is inherently changeable and corruptible, because he is not himself absolute being, and that the quality of unchangeability ascribed to him in these two letters is itself an added gift of the Father, a feature of divine being that belongs inherently only to the infinite God, but in which the Son participates by grace. Whatever Arius may have taught in detail, the basic logic of his position is familiar and clear: the Son is neither a part of the created

---

[9] *De Synodis* 16.4 (*Ath. Werke* 2.244), trans. Hardy, 333.  [10] *De Synodis* 16.4.
[11] *De Synodis* 16.4 (*Ath. Werke* 2.244), trans. Hardy, 333–4 (corrected).
[12] Again, the verb is ὑποστῆναι, cognate with *hypostasis*. He "became a concrete individual."
[13] Arius, *Letter to Eusebius of Nicomedia* (in Theodoret, *Church History* 1.5.3 (SChr. 501.192), trans. Hardy 330 (altered). Hardy prefers to take πλήρης θεός—literally "a full god"—as an elliptical reference to John 1.14: "full [of grace and truth], divine."

world as we know it, nor is he the same as the absolute, uncaused source of all things whom we call God; he is a kind of super-creature, brought forth purposefully by God before created time, in order to act as God's agent and delegate in producing and ordering this spatio-temporal world. Even before the Word becomes flesh, his very existence as Word is a part of the divine economy, and thus dependent on God's sovereign will.

Scholars have offered various hypotheses about the main inspiration for Arius's way of conceiving God the Son. Were there Judaeo-Christians still present in Alexandria, who convinced him that the biblical tradition is incompatible with the confession of a Son who is co-eternal, primordially divine along with the Father?[14] Was his inspiration rather the cosmological tradition of Middle Platonism and Neo-Pythagoreanism, as represented in writers such as Numenius, a philosophical approach Arius applied, in a popularizing way, to the Christian confession of Jesus as Word and Savior?[15] Was Arius, as Rowan Williams has argued, simply "a committed theological conservative; more specifically a conservative *Alexandrian"*—in the tradition of Philo, Clement, and Origen?[16] Was his background, in other words, specifically and traditionally *Christian*—predictable within the confines and terms of a biblical Greek monotheism, which struggled to harmonize the Old Testament confession of a unique, nameless, invisible God with the early Christian recognition that God's Word, God's creative and saving Wisdom, had taken human form in Jesus, in order to heal us of our sins?

Controversy, in any case, over how to conceive and articulate the relation of Jesus, the Savior, to the one God of Israel soon spread beyond Alexandria and engulfed the whole Church. The age of official persecution was over; Christian internal disputes were rapidly becoming public. At the Council of Nicaea, summoned by the Emperor Constantine in the summer of 325 to deal with this and other pressing issues dividing the Empire's newly legitimized Christian population, bishops from all over the Mediterranean world struggled to find a formula that would pick up the central thread of both biblical monotheism and faith in the unique mission and person of Jesus. Its creedal formula, doubtless building on earlier baptismal creeds from Syria and Palestine, laid the groundwork for decades of further theological controversy, detailed parsing of traditional texts, and political maneuvering, by affirming the Church's faith in "one Lord Jesus Christ, the unique ($\mu o \nu o \gamma \epsilon \nu \acute{\eta} s$)[17] Son of

---

[14]  So, for instance, Rudolf Lorenz, *Arius Judaizans? Untersuchungen zur dogmengeschichtlichen Einordnung des Arius?* (Göttingen: Vandenhoeck & Ruprecht, 1979).

[15]  So Friedo Ricken, "Nikaia als Krisis des altchristlichen Platonismus," *Theologie und Philosophie* 44 (1969), 321–41; "Zur Rezeption der platonischen Ontologie bei Eusebios von Kaisareia, Areios und Athanasios," *Theologie und Philosophie* 53 (1973), 321–52.

[16]  *Arius* (rev. edn; Grand Rapids, MI: Eerdmans, 2001), 175.

[17]  The usual English translation of this word, "only-begotten," is in fact a confused rendering, as later fourth-century debates about the uniqueness of the Son would make clear. $Mo\nu o \gamma \epsilon \nu \acute{\eta} s$,

God, begotten from the Father—that is, from the essence (οὐσία) of the Father."[18] The formula goes on, in a kind of explanatory parenthesis, to describe this relationship of Son to Father in images and distinctions that were to form the heart of later debate: "that is, from the essence (*ousia*) of the Father: God from God, light from light, true God from true God, begotten [but] not made, of the same substance (ὁμοούσιος) as the Father, through whom all things came to be, things in heaven and things on earth."[19] The Son is clearly understood here to come forth from the very central reality, the "substance," of God, in order to serve as the agent of the creation willed by God; the question to Nicaea's interpreters is not his role, his "mediation" in the history of creation and redemption, but his relationship with the one God at the heart of all things: the God of Israel and of the philosophers, whom Jesus and the Church would come to call "Father." And the explanatory phrases that are included here seem to be meant to remove all notion of temporal sequence and difference in grades of being from that relationship of Father and Son; the Son is "begotten" (γεννηθείς)—generated—"but not created (οὐ ποιηθείς)," as are all other things.

The lawyer Socrates, in his *History of the Church*, written a little over a century after Nicaea, describes the events and documents of the Council in perhaps the fullest detail of any ancient writer.[20] He tells us that all but five of the three hundred and eighteen bishops present agreed to affirm the proposed formula of faith; these five, however—including Eusebius of Nicomedia and the Libyan Secundus of Ptolemais, both early sympathizers with Arius and his theological position—balked at the image of the relationship of Son to Father suggested by this section of the creed.

> For, they said, since something is "consubstantial" which is from another either by division, derivation or germination—by germination, as a shoot from the roots; by derivation, as children from their parents; by division, as two or three vessels of gold from a mass—and since the Son is from the Father by none of these modes, therefore they declared themselves unable to assent to this creed.[21]

combining μόνως, "uniquely," and γενής, "produced," indicates that God has only one eternal Son or Word, who becomes flesh in Jesus. "Only-begotten" would suggest μόνως and γεννής, from γεννάω, "give birth to," which is a somewhat narrower notion. The distinction between "producing" and "begetting," which would play a significant role in Athanasius's thought, is already anticipated in the Nicene creed's phrase, "begotten, not made," but the older, widely used term *monogenēs*, the term that appears here in the Nicene formula, probably was not yet understood to imply such a distinction. The term *monogenēs*, in the sense of "unique," "one of a kind," was already widely used in classical Greek: see, for example, Hesiod, *Works and Days* 376; Herodotus, *History* 7.221; Plato, *Timaeus* 31b.

[18] For Greek text, see Council of Nicaea, "Profession of Faith of the 318 Fathers," Alberigo/Tanner, 5.
[19] Alberigo/Tanner, 5.  [20] Socrates, *History of the Church* 1.7–10.
[21] *History of the Church* 1.8, trans. A. C. Zenos (NCNF II/2) (Grand Rapids, MI: Eerdmans, 1983), 10.

"Consubstantial," in other words, seemed to one small but influential group of bishops at Nicaea to lack the precision necessary for expressing the position of the Word or Son of God in the divine creative process. It seemed to suggest that the Son is made of the same transcendent "stuff" of which the Father consists, and that the Son can only be "the same thing" as the Father if the Father's substance has been *divided* materially, or multiplied—cloned, we might say—organically, as creatures in the world are reproduced.

The historian, exegete, and theologian Eusebius of Caesaraea, who had inherited much of the influence, as well as the considerable library, of Origen, in becoming head of the see of Caesaraea in Palestine, where Origen lived and worked later in life, himself sympathized with Arius's approach and originally resisted the formulation of the majority at Nicaea. But, as he explained to the people of his Church in a letter written shortly after the conclusion of the Council, he came to accept the wording of the Council's creed as orthodox when it was explained, at Constantine's suggestion, that *homoousios* and related substance-language in the formula should not be taken in a corporeal sense, "and consequently that the Son did not subsist from the Father either by division or sublation—for, said [Constantine], a nature which is immaterial and incorporeal cannot possibly be subject to any corporeal affection, and hence our conception of such things can only be in divine and mysterious terms."[22] Even Athanasius of Alexandria, who was present at the Council in a junior role and who was later, as bishop, to become its most passionate apologist, insists in his *Defense of the Nicene Definition* or *De Decretis*, written probably in 350 or 351 to allay lingering concerns about the Council's theology, that *homoousios* and similar expressions in the creed were not meant to promote a material conception of the Son's relationship to the Father—a process of material division or iteration; they were only intended to underscore the idea that the Son is "from" God in a more literal, mysteriously undivided sense than created things are said to be—"that we might believe the Word to be other than the nature of originate things (*genēta*), being alone *truly* from God."[23] For both Eusebius and Athanasius, opposed as they were in their understanding of the Son's identity as mediator, the Nicene injection of "substance" language into a traditional confession of faith was only acceptable if not taken in a material sense; the very fact that both emphasize this suggests that such a sense may have been the first thing the definition's language would have suggested to the ordinary reader.

---

[22] *History of the Church* 1.8, trans. Zenos (altered).

[23] Athanasius, *Defence of the Nicene Definition* 19, trans. John Henry Newman (NPNF II/4) (Grand Rapids: Eerdmans, 1980) 163, altered. *Genēta* are "things that have been produced": i.e. creatures, made from nothing at God's will, or what Newman translates here as "originate things."

One of the main difficulties, in fact, at Nicaea and through the half-century of fierce theological controversy and ecclesiastical maneuvering about its reception that followed, was that there was no clear consensus on the meaning of the word *ousia*, which we usually translate in English as "substance" or "essence." The word's origins were in classical Greek philosophy. Aristotle, for instance, uses οὐσία—a word formed from the root of the Greek verb "to be"— to refer to the stable identity or reality of a thing, what the thing really *is*, as opposed to its changeable or incidental qualities or "accidents."[24] It had often been used as a synonym for φύσις, *physis*, customarily translated as "nature" and related to the Greek verb meaning "to put forth" or "to make grow" (φύειν)—to express one's being dynamically. For Aristotelian philosophy, a thing's "nature" is its potential to act or develop in a certain predictable way—a kind of built-in "program" for specific behavior that is derived from the thing's very identity. The Nicene statement of faith also identifies the "substance" or "essence" shared by Father and Son with their "hypostasis": a term without such a well-defined philosophical history, originally used in medical or scientific treatises to signify a particular "substance" in a concrete, more material sense—an individual, concrete thing as we encounter it empirically. So the anathema appended to the Council's creedal statement affirms— confusingly, to later Chalcedonian ears:

> But those who say "there was a point when he was not" and that "before he was begotten he was not," and that he is from what is not, or that the Son of God is of a different *hypostasis* or *substance* (οὐσία), or changeable or alterable, these the Catholic and Apostolic Church anathematizes.[25]

In contrast to Arius's assumption that since the Son is *produced* or begotten by the Father he is a *creature*, even if one of a unique kind, the bishops at Nicaea apparently intended to affirm above all that the Son is *truly God* in the full sense, and thus *not* simply a derived being, brought into being by God to accomplish his will. But *how* this relationship was precisely to be understood, without compromising the distinct personal identity of the Son as the Word who was made flesh—the one whose filial obedience lays out a path for those creatures who want to become themselves sons and daughters of God with him—was not clearly defined at Nicaea, and perhaps not even clearly perceived as a problem by most participants in the discussion. And the thought that "substance" (οὐσία)-language could also be used theologically in a way subtly different from "hypostasis"-language, so that one might conceive of Father, Son

---

[24] See *De Partibus Animalium* 641b32, 643a27; *Metaphysics* 1003b7. In his famous statement in *Met* 1017b22, Aristotle defines *ousia* as "that which a being is" (τὸ τί ἦν εἶναι). See also Plato, *Phaedrus* 65d, 92d; *Republic* 509b.

[25] Alberigo/Tanner, 5 (trans. altered). These statements were apparently all understood to be major implications of Arius's teaching.

and Holy Spirit as *distinct hypostases* which share and constitute a *single divine substance* or reality, seems not yet to have been clearly in anyone's mind.[26]

## MARCELLUS OF ANCYRA

Another participant in the discussions about the status of God the Son and Word at the Council of Nicaea was Marcellus, bishop of Ancyra (today's Ankara) in central Asia Minor. None of Marcellus's major writings has survived whole, under his own name; our knowledge of his thought depends mainly on fragments quoted by other authors—notably the hostile witness Eusebius of Caesaraea, in his tract *Against Marcellus*—and also a few important works traditionally attributed to other authors, which may in fact be his.[27] Marcellus's main concern as a theologian, it seems, was to safeguard the biblical and philosophical tradition of monotheism, by insisting that if creation and salvation are both works of the one God, the agent of them cannot be ontologically distinct from the transcendent heart of all reality. In the

[26] For further reflection on the history and use of these critically important terms, see especially Marcel Richard, "L'Introduction du mot 'hypostase' dans la théologie de l'incarnation," *Mélanges de science religieuse* 2 (1945), 5–32, 243–70 (= *Opera Minora* II, No. 42); André de Halleux, "'Hypostase' et 'personne' dans la formation du dogme Trinitaire," *Revue d'histoire ecclésiastique* 79 (1984), 3110–369, 623–67 [= *Patrologie et oecuménisme: Recueil d'études* (Leuven: Leuven University Press, 1990), 113–214]. For thoughtful reflections on apparent differences between early Christian use of *ousia* and *hypostasis* and that of Platonic and Stoic philosophers, see Christoph Markschies, "Was bedeutet οὐσία? Zwei Antworten bei Origenes und Ambrosius und deren Bedeutung für Bibelerklärung und Theologie," *Origenes und sein Erbe: Gesammelte Studien* (Berlin: De Gruyter, 2007), 173–93.

[27] For modern attempts to identify Marcellus as the author of a number of works attributed to Athanasius in the manuscripts, whose Athanasian origin has long been questioned, see Martin Tetz, "Zur Theologie des Markell von Ancyra I. Eine Markellianische Schrift 'De Incarnatione et contra Arianos'," *ZKG* 75 (1964), 215–70; "Zur Theologie des M. von A. II: Markells Lehre von der Adamssohnschaft Christi und eine pseudoklementinische Tradition über die wahren Lehrer und Propheten," *ZKG* 79 (1968), 3–42; "Zur Theologie des M. von A. III: Die pseudoathanasianische Epistula ad Liberium, ein Markellischer Bekenntnis," *ZKG* 83 (1972), 145–94; "Markellianer und Athanasios von Alexandrien: Die markellianische *Expositio Fidei ad Athanasium* des Diakons Eugenios von Ankyra," *ZNTW* 64 (1973), 75–121; "Zum altrömischen Bekenntnis: Ein Beitrag des Markellus von Ancyra," *ZNTW* 75 (1984), 107–27.

In his careful collection of the well-attested fragments of Marcellus, Markus Vinzent includes all the texts Eusebius cites, plus Marcellus's brief "Letter to Julius of Rome," which is preserved by Epiphanius of Salamis in his anti-heretical collection, the *Panarion*. Vinzent suggests that the fragments assembled by Eusebius are all taken from a large work of Marcellus's against Asterius, the supporter of Arius, of which the title remains unknown. See Vinzent, *Markell von Ankyra: Die Fragmente* (Leiden: Brill, 1997), esp. lxxvi–lxxxi. For a broad, sometimes speculative reconstruction of Marcellus's theology, see also Klaus Seibt, *Die Theologie des Markell von Ankyra* (Berlin: De Gruyter, 1994). For a clear and authoritative summary of what the sources reveal, see Joseph T. Lienhard, *Contra Marcellum: Marcellus of Ancyra and Fourth-Century Theology* (Washington, DC: Catholic University of America Press, 1999).

language of early fourth-century debate, the Father and the Son of the Gospels cannot, according to Marcellus, be separate "hypostases"—distinct individuals or actors—if both of them really do what only God does. In the view of Marcellus, in fact, the main error of Arius and his generation of followers, especially the "sophist" or grammarian Asterius, was their insistence that Father and Son have remained permanently distinct divine agents—that "the Father is Father and the Son is Son" in the work of both creation and redemption, with the Son *produced* and delegated to carry out the Father's will. If a "hypostasis" is a distinct reality, a being that exists in and for itself and that can be identified as such, then to suggest Father and Son are *different hypostases* is to affirm not only that they have distinct roles in history, but that they are two Gods; this, in turn, would imply that one of them must be divine in a more authentic, more original, sense than the other.[28]

For Marcellus, and probably also for those who first crafted Nicaea's statement of faith, the crucial point to affirm was rather that a single God— the God of the Bible—lies behind creation and redemption, that a single God works through human history and stands as its goal and fulfillment. In one of the fragments quoted by Eusebius in his *Contra Marcellum*, Marcellus expressly insists that this excludes the possibility of Father, Son, and Holy Spirit being *distinct hypostases*.[29] God affirms, for example, in Isaiah 45.21 that "there is no other God besides me, just and a savior." For Marcellus, this is a clear statement of God's single identity as agent of salvation;[30] the ontological oneness of the divine monad takes priority over human encounters with God's distinct "faces," God's personal appearances within the history of Israel and the Church. Marcellus concludes that "the triad previously originated from the monad":[31] the three divine agents recognized in biblical history are really three distinct personifications in which God has revealed himself in time, ways in which the single transcendent Monad for our sake "broadens forth into a triad, yet without undergoing division."[32]

In Eusebius's polemical presentation, Marcellus is simply reviving the classical anti-Trinitarian heresy associated with the notorious Sabellius in the early second century: he is denying any real identity to Father, Son, and Holy Spirit, and instead sees all three of them as simply the "modalities" in which God has manifested his single being in history. So John's reference to the Logos who became incarnate in Christ, in this interpretation, would simply be a functional way of talking about how the one God works to reveal himself:

---

[28] For further reflection on Marcellus's understanding of "hypostasis" in God, see Colm Luibhéid, *Eusebius of Caesaraea and the Arian Crisis* (Dublin: Irish Academic Press, 1981), 68–72.

[29] See Frag. 76 Klostermann (97 Vinzent).

[30] See Frag. 76 Klostermann (97 Vinzent); also Frags. 78 Klostermann (92 Vinzent), 80 Klostermann (124 Vinzent).

[31] Frag. 66 Klostermann (47 Vinzent).     [32] Frag. 67 Klostermann (48 Vinzent).

the Logos would be a "mere Word" in the transcendent divine mind, taking human shape by forming and guiding the human Jesus. In fact, Eusebius seems to be over-simplifying here: Marcellus is critical of Sabellius in one fragment of his work, for being unaware of the active divine reality of the Logos.[33] On the other hand, Marcellus does often sound like a classic "modalist," in the excerpts we have of his works. He seems, for example, to have interpreted those passages in Scripture that speak of the Logos as a distinct, historically perceptible divine actor—Proverbs 8.22–30, for example, which describes the activity of God's Wisdom in forming the earth and guiding the human race—as referring primarily to the *human* Jesus, God's Logos enfleshed; it is the *incarnate* Word, he suggests, who is "the image of the invisible God," referred to by Colossians 1.15. Marcellus is clearly reluctant to emphasize the permanent, identifiable reality of God the Son in terms that might suggest the Son possesses any particular ontological "density" of his own within the Mystery of God. To the extent the Son is recognized as "something different" from the Father in any radical sense, the Son is simply the Father's own Word, made flesh.

## EUSEBIUS OF CAESARAEA

Marcellus's chief opponent in his own times was Eusebius, bishop of Caesaraea (before 265–339/40), whom we have already mentioned as a prominent if questioning participant at the Council of Nicaea. Perhaps best known by modern readers as the first Christian author to attempt a chronicle of Graeco-Roman civilization centered on the coming of Christ, Eusebius, as we have seen, was a native of Caesaraea, the capital of the Roman Province of Palestine—the city where Origen had spent the last two-and-a-half decades of his life—and eventually became its bishop. Thanks to his own extensive liberal education, Eusebius was uniquely qualified to be a historian of culture and an interpreter of the Christian Scriptures in the Origenist mold, as well as a constructive theological thinker.

As the controversy between Arius and his own bishop Alexander erupted into an Empire-wide debate about the person of the Savior, Eusebius was originally sympathetic with the Alexandrian presbyter, and apparently defended him from the charge that he conceived of the Son of God simply as a creature with all the rest.[34] At the Synod held in Antioch to respond to the controversy over Arius's

---

[33] Frag. 44 Klostermann (69 Vinzent).
[34] See the Greek fragments of his letter to Alexander of Alexandria, defending Arius: H. G. Opitz, *Athanasius' Werke* 3/1 (Berlin: De Gruyter, 1934), 14–15 [=Urkunde 7]. See also the fragments of an earlier letter to Euphration of Balanaea: *Athanasius' Werke* 3/1, 4–6 [= Urkunde 3].

views, early in 325—a synod which condemned what was understood to be Arius's position, and strongly affirmed the eternal, immutable reality of the Son, "who did not come into being by [God's] volition or by adoption," but always exists with his Father as God's perfect image[35]—Eusebius was one of three bishops who refused to sign the final profession of faith. The historian Sozomen tells us that Eusebius and two Palestinian colleagues confirmed Arius's canonical status as a presbyter when his own bishop, Alexander, had withdrawn it.[36] As we have seen already, later that year Eusebius came to accept Nicaea's profession of faith, with its affirmation that the Son is "of the same substance and hypostasis" as the Father, but only as a result of assurances that this language was intended to assert the difference between the Son and the created world, not to affirm that there is no real and lasting distinction between him and the one transcendent God who generates him. Eusebius was clearly concerned, as Origen and many third- and fourth-century writers were, to underscore both the uniqueness and inconceivable self-sufficiency of the God of Israel, and the dependence of his Son and his Spirit on him and on his will, in carrying out their saving and sanctifying roles in the history of creation. To accept Nicaea, Eusebius apparently had to swallow hard!

Eusebius's underlying concern, it seems, in writings of various kinds spanning his long career, is to emphasize the identity of the biblical God of Israel, whom Jesus calls "Father," with the unique, transcendent, ineffable source of all reality generally recognized by Greek philosophy.[37] So, for instance, in his *Theophany*—an apologia for Christian faith written in the 330s, towards the end of Eusebius's life (he died in 339 or 340), which echoes themes from his pre-Nicene works, *Preparation for the Gospel* and *Demonstration of the Gospel*—Eusebius emphasizes the ultimacy and absolute transcendence of the one God:

> The divine doctrine declares that He who is above all that is good, the same one is the efficient cause of all, and is beyond all comprehension; and that on this account he cannot be described, enunciated or named; and not only that he is elevated above all verbal description, but also above all mental apprehension; that

---

[35] See the letter of the Synod of Antioch of 325, preserved in Syriac and translated back into Greek by Eduard Schwartz: Urkunde 18.10 (Opitz III/1, 39).

[36] Sozomen, *Church History* 1.15.

[37] On the philosophical concerns of Eusebius—who also saw himself, like Origen, as a professional interpreter of the Christian Scriptures—see Alois Dempf, "Der Platonismus des Eusebius, Victorinus, und Pseudo-Dionysius," *Sitzungsberichte der Bayrischen Akademie der Wissenschaften, phil.—hist. Klasse* 3 (Munich, 1962); Friedo Ricken, "Der Logoslehre des Eusebios von Caesaraea und der Mittelplatonismus," *Theologie und Philosophie* 42 (1967), 341–58; Holger Strutwolf, *Die Trinitätstheologie und Christologie des Euseb von Caesaraea* (Göttingen: Vandenhoeck & Ruprecht, 1999), esp. 87–194. See also Beeley, *The Unity of Christ*, 49–104; Beeley proposes Eusebius, rather than Athanasius, as "the most influential church leader of the fourth century" (49), and as more authentically representative of the longer Patristic tradition on the person of Christ.

he is neither contained in a place nor existing in a body, neither in the heavens, nor in the aether, nor in any one portion of this whole.[38]

This transcendent source of all things Eusebius compares to a king, sitting enthroned and inaccessible within a hidden chamber, "governing and ordering all, solely by the power of his own will."[39] This God, being essentially good, freely and providently generates his Word, who comes out of God's own substance to realize the work of creation and salvation God desires:

> He, therefore, by whom all things are—the Word of God—proceeded forth from above, from his good Father, as a river ever flowing from an unlimited fountain, and descending as rain, in words unutterable, to those who were perishing, completely produced for the common salvation of all.[40]

As our own minds only become accessible to others in the words we speak, so "the only Word [of God]...openly publishes those things which its Father has considered in secret; and passing on into the hearing of all, brings to full effect his will."[41] The role of the Word or Son of God, then, is precisely to be the life-sustaining *link* between the hidden God and all other things, which depend on God's goodness and will for their existence: "and therefore it is, we say, that he first before all things was *made* by the Father, as something one in form, the instrument of every existence and nature, alive and living—nay divine, life-giving and all-wise..."[42]

God, in his primordial being, is beyond all perception and communication, and so can have no effective contact with creatures. It is only because the

---

[38] Eusebius, *Theophania* 1.21, ed. and trans. Samuel Lee (Cambridge: Cambridge University Press, 1843), 11(altered). This work of Eusebius exists in fragments in Greek, but is completely preserved only in a Syriac translation, which Lee edited and published from a manuscript copied by a certain Jacob of Edessa and dated A.D. 411—the oldest dated Syriac manuscript known. This manuscript—British Library Add. 12150—is a miscellaneous collection of third- and fourth-century theological and hagiographical works translated from the Greek, and includes the *Clementine Recognitions*, Titus of Bostra's treatise against the Manichees, and works of Eusebius on the martyrs. Eusebius's *Theophania* occupies ff. 171b–235a. See W. Wright, *Catalogue of the Syriac Manuscripts in the British Museum* 2 (London, 1871), 632: entry no. 726.

[39] *Theophania* 1.21 (trans. Lee, 11) In his earlier apologetic work, the *Proof of the Gospel*, probably dating from 314–18, Eusebius offers this same classical conception of the one supreme God: "There is one principle of the universe—in fact, one even before the principle and born before the first, and of earlier being than the Monad, and greater than every name, who cannot be named nor explained nor sought out, the good, the cause of all, the creator, the beneficent, the foreknowing, the saving, himself the one and only God, from whom are all things and for whom are all things...And the fact that he wills it is the sole cause of all things that exist coming into being and continuing to be. For it comes of his will, and he wills it, because he happens to be good by nature. For nothing else is essential by nature to a good person, except to will what is good. And what he wills, he can effect" (*Proof of the Gospel* 4.1, trans. W. J. Ferrar [Grand Rapids, MI: Baker, 1981], 1.164]) (slightly altered). For Eusebius, the classical Greek conception of a "monad" at the base of all multiplicity in the world refers to the *Word of God* in his creative role; he acts as a mirror and dynamic representation of the ineffable unity of God: see *Proof of the Gospel* 4.6.

[40] *Theophany* 1.23 (trans. Lee, 12 [altered]).

[41] *Theophany* 1.23 (trans. Lee, 12 [English slightly altered]).

[42] *Proof of the Gospel* 4.4 (trans. Ferrar, 169).

Word is produced from this transcendent divine source for the sake of creation that he can then mingle with creatures, and communicate to them the energies and qualities of God, which preserve their life:

> For though he was in the most certain and the closest association with the Father, and equally with him rejoiced in that which is unspeakable, yet he could descend with all gentleness, and conform himself in such ways as were possible to those who were far distant from his own height, and who through their weakness crave amelioration and aid from a secondary Being: that they might behold the flashings of the sun falling quietly and gently on them, though they are not able to delight in the fierce might of the sun because of their bodily weakness.[43]

Essential, then, to Eusebius's carefully developed position on the relation of the Son—who became flesh as Jesus—to the eternal and ineffable God is both the Son's distinct, dependent character within the divine Mystery, and the fact that he exists because the Father has *willed* to beget him as unique mediator, the bridge between God and the rest of creation.

> The Father precedes the Son, and has preceded him in existence, inasmuch as he alone is unbegotten. The one, perfect in himself and first in order as Father, and the cause of the Son's existence, receives nothing towards the completeness of his Godhead from the Son. The other, as a Son begotten of him that caused his being, came second to him, whose son he is, receiving from the Father both his being and the character of his being. And, moreover, the ray does not shine forth from the light by its [the light's] deliberate choice, but because of something which is an inseparable accident of [the light's] essence: but the Son, by contrast, is the image of the Father by [the Father's] intention and deliberate choice. For God willed to beget a Son, and so established a second light, in all things made like unto himself.[44]

Son and Father are radically related in their Being: the Son is the unique image and likeness of the Father—in the words of the Letter to the Hebrews, "the brightness of his glory and the exact imprint ($\chi a \rho a \kappa \tau \acute{\eta} \rho$) of his individual being ($\acute{\upsilon} \pi \acute{o} \sigma \tau a \sigma \iota s$)."[45] As such, the Son must be thought of as a *distinct* hypostasis, an individual in and for himself; to that extent, Nicaea's image of light radiating from a glorious center is not strictly accurate, in Eusebius's thinking. For

> the radiance is inseparable from the light of sense, while the Son exists in himself in his own essence (*ousia*), apart from the Father. And the ray has its range of activity solely from the light, whereas the Son is something different from a channel of energy, having his being in himself.[46]

---

[43] *Proof of the Gospel* 4.6 (trans. Ferrar, 173–4 [slightly altered]).
[44] *Proof of the Gospel* 4.3 (trans. Ferrar, 167).     [45] Heb. 1.3.
[46] *Proof of the Gospel* 4.3 (trans. Ferrar, 166). See also our preceding excerpt, part of the same Eusebian critique of the image of light for the generation of the Son. Here, clearly, as in the anathema attached to the Nicene profession of faith, *hypostasis* and *ousia* are not distinguished in meaning, and are apparently assumed to be synonyms.

So the *manner* of the Son's begetting, for Eusebius, defies philosophical explanation or mental images. In the beginning of Book 5 of his *Proof of the Gospel*, Eusebius excludes both the notion that the Son is "unbegotten for infinite ages and without beginning within the Father," like a part or aspect of God that is later detached and produced to act in the world on his own, and also the notion that he is "begotten of things that were not, similarly to other begotten beings—for the *generation* of the Son differs from *creation through the Son*." The generation of the Son remains one of the great Mysteries that confront our minds, and "we have nothing else to say or to think of him except 'Who shall declare his generation?' (Isa. 53.8 [LXX])"[47]

These passages suggest a fairly clear sense, on Eusebius's part, of what the Word or Son is, in relation to the Father: he is a distinct being, a separate hypostasis, "existing in himself"; he is unique, and mirrors or represents the being of the Father exactly in his qualities; he is dependent wholly on the Father, brought forth simply by the Father's will, and therefore is in some way "subsequent" to the Father; yet he is clearly *with* the Father since before all spatial and temporal reality, ready to do the Father's will in this relationship of causal dependence. Although Eusebius often makes use himself of the images of light from a source, or a fragrance from a flower or a jar of ointment, to suggest the Word's role in communicating the Father's being without dividing or lessening it, he concedes that such images are of limited accuracy.

> The scope of the theology we are considering far transcends all illustrations, and is not connected with anything physical, but imagines with the acutest thought a Son begotten: not at one time non-existent, and existent at another afterwards; but existent before eternal time, and pre-existent, and ever with the Father as his Son; and yet not unbegotten, but begotten from the unbegotten Father, being the Only-begotten, the Word, and God of God . . . , unspeakably—and unthinkably to us—brought into being from all time, or rather before all times, by the Father's transcendent and inconceivable will and Power. "For who shall describe his generation?" (Isa. 53.8)[48]

In Eusebius's view, this unique divine dialectic of dependence and independence, shared divinity and clear ranking in terms of causality and priority, suggests that the Son's godhead, while authentic, is, in fact, his by *participation*, rather than simply the foundation of all other being, as the Father's godhead is.

---

[47] *Proof of the Gospel* 5.1 (trans. Ferrar, 232–3).

[48] *Proof of the Gospel* 5.1 (trans. Ferrar, 168). In *Ecclesiastical Theology* 2.14, a work written against Marcellus of Ancyra in the 330s, Eusebius draws on John 1.1 to suggest, in even more explicit terms, that the Son is generated eternally by the Father's *will*. In *Proof of the Gospel* 5.1 Eusebius makes it clear that the Son is "not unbegotten, for ages infinite and without beginning within the Father" (trans. Ferrar, 232–3)—not simply existing as a part within a whole, or as an element of the Father which was later hypostatized, changed, and extruded; such material conceptions are not part of his understanding of their eternal relationship.

The Father possesses deity *naturally and by right*; it is "proper" (οἰκεῖα) to his concrete being (*hypostasis*).[49] The Son and the Spirit are truly God, but only because they have *received* being, personhood, and even deity from the Father. So Eusebius writes of the Word:

> Thus therefore him also—as being the only Son and the only image of God, endued with the powers of the Father's unbegotten and eternal essence according to the example of likeness . . . —the holy Scriptures salute as God, as one worthy of receiving the name of the Father with his other (names), but as one who receives it and does not possess it in his own right. For the one gives and the other receives, so that strictly the first is to be reckoned God, alone being God by nature, and not receiving divinity from another. And the other is to be thought of as secondary, and as holding a divinity received from the Father, as an image of God.[50]

The Son's distinctive identity, in fact—the key to his own particular "essence" and to his hypostasis—is to be the perfect *image* of the Father. It is this that allows him to be called God in a genuine, but clearly participated sense: he is God by begetting, by sharing in the original fullness of the Father's being.[51]

In Eusebius's conception of Christian theology, then, the Son or Word of God has been produced from the Father before anything was created, by a process of generation that is hidden within the Mystery of God, in order to be

> the commander-in-chief of the rational and immortal host of heaven, the messenger of Great Counsel, the executor of the Father's unspoken will, the creator with the Father of all things, the second cause of the universe after the Father, the true and only-begotten Son of God, the Lord and God and King of all created things, the one who has received dominion and power with divinity itself, and with might and honor, from the Father.[52]

As God's creative Wisdom, the Son is "a certain substance (*ousia*) which lived and had concrete existence (ὑφεστῶσα) before the world, and which ministered to the Father and God of the universe for the formation of all created things."[53] Eusebius clearly wants to emphasize the Son's mediatory role in the

[49] So in *Ecclesiastical Theology* 1.11, Eusebius asserts that θεότης, divinity, is proper only to the Father; it is this that preserves the "monarchy" of orthodox faith. See also *Eccl. Theol.* 2.7; and Jon M. Robertson, *Christ as Mediator: A Study of the Theologies of Eusebius of Caesarea, Marcellus of Ancyra, and Athanasius of Alexandria* (Oxford: Oxford University Press 2007), 163–4.
[50] *Proof of the Gospel* 5.4 (trans. Ferrar, 246–7).
[51] See also *History of the Church* 1.2.3; *Ecclesiastical Theology* 1.20; 2.14.
[52] *History of the Church* 1.2.3, trans. Arthur C. McGiffert (NPNF II/1.82). Eusebius begins his history with an account of the coming of Christ, which itself must begin with an affirmation of the distinct, pre-cosmic existence of the Son.
[53] *History of the Church* 1.2.14 (trans. McGiffert, 83).

creation and preservation[54] of the world; unlike Marcellus, however, who draws on this same biblical tradition, Eusebius emphasizes that the Son is a distinct, "hypostatic" being, in active relationship to the Father, and not simply a function of the one God's divine activity.

> Intermediate, as it were, and attracting the created to the uncreated essence, this Word of God exists as an unbroken bond between the two, uniting things most widely different by an inseparable tie. He is the Providence which rules the universe; the guardian and director of the whole; he is the power and Wisdom of God, the only-begotten God, the Word begotten of God himself.[55]

As will be obvious from the texts we have quoted, Eusebius's primary concern, in speaking about God the Son, is to emphasize his unique position in the realization of God's activities: related to the transcendent source of all things as first to issue forth; produced from the heart of God as Son from Father; commissioned by the will of the Father to form, moderate and heal the whole world of reality outside God. In origin and activity he is divine, but divine by derivation, participation, and designated role; he shares and represents the Father's benevolent will, but for that reason is always distinct from the Father in being, always obeys the Father's original will.

Eusebius's emphasis in these passages is mainly on the pre-historical existence of the Word, the role of the Word in the formation and continuing ordering of the cosmos. However, he is also concerned to give an account of the Word's Incarnation as Jesus of Nazareth. His approach, like that of his contemporary Athanasius, is to stress the importance of the Incarnation both as revelation and as a medium of healing the ills of creation. The human race, he reminds us in his *Oration in Praise of Constantine* [335], showed since its origins an increasing alienation from God and his Word, expressed in false worship and immoral activity. After reaching out repeatedly to humanity through the events and prophets of Israel's history, and failing to win their attention, the Word finally chooses to become flesh and so "to associate and converse with men and women, desiring, through the medium of their own likeness, to save our mortal race."[56] Through his teaching, his miracles, his

---

[54] Like Athanasius, Eusebius emphasizes that the role of the Logos in creation is not simply apparent at the beginning of things, but is a constant one: preserving order and so giving healthy life to the world. So he is σωτήρ, "savior" or "preserver," as well as efficient cause. See his *Oration in Praise of Constantine* 11.2, 5, 15; 12.2–7; see also the *Oration of Constantine to the Assembly of the Saints* 11: "Since the world and all things that it contains exist, and are preserved (= 'saved'), their preserver (= savior) must have had a prior existence; so that Christ is the cause of preservation, and the preservation of things is an effect, even as the Father is the cause of the Son and the Son the effect of that cause" (trans. Ernest C. Richardson; NPNF II/1.569). This work, which exists in what seems to be a Greek translation of a Latin address given by Constantine, shows marked similarities to Eusebius's own understanding of the role of the Son in the world, and may well have been drafted by Eusebius himself.

[55] *Oration in Praise of Constantine* 12.7, trans. Ernest C. Richardson (NPNF II/1.599).

[56] *Oration in Praise of Constantine* 13.16 (trans. Richardson, 603).

example, and finally his resurrection after suffering real human death, the Word touches and heals us, without ceasing to exercise his cosmic role as ruler and guide,[57] and so offers us hope for a share in his own everlasting life.[58]

In his roughly contemporary *Theophany*, Eusebius explains the reasons for the Incarnation of the Word in similar, if somewhat simpler terms: having acted throughout history as the unseen, though constant, guide of creation,

> [the Word] has, by means of a mortal vessel—not unlike a king who acts through an interpreter—openly declared his edicts and methods of government among men and women, in order that he might reveal his providential care for mortals, by what was like themselves, that they might find life.[59]

Eusebius emphasizes, however, that in this new encounter with humanity through sharing their flesh, the Word does not suffer any diminution of his own divine being, or undergo any loss through his human suffering.[60] Rather, the Word comes to dwell in a human body, as in a "Temple" or "bodily vessel," which it penetrates with its divinity as light penetrates material realities;[61] his person forms the human instrument which it reshapes into "the divine image, [as] the dwelling place of the Word of God, and the holy Temple of the holy God."[62] Like Orpheus charming the beasts with his lyre,

> the only Word of God, who availed himself of a human instrument and set up his own interpreter, administered everything for the healing of men and women, by the will of the Father, [yet] still remaining immaterial and incorporeal, just as he formerly was, with his Father. By means of a man also, he showed forth God to human beings, through mighty acts and wonderful works.[63]

In the Iconoclast controversy of the eighth and ninth centuries, one of the sources often cited by those who opposed the making and veneration of sacred images was a letter attributed to Eusebius and addressed to the Emperor's half-sister, Constantia.[64] Allegedly, the royal lady had asked the Palestinian bishop

---

[57] *Oration in Praise of Constantine* 14.7–8. See also *Theophany* 3.39.

[58] *Oration in Praise of Constantine* 15.6–10. In this same chapter, Eusebius also develops the Scriptural idea that Jesus' death was a sacrifice offered to the Father, to defeat false religion and the power of the evil spirits over humanity (see 15.11–12). See also *Theophany* 3.58–9.

[59] *Theophany* 3.39 (trans. Lee, 175).     [60] *Theophany* (trans. Lee, 177, 179).

[61] *Theophany* (trans. Lee, 176–7).

[62] *Theophany* (trans. Lee, 177). In the next chapter, Eusebius suggests that it is not the human Jesus, the dwelling-place and instrument of God the Word, who is actually the image of God, but rather that Jesus is the dwelling-place of God's true image: so Jesus revealed "how he, who was immortal, conversed with mortals; how the Image (of God), which is incorporeal, became vested with the nature which is human; and how the image of God, which was in him [=Jesus], moved [him]" (*Theophany* 3.40; trans. Lee, 181).

[63] *Theophany* 3.40 (trans. Lee, 180–1, slightly altered). This same comparison of Christ with Orpheus is offered by Clement of Alexandria in his *Protreptic Discourse* 1.

[64] Constantia was married in 313 to Constantine's early colleague and co-emperor, Licinius; after the Council of Nicaea and the death of Licinius, she lobbied to have Arius restored to communion with the Church. (Socrates 1.2; Philostorgius 1.9) The text of this letter, attributed to

to send her a painted icon of Christ for her devotions. Eusebius, in his reply, politely refused to cooperate. The only adequate and true earthly representation of Christ, he insists, is his active portrayal in the Scriptures.[65] As he had emphasized in the *Proof of the Gospel*, the true spiritual icon of God, which we find fully even in the pre-incarnate Son, is

> a kind of living image of the living God, in a mode that is beyond our words and reasoning, and exists in itself immaterially and unembodied, and is unmixed with anything opposite to itself; he is not such an image as we connote by the term, which differs in its essential underlying reality and is other in form [than its original], but he is completely the same form and is like in his own essence to the Father...[66]

Although Eusebius's authorship of the *Letter to Constantia* continues to be questioned, the position embodied both in this and in his certainly authentic texts is similar, and represents clearly one key aspect of his conception of Christ as the image of God: it is the pre-incarnate Word, the mediator of creation, depicted for us textually in the written words of Scripture, who is God's full and true image and likeness. The human Jesus is the image of this original Image:

> the image, filled with every excellence—the divine image, the dwelling place of the Word of God, and the holy temple of the holy God—was prepared by the power of the Holy Spirit, in order that he who resided in it might become known among mortal men and women by means of one who was their equal: by a kind of interpreter.[67]

The role of Christ, in other words, as Word first made text and ultimately made flesh, is to contain and embody, to represent in human flesh, the essentially immaterial form of the divine mediator, whom God has commissioned to be his agent in history. It is to make available the self-communicating reality of God, to

---

Eusebius, is preserved, possibly in incomplete form, only in the treatise criticizing it and a few other texts by Nicephorus, patriarch of Constantinople in the early ninth century. Nicephorus's work is edited by J. B. Pitra, *Spicilegium Solesmense* 1 (Paris, 1852), 383–6, and the letter of Eusebius is reprinted in PG 20.1545–9. Arguments about Eusebius's authorship continue: see George Florovsky, "Origen, Eusebius and the Iconoclastic Controversy," *Church History* 19 (1950), 77–96; Sr. Charles Murray, "Art and the Early Church," *Journal of Theological Studies* NS 28 (1977), 303–45; Klaus Schäferdieck, "Zur Verfasserfrage und Situation der Epistula ad Constantiam de Imagine Christi," *Zeitschrift für Kirchengeschichte* 91 (1980), 177–86; Stephan Gero, "The True Image of Christ: Eusebius's Letter to Constantia Reconsidered" *Journal of Theological Studies* NS 32 (1981), 460–70.

[65] See PG 20.1550 A4–7. For further discussion and citation of this letter attributed to Eusebius, see chap. 10 pp. 235–236.

[66] *Proof of the Gospel* 5.1 (trans. Ferrar, 234, altered).

[67] *Theophany* 3.39 (trans. Lee, 177, altered). For a discussion of Eusebius's treatment of the Son as the image of God, see especially Anton Weber, *Archē: Ein Beitrag zur Christologie des Eusebius von Cäsarea* (Rome: Verlag Neue Stadt, 1964), 95–108.

express the divine, saving will by obedient action, and to heal human creatures by the life-giving touch of his human instrument. The human Jesus, in whom the Word dwells, is the mediator of God's Mediator, the temporal inflection of God's all-powerful Word.

## ATHANASIUS

Our final figure from this early fourth-century controversy, St. Athanasius, worked for some forty-five years as bishop of an Alexandria that seems to have been decidedly more polarized, less pluralistic in its religious atmosphere than it had been before the end of imperial persecution. Athanasius inherited leadership of the Church of Alexandria from the embattled bishop Alexander in 328, apparently without the full consensus of Egyptian bishops usually required for valid episcopal succession; as Alexander's deacon and chief assist-ant, he had been unofficially designated his ecclesiastical heir, and quickly took control of the Church.[68] Athanasius was certainly familiar with the language and concepts of the eclectic Platonism that formed part of an educated person's thought world in the fourth century; he sometimes draws on the philosophical tradition in his arguments, although his inclinations are to rely on Scripture and the Church's liturgical tradition rather than on metaphysics.[69] More importantly, Athanasius clearly knew Origen's work, and despite the serious criticisms that had been leveled against some aspects of it by the early fourth century, he recognizes Origen's authority and at times defends his memory.[70] It seems highly likely, too, that he was influenced by Irenaeus's thought, although he does not mention him by name.[71] Yet Athanasius developed his own understanding of Christ in very different theological circumstances from those two earlier writers: although Gnostic speculation still exercised a strong attraction for some ascetics in the Egyptian desert,[72] apparently it seems to have

---

[68] On the troubled early years of Athanasius's long tenure as bishop, with careful evaluation of the credibility of the evidence for various charges that have later been made, see Duane W. H. Arnold, *The Early Episcopal Career of Athanasius of Alexandria* (Notre Dame. IN: University of Notre Dame Press, 1991).

[69] On Athanasius's use of the anthropological assumptions of Middle and Neo-Platonism, see Johannes Roldanus, *Le christ et l'homme dans la théologie d'Athanase d'Alexandrie: Etude de la conjonction de sa conception de l'homme avec sa christologie* (Leiden: Brill, 1968).

[70] See *De Decretis* 27.

[71] See the arguments of Khaled Anatolios, "The Influence of Irenaeus on Athanasius," *Studia Patristica* 36 (2001), 463–76. The influence of Irenaeus's thought on later Greek Patristic theology, from Clement of Alexandria to Maximus Confessor, and even on Augustine, seems to have been considerable; like most pre-Nicene Fathers, however, he is seldom mentioned by name or cited by later authors or councils.

[72] The collection of Coptic texts discovered at Nag Hammadi in Upper Egypt in December, 1945—now our main source for a first-hand understanding of early Christian Gnosticism—were

been less of a competitor for Alexandrian religious minds than it had been a century before. Manichaeism, a later and more syncretistic form of Gnostic religion, was also certainly an active force in fourth-century Egypt, as it was in many parts of the Roman Empire. But the real enemy Athanasius saw himself facing was the ingrained tradition of Platonic and earlier Christian thought—a tradition Origen also represented, in some ways—that imagined God's action in the world as always mediated in ontological steps, and that conceived of the Son and the Holy Spirit as produced, even "created," by the transcendent Father to be his agents then in creating, redeeming, and sanctifying all other things. They were agents who were necessarily *less* than the Father in being and status, but who *participated* in his Godhead to such a pre-eminent extent that they could legitimately be called "divine." The main representatives of this tradition, as we have already seen, were the presbyter Arius and his supporters, as well the more moderate Eusebius, who carried on Origen's scholarship and tradition. This was the accepted background against which most fourth-century Greek discussion of Christ was carried out.

In a fine study of Athanasius's work as a whole,[73] Khaled Anatolios has convincingly argued that despite the often polemical and occasional character of Athanasius's writings, his theological work is held together by a certain perspective, a certain way of thinking about God and the world and human history, which runs through every period of his long life, and which stands in contrast to this widespread assumption of graduated mediation between God and creation. Rather, as Anatolios shows, Athanasius generally emphasizes the beneficent, life-giving *presence* of the eternal, transcendent Logos of God *within* the created order: his presence as one who is not simply a lesser mediator or a derived participant in God's being, but fully God, and therefore wholly "other" than creation; yet also a presence as one who is so actively involved in the world, and finally so intimately identified with the world by his Incarnation, that he can direct history, order the cosmos, and heal the ills of a fallen humanity from within.

In his early apologetic work, the coordinated pair of treatises *Against the Pagans* and *On the Incarnation*, probably written in the early or middle 330s,[74]

---

probably copied in the mid-fourth century by monks of one of the nearby Pachomian monasteries, and later hidden. The reason they were copied, like the reason they were hidden in a cave, remains a mystery.

[73] Khaled Anatolios, *Athanasius: The Coherence of his Thought* (London: Routledge, 1998).

[74] The dating of these two treatises has long been debated. The earlier idea that since they make no mention of Arius or the controversy that surrounded him, they must have been written before 321, when Athanasius would have been scarcely over 20 himself, is not widely held today. For other conjectures, see Anatolios, *Athanasius*, 26–7 and the references there. It seems safest to place it at some point in the early or middle 330s, before the deaths of Constantine (337) or Eusebius (339/40), but after Athanasius's own rise to influence as bishop and theologian. The apologia these treatises present for the Christian understanding of God's work in history is, in many ways, strikingly similar to what Eusebius offers in the *Theophany*, yet from a Nicene

Athanasius sets out, as he tells us in the first chapter of *Against the Pagans*, to defend faith in Christ as Savior and refute those who "scoff at the cross" by showing that "the one who ascended the cross is the Word of God and Savior of the world."[75] In the rest of that first treatise, Athanasius sets out to sketch the broad narrative background for the coming of Christ—his own version of the biblical "meta-narrative." God has created the human race, he reminds his readers, in his own image, even giving humans the ability to know God in his eternity, and in that knowledge to be joined with other intelligent creatures and "have communion with the Deity" by knowing the Father in his Word.[76] But humanity declined from its original state by a making series of fatal choices: abandoning the contemplation of God, humans became preoccupied with gratifying sensual desires, turned to idolatry, the projection of those desires into religion, and identified God with material things.[77] Yet the human mind, Athanasius insists, remains capable of knowing God as he is, and so of finding life.[78] It simply needs to rediscover God's creative Word as a present force in the world, as the giver of the harmony and order that is the central principle of continuing organic life.[79]

In the second of these two treatises, *On the Incarnation*, Athanasius sets his version of the Christian story of salvation through Jesus, crucified and risen, against this wider philosophical and biblical background. God, he states, originally made the world and all its inhabitants out of nothing, simply because of his goodness. He took special pity on the human creatures, because of their obvious natural vulnerability and variability of behavior, which made a tragic background for their obvious gifts. So, after the first gift of creation, God immediately bestowed on humanity a "second gift," an inner grace beyond mere movement and sensation:

> [God] made them after his own image, giving them a portion even of the power of his own Word (*Λόγος*), so that having, as it were, a kind of reflection of the Word and being made rational (*λογικοί*), they might be able to abide ever in blessedness, living the true life which belongs to the saints in paradise.[80]

Humans were no longer simply cunning in an instinctive way, as the other animals are, but now could know God, which is the basis of participation,

---

perspective. It is possible they are intended as Athanasius's response to Eusebius's late work. On the date and original intent of these two treatises, see Wolfgang Bienert, "Zur Logos-Christologie des Athanasius von Alexandrien in *Contra Gentes* und *De Incarnatione*," *Studia Patristica* 21 (1989), 402–19.

[75] *Contra Gentes* (CG) 1.5. On these two works as constituting an *apologia crucis*, see Anatolios, *Athanasius*, 28; John Behr, *The Nicene Faith* 1 (Crestwood, NY: St. Vladimir's, 2004), 171, 181–3.

[76] CG 2.   [77] CG 3–8.   [78] CG 30.   [79] CG 35–8.

[80] *De Incarnatione* [DI] 3 (trans. Archibald Robertson, *Nicene and Post-Nicene Fathers*). In quoting from this work, we shall make use of this translation, but will modernize it slightly.

everlasting life. But recognizing the moral instability of his human creatures, Athanasius suggests, even with their new gift of rationality, God "secured the grace given them by a law;"[81] his plan was that if they could abide within the Law's structure—which kept them "rational"—and were content to live within the Garden where he had placed them, they would continue to be incorruptible, because they knew and conversed with God. If they broke the law, however, all these blessings of "the second gift" they had received would be lost, as well: humans would again experience the weight of their own mortal, animal natures, be excluded from the Garden and its delights, and would lose not only their knowledge of God and his will, which made them "reasonable" in the image of God's own Word, but would lose the natural incorruptibility that came as a result of that knowledge.[82]

Athanasius describes poignantly the epidemic of corruption that, in fact, has followed humanity's abandonment of God and his laws: increasing sensuality and materialism, a loss of practical rationality, and with it a loss of vital energy—all frustrating God's original plan, and placing humanity under the "legal" and actual hold of death.[83] The only remedy, Athanasius argues, was for the Logos, our divine source of rationality and of communion with God, to enter the world himself on human terms and to "meet us halfway:"[84] to take on human corruptibility and mortality himself, in a mortal human body, in order to overcome death at first hand, in his own person, and so reveal his glory to dulled human minds in inner-worldly terms they could understand.

> To this end he took to himself a body capable of death, that it, by partaking of the Word who is above all, might be worthy to die in the stead of all, and might, because of the Word which had come to dwell in it, remain incorruptible, and that from then on corruption might be kept from all by the grace of the resurrection.[85]

But salvation was not simply accomplished by the sacrificial death of the Word in the mortal human body he had assumed—in which, Athanasius even says, "he disguised himself."[86] It was accomplished also by the Word's revelation of himself to the human race, which required not only his death, but the life and words and works that preceded and followed it, all of which showed him to be both human and divine:

> For by his becoming human, the Savior was to accomplish both works of love: first, in putting away death from us, and renewing us again; second, being unseen and invisible, in manifesting and making himself known by his works to be the Word of the Father, and the ruler and king of the universe.... For just as, though invisible, he is known [in the world] through the works of creation; so, having

---

[81] DI 3.    [82] For Athanasius's development of this view, see DI 4–5, 11, 12, 13.
[83] DI 5–6.    [84] DI 15.    [85] DI 9.    [86] DI 16.

become human, and being in the body [still] unseen, it may be known from his works that he who can do these is not human, but the power and Word of God.[87]

Here and in many other passages in the treatise, Athanasius sees the effect of the Incarnation of the Word, worked out in the life and actions of Jesus as well as in his death and resurrection, essentially as a demonstration of the Word's present creative, life-giving power, realized in the establishment of order and stability in a material universe that is otherwise prone to dissolution. In the wider cosmos, that effect of the Word's presence can be seen in the constant, orderly course of the planets and stars; in a renewed humanity—the community of those who believe in the incarnate Word and join in accepting his lordship—it is seen rather in the demise of ancient idolatry and all its attendant superstitions, in the courage of ordinary humans to face martyrdom and to undertake the toils of Christian asceticism, and in the growth of a new community of peace and law and self-control—the Church—even among peoples formerly known as barbarians.[88] All of this, argues Athanasius, reveals the nearness of God the Word through his works in ordering creation: a manifestation that of itself communicates a share in his divinity, his unending life and virtue and intellectual light, to those who can accept it for what it is:

If, then, anyone should wish to see God, who is invisible by nature and not seen at all, he may know and apprehend him from his works...And if [Christ's works] be human, let him scoff; but if they are not human, but of God, let him recognize it, and not laugh at what is not matter for scoffing; but rather let him marvel that, by so ordinary a means, divine things have been manifested to us, and that by death immortality has reached to all, and that by the Word becoming human, universal providence has come to be known, along with its giver and artificer, the very Word of God. For he was made human that we might be made God; and he manifested himself by a body that we might receive the idea of the unseen Father; and he endured human insolence that we might inherit immortality.[89]

This pattern of argument, which Athanasius develops far more amply in this double apologetic work than we have been able to report here, runs also through many of his other writings, from every stage of his career. A striking instance of it can be seen in his celebrated *Life of Antony*, probably written in the late 350s, where the ascetic—whom Athanasius carefully depicts as a simple, unlettered man—is presented as renewed and vivified, in body and in mind, by his utterly selfless, often heroic personal dedication to Christ.[90]

---

[87] DI 16, 18. For another, strongly argued explanation of the saving work of the incarnate Word, in terms of both self-revelation through his works of power, and the overcoming of death in the place where death had gained its hold—the human body—see DI 44.

[88] For a description of this effect of faith, see DI 29–31, 46–54.     [89] DI 54.

[90] For a discussion of the *Life of Antony* as an elaborate paradigm of the effects of sincere, practical faith in the incarnate Word, see Johannes Roldanus, "Die Vita Antonii als Spiegel der

Even at a point when Christ had seemed absent, and Antony felt himself utterly alone in his combats with the demons that surrounded and harassed him, the Lord unexpectedly appeared to him as a bright light, and assured him, "I have been here, but I have been waiting to watch your struggle."[91] And when Antony emerges from his solitude to greet his friends, after twenty years of enclosure, they find him, as Athanasius describes the scene, to be the perfect example of human health and order: physically fit and apparently unaged, balanced and serene in manner, easily able to communicate with others and to help them in their own troubles, "like someone who was governed by reason and had come to stability in his natural state."[92] Throughout the *Life*, the Word reveals his presence in Antony by making possible the monk's ability to overcome evil spirits and give reliable counsel—he is active even in this obscure Egyptian peasant to heal and order creation.

It is the disciple's "active faith"[93] in Christ (ἡ ἐνέργεια πίστεως), Antony later assures a group of pagan philosophers who visit him, that has enabled him and his fellow Christians, even without the support of elaborate theoretical proofs, to be men of reason: to "recognize the universal providence of God in all things" and to live, free of crippling superstition, in a new commonwealth of faith spreading all over the world.[94] So he questions his visitors:

> "In knowledge of reality, especially knowledge of God, how do we come to accurate conclusions? Through verbal demonstrations or through the activity of faith? And which is more authoritative—faith actively lived out, or verbal demonstrations?" And when they answered that faith lived out actively must take first place, and that this *is* accurate knowledge, Antony said, "You are right! For faith grows out of the condition of the soul, but dialectics belongs to the realm of conventional skills. So that if someone possesses an active faith, demonstration is not necessary, or is perhaps superfluous."[95]

Theologie des Athanasius und ihr Weiterwerken bis ins 5. Jahrhundert," *Theologie und Philosophie* 58 (1983), 194–216; also Anatolios, *Athanasius*, 177–95. Roldanus points out (211–16) that other important early monastic lives, influenced strongly by the *Life of Antony*, such as Sulpicius Severus's *Life of Martin* or Callinicus's *Life of Hypatius*, draw heavily on the ascetical and demonological features of Athanasius's narrative, but neglect its underlying Christological and soteriological emphasis. The latest full edition of the Greek text is by G. J. M. Bartelink, SChr. 400 (Paris, 1994).

[91] *Vita Antonii* [VA] 10.

[92] VA 14: ὡς ὑπὸ τοῦ Λόγου κυβερνώμενος. The first part of this phrase may also be translated: "like someone governed by the Logos." The ambiguity of *Logos* and *logos* may be part of Athanasius's point.

[93] VA 77–9. At some places in this passage, Antony refers to "the activity accomplished by faith" (ἡ διὰ πίστεως ἐνέργεια), at others "faith working through action" (ἡ δι' ἐνεργείας πίστις). Both kinds of expression seem to mean the same thing: a practical, rather than simply a theoretical, grasp of God's reality and presence.

[94] VA 78. See also his depiction of the growing community of Christian disciples, in *On the Incarnation*.

[95] VA 77 (SChr. 400.332).

To know the Word in his own flesh, by the direct experience of living in a community of faith in Christ the Word, is, for Antony, to experience directly the life-giving power of the one God.[96]

The principal criticism leveled in recent decades against Athanasius's portrait of Christ has been that the *human* side of that portrait can seem seriously incomplete. Grillmeier sees in Athanasius's work a developed form of the earlier "word-flesh" Christology, which at times steers close to what would later be deemed heretical. In Athanasius, he admits, "the soul of Christ retreats well into the background, even if it does not disappear completely";[97] it is certainly not "a theological factor" in Athanasius's thought, Grillmeier suggests, and Athanasius leaves it unclear in places whether a human soul is even "a physical factor" in the life and actions of Jesus.[98] As a result, Grillmeier complains, "there is not always a distinction between the mediation of natural and supernatural life" in Athanasius's conception of the Incarnation; the Logos is the source of all that Jesus does, so that even "the mediation of natural life to the flesh imperceptibly becomes *soteria*, which from a biblical point of view must be regarded as supernatural."[99] Athanasius, in other words, does not distinguish with sufficient theoretical clarity between the human and the divine in Jesus, as principles of his actions: he does not mark off, as scholastic theology later would, the two "natures" possessed by his single "person." More recently, Bishop Richard Hanson has gone so far as to describe Athanasius's approach as a "space-suit Christology": just as an astronaut puts on a special suit to be able to live and act in an environment that is not his own, "so the Logos put on a body which enabled him to behave as a human being among human beings. But his relation to this body," which Athanasius (like Eusebius) often refers to as an "instrument" (ὄργανον) of the Logos's saving work, says Hanson, "is no closer than that of an astronaut to his space-suit."[100]

A number of still more recent scholars, however—notably Alvyn Pettersen[101] and Khaled Anatolios—have argued convincingly that such judgments of Athanasius's Christology (which were not shared by most ancient writers) distort his intentions, by imposing on them linguistic and conceptual expectations he never intended to meet. In his anti-Arian works, especially, where

---

[96] See also *Festal Letter I*, 6 (329), in which Athanasius refers to the words and the vision of God as the only all-sufficient nourishment for angels or humans; also *Letter to Adelphius* 8 (probably from the late 350s); *Letter to Maximus* 3 (from about 371).

[97] Aloys Grillmeier, *Christ in Christian Tradition*, I: *From the Apostolic Age to Chalcedon (451)* (2nd edn; London: Mowbray, 1975), 308.

[98] *Christ in Christian Tradition*, 325.       [99] *Christ in Christian Tradition*, 312–13.

[100] R. P. C. Hanson, *The Search for the Christian Doctrine of God* (Edinburgh: T. and T. Clark, 1988), 448. For a critical response to Grillmeier and Hanson on the question of Athanasius's term "instrument" for the body of Christ, see Khaled Anatolios, " 'The Body as Instrument': A Reevaluation of Athanasius' Logox-Sarx Christology," *Coptic Church Review* 18 (1997), 78–84.

[101] Alvyn Pettersen, *Athanasius and the Human Body* (Bristol: Bristol Press, 1990); *Athanasius* (London: Geoffrey Chapman, 1995), esp. 109–35.

such an "instrumental" conception of Christ's humanity is perhaps most often expressed, Athanasius's interest is quite different from that of Leo and the framers of the Chalcedonian formula a century later. He is concerned above all to argue that the redeeming Logos, despite the shocking Christian confession that he has "become flesh" and taken on himself all the human passibilities associated with that flesh, is not himself a creature, and therefore is not himself either passible or changeable. Athanasius expresses the "otherness" of Jesus' humanity from the Logos in a variety of ways: he speaks of the Logos as taking on himself real flesh, or a real body, as his "garment";[102] of his clothing of his body with divine life;[103] of his "putting on our passibilities," making a human body "his own";[104] of his taking on a "human being";[105] of his dwelling in a human body as his "temple."[106] Only because he is the transcendent Word, in fact, who brings a "wholly other" material creation into being and is always present within it, to supply it with order and stability, can the incarnation of this Word in a human body become a way of reversing the disease of death in *our* fleshly bodies, of putting us into full touch, on the sensible and cognitive as well as the spiritual level, with his divine creative power.

In service of this central theological concern—emphasizing our encounter with God here, in and through our own flesh—Athanasius develops what is essentially a rhetorical rather than an analytical or scholastic Christology, a Christology of paradox, constructing what Anatolios calls a "dialectic 'focused on extremes'."[107] This is a way of speaking about the Mystery of Christ that emphasizes the dramatic contrast of Word and flesh, creator and creature, whose very ontological distance from one another—whose infinite inequality— is the very foundation for our seeing in the story of Christ the wonder of our own salvation. In fact, it seems likely that Athanasius's failure to refer to a human soul or mind in Christ, except in a fairly late, official document of 362, the *Tomus ad Antiochenos*, was probably a deliberate way of avoiding any suggestion—even of the kind found earlier in Origen—that a created entity, intellectual or material, might be able to mediate between the Word of God and the physical, fallen humanity he has taken on himself, to refashion and save it. As Pettersen gently suggests, if one takes seriously the fact that Athanasius is writing as "an Alexandrian of his time," then it is "the commonly received opinion" of Grillmeier and Hanson, in fact, that is "more a mirage than actuality."

---

[102] See, for instance, DI 45; *Letter to Adelphius* 3; cf. *Contra Arianos* [CA] 2.55.
[103] See, for instance, DI 44.       [104] See, for instance, CA 3.32.
[105] See, for instance, DI 14, 15, 16, 17, 41, 43, 44, 54.
[106] See, for instance, DI 9 ("offering his own temple and corporeal instrument"); *Letter to Adelphius* 3, 7–8.
[107] Anatolios, *Athanasius*, 73.

One must consider (Pettersen says) whether the "body" which the Logos enlivens and controls, to which passions, both psychological and physiological, are attributed, and from which the Logos is loosed in death, is indeed a "body," as opposed to a soul, or whether it is the assumed, creaturely humanity, in contrast with the incorporeal, creator God. For the terminology may originate from Scripture and tradition, and not from anthropological debate . . . One must reflect upon whether Christ's death, in which the Logos is loosed from its body, is to be interpreted anthropologically, akin to a person's, in which the soul is separated from its body, or theologically, akin to a person's whose death, evidenced in the soul's separation from the body, occurs through the withdrawal of the life-giving Logos, his no longer holding that person in unified being upon this earth.[108]

The presence of the creative and ordering Word of God in the human Christ, in other words, is what makes his embodied experiences and actions salvific; his immediacy to each of us is ultimately what keeps our own souls and bodies alive and functioning well.

## CONCLUSION

Clearly, I have not intended to offer in this chapter a complete picture of the understanding of Christ that these early fourth-century theologians present to us in their writings; I have merely tried to point out certain features of what *we* identify as their Christology, features that I think do connect them with each other in important ways, and that can appear all the more interesting and powerful to us when we look at them apart from the Chalcedonian—or the modern dogmatic or historicist—lens. Clearly, too, they differ in important ways. For *Arius*, the earnest pastor steeped in traditional Hellenistic thought and Alexandrian theology, it was clear that Jesus had to be, in some fundamental sense, a part of this created cosmos in need of salvation—changeable, capable of growth, bounded by time—if he was to be its savior. He must be the first and noblest of creatures, if he is to be the beginning of a "new creation." For *Eusebius*, the learned Origenist biblical scholar and historian—still more familiar with Middle Platonic ontology than Arius was, still more inclined to think in Platonic terms about the relationship of the world to its divine source—Christ, the mediator between God and creatures, can only be fit into the biblical narrative if we understand him to be in some way produced ($\gamma\epsilon\nu\eta\tau\delta s$) and delegated by God to carry out his mission. While not simply an Arian, Eusebius was also hesitant to make Nicaea's language his own; the Son, for him, is not simply "the first of creatures," but also stands above them; at the same time, he must clearly be of a different rank, in activity and in being, from the one who

---

[108] Pettersen, *Athanasius*, 131.

begot him. He is God "by participation," and so—as divine Wisdom—he can enable intelligent creatures to participate in God, as well.

*Marcellus*, on the other hand, seems to have begun his reflection on Christ from the Nicene assumption that only God, as God, can save the world; the Scripture passages that seem to rank the Son as in some way less than, and dependent on, the Father, must all be referring to his incarnate state. As a divine agent, the Son is acting on his own as God, rather than simply carrying out a commission from his Father; so his generation, his sonship, must be truly eternal, must occur within the mysterious bounds of God's being; his relationship with the God of Israel must be, as Nicaea had labeled it, that of "one substance," "one hypostasis." In his root identity, Jesus the divine Savior is indistinguishable from the one he refers to as "Father" and "Lord."

*Athanasius* takes from his culture's Middle Platonic tradition the understanding that it is the constant, active presence of the divine Logos in the world, and in each created intellect, that holds all things in physical and moral order: that preserves us from dissolution, makes us "reasonable," guides our decisions towards the right goals, and enables us to know God as he is. The Incarnation of the Word has made that divine gift of order and vitality accessible to a fallen race: Jesus healed the sick, drove out the evil spirits of disorder, revealed in human terms the life-giving knowledge of God that assures us of our kinship with him. But except for some important passages in Athanasius's *Third Oration against the Arians*,[109] neither he nor the other authors we are considering shows much interest in the human psychology of Jesus, or even in the "structure" of his personal being, understood in abstract terms. Like the rest, Athanasius is mainly interested in explaining how the Word has *done* for us what he came to do. Khaled Anatolios characterizes the Christology of Athanasius, tellingly, as "a ἵνα-Christology": a Christology arranged by God "in order that," which sets out to explain what the Word has become, not in terms of natures and person, but in terms of *why* he has come at all—of final causality, perhaps, rather than efficient or formal causality.[110] For all of these authors, in fact, God's Word, as person and as Scripture, cannot really be separated from God's saving promise, fulfilled finally in Jesus.

We have grown used to thinking of Christ, to puzzling about his identity, in more static and metaphysical terms. We cannot, perhaps, simply return to the narrative style of pre-critical theology and exegesis to talk about the great work

---

[109] See, for example, CA III, 32–5; 39–43; 49–51. In all of these texts, Athanasius struggles to explain the ignorance and internal sufferings of Jesus mentioned in the Gospels.

[110] Anatolios, *Athanasius*, 147. He gives as an example of this kind of explanation a sentence in Athanasius's *Letter to Epictetus* 9: "The Word has become flesh, not by reason of an addition to the Godhead, but in order that the flesh may rise again." One kind of causal explanation is rejected here as inadequate, but the explanation then put forward points to a wholly different kind of "cause."

of God in history, as if either of those terms—"God" and "history"—were problem-free. Yet we, too, live in a culture where various forms of Gnostic revisionism are still alive and well. Retellings of present human needs and possibilities in the cosmogonic or psychoanalytic narratives of Marx or Freud or Foucault, of capitalist political economics or of post-colonial history, or even in terms of the cosmic after-effects of the "big bang," all have a determining effect on how we understand the value and the possibilities of our human life, how we understand who we really are. What Arius and Eusebius, Marcellus and Athanasius suggest to us, in their approach to the person of Christ, is that one of the main functions of Christology, too, is to tell us who we really are and can be, where we come from and where we are invited to go—and to remind us that the very vision we have of Christ, in our "active faith," is enough to change both ourselves and our world.

# 5

## Apollinarius, Gregory of Nazianzus, and Gregory of Nyssa

### Towards a Christology of Transformation

In the commonly received narrative of the history of Christology, the first specifically "Christological" challenge raised to traditional teaching in the post-Constantinian Church was the proposal of Apollinarius of Laodicaea, in the 360s and later, that in Jesus, the divine Logos took the place of a created human mind. The controversy over Arius's insistence that the Logos must be a creature, with some kind of temporal beginning, if he was truly "generated" by the God he called "Father," and truly involved in the world of temporal creatures as mediator, is usually classified as a controversy about the Christian understanding of *God*. So the affirmation of the Nicene creed that the Son is "of the same substance" as the eternal, transcendent Father has normally been understood as the first step towards that paradoxical summary of Christian theism we call the doctrine of the Trinity. Later polemics between Athanasius and his allies, on the one hand, and those critics who felt the Nicene formula steered dangerously close to a traditionally "modalist" understanding of God— for many early Greek Christians a position still more alien to Christian thinking than the teachings of Arius had been—or else the struggle between supporters of Nicaea and the more radical "Neo-Arians," identified with Aetius and Eunomius, from the late 350s on, are usually thought of as really part of a debate about God's being, despite the fact that they center on the identity and status of the Son.[1]

---

[1] For a thorough discussion of the details of these controversies, see now Michel Barnes, *The Power of God: Dynamis in Gregory of Nyssa's Trinitarian Theology* (Washington, DC: Catholic University of America Press, 2001); John Behr, *The Nicene Faith* (Crestwood, NY: St. Vladimir's, 2004); Lewis Ayres, *Nicaea and its Legacy* (Oxford: Oxford University Press, 2004); and Khaled Anatolios, *Retrieving Nicaea: The Development and Meaning of Trinitarian Doctrine* (Grand Rapids, MI: Baker Academic, 2011). See also the earlier, now partly superseded work of R. P. C. Hanson, *The Search for the Christian Doctrine of God* (Edinburgh: T. and T. Clark, 1988), 557–636. The question has also been raised of whether the term "Arian" is really a helpful

It is only with Apollinarius's dogmatic insistence on what had been, especially in Alexandria, the commonly accepted picture of Christ for two centuries—what Grillmeier calls the *logos-sarx* or "word-flesh" model of conceiving the Savior— that theological debate came to be focused, it is often said, in a more explicitly *Christological* way: not simply focused on whether or not the Son is "divine" in the same sense in which the God of Israel is divine, but on the structure of the Son's own *person*, as God and as a human being. In response to Apollinarius's understanding of Christ, it is often argued, the Cappadocian Fathers suddenly became more deeply aware of the crucial importance of the human *soul* of Jesus, of his human consciousness and freedom, as central to the full content of Christian faith. As Gregory of Nazianzus wrote to his vicar Cledonius, echoing a point made already in the early third century by Origen and others, "What has not been assumed has not been healed, but what is united to the Godhead is also saved."[2] If Jesus has no human inner life, no human mind, then the minds of all humanity, the conscious center in each of ourselves, must remain outside the range of God's healing touch through the Incarnation; God heals us, we believe, by drawing close to us, and if Jesus, as Word incarnate, is not fully like us, he cannot really help us. And it is only with this turn in the debate, so our common understanding goes—only with the recognition that the Apollinarian version of a "logos-sarx" Christology is seriously deficient, even heretical—that mainstream Christology, expressed in the formula of Chalcedon and later Western theology, really begins.[3]


APOLLINARIUS OF LAODICAEA

There is, of course, much truth in the story with which this chapter opens. And yet, as often happens, a deeper look at the ancient evidence reveals that things

category for describing a long and rather varied series of anti-Nicene theological positions: see especially Joseph T. Lienhard, "The 'Arian' Controversy: Some Categories Reconsidered," *Theological Studies* 48 (1987), 415–37; Michel R. Barnes, "The Fourth Century as Trinitarian Canon," in Lewis Ayres and Gareth Jones (eds), *Christian Origins: Theology, Rhetoric and Community* (London: Routledge, 1998), 47–67.

[2] Gregory of Nazianzus, Ep. 101.32 (SChr. 208.50). For the background of this familiar phrase, see n. 29.

[3] Basil Studer, *Trinity and Incarnation: The Faith of the Early Church* (Edinburgh: T. and T. Clark, 1993), 193–4, for instance, asserts that "around 360, the lengthy debate on Christ's divinity finally came to an end." It was at the synod of Alexandria in 362, the synod where first official notice is taken of the Apollinarian party in Antioch and their view of Christ's person, that "the *christological problem* was raised for the first time," and "*Christology* had become a matter of public discussion" (italics mine). Although Aloys Grillmeier does not state things quite so baldly, this same dogmatic sequence seems to be implied in *Christ in Christian Tradition*, I: *From the Apostolic Age to Chalcedon (451)* (2nd edn; London: Mowbray, 1975), 345–7.

were not quite so simple. For one thing, although Apollinarius of Laodicaea was clearly regarded as a troublesome figure by many leading orthodox Churchmen of Syria, Palestine, and Asia Minor in the 370s and 380s, as well as later—so much so that the first canon of the Council of Constantinople of 381 adds "the Apollinarians" to the growing canonical list of fourth-century groups to be excluded from communion[4] and Gregory of Nyssa, shortly afterwards, will say that Apollinarius should win first prize in any contest of heretics, even when compared with the neo-Arian arch-heretic Eunomius[5]— still the label "heretic" never adhered to Apollinarius himself with the archetypal force with which it clung to a Paul of Samosata or an Arius. The dogmatic statement of the Council of Chalcedon (451) may have had Apollinarius as well as Eutyches in view, when it rejected any conception of Christ that "introduces confusion and mixture, and foolishly imagines that the nature of the flesh and the divinity is one";[6] the Second Council of Constantinople (553) linked Apollinarius with Eutyches in supporting a notion of union in Christ that "confuses the elements which have come together,"[7] and the Third Council of Constantinople (680–1), rejecting a Christology that finds Christ's unity in a single divine will and single divine flow of natural activity or energy in all he does, named Apollinarius, along with Severus the other opponents of Chalcedon, as the source of this "wicked and insane belief."[8] But in the scale of ancient invective, it must be said that the reproaches heaped on Apollinarius in his own time for his understanding of Christ are relatively light. Although his way of conceiving Christ—as a single, organic unity of Logos and sentient flesh, as the divine and universal mind controlling a living, ensouled human body as one organism—was generally understood to be defective from the 380s on, Greek-speaking theologians seem to have recognized that his position was not so radically different from that of the mainstream, as found in Irenaeus and Eusebius and Athanasius, to say nothing of Arius and Marcellus, as to make its author into a major heresiarch. It was expressed too baldly, perhaps; but it was more or less the way most Christians, up to the 370s, tended to imagine their Savior.

---

[4] Canon 1 (Alberigo/Tanner, 31, ll. 14–15), which confirms "the faith [= creedal formula] of Nicaea," anathematizes Eunomian Arians, "semi-Arians" (who reject the divinity and hypostatic distinction of the Spirit), Sabellians and Marcellians, followers of Photinus of Sirmium (another modalist), and Apollinarians. See also canon 7 (Alberigo/Tanner, 35, l. 13), which included them with Trinitarian heretics, Manichaeans, and Novatianists, who were ecclesiological rigorists. The Emperor Theodosius I outlawed the Apollinarian sect in decrees of 383, 384, and 388.

[5] *Antirrhetikos* 44 (GNO III/1, 205.21–206.9).

[6] Alberigo/Tanner, 84, ll. 40–3; see also the list of rejected Christological positions, further on in the statement, which includes "those who imagine a *mixture or confusion* between the two natures of Christ" (Alberigo/Tanner, 6, l. 4–6).

[7] Constantinople II, Canon 4 (Alberigo/Tanner, 115, ll. 29–32); this position is contrasted immediately with the overly divisive Christology of Theodore of Mopsuestia and Nestorius.

[8] Alberigo/Tanner, 126, ll. 4–11.

It seems likely, in fact, that opposition to Apollinarius and his followers originally centered on their Church politics, as much as it did on their Christology. A person of prodigious intellectual energy, a gifted writer deeply engaged in the project shared by many well-educated Christians, in the decades after Julian, to create a new body of Greek literature with an explicitly Christian content, Apollinarius seems to have been the center of a growing circle of disciples in the Eastern Mediterranean provinces by the 370s, who were intent on cultural and structural Church reform. Their main theological concern, recent scholarship has shown, seems to have been Nicene orthodoxy: elaborating an understanding of God that strongly affirmed the full, substantial divinity of Son and Spirit, as Athanasius had done, but that also avoided the suspected modalism of Marcellus of Ancyra, by insisting that Father, Son, and Spirit are irreducibly three figures, three concrete entities or hypostases, which share fully the single substance of God.[9] Apollinarius's distinctive understanding of the person Christ may well have originated, in his mind, as simply a corollary to his emphasis on the distinct, divine individuality of the Son, who is incarnate as our Savior. A modalist understanding of Father, Son, and Holy Spirit, after all, tends to conceive of Jesus as a human being filled with the power and wisdom of God, but not as the incarnation of the eternal Son, who is not, in such a view, a distinct person.

Apollinarius and his disciples seem also to have been activists: anti-Arian and anti-modalist crusaders. Their activity first aroused concern in the Church of Antioch during the late 350s—a Church already divided into several rival Christian groups. The supporters of Nicaea in Antioch had already split into a larger community, led by bishop Meletius, who tended—despite their eventual support of Nicene Christology—to emphasize the distinction and hierarchical ordering of Father, Son, and Spirit within the Mystery of God, and who were on good terms with the Cappadocians, and a smaller group led by bishop Paulinus, whose sympathies were more in the modalist direction, and who found external support from Alexandria and the West.[10] Although Apollinarius's own origins are somewhat murky, it seems likely that he began his career in the Antiochene Church as a supporter of Meletius, but raised the suspicions, and eventually the hostility, of Meletius's faction by asserting his own version of Nicene orthodoxy, and perhaps his own ambition for leadership, too strongly. G. L. Prestige suggested in the 1950s that Apollinarius, who had been engaged in friendly correspondence with Basil of Caesaraea, and was a

---

[9] See especially Kelly McCarthy Spoerl, "Apollinarius and the Response to Early Arian Christology," *Studia Patristica* 26 (1993), 421–7; "Apollinarian Christology and the Anti-Marcellan Tradition," *JTS* 43 (1994), 545–68; "The Liturgical Argument in Apollinarius: Help and Hindrance on the Way to Orthodoxy," *Harvard Theological Review* (1998), 127–52.

[10] See my article, "The Enigma of Meletius of Antioch," in Ronnie J. Rombs and Alexander Y. Hwang (eds), *Tradition and the Rule of Faith in the Early Church*, Festschrift for Joseph Lienhard (Washington, DC: Catholic University of America Press, 2010).

solicitous admirer of the elderly Athanasius, first aroused opposition in the Churches outside Antioch in the 370s when, himself now a bishop, he tried to extend his influence in the surrounding provinces by uncanonically ordaining bishops who would be sympathetic to his views.[11] John McGuckin, in his biography of Gregory of Nazianzus, suggests that all three "Cappadocians" were probably sympathetic to Apollinarius's strongly Nicene position until the late 370s, and that it was the Meletian faction in Antioch—perhaps with help from Diodore of Tarsus—who persuaded the two Gregories that the Apollinarians were both over-ambitious and theologically dangerous, and enlisted their help in opposing them.[12]

The Christology of the Apollinarians, which eventually became the intellectual icon of their movement, had deep roots in earlier tradition, as we have already observed. Rowan Greer has argued convincingly for the similarity between Apollinarius's understanding of Christ and that of Irenaeus:[13] both centered on the Pauline picture of the Savior as the Adam of a new humanity, particularly as it is presented in I Corinthians 15.45–9, where Paul contrasts "the man from the earth," "the man of dust," whose image we now bear, with the second Adam, "a life-giving spirit," the "heavenly man, in whose image we are being renewed." Apollinarius develops this understanding of Christ with great subtlety of thought and linguistic skill—so much so that it is often hard to draw a single, unblurred portrait of Christ from his and his disciples' many writings. Still, the overall emphasis of the Apollinarians is clear and distinctive: the Incarnation of the divine Word in Jesus means that even as a human being, an *anthrōpos*, Jesus is unique in every way. Since he was conceived by the "overshadowing of the Most High and the power of the Holy Spirit" (Luke 1.35), "it is not possible to take his body separately and call *it* a creature, since it is altogether inseparable from him whose body it is."[14] Rather, the incarnate Son of God, in the Apollinarian view, forms a single, organic unity analogous to that of mind, soul, and body in the ordinary human individual, "so that *one nature* is constituted out of the parts severally, and the Word contributes a special energy to the whole, together with the divine perfection."[15] In some passages, Apollinarius is willing to affirm, on the one hand, that the *whole*

---

[11] G. L. Prestige, *St. Basil the Great and Apollinarius of Laodicaea*, ed. Henry Chadwick (London: SPCK, 1956), 14–16.

[12] John A. McGuckin, *St. Gregory of Nazianzus: An Intellectual Biography* (Crestwood, NY: St. Vladimir's, 2001), 231–2, 392–3.

[13] Rowan A. Greer, "The Man from Heaven: Paul's Last Adam and Apollinaris's Christ," in William S. Babcock (ed.), *Paul and the Legacies of Paul* (Dallas, TX: Southern Methodist University Press, 1990), 165–82.

[14] Apollinarius, *On the Union in Christ of the Body with the Godhead* 2, in Hans Lietzmann, *Apollinarius von Laodicaea und seine Schule* (Tübingen: Mohr Siebeck, 1904), 186, trans. Richard A. Norris, *The Christological Controversy* (Philadelphia, PA: Fortress, 1980), 103.

[15] *On the Union in Christ* 5 (Lietzmann 187.5–14; Norris, 104). By "one nature" Apollinarius seems to have meant "one natural thing," one dynamic, functioning unit. His stress here on the

Christ, flesh and spirit, can be said to be "of one substance" with both God and humanity;[16] yet in virtue of their unified activity, these two utterly distinct realities have also become a new, operative thing with its own structure: "a single essence" or "substance" in itself.

> God, who has taken to himself an instrument of activity, is both God, insofar as he activates, and human, with respect to the instrument of activity which he uses. Remaining God, he is not altered. The instrument and its user naturally produce a single action, but if the action is one, the essence (*ousia*) is one also. Therefore, there has come to be one essence of the Logos and his instrumental means of activity.[17]

One of Apollinarius's more dramatic conclusions is that orthodox Christianity cannot call Christ a "human being" without careful qualification. "The human being who has come down from heaven is not, he says, a human being from earth; yet, though he came down from heaven, he *is* a human being, for in the Gospels the Lord does not repudiate this title."[18] He is the "Lordly human," the κυριακὸς ἄνθρωπος—a title welcomed by later writers in a variety of Christological traditions.[19] In a typically complex passage of his *Anakephalaiosis* or doctrinal "summary," Apollinarius first develops a chain of syllogisms, each leading to the provocative conclusion, "Christ is *not* a human being (*anthropos*)." In the second section, he goes on, in the same syllogistic style, to argue that he is "not a human being in whom God *dwells*," but that he is "God *and* a human being (Θεὸς καὶ ἄνθρωπος)." Finally, as if to resolve the conundrum, he argues by similar syllogisms that Christ is *not what each of us is*: "a human being joined to God (ἄνθρωπος Θεῷ παραζευχθείς)," which is probably the main point he had wished to make all along.[20] Christ's humanity, precisely in the way it is identified with God the Son, is *different* from the humanity all of us share.

Apollinarius explains his understanding of this "Lordly" humanity of Jesus in two principal ways. One was to insist, as is well known, that in Christ the Logos, the eternal and transcendent "mind" of God that rules and orders the universe, served as the νοῦς or rational mind—as the "governing part" or ἡγεμονικόν—of Jesus' humanity, and that therefore Jesus cannot have had a

---

unified "special energy of the whole" anticipates the "monenergist" position of Patriarch Sergius in the 630s and 640s.

[16] *On the Union in Christ* 8 (Lietzmann 188.9–12; Norris, 105); cf. Fragment 126 (Lietzmann 238.9–12; Norris, 111).

[17] Fragment 117 (Lietzmann 235.24–236.2; Norris, 110).

[18] Fragment 17 (Lietzmann 209.17–20; Norris, 108).

[19] The use of this phrase by others is first witnessed by Gregory of Nazianzus, Ep. 101.12. For the history of the phrase, see Aloys Grillmeier, *"Kyriakos anthropos*: Eine Studie zu einer christologischen Bezeichnung der Väterzeit," *Traditio* 33 (1979), 1–63 [= *Fragmente zur Christologie* (Freiburg: Herder, 1997), 152–214].

[20] *Anakephalaiosis* (Lietzmann 242.24–245.30).

human, created mind. Apollinarius seems to have been willing to concede that Jesus, like the rest of humanity, had a lower, animating soul—a ψυχή –which organized his sensory and vital functions; but he argues, in several places, that if there were a created intellectual mind in Christ, a fully active, free human center of knowing and willing, this created mind would either have been totally dominated by its union with the Logos, and thus would have lost its normal God-given role as the self-determining factor in the human composite, or else it would have been in constant conflict with the mind and will of God.[21] In Apollinarius's view, Christ acts as our Savior, as the new Adam of a God-centered race, first of all by being the one man whose unruly flesh and sense-faculties are ruled not by a weak and fallible created mind, but by the Logos himself. We are saved by contemplating and imitating him. He writes:

> If together with God, who is intellect, there was also a human intellect in Christ, then the work of the incarnation is not accomplished in him. But if the work of the incarnation is not accomplished in the self-moved and undetermined intellect, then this work, which is the destruction of sin, is accomplished in the flesh, which is moved from without and energized by the divine Intellect. The self-moved intellect within us shares in the destruction of sin, insofar as it assimilates itself to Christ.[22]

Second, Apollinarius seems to have so emphasized the intrinsic, dynamic unity of the divine mind with the living, fleshly body of Christ that he was understood by most of his contemporaries to have taught that the *flesh* of Christ is itself eternal, itself is in some way an integral part of "the man who came down from heaven" (John 3.13). So Apollinarius was understood to argue that Christ's flesh was not genuinely taken from Mary's human flesh, but only passed through her, as through a channel. In some extant passages of his works, it must be said, Apollinarius strenuously denies that the flesh of Christ is heavenly or eternal *of itself*, even though it is to be adored as "God's flesh."[23] Greer has suggested that Apollinarius may really have intended only to emphasize the mutual predicability of divine and human attributes in Christ— what later would be called the "communication of idioms"—as strongly as possible, and may have done so in dramatic, experimental language that was easily misunderstood, especially since he apparently neglected to mention that this union of attributes only came to be real in the course of created history. In any case, this was, certainly, the main charge levelled against the Apollinarian party in the late fourth century; so Athanasius, towards the end of his life, is

---

[21] See, for example, fragments 87 and 150 (Lietzmann 226 1–6 and 247.22–27; Norris 109–10).

[22] Fragment 74 (Lietzmann 222.6–12; Norris 109).

[23] Fragment 9 (Lietzmann 206.20–207.4; Norris 107f.). See also *Epistula ad Dionysium* 7 (Lietzmann 259.5–9); *Tomus Synodalis* (Lietzmann 262.27–263.4), both of which are apologetic works, intended to make the Apollinarian position acceptable to the wider Church.

sharply, if somewhat confusingly, critical of such a position in his *Letter to Epictetus*, although he does not mention Apollinarius by name;[24] and Gregory Nazianzen presents the eternity of Christ's human flesh as the central Apollinarian error:

> He [Apollinarius] asserts that the flesh, which the only-begotten Son assumed in the incarnation for the remodeling of our nature, was no new acquisition, but that that carnal nature was in the Son from the beginning....As though even before he came down, he was the Son of Man, and when he came down he brought with him that flesh, which it appears he had in heaven, as though it had existed before the ages and had been joined with his essence.[25]

In Apollinarius's version of Nicene Christology, as it developed, both the mind and the flesh of Christ have important soteriological implications. Christ's heavenly mind rules over his senses and his flesh, Apollinarius argued, delivering them from the possibility of sin and from the death that sin causes, as the mind is always intended to do. So "we, sharing in his right activity by faith, are saved and become heavenly *by likeness* with the heavenly man."[26] Beyond this union with Christ in faith, the fact that his very flesh is "heavenly flesh" also means that our sacramental appropriation of it in the Eucharist communicates nothing less than God's healing life to us:

> His flesh gives us life through the divinity which is united substantially with it; and what gives life is divine. It is divine flesh, then, because it is joined to God. And it saves, since we are saved by sharing in it as food...[27]

Although he is radically unlike us, then, in mind and even in flesh, Apollinarius's Christ was both a model of holiness, for our distant imitation, and a sacramental source of life.

## GREGORY OF NAZIANZUS

Once they had been made fully aware of the full dimensions of Apollinarius's picture of Christ—probably in the early 380s—Gregory of Nazianzus and his friend Gregory of Nyssa responded to it critically, with increasing clarity and energy. Gregory Nazianzen's classic attack on the views of Apollinarius, and on other troubling conceptions of the Savior, in his *First Letter to*

---

[24] *Epistula ad Epictetum* 2, 4f.
[25] Epistle 202, to Nectarius, 10–14 (SChr. 208.90–92), trans. Charles Gordon Browne and James Edward Swallow, repr. in Edward Rochie Hardy (ed.), *Christology of the Later Fathers*, Library of Christian Classics 3 (Philadelphia, PA: Westminster, 1954), 231 (altered).
[26] In Leontius of Byzantium, *Adversus Fraudes Apollinaristarum* 1.11 (emphasis mine).
[27] *Adversus Fraudes Apollinaristarum* 2.12.

*Cledonius*, is perhaps the polemic best remembered. Insisting that "*we*"—Nicene Christians—"do not sever the human being from the godhead," and pointing out that the saving, paradoxical union of the divine Son with our humanity is not eternal, but has taken place "in these last days for our salvation,"[28] Gregory focuses his argument, in the first two-thirds of his letter, on the importance of Christ's human mind (νοῦς) to the integrity of the Gospel message:

> If anyone has put his trust in him as a man without a human mind, he is really bereft of mind, and quite unworthy of salvation. For that which he has not assumed he has not healed; but that which is united to his Godhead is also saved.[29] If only half Adam fell, then that which Christ assumes and saves may be half also; but if the whole of his nature fell, it must be united to the whole nature of Him that was begotten, and so be saved as a whole. Let them not, then, begrudge us our complete salvation, or clothe the Savior only with bones and nerves and the likeness of humanity.... But, says such a one, the Godhead took the place of the human mind. How does this touch me? For Godhead joined to flesh alone is not a human being, nor to soul (ψυχή) alone, nor to both apart from mind (νοῦς), which is the most essential part of the human person. Keep, then, the whole human being, and mingle God with it, that you may benefit me in my completeness.[30]

It is worth noting that here, as in virtually all of his works, Gregory avoids the technical language of "substance" or "nature," "individual" or "hypostasis," which his colleagues Gregory of Nyssa and Basil of Caesaraea had endeavored, during the previous decade, to canonize with respect to the relationships of Father, Son, and Holy Spirit. Always self-consciously concerned with "realities" (πράγματα) rather than simply "terminology" (ὀνόματα),[31] but always

---

[28] Epistle 101.13 (SChr. 208.40–2; Hardy, 216). It is worth quoting the full passage (Ep. 101.13–15): "For we do not sever the human being from the Godhead, but we lay down as a dogma the unity and identity of the one who of old was not human but God, and the only Son before all ages, unmingled with body or anything corporeal; but who in these last days has assumed humanity also for our salvation; passible in his flesh, impassible in his Godhead; circumscribed in the body, uncircumscribed in the Spirit; at once earthly and heavenly, tangible and intangible, comprehensible and incomprehensible; that by one and the same, who was perfect human and also God, the entire humanity, fallen through sin, might be created anew." Gregory suggests that the Apollinarian affirmation of the eternal unity of a hybrid Christ implicitly lessens the central paradoxes that make the Mystery of salvation what it is.

[29] This phrase, a classic maxim in the development of the Orthodox understanding of Christ, was not entirely original with Gregory, but drew on a tradition of insisting that Christ saves us from our weakness and sin primarily by becoming "like us in all things but sin" (cf. Heb. 4.15). This principle is expressed in the early Church by Irenaeus, *Adv. Haer.* 5.14.1–2, and by Tertullian, *De carne Christi* 10 and *Adv. Marc.* 2.27. It is explicitly formulated by Origen in *Dialogue with Heracleides* 7 (SChr. 67.70.17–19), and later applied by Maximus the Confessor to the defense of Christ's two natural wills (Opusc. 9 [PG 91.128D–129A]), where Maximus explicitly cites Gregory of Nazianzus. See the excellent little article by Aloys Grillmeier, "Quod non assumptum—non sanatum," *LThK* (Freiburg: Herder, 1957– ) 8.954–6.

[30] Epistle 101.32–4, 36 (SChr. 208.50–2; Hardy, 218–19 [altered]).

[31] See Oration 32.20, 24 (SChr. 250.312–14, 320–2); Oration 39.13 (SChr. 358.172–6); for the same claim, see Gregory of Nyssa, *Catechetical Oration* 26 (SChr. 453.262–4).

first of all the rhetorician, Gregory prefers to use a narrative style, concrete images, and dazzling paradoxes[32]—sometimes even drawing simply on the resources of an inflected language—rather than abstract philosophical categories, to convey a sense of what is one and what is two in Christ, and how their coming-together in time is the source of our salvation: a fact often obscured by English translators eager to square his thought with Chalcedon.[33]

So for Gregory, Christ is "double": something revealed to us by his experiences, as Son of God, of human weakness. His "mission" from the Father, fulfilling the Father's good pleasure, explains his human coming, and even applies to his divine identity, "for he refers all that is his own back to him [the Father], and honors him as his timeless origin."[34] Gregory's favorite term for the unity of the divine and the human in Christ is "mixture"—in Greek, *krasis* or *mixis* and their various verbal cognates: a blending not of two equally powerful ingredients to make a third, but rather a blending in which an immeasurably more powerful agent penetrates, and so transforms, a weaker one. So in the third of his "Theological Orations" he sums up the mystery of the Incarnation in terms that would be for him characteristic:

> There was a time when the one who now seems contemptible to you was in fact above you: the one who is now human was in fact uncompounded. What he was, he remained; what he was not, he took on himself. In the beginning he was, without cause: for what can be a cause of God? But later he also came to be, for a cause: and that cause was that you, his calumniator, might be saved—you who think little of his divinity because he took on your coarseness, associating himself with flesh through the mediation of a mind; and the human being from our world became God, since he was mixed together with God, and became one subject— the stronger overcoming the weaker, so that to the degree that he has become human, I might become God.[35]

---

[32] For a highly original study of Gregory's way of conceiving the Mystery of Christ through reflection on the details of his own life—especially in his poems—see Andrew Hofer, OP, *Christ in the Life and Teachings of Gregory of Nazianzus* (Oxford: Oxford University Press, 2013).

[33] An example can be found in the standard Browne and Swallow translation of Gregory's Oration 38, *On the Theophany, or the Birthday of Christ*: where Gregory says, "Coming forth as God, along with that which he had assumed, he was one out of two opposed things, flesh and Spirit—the one of which divinized, the other was divinized," they translate: "He came forth then as God with that which he had assumed, one Person in two Natures, flesh and spirit, of which the latter deified the former" (13). Again later, at the start of chapter 15, Gregory writes: "He was sent, but as a human being—for he was twofold;" Browne and Swallow translate: "He was sent, but as man, for He was of a twofold Nature." Such subtle, doubtless unintentional dogmatic corrections distort Gregory's effort to speak in pastoral, non-technical terms—and to avoid some of the rising difficulties in defining and using technical language!

[34] Oration 38.15 (SChr. 358.138).     [35] Oration 29.19 (SChr. 250.216–18).

In the fourth oration, he uses similar language to explain the saying of the Letter to the Hebrews that Jesus "learned obedience through what he suffered" (Heb. 5.8):

> As Word, he was neither obedient nor disobedient...But as "the form of a servant," he stooped down to his fellow servants—who *were* servants—and took on a form foreign to himself, bearing me, with all that is mine, completely in himself, that in himself he might consume what is worse—like a fire consuming wax, or the sun a mist—and that I might receive, in return, what is his, as a result of the mixture (σύγκρασις).[36]

Gregory's talk of "mixture" in these two passages seems to be less an attempt to co-opt Stoic theories about the exchange of properties between two substances (as Grillmeier has suggested)[37] than a striking and concrete metaphor; like his language elsewhere about the exchange of "forms"—clearly an echo of Philippians 2—his purpose is to find a non-technical way to capture the paradoxical yet ontologically real encounter of two wholly unequal realms of being, which is the heart of the Christian message of the Incarnation. In a famous passage of his homily on the Nativity of Christ, Gregory can simply wonder:

> O new mixture! O paradoxical blending! The one who is comes to be, the uncreated is created, the uncontained contained, through the medium of a rational soul, which brings together divinity and coarse flesh. And the one who is rich becomes a beggar (II Cor. 8.9), for he beggars himself in my flesh that I might be rich with his Godhead. And the one who is full is becomes empty, for he "emptied himself" (Phil. 2. 7) of his own glory for a while, that I might share his fullness.[38]

In Gregory's highly personal, intensely emotional style, the soteriological purpose of the incarnation can never be put in simply objective terms; it is the story of what "my Jesus," "my Christ" has done,[39] the mystery of *my* salvation. It is a mystery still more wonderful than that of our first creation, by which God destined us for deification by letting us share in his image, because here God has humbled himself to share in our weakness:

> What are the riches of his goodness? What is this mystery concerning me? I had a share in the image, and did not preserve it; he shares in my flesh, so that he might both save the image and make the flesh immortal. He establishes

---

[36] Oration 30.6 (SChr. 250.236).     [37] *Christ in Christian Tradition* I, 368–9.
[38] Oration 38.13 (SChr. 358.134).
[39] See, for example, the beginning Gregory's Epiphany sermon, "On the Holy Lights" (Or. 39.1) (SChr. 358.150); also *Poemata Dogmatica* 32 (PG 37.511); *Poemata de seipso* 24 (PG 37.1286), 33 (PG 37.1305), etc.

a second communion, much more paradoxical than the first: then he gave a share in what is better, but now he takes a share in what is worse. This is more divine in form than the first communion; this, to those who have sense, is more lofty![40]

Like Irenaeus and Athanasius, Gregory Nazianzen strongly emphasizes the "communion," the κοινωνία, which the Incarnation of the Word establishes between God and humanity, as the fundamental purpose of both creation and redemption: *we* are meant to share in what God is. Like them, and Origen, too, he often emphasizes the saving effect simply of the Logos's manifestation of himself to our human contemplation, both in the person of Christ and in the Scriptures as interpreted through Christ: to reveal himself is to begin that communion. The "innovation" of the Incarnation, the newness of the coming of Christ, Gregory insists in his great Epiphany sermon, is "that the incomprehensible might be comprehended, conversing with us through the mediation of the flesh as through a veil."[41] Yet the communion is only achieved through paradox, the revealing presence of the Word in Jesus only known in the renewed yet fully normal humanity that is his.

To learn how to interpret the various things in the Scriptures that are said of Christ, to meditate on each event in the life of Jesus as something that involves us in his passage to life through the world of death, is a discipline that eventually will enable us to "look at and be looked at by God,"[42] to "ascend with his Godhead and no longer remain among visible things, but be raised up to the intelligible realm, and know what is said of his nature [as God], and what of his saving incarnation."[43] So at the end of his "Fourth Theological Oration," after briefly commenting on the various Scriptural titles (*epinoiai*) of Christ in good Origenistic fashion, Gregory concludes:

These are the titles of the Son. Walk through those of them that are lofty in a way befitting God, and through the bodily ones with compassion—or rather, walk through all of them divinely, so that you may become God, rising up from below through the one who for our sake came down from above.[44]

To know the full Mystery of Christ, "'the same yesterday and today' in bodily form, and spiritually 'for all ages',"[45] is already to share in what that Mystery promises.

---

[40] Oration 38.13 (SChr. 358.134). See also Oration 30.5 (SChr. 250.232–4), where Gregory explains the "submission" of Christ, famously referred to in I Cor. 15.28, and his obedience unto death on the cross, in terms of his identification of himself with us in our disobedience, turning it into obedience by his own actions.

[41] Oration 39.13 (SChr. 358.176).     [42] Oration 38.18 (SChr. 358.148).

[43] Oration 29.18 (SChr. 250.216).     [44] Oration 30.21 (SChr. 250.274).

[45] Oration 30.21 (SChr. 250.274), alluding to Hebrews 13.8.

## GREGORY OF NYSSA

As is true on most subjects, Gregory of Nyssa's approach to the person of Christ shows great similarities to that of his friend and namesake from Nazianzus: greater similarities in argument and basic understanding than their obvious differences in style and literary form might at first suggest. Gregory of Nyssa, too, when speaking of the Mystery of Christ's person and work, generally avoids the technical language of person and substance that he uses so prominently in some of his anti-Arian polemics;[46] although well acquainted with both the technical philosophy and the natural science of his day, he is, first of all, an accomplished rhetorician. Like his namesake and friend, as we shall see, he also tends to speak of the complex reality of Christ in the category of "mixture": God the Word "blending" himself inextricably and potently into the whole of our human composite, to overwhelm our weaknesses and suffuse them with his power. And Gregory of Nyssa understands the Incarnation as a *theophany*, a revelation of the life-giving glory of God in a form adapted to minds dulled by their preoccupation with mundane things; if everyone had the purity of heart Moses or Paul had, he remarks at one point, or the visionary qualities of the great Old Testament prophets, "there would be no need for the appearance of our God in the flesh."[47] For these two Cappadocians, as for much of the earlier Greek Christian tradition, the healing of what is infirm in the human condition is, to a great extent at least, the restoration of our ability to see and know God as he is.

Some of Gregory of Nyssa's most carefully developed reflection on the person of Christ appears in his polemical works against Apollinarius and his disciples: his brief letter critical of Apollinarian theology and propaganda in Palestine, written to three ascetical women there some time after Gregory's visit to Jerusalem in 379 (Epistle 3, listed in older editions as Epistle 17);[48] his letter to Theophilus, bishop of Alexandria, probably written shortly after 385, refuting Apollinarian charges that Gregory and his colleagues in Asia teach "a duality of Sons";[49] and his longer polemical treatise, the *Antirrhetikos* or *Refutation*, probably written in 387, which goes passage by passage through Apollinarius's own *Apodeixis*, his *Exposition of the Divine Incarnation in Human Likeness*.[50] In all of these works, Gregory insists that the one whom

---

[46] There are exceptions, however: note his discussion of whether Christ is or is not "of one substance" with other humans: *Antirrhetikos* (GNO III/1, 165.7–28).

[47] *Ad Theophilum* (GNO III/1, 124.7–9).

[48] GNO VIII/2.19–27, esp. chaps. 15–22 (pp. 23–6).          [49] GNO III/1, 119–28.

[50] GNO III/1, 131–233. For the chronology of Gregory's works—always a highly speculative business—see G. May, "Die Chronologie des Lebens und der Werke des Gregor von Nyssa," in M. Harl (ed.), *Écriture et culture philosophique dans la pensée de Grégoire de Nysse* (Leiden: Brill, 1971), 51–66. See also Pierre Maraval, "Chronology of Works," in L. F. Mateo-Seco and G. Maspero, *The Brill Dictionary of Gregory of Nyssa* (Leiden: Brill, 2010), 152–69.

God the Word "took up" was a "human being," an *anthropos*, and not merely vitally ensouled flesh; "if one removes the chief characteristic of the human person—namely, the mind," he argues in the *Antirrhetikos*, "one has shown that what remains is simply a beast of burden (κτῆνος), and a beast of burden is not a human being!"[51] In one passage in the same work, he even develops at some length an argument for two functioning *wills* in Christ, based on Jesus' prayer in Gethsemane, and concludes:

> Since, then the human faculty of will is one thing, and the divine another, he who has made our vulnerabilities his own speaks, from his role as a man (ὡς ἐκ τοῦ ἀνθρώπου), what befits the weakness of nature; but he adds a second voice, willing that the exalted, the godly will should prevail over the human, for the sake of human salvation.[52]

Here, without the terminological apparatus of the next three centuries, Gregory echoes the thought of his contemporary, Augustine, and anticipates the argument of Maximus Confessor and the Council of 681.

Clearly, though, Gregory is concerned with much more in his anti-Apollinarian argument than simply the question of Jesus' human mind. He is concerned with articulating the relationship between the divine Logos and a fully human Jesus in terms that will make it clear the incarnate Word is not simply a unique hybrid of divine mind and created body but a coming together, as one agent, of two utterly incommensurable, yet complete, living realities. In Christ, as Gregory conceives him, the one who is infinitely greater—God the Word—so makes a creature his own, that the creature is utterly transfigured, thereby beginning a process of transformation or divinization that is intended to be shared, ultimately, by every created intellect. It is in what one might call his "Christology of transformation" that Gregory of Nyssa develops his real reasons for rejecting the Christology of Apollinarius.[53]

The key to this Christology, perhaps, lies in the contrast Gregory often draws between the unchangeability of God, who always simply *is*, and the innate changeability of every creature, which is rooted in the created world's finitude and composition. One of the basic convictions Gregory admits to sharing with Apollinarius, in fact, is that Christian faith in the Incarnation proclaims precisely this contrast:

> Scripture says "the Word was made flesh" (John 1.14), and "glory has made its dwelling in our land," (Ps. 84.10), and "God has appeared in flesh" (I Tim. 3.16),

---

[51] GNO III/1, 165.26–8.     [52] GNO III/1, 181.18–23.

[53] See my articles, "Divine Transcendence and Human Transformation: Gregory of Nyssa's Anti-Apollinarian Christology," *Studia Patristica* 32 (Peeters: Leuven, 1997), 87–95 [= Sarah Coakley (ed.), *Re-Thinking Gregory of Nyssa* (Oxford: Blackwell, 2003), 67–76]; and "'Heavenly Man' and 'Eternal Christ': Apollinarius and Gregory of Nyssa on the Personal Identity of the Savior," *Journal of Early Christian Studies* 10 (2002), 469–88.

so that through each of these texts we might learn that the divine being, ever changeless and unvarying in essence, has come to be in a changeable and alterable nature, so that by his own unchangeability he might heal our tendency to change for the worse.[54]

In Gregory's theology, mutability is one of the defining aspects of created being: creatures are always *becoming*, always growing to be either more or less of what they are made to be; so he observes in the *Catechetical Oration*:

> Uncreated nature is incapable of the movement implied in mutability, change, and variation. But everything that depends upon creation for its existence has an innate tendency to change. For the very existence of creation had its origin in change, non-being becoming being by divine power.[55]

This, in turn, is the basis for Gregory's characteristic understanding of created perfection, especially the human moral and aesthetic perfection the Greek tradition had long assumed as the basic conception of virtue (ἀρετή). In Gregory's view, the virtue of creatures is a participation in the goodness of God, who "is himself absolute virtue."[56] As a result, the perfection of creatures is always a process of growth in this participation—a growth that never comes to an end, precisely because the finite can never completely possess the infinite. So Gregory challengingly writes, in his *Life of Moses*, that in creatures, "the one limit of virtue is the absence of limit."[57] This endless growth, in intelligent creatures, involves also the unquenchable desire for a greater share in the divine goodness; so Gregory remarks, in the prologue to his *Life of Moses*, "Perhaps, after all, the perfection of human nature is this: to be so disposed that one always wishes to have a greater share of the Good."[58]

This understanding of an endlessly expanding human perfection is, in Gregory's works, itself rooted in an ontology which conceives of created beings as composed simply of the sum of all their qualities, their ἰδιώματα. Unlike virtually all other early Christian thinkers, including Origen, Gregory completely rejected the Aristotelian notion of "prime matter," a continuing substratum in the reality of limited creatures, wholly without its own characteristics, which serves as the recipient of qualities that may come and go; although Gregory took over Origen's idea of a permanent "perceptible form" or εἶδος in material beings, which enables a thing to remain recognizable through all the changes it

---

[54] *Antirrhetikos* (GNO III/1, 133.4–9).

[55] *Catechetical Oration* 6 (GNO III/4, 24.3–6), trans. Cyril C. Richardson, in Hardy (ed.), *Christology of the Later Fathers*, 280. Cf. *Life of Moses* II, 2–3 (GNO VII/1, 33.19–34.14); *On Perfection* (GNO VIII/1, 213.1–214.6).

[56] *Life of Moses* I, 8 (GNO VII/1, 4.11–12); for the idea that "God is virtue," cf. *Hom. in Cant.* 9 (GNO VI, 285.17); *De Anima et Resurrectione* (GNO III/3.76.13–14; trans. Catherine Roth 86); *Contra Eunomium* III, 7.60–64 (GNO II, 236.10–237.18); *De Beatitudinibus* 4 (GNO VII/2, 122.12–19).

[57] *Life of Moses* I, 5 (GNO VII/1, 4.18).     [58] *Life of Moses* I, 10 (GNO VII/1, 5.2–4).

undergoes,[59] he saw this form simply as the sum total of the thing's characteristic properties, rather than as joined to a passive, formless principle of continuing identity.[60] As a result, in Gregory's view human change—including the unending change for the better that is his definition of perfection—is always understood to be simply *qualitative* change: the acquisition of some properties (ἰδιώματα) and the atrophy or deliberate alteration of others.

It is this metaphysics of change which underlies Gregory's distinctive Christology and soteriology. To refute the Apollinarians' charge that he and his colleagues preach "two Sons" in Christ by claiming he is both the divine Logos and a complete human being, Gregory invokes not the ontological categories of individual and substance, *hypostasis* and *ousia*, in which he and his colleagues had become accustomed to speak of the divine Persons, but argues rather in terms of qualitative change:

> If the divine, having come to be in the human, and the immortal, having come to be in the mortal—and the powerful in the weak, and the unchanging and incorruptible in the changeable and corruptible—had allowed the mortal to persist in a state of mortality or the corruptible to persist in corruption and the other qualities to remain in the same way as they were, one might justifiably see a duality in the Son of God, numbering each of the opposed aspects we recognize in him as something peculiar and independent. But if what is mortal, situated in the immortal one, has *become* immortality, and if the corruptible has similarly changed into incorruptibility, and all the other qualities, in the same way, have been transformed into what is free from passivity and divine, what argument will be left to those who want to divide what is one into dualistic distinction?[61]

Gregory's understanding of the Incarnation, in other words, is that in Christ, God has taken up a complete human being and made him his own, so that his human qualities might be thoroughly and ceaselessly *changed* into divine ones by the divine presence, and that this process of transformation might then radiate out from that one human individual into the entire human race: "he was mingled with a human being," Gregory writes in his *Antirrhetikos*, "and received our entire nature within himself, so that what is human (τὸ ἀνθρώπινον) might mingle with what is divine and be divinized with it, and that the

---

[59] See Origen, *On First Principles* 2.10.2; fragment of *Commentary on Psalm 5* quoted by Methodius (Epiphanius, *Panarion* 64.14.2–6).

[60] See Gregory of Nyssa, *De Hexaemeron* (PG 44.69 BC); *De Hominis Opificio* 24 (PG 44.212–213); *De Anima et Resurrectione* (PG 46.124.B9–D5; GNO III/3, 93, 1.14–94, 1.15); on the possibility of a continuing "perceptible form," see *De Hominis Opificio* 27.3. Origen affirmed the probable existence of prime matter, but denied that it is eternal: *De Principiis* 4.4.6–7; *Contra Celsum* 6.77; *De Oratione* 27.8. In Richard Sorabji's phrase, Gregory conceives of all material things as essentially "bundles of properties," thus anticipating the ontology of George Berkeley and the German idealists: see *Matter, Space and Motion* (Ithaca, NY: Cornell University Press, 1988), 520–55.

[61] *Ad Theophilum* (GNO III/1, 124.21–125.10).

whole mass of our nature might be made holy through that first-fruit."[62] The very inequality between God and the creature implies that their "mixture" is itself a one-sided process: God has taken up a whole human individual as his own, so that it might begin to lose all the corruptible characteristics that define the present state of humanity, and might take on the glorious characteristics of God. Because God and the creature remain always infinitely distant from each other, Gregory understands that this process of assimilation will never be complete—not even, presumably, in the transfigured humanity of Christ. So he writes to Theophilus of Alexandria:

> He who is always in the Father, and who always has the Father in himself and is united with him, is and will be as he was for all ages, and there neither was another Son beside him, nor has one come into being, nor shall there ever be one. But the first-fruits of the human nature which he has taken up, absorbed—one might say figuratively—by the omnipotent divinity like a drop of vinegar mingled in the boundless sea, exists in the Godhead, but not in its own proper characteristics. For a duality of Sons might consistently be presumed, if a nature of a different kind could be recognized by its own proper signs within the ineffable Godhead of the Son, so that the one element were weak or small or corruptible or transitory, while the other were powerful and great and incorruptible and eternal. But since all the traits we recognize in the mortal one we see transformed by the characteristics of the Godhead, and no difference of any kind can be perceived— for whatever one sees in the Son is Godhead, wisdom, power, holiness, freedom from passivity—how could one divide what is one into double significance, since no difference divides him numerically?[63]

This striking image for how divine and human are related in the incarnate Word has several important implications for Gregory's Christology. One is that if one defines "humanity" simply in terms of its recognizable characteristics, then the Son—who is always the "Christ," always anointed by the Spirit, and always "Lord" over creation—can authentically be called "human" and "fleshly" only during the time of his earthly life:

> We say that he is always the Christ, both before the economy and after it; but he is human neither before it nor after it, but only during the time of the economy. For the flesh, in its own proper characteristics, did not exist before the Virgin, nor after his ascent into heaven. "For even if we once knew Christ according to the flesh," Scripture says, "we no longer know him thus." (II Cor. 5.16)[64]

---

[62] *Antirrhetikos* (GNO III/1, 151.14–20).
[63] *Ad Theophilum* (GNO III/1, 126.14–127.10). The continuing operation of two distinct natures, recognized in the words and actions of the one Jesus, which Gregory identifies here as indicating "two Sons," is precisely what Pope Leo and the Chalcedonian formula, sixty years later, would insist on as central to orthodox Christology—and what would be rejected at that time as "Nestorian" by many devout Eastern Christians.
[64] *Antirrhetikos* 53 (GNO III/1, 222.25–223.1).

Second, Gregory insists that the growth attested to in the Gospel accounts of Jesus, and the gradual revelation of his divine power and identity to his disciples, should not be taken to imply that his own humanity was only gradually divinized, as ours are destined to be; since Jesus' humanity was always free from sin, it did not need to be healed in him, restored to its original condition, in the same way that it needs to be healed and restored in us.[65] Rather, the transformation of the human in Christ, of which one reads evidence in the Gospel, culminating in his resurrection from the tomb, is to be understood, in Gregory's view, as the gradual *revelation* of a dynamic presence which had been there from the beginning, like the element of fire present but hidden in a piece of wood (according to ancient physics), which only becomes perceivable when the wood is set ablaze by contact with an external source; so

> he who thought little of human shame, because he is Lord of glory, concealed, as it were, the flame of life within his bodily nature in the course of events (οἰκονομία) that led to death, but he enkindled it and fanned it into flame again by the power of his own divinity, warming the body that had died and so infusing that meagre first-fruit of our nature with the infinity of divine life, and made that, too, into the thing he himself was . . . , making everything that is religiously understood to be in God the Word also to be in the one assumed by the Word.[66]

Thirdly, Gregory understands the divine purpose of the Word's incarnation to be that of bringing about in all of us—the whole human "harvest," the entire "mass of dough" that will become with him one bread—the same transformation of our humanity which we now perceive in Christ. This transformation begins for us in the healing of weakness and sin, flowers in the virtues we develop by consciously imitating Christ, and will reach its fulfillment, as far as our bodily nature is concerned, in our own resurrection from the dead— although, as we have said, the transformation of our whole being in the image of Christ, in Gregory's view, will, because of our finitude, never reach completion.

At the end of his *Catechetical Oration*, Gregory considers at some length the steps or means by which this transformation normally begins for the Christian believer. The first, not surprisingly, is *baptism*: building his interpretation mainly upon Paul's treatment of baptism in the sixth chapter of Romans, Gregory sees in the rite's triple immersion an "imitation" (μίμησις) of the death of the Savior, the purpose of which, first in him and now in us, is "to refashion us once more by means of the resurrection into a sound creature, free from passion, pure and with no admixture of evil."[67] This sacramental

---

[65] Epistle 3.16–19 (GNO VIII/2, 24.6–25.8).
[66] *Contra Eunomium* III,3.68 (GNO II, 132.14–25).
[67] *Oratio Catechetica* 35 (SChr. 453.306.52–5; trans. Richardson, 315).

representation, plus the inner repentance required of the candidate for baptism, means the beginning of a new life assimilated to Christ, in growing freedom from sin and from the passions.[68] The second means of transformation, in Gregory's view, is the reception of the *Eucharist*, in which the body of the risen Christ becomes food for the baptized believer's nourishment: "For as the Apostle observes (I Cor. 5.6), a little yeast makes a whole lump of dough like itself. In the same way, when the body which God made immortal enters ours, it entirely transforms it into itself."[69] Third, Gregory emphasizes that neither of these sacramental encounters with Christ works its effect in us unless we are ourselves fully engaged by faith in receiving the grace of this transformation. The faith we profess in our baptismal creed is an expression of the free choice we each must make to have God as our Father, and so to be incorporated with the glorified Christ, through the action of the Spirit, into the life of the Trinity.[70] If the baptized Christian does not live this faith by leading a virtuous life, Gregory insists,

> if the washing has only affected the body, and the soul has failed to wash off the stains of passion, and the life after initiation is identical with that before, despite the boldness of my assertion I will say without shrinking that in such a case the water is only water, and the gift of the Holy Spirit is nowhere evident in the action ... If, then, you have received God and become his child, let your way of life testify to the God within you; make it clear who your Father is![71]

To be transformed as the human Jesus was, we must choose to live as he lived.

Gregory of Nyssa's strong emphasis on the inner, organic unity of Word and humanity in Christ, a unity in which the human is clearly both preserved and overwhelmed by the divine in such a way that God's life and goodness transform and suffuse Jesus' inner life and even his bodily characteristics, clearly bears many similarities to the Apollinarian Christology Gregory and his fellow Cappadocians opposed. Despite these similarities, however, there are at least four ways in which their Christology substantially differs from the Apollinarian approach.

1. One is in its underlying *soteriology*. For Apollinarius, Christ is always fundamentally different from us: not an ἄνθρωπος, not even one to whom God is closely joined[72]—"not a God-bearing man," as Gregory Nazianzen reports the Apollinarian slogan, "but a flesh-bearing God."[73] Salvation from sin, and from the disorders that follow in its wake, the Apollinarians argued, comes to the disciple either by following and

---

[68] *Oratio Catechetica* 35 (SChr. 453.312.117–24; trans. Richardson, 317).
[69] *Oratio Catechetica* 37 (SChr. 453. 316.21–6; trans. Richardson, 318).
[70] *Oratio Catechetica* 39 (SChr. 453.326.16–327.33; trans. Richardson, 321–2).
[71] *Oratio Catechetica* 40 (SChr. 453.332.22–334.36; trans. Richardson, 324).
[72] See above, p. 131 and n. 20.          [73] Ep. 102.18 (SChr. 208.80.3–4; Hardy, 227).

imitating Christ in faith,[74] or by being nourished by his life-giving flesh in the Eucharist;[75] yet in Apollinarius's approach they seem to leave the disciple still at some distance from the person of the Savior. Gregory of Nyssa, in contrast, emphasizes that the salvation worked by Christ is nothing less than a healing of humanity's ills from within, a transformation of our present mental and material nature in virtue and freedom modelled on that of the human Jesus, and a regeneration that will end for us, too, in resurrection and eternal, endlessly growing life. Because the human being taken up by the Word is exactly what we are, the divine overshadowing that gave Jesus' life its unique character is communicated to us, soul and body, "so that our salvation throughout every element may be perfect."[76]

2. Second, Gregory of Nyssa also differs from Apollinarius in his *anthropology*—his view of the human person. Rowan Greer has rightly observed, I think, that the anthropology implied in his understanding of Christ is considerably more optimistic than that of Apollinarius, who saw the human mind as naturally unstable, hopelessly enmeshed in passions, without the new model of the "man from heaven."[77] Gregory, as we have seen, regards change (τροπή) in all creatures—even radical changes such as birth and death—as natural and morally neutral, the basis for improvement as well as for decline.[78] Sin, he insists, is not proper to human nature at any stage, but is simply a defect in the condition nature, a kind of illness;[79] "If God is truly virtue," he observes in his *Catechetical Oration*, "there is nothing in the human constitution which is opposed to the principle of virtue."[80] And because created nature is limited in its power and duration, and the evil which creatures do thus limited as well, Gregory sees it as ontologically necessary that evil and sin will everywhere come to an end, and that God's healing action in Christ will lead to universal salvation.[81]

3. Gregory of Nyssa's Christology also differs significantly from that of Apollinarius in its *eschatological* orientation: in Gregory's Christ, a process of change has begun that will lead to the eternal transformation of human creatures, that points to eternal fulfillment. One of the weaknesses of

---

[74] Fragment 165 (Lietzmann 262.28–263.14).   [75] Fragment 116 (Lietzmann 235.8–17).
[76] Epistle 3.22 (GNO VIII/2.26.5–6).
[77] Greer, "The Man from Heaven", 172, with further references.
[78] See, for example, *Oratio catechetica* 6 and 16 (SChr. 453.176–8; 220–2); see also Jean Daniélou, *L'Être et le temps chez Grégoire de Nysse* (Leiden: Brill, 1970), 95–115.
[79] *Oratio catechetica* 7–8 (SChr. 453.182–92; 200); Epistle 3.17–18 (GNO VIII/2. 24.19–25.1).
[80] *Oratio catechetica* 15 (SChr. 453.220).
[81] *Oratio catechetica* 26 (SChr 453.262–4); *De anima et resurrectione* (GNO III/3.66.9–71.12); see Jean Daniélou, "Le comble du mal et l'eschatologie de S. Grégoire de Nysse," in E. Iserloh and P. Manns (eds), *Festgabe Joseph Lortz* 2 (Baden-Baden: Bruno Grimm, 1958), 27–45.

Apollinarius's portrait of Christ—as Rowan Greer has observed—is its peculiarly *timeless* quality:[82] he seems to have conceived the Son's role as "new Adam" for the human race as an eternal characteristic, as part of the Son's personal constitution, and so was suspected of holding that even Christ's flesh "came down from heaven." Apollinarius, in turn, criticized his opponents—probably including, in the end, Gregory himself—of holding too ethereal, too bodiless a notion of the Lord's glorified state: "if after the resurrection he has become God and is no longer human," Apollinarius asked, "how will the Son of Man send out his angels? And how shall we see the Son of Man coming on the clouds?"[83] This concrete, rather literal way of imagining the eternally embodied Christ and his coming parousia may be one of the reasons the Apollinarians were charged, in several contemporary sources, with having millenarian expectations.[84] In any case, Gregory responds disdainfully that the Apollinarians have a "low, stunted notion of God," imagining that the Lord still has "hair and nails, a physical shape and a circumscribed bulk."[85] Unlike even Gregory of Nazianzus, who believed that Christ would come again in a visible, if spiritualized body, "such as he was seen by his disciples on the Mount,"[86] Gregory of Nyssa seems to have understood the final state of both Christ and the believer as something completely beyond our present categories of sense and thought, and to have seen movement towards such a state as central to God's plan of salvation.[87]

4. Perhaps Gregory of Nyssa's greatest difference from Apollinarius, however, is in the *theology*, the conception of God, that each of their portraits of Christ presupposes. For Apollinarius, the divine Logos is clearly a supremely powerful, supremely holy mind, which gives to the flesh of the new Adam the vitality and the moral direction it needs to become for us all a source of life and teaching, an example of redemption. For Gregory, however, who always tends to emphasize the ineffable side of our

---

[82] Greer, "The Man from Heaven", 171.

[83] Quoted by Gregory of Nyssa, *Antirrhetikos* (GNO 3.228.18–22).

[84] See Gregory of Nyssa, Epistle 3.24 ((GNO VIII/2.26.20–5); Gregory of Nazianzus, Ep. 101.63–4 (S Chr. 208.64); Ep. 102,14 (S Chr. 208.76); Basil of Caesaraea, Ep. 263.4 (ed. Y. Courtonne [Paris: Belles Lettres, 1966], 124–5; 265.2 (Courtonne, 128–31); Epiphanius of Salamis, *Panarion* 77.36–8 (GCS 37.448–51). For further references, see my *Hope of the Early Church* (Cambridge: Cambridge University Press, 1991), 80.

[85] *Antirrhetikos* 228.26–229.1.

[86] Ep. 101.29 (SChr. 208.48; Hardy, 218); cf. Oration 40.45 (SChr. 358.306): Christ will come again as judge, "no longer flesh, yet not without a body, according to the laws which he alone knows of a more godlike body, that he may both be seen by those who pierced Him, and may remain as God without material coarseness."

[87] See the final section of his dialogue *On the Soul and the Resurrection* (GNO III/3, 111.16–123.16).

experience of God, and to speak of God in apophatic or negative terms,[88] stressing God's transcendence over all limited, intelligible categories, any suggestion of limit or circumscription in the Incarnation—even the active circumscription of a mind by a body—is impious.

> For if human nature receives, indifferently, either our kind of mind or God in place of a mind, these must be of equal proportions and equal weight with each other—if a mind is received within the same one in whom divinity, too, could be contained. If someone should measure out wheat or some other seed in an empty pail, for instance, we would not say that what bulks equally large in the same container differs in quantity from the other; for one variety of wheat is equal to the other, whenever one kind of seed is emptied from the pail, only to have the other take its place. So then if the Godhead comes to take the place of the mind, one would not be able to say that the Godhead surpasses the mind, since the latter and the former can be received by nature in the same way. Either, then, the mind is equal to the Godhead, as Apollinarius wants to say, and [the Word] was not changed when moving from one role to the other; or, if the mind is inferior in comparison with the divine, then the one who came to be the former from being the latter has undergone a change to a less valuable status.[89]

If God truly transcends all created categories, God's "owning" a human individual, for our salvation, cannot be conceived in terms of the presence of a divine mind in a material, living body; it is a relationship of two realities far more unequal than simply spirit and matter as we know them—a relationship that can be recognized through its effect on the human creature who has been so taken up and transformed, and eventually through its effect on the rest of the human family, but not described in more definite terms. Apollinarius's conception of Christ, from Gregory's perspective, imagines the relation of the divine and the human far too clearly to do justice to the transcendent reality of God.[90]

---

[88] See, for example, *Life of Moses* II, 234–5 (SChr. 1bis.102); Homilies on Ecclesiastes 7–8 (SChr. 416.374–86); Homilies on the Beatitudes 6 (GNO VII/2. 136–48).

[89] *Antirrhetikos* 50 (GNO III/1, 227.23–228.7). Cf. *Antirrhetikos* 18 (156.26–157.9); 35 (185.7–10).

[90] One might compare with Gregory's criticism on this point the indignant report Gregory of Nazianzus to his successor at Constantinople, bishop Nectarius, in which he accuses the Apollinarians of teaching that the Son's "carnal nature was from the beginning," that the Godhead "fulfills the function of mind" in the "man from heaven," and—"most terrible of all"—that "the only-begotten God, the judge of all, the prince of life, the destroyer of death, is mortal, and underwent the Passion in his proper Godhead" (Ep. 202.15–16 [SChr 208.90–2]). However exaggerated such a representation of Apollinarius's real Christological intentions may be, Gregory of Nazianzus is objecting to what he sees as implied in the Apollinarian model: that God the Son has been deprived of his transcendence in the effort to give too clear a picture of his union with the human Jesus.

## CONCLUSION

The Christology of Gregory of Nazianzus and Gregory of Nyssa, as each developed it in response to the Apollinarian model, has never been easy to fit into the story of a developing conception of Christ relentlessly zig-zagging towards Chalcedon. The historian of doctrine Joseph Tixeront, early in the last century, for instance, was puzzled by the fact that Gregory of Nyssa sometimes sounds like a Nestorian, speaking as if there were two "persons" in Christ, while at other times he shows disturbingly "monophysite" tendencies.[91] In Tixeront's view, these "obscurities" are symptoms of the fourth century's need for greater conceptual precision, "in order to bring the Christological problem to a perfectly satisfactory and definite solution"[92]—something Tixeront apparently takes to have been achieved in the Chalcedonian formula. Grillmeier, too, taxes both Gregories with "insufficient definition of the relationship between substance and hypostasis (*prosopon*)," and with continuing to use "material categories" such as "mixture," rather than consistently employing the terms in which they themselves had analyzed Trinitarian relations.[93] J. N. D. Kelly recognizes many positive features of their works against Apollinarius, but criticizes Gregory of Nazianzus, especially, for failing to "make adequate use" of the human mind of Christ in interpreting Gospel reports of his suffering, ignorance and fear.[94]

Fair as these criticisms may be from the standpoint of what was to become the classical Christology of the West, they seem largely beside the point when one reads the works of these two fourth-century theologians as expressions of what they considered most important in Jesus Christ. For all their philosophical sophistication, both of them remained profoundly suspicious of the power of analytical formulas and technical terminology to express the genuine concerns of theological language. Both of them were preachers, letter-writers, rhetoricians, even (in Gregory Nazianzen's case) poets, rather than "scholastics" in the mold of Aëtius or Eunomius; their purpose in using words was to bring about *change* in those who heard or read them. For both of them, the Incarnation meant change, too—the beginning of something utterly new, utterly crucial in human history: a kind of unparalleled divine rhetoric addressed to created history. It was the coming of the eternal, transcendent Word of God among us, as the "man-bearing God,"[95] in order to begin—by the unresolved paradox of his "double" being, by his

---

[91] *Histoire des dogmes dans l'antiquité chrétienne* II (Paris: Lecoffre, 1912), 128; English translation: *History of Dogmas* II (St. Louis, MO: Herder, 1914), 127.

[92] *Histoire des dogmes*, 130 (Eng. trans. 129f.); cf. 126 (Eng. trans. 126).

[93] *Christ in Christian Tradition* I, 369.

[94] *Early Christian Doctrines* (5th edn; London: A. and C. Black, 1977), 298.

[95] Gregory of Nazianzus, Ep. 102.18–20 (SChr. 208.80).

"strange conjunction"[96]—a new "communion"[97] of God and humanity in all their incommensurability. This communion marked the beginning of transformation for all humanity, first in Jesus but ultimately in all of us, and a promise that the future course of this communion would lead to our endless immersion into the Mystery of God.

Both Gregories used the story of Moses' ascent up Mount Sinai as a metaphor for the human mind's urgent, driving desire to be in touch with God. Both interpreted the grace given Moses, to "see the back parts of God," as an expression of the only kind of knowledge available to creatures: not to see God "face to face," as he is in his own transcendent nature, but to glimpse the traces he has left behind in the created world (so Gregory Nazianzen),[98] and to follow him as one who is always ahead of us, always eludes our intellectual grasp (so Gregory of Nyssa).[99] For both of them, it was significant that when God reveals his glory to Moses on the mountain, in Exodus 33–34, he places him "in a cleft of the rock," where Moses can find shelter from annihilation while God passes by: as Paul writes in I Corinthians 10.4, after all, "the Rock was Christ." For Gregory of Nazianzus, the humanity of Christ was shelter, a protective veil that allowed us to know enough of the reality of God to find life, but shielded us from the overpowering light of the Godhead, and from the destructive effects of wanting to know more about God than can be known.[100] For Gregory of Nyssa, it was also the rock on which we can find a secure foothold in our unending ascent towards God, the solidity of "perfect virtue" revealed in human form: "For since Christ is understood by Paul as the Rock, and since all hope of good things is believed to lie in Christ, in whom, as we have learned, 'all the treasures of good are hidden' (Col. 2.3), whoever shares in any good thing is surely in Christ, who holds all good together."[101] Knowing Christ, in the category-shattering paradox of his person, was for the Cappadocians a kind of constant initiation into the healing, transforming presence of a God who is utterly beyond knowledge, but whose very nearness in Christ, our Good, is the Mystery that saves us.

---

[96] See Gregory of Nazianzus, Oration 38.13 (SChr. 358.134); see Oration 38.15 (SChr. 358.140).

[97] Oration 38.13 (SChr. 358.134).     [98] Oration 28.3 (SChr. 250.104–6).

[99] *Life of Moses* II, 221–39 (SChr. bis.103–9).     [100] See Oration 39.13 (SChr. 358.176).

[101] *Life of Moses* II, 248 (SChr. 1bis.112).

# 6

---

# Augustine of Hippo

## Christology as the "Way"

Perhaps the most remarkable thing about St. Augustine's Christology is that it seems, at least to a modern reader, so unremarkable. In other areas of theology, after all, the Augustine most of us immediately think of is Augustine the controversialist: Augustine debating with representatives of the old Roman aristocracy about the role of religion, pagan and Christian, in Roman history, or with representatives of the classical philosophic tradition about human certainty, human freedom, and the ways of purifying the soul from guilt and leading it to contact with the divine; Augustine refuting the Manichean understanding of the substantial character of evil and the materiality of God; Augustine arguing for a conception of the Christian Church as a worldwide community united by love and mutual forbearance, and for the unrepeatability of baptism, against Donatist regionalism and exclusivism; Augustine defending the now-normative conception of God as a Trinity of equal persons in a single transcendent substance, against various forms of Arian theology, whose voice still echoed in the West; Augustine engaging in a long, increasingly complex debate with Pelagius and his disciples on the relative weight to be assigned God's initiative and ours in the process of human salvation and sanctification. From Augustine's enormously productive pen, theological arguments and positions were produced in these and other debates which have become classical in Western Christian thought, setting the agenda for theological reflection not only in the late antique world but in the medieval schools, the Churches of the Reformation era, and even in the twenty-first century. Yet Augustine is not generally thought of as one of the formative thinkers in the development of Christology: above all, perhaps, because the controversy over the structure and unity of Christ's person, which for many modern readers was definitively resolved at Chalcedon a little over twenty years after Augustine's death, was one of the few doctrinal debates of early Christianity in which he took almost no direct part. Apollinarianism had been included in the list of canonical heresies by the Council of Constantinople in 381, six and a half years before Augustine's baptism, and the war of words over Christ's personal unity between Cyril of Alexandria and Nestorius of Constantinople was just coming to a boil while Augustine lay dying in Hippo, in the summer of 430. From the perspective of the history of Christian dogma, in which so many of our modern theological assumptions are formed, Augustine's role in the formation of orthodox Christology seems uncharacteristically marginal.

This judgment of modern scholarship is all the more strange, however, when one recognizes that Augustine's thought, on almost every major theological subject, is strikingly and explicitly centered on Christ: his understanding of God as Trinity, his conception of the relation of God's grace to human freedom, his view of the Church and its sacraments as constituting a single, trans-historical "person" with him, his approach to the interior struggles of our present life—all take their point of departure from his understanding of the unique identity and role of Christ in created history, as God's Word made flesh. And although Augustine had relatively little to say on the major Christological controversies that historically framed his own life as a theologian, rich and moving reflections on Christ himself appear, often somewhat unpredictably, in the midst of other discussions: usually couched in terms that sound so classical, so balanced and well-rounded, so orthodox, that one tends to forget they were written twenty to forty years before Leo's *Tome* and the Chalcedonian formula.

## AUGUSTINE'S VIEW OF THE PERSON OF CHRIST

Many of Augustine's allusions to Christ are deliberately phrased, it seems, to bring out the central paradox of Christ's person, as the Christian tradition proclaims it, and to do this by rhetorical means rather than technical terminology.[1] In many of his works, particularly earlier writings, Christ is referred to simply as "the man-God" (*homo Deus*) or "the God-man" (*Deus homo*). In a homily on Psalm 56, probably delivered while he was still a presbyter at Hippo in 393 or 394, Augustine sums up the Mystery of the Incarnation in terms so simple they defy elegant translation:

> The Word took up a complete human being, and the complete human being was made the Word...So a soul was there, flesh was there, a whole human being was there; and the whole human being was with the Word, and the Word with a

[1] For a list of such phrases, see Tarcisius J. Van Bavel, *Recherches sur la christologie de saint Augustin*, Paradosis 10 (Fribourg: Éditions universitaires, 1954), 41–4. Although Van Bavel's work is constructed along conceptually scholastic lines, it remains the most ample, accurate, and thoroughly documented modern study of Augustine's Christology, and is still an invaluable guide to any study of the subject.

human being, and the human being and the Word were one human being, and
the Word and the human being were one God."[2]

In the *Enchiridion*, Augustine's catechetical "handbook" on the essential
contents of Christian faith, hope and charity, written for an inquirer named
Laurentius almost thirty years later, in the early 420s, we find similar language;
commenting on Philippians 2.6–7, the crucial Pauline text on the divine self-
emptying of the Incarnation, Augustine writes:

> In this way he was made less, yet remained equal, one being now both, as
> Scripture says. But one thing is said because of the Word, the other because of
> the human being: because of the Word, he is equal to the Father, because of the
> human being, he is less. There is one Son of God, and the same one is Son of Man;
> there is one Son of Man, and the same one is Son of God. There are not two Sons
> of God, one divine and one human, but one Son of God—God without beginning,
> human from a definite beginning—our Lord Jesus Christ![3]

One could multiply examples of such balanced, almost incantatory language
about the Mystery of Christ, from every period of Augustine's life: it seems
simply to have been the way in which, rhetor that he was, he preferred to
meditate out loud on the asymmetrical, irreducible paradox of the Incarnation.

This very balance of language, of course, also reveals Augustine's expressly
balanced understanding of who and what Jesus is, despite the radical dominance of God in him: he is *complete* both as a divine and a human being. So, to
use Grillmeier's term, the soul of Christ *is* very definitely a "theological factor"
in Augustine's Christology. Augustine explains, in an important passage in
Book VII of the *Confessions* to which we will return shortly, that even in the
days before his baptism, when he was a skeptical ex-Manichee looking for
reasons to draw closer to the Church of his origins, he took it for granted that
Jesus had a human soul and mind as well as a human body, simply because
Jesus underwent the physical and emotional changes that could only be
explained by his full sharing in our composite human structure. At the same
time, he suggests here, one of the barriers to his accepting the Catholic faith
was that both he and his friend Alypius had the impression that the normative
Catholic position was a strong "word-flesh" Christology (to borrow Grillmeier's term), similar to that of Apollinarius, which effectively excluded a human

---

[2] *Enarratio in Psalmum* 56.5 (CCL 39.698). The exact date of this sermon is uncertain. The
chronology of Augustine's works, in fact, like that of all Patristic writings, remains conjectural,
although in his case it is founded on such external criteria as Possidius of Calama's biography of
Augustine, and on his own *Retractationes*. Because Augustine's thought develops so markedly, in
many respects, throughout his long career, I have included the possible or probable dates of his
works in square brackets after citations, where possible. These dates are based on the summary
lists in Allan Fitzgerald (ed.), *Augustine through the Ages: An Encyclopedia* (Grand Rapids, MI:
Eerdmans, 1999), xliii–il.

[3] *Enchiridion ad Laurentium de fide, spe et caritate* 35 [421–2].

mind in Christ—a position both of them found unacceptable. Only later did they discover that the Catholic Church of both East and West also considered the Apollinarian model unacceptable, including Apollinarius among the heretics at the Council of 381, a few years before their baptism.

Augustine himself, drawing on the Neoplatonic tradition, generally assumed that the rational soul or *mens*, in every human being, is a complete spiritual substance: physically not localized in any part of the body or identified simply as a bodily function, but giving the whole human being life and direction; he also identified this *mind*, in its psychological totality, as the "inner self" of every individual. "The human person," Augustine wrote in one of his earliest works, "is a rational soul using a mortal and earthly body."[4] It is understandable, then, that Augustine assumed, throughout his career—as Origen and Origen's followers had—that the human mind of Christ, as a superior intellectual being, was the connecting link between the transcendent divine Logos and his human, historical body—even though Augustine's reasons for assuming this were somewhat different from Origen's. As he wrote to the young pagan aristocrat Volusianus in 412, in a letter that is in fact one of Augustine's few documents devoted almost exclusively to the person and work of Christ,

> the combining of two immaterial realities ought to be easier to believe in than the combination of one that is immaterial with another that is material. Unless the soul is mistaken in its understanding of its own nature, it is immaterial; much more immaterial is God's Word. Therefore the combining of God's Word with a human soul ought to be more believable than the combining of a soul and a body.[5]

Throughout his career, too, Augustine continued to conceive of the death of Christ as the separation of his soul, united inseparably to the divine Logos, from his human body: "What more could his passion and death do," he asks in one of his sermons on John's Gospel, "than separate the body from the soul? It did not separate the soul from the Word."[6] Like the Apollinarians and (later)

---

[4] *De moribus ecclesiae Catholicae et de moribus Manichaeorum* 1.27.52 [387–9] (PL 32.1332). Augustine would later describe the human composite in a more complex and ontologically balanced way; see, for instance, *Confessions* 10.6.9: "Then I turned towards myself and asked, 'Who are you?' And I answered my own question: 'A human being.' See, here are the body and soul that make up myself, the one outward and the other within" (trans. Maria Boulding; London: Hodder and Stoughton, 1997; 243 [altered]). For Augustine's understanding of the soul, see especially Ernest Fortin, *Christianisme et culture philosophique au cinquième siècle: La querelle de l'âme en Occident* (Paris: Études Augustiniennes, 1959).

[5] Epistle 137, to Volusianus, 11 [412].

[6] *In Joannis Evangelium Tractatus* 47.10 [413]; see also Sermo Denis 5.1 (*Miscellanea Augustiniana* 1.26); *Contra Faustum* 12.35 [397–8]; Ep. 164.5.14 [c.414]; and see Leporius, *Libellus emendationis* 9, ll. 35–46 (CCL 64.121), a document from about 418, which, as we shall see, received Augustine's approval and was probably composed with his help.

Cyril of Alexandria—although doubtless apart from their influence—Augustine, in fact, came to use the commonly accepted understanding of the soul's relationship to its body as the most convenient model for explaining the non-spatial, all-pervasive, dominant relationship of God the Word to the human being he had made his own; so in a sermon on John's Gospel from about 413, he writes:

> The Son of Man has a soul and has a body. The Son of God—that is, God's Word—has a human being in the way a soul has a body. Just as a soul in possession of a body does not make two persons, but one human being, so the Word in possession of a human being does not make two persons, but one Christ.[7]

And just as the soul is the core of the body's life and continuing existence, the Word—who for each of us, in Augustine's terms, is meant to be "the life of the life of my soul"—is most properly the "true life" of the human Jesus.[8]

Another point in which Augustine's understanding of the person of Christ undoubtedly anticipated the later, Chalcedonian portrait is his gradual, if limited, adoption of the language of "substance" and "person," in his mature writings, to refer, respectively, to what is double and what is single in him. In his earlier works, Augustine tends to use the term *persona*, especially in exegetical contexts, in what one might today call a functional rather than a metaphysical sense—a sense derived, perhaps, from the word's earlier association with the theatre and the law-court: to signify the outward "role" assumed by a speaker, especially in the biblical narrative. So David, in composing the Psalms, sometimes speaks "from the person of the Lord" (*ex persona Domini*), Augustine observes, and sometimes "from his own person" (*ex persona sua* or *ex persona Prophetae*);[9] but when the Psalmist, "from the person of Christ," exclaims about God, "he sent from heaven and saved me" (Ps. 56.5), "he—Christ—is now speaking from the person of the one praying, from the person of humanity, from the person of the flesh."[10] The "person" in all these cases is really a voice, a character in the drama of humanity's complex relationship to God. In his early treatise *On the Christian Struggle* [396], Augustine remarks that "it is one thing simply to become wise through the Wisdom of God,

---

[7] *In Jo. Ev. Tr.* 19.15 [413]; Ep. 137.8.

[8] Sermon Denis 5.7 (*Misc. Aug.* 1.28); on God as the "true life" of every soul, see, e.g., *De libero arbitrio* 2.16.41.163 [388–95]; *Conf.* 7.1.2; 10.6.10; 10.17.26; *De civ. Dei* 19.26 [425].

[9] *Enar. in Ps.* 56.13 [393–4?]. Although we do not usually speak in English of acting "from the person" of anyone, this literal translation of the Latin phrase *ex persona* seems better to grasp the ancient assumption about what playing a role implied: taking on a position or starting-point, in some transaction, which is not actually one's own.

[10] *Enar. in Ps.* 56.8: "ex persona precantis, ex persona hominis, ex persona carnis dicit." For a thorough and carefully nuanced study of the "voices" Augustine hears in the Psalms, as they are sung and prayed by the Church "which is his body," see especially Michael Fiedrowicz, *Psalmus Vox Totius Christi: Studien zu Augustins "Enarrationes in Psalmos"* (Freiburg: Herder, 1997).

but another thing to carry out the very role of God's Wisdom (*ipsam personam sustinere Sapientiae Dei*)," as Christ did.[11]

Hubertus Drobner has argued convincingly, however, that Augustine's use of the language of "person" and "substance" or "nature"—language that had been current in the Latin theological vocabulary since Tertullian for speaking of the specific roles of Father, Son, and Holy Spirit in sacred history—began to take on a more technical, ontological coloring about 412, with his letter to Volusianus (Ep. 137), which we have already mentioned.[12] Here, for the first time, Augustine depicts the unique, world-transforming event of the Incarnation in terms that would sound familiar to the later dogmatic tradition:

> Now a "Mediator between God and humanity" (I Tim. 2.5) has appeared, such that he might join both natures in the unity of a person, and raise up the ordinary by extraordinary things, and moderate the extraordinary by the ordinary ... For as soul is joined to body in the unity of a person, so that a human being might result, so God is united to a human being, that Christ might be the result. In the one person, there is a mixture of soul and body; in this person there is a mixture of God and a human being.[13]

It is clear, on the one hand, that Augustine uses this philosophical and anthropological vocabulary more and more frequently during the last two decades of his life; but on the other hand, he never precisely defines the ontological criteria regulating his use of "person" and "nature" with reference to Christ. Rather, he seems to use them in a kind of dialectical pattern that suggests by "natures" the very different, incommensurate ontological and dynamic realities which have come together in Jesus, and by "person" the unified, acting individual encompassing them—clearly the Word of God— through whom both those incomparable realities are encountered together. So in his little treatise *Against an Arian Pamphlet*, written in 418 or 419 as a critical analysis of a Latin "Homoean" manifesto he has received from a friend, Augustine writes of the effect of this "personal" union of divergent realities on the way we speak of Christ, an effect that in later Christology is often referred to as "an exchange of characteristics (*communicatio idiomatum*)":

> Through this unity of "person," understood to be in both natures, the Son of Man is said to have 'come down from heaven' (John 3.13), although he has been taken up from the Virgin who lived on earth; and the Son of God is said to have been

---

[11] *De agone Christiano* 20.22 (CSEL 41, 122) [396]. See also the *Exposition of the Letter to the Galatians* 27 [394–5], where Augustine remarks that unlike the rest of us, who only participate in the divine Wisdom, Christ is suited "by the unique and surpassingly powerful way in which he [= the man Jesus] was assumed, naturally to *have* and to *play the role of* Wisdom (*ad habendam naturaliter et agendam personam Sapientiae*)" (PG 35.2125.5–7).

[12] See Hubertus Drobner, *Person-exegese und Christologie bei Augustinus: zur Herkunft der Formel "Una Persona"* (Leiden: Brill, 1986).

[13] Ep. 137.9, 11 (PG 33.519–20) [411–12].

crucified and buried (cf. Mark 15.39; I Cor. 2.8), although he suffered these things
not in that divinity by which he is the Only Son, co-eternal with the Father, but in
the weakness of human nature ... The holy Apostle shows that this unity of the
"person" of Christ Jesus our Lord is so joined together from both natures—that is,
from the divine and the human—that each of them can apply its own nomen-
clature to the other: the divine to the human, and the human to the divine.[14]

In this style of his Christological vocabulary, Augustine clearly anticipates the
language of Chalcedon, and even the later "scholastic" tradition of East
and West.


## AUGUSTINE AND LEPORIUS

Besides a brief early critique of the Apollinarian conception of Christ, in his
*Eighty-three Different Questions* [395],[15] however, Augustine's one foray into
the thick of contemporary Christian controversy over the structure of Christ's
person was at best an indirect one. Around 418, a monk named Leporius, with
two companions, arrived in Africa from southern Gaul, where they seem to
have been excommunicated by their local bishop for defending, in writing,
what were thought to be inadequate opinions on who Christ really was—
opinions now lost to us. After conversations with Augustine, however, Leporius had apparently been led to see the error of his position, and with his
companions signed a lengthy profession of faith, witnessed by Augustine and
three other African bishops, who sent him home with a covering letter to
vouch for the sincerity of his self-correction.

Leporius's original difficulty seems to have been essentially a philosophical
scruple about the Christian notion of a genuinely incarnate God—a scruple
shared at the time by a number of Greek theologians who belonged to what we
know today as "the school of Antioch." This was, in fact, a concern that seems
to have been Augustine's own, in his pre-Catholic years, but one which came
to represent for him the main criterion for distinguishing a simply rational or
philosophical view of God from genuine Christian faith. Leporius, Augustine
explains in his covering letter, "denied that God had been *made* a human
being, lest change or corruption unworthily attach itself to the divine substance, by which the Son is equal to the Father."[16] As a result, Leporius had
argued that Christ was simply an inspired and exalted human, a person
distinct from the divine Son; so he suggested that Jesus was "a man born
with God," not realizing that one implication of such a view would be to

---

[14]  *Contra sermonem Arianorum* 8 (PL 42.688) [419].
[15]  *De diversis quaestionibus LXXXIII*, quaest. 80 [probably c.395] (CCL 44A, 232–8).
[16]  Augustine, Ep. 219 [426] (CCL 64.104).

introduce a fourth "person" into the Trinity, after the ascension and exaltation of this same Jesus.[17] Augustine characterizes Leporius's position as representing, in his lapidary phrase, "a devout concern, but a careless mistake" (*pius timor, sed incautus error*): "he piously saw that the divinity cannot change, but he carelessly assumed that the Son of Man can be separated from the Son of God, so that one is one subject and the other another, and either that one of them is *not* Christ or that Christ is two subjects!"[18]

Leporius's profession of faith, creedal in form but showing many similarities in content to Augustine's own mature discussions of Christology, develops at some length the inescapable paradox that Augustine had already come to put forward, in sermons and in his *Confessions*, as the central proclamation of Christian faith:

> Therefore we confess that our Lord and God Jesus Christ, the only Son of God, who was born of the Father before the ages, in most recent time has been made human from the Holy Spirit and Mary, ever a virgin, and as God has been born; and confessing both substances, that of flesh and that of the Word, we accept with the reverent readiness of faith that one and the same has been born, inseparably, as both God and a human being. From the time of his taking up of the flesh, we say, everything that belonged to God has now passed over into the human being, in such a way that all that belonged to the human might come to God.[19]

The "mixture" that results from the Incarnation is not to be thought of as mere conflation, nor as a combination of equal ingredients into a new whole that is both at once, but neither completely. As Gregory of Nyssa, too, had recognized, the person of Christ is always a highly asymmetrical synthesis: "through the merciful outpouring of his power," Leporius confesses, "God has mingled with human nature, but human nature has not mingled itself with the divine. The flesh, therefore, advances towards the Word; the Word does not advance towards the flesh."[20] The initiative, the origin of the movement that saves us, lies wholly with God. And the result is not a generic union of divinity and humanity, but something unique, individual, and so (in our modern sense) personal: a particular, historical human being (*homo*), in a way that exceeds our power of imagining, is now made one, not with the Father or the Spirit, as Augustine explains elsewhere, but with the particular divine hypostasis of the Son, who has "taken him [Jesus] up" and has expressed his own eternal personhood in precisely these—and no other—human terms.

> Because God the Word, in graciously taking up a human being, came down into a human, and through that assumption by God a human being ascended to God the Word, God the Word as a whole became a whole human being. For God the

---

[17] Ep. 219 [426] (CCL 64.104); see also Leporius, *Libellus emendationis* 2 (CCL 64.114).
[18] Augustine, Ep. 219 (CCL 64.105).     [19] Leporius, *Lib. Emend.* 3 (CCL 64.114).
[20] *Lib. Emend.* 4 (CCL 64.115).

Father was not made human, nor was the Holy Spirit, but rather the Only-begotten of the Father. And therefore we must accept one person comprising both flesh and Word, so that we may truly believe, without any hesitation, that the one single Son of God—he who is also called "the twin-substanced giant"[21]— always remaining inseparably single, both truly underwent all that belongs to a human person "in the days of his flesh" (Heb. 5.7), and truly possessed what belongs to God.[22]

Leporius's profession of faith in the Mystery of Christ's person (presumably written by Augustine, or at least with Augustine's help) expresses, in the formal and rather abstract language of a creed, a vision of what Augustine himself apparently had come to see more and more clearly, as he grew older, as both the central challenge and the central promise of being a Christian: an understanding of the paradox of Christ, expressed in terms that may sound to us like the familiar rhetoric of Chalcedonian dogma, but which already, in Augustine's pre-Chalcedonian view, challengingly lies at the heart of Christian faith and practice, and even of the Church's understanding of itself and its mission.

## CHRIST AS MEDIATOR

As sometimes happens with other subjects, there is a section in the *Confessions* —the last four chapters of Book VII—which seems to sum up, more dramatically and more poignantly than in his later works, the importance Augustine saw, throughout his career, of rightly understanding the Mystery of Christ. He is writing here about his experiences in Milan, as a rising young professor of rhetoric in the early 380s. Having abandoned the Manichaean sect after several years of growing intellectual dissatisfaction, and having lived uncomfortably for several years as a philosophical skeptic, Augustine finds himself increasingly drawn to take part again in the Catholic community of his childhood. In spite of discomfort with the apparently impenetrable mysteries of parts of the Old Testament, Ambrose's preaching has opened for him a new sense of the depth of meaning hidden in the biblical text. The study of Neoplatonism, he has told us earlier in the same book, has finally resolved two of his main

---

[21] This is a phrase borrowed from Ambrose's Christmas hymn, "Intende, qui regis Israel," based on Ps. 18.5 (which seems itself to have been used in the fourth-century Latin Christmas liturgy)—a phrase beloved by Augustine. For Augustine's own use of the phrase, *gigas geminae substantiae*, and its importance in his growing articulation of the mystery of Christ, see my article, "The Giant's Twin Substances: Ambrose and the Christology of Augustine's *Contra sermonem Arianorum*," in Joseph T. Lienhard, Earl C. Muller, and Roland J. Teske (eds), *Augustine: Presbyter factus sum*, Collectanea Augustiniana (New York: Peter Lang, 1993).

[22] Leporius, *Lib. Emend.* 6 (CCL 64.117).

other intellectual difficulties with biblical faith: the question of the ontological status of evil in the world, and the related question of how to conceive of the being of God, and of God's presence in creation, in terms that were not spatial or temporal. Yet, Augustine writes near the end of Book VII, although these major hurdles had been cleared, he still found himself unable to take the final steps towards full membership in the Church. He describes his plight, at this point, as a kind of spiritual weakness due to lack of "nourishment":

> I sought a way to obtain strength enough to enjoy you, but I did not find it until I embraced "the mediator between God and man, the man Christ Jesus" (I Tim. 2.5), "who is above all things, God blessed forever" (Rom. 9.5). He called and said "I am the way and the truth and the life" (John 14.6). The food which I was too weak to accept he mingled with our flesh, in that "The Word was made flesh" (John 1.14), so that our infant condition might come to suck milk from your wisdom, by which you created all things. To possess my God, the humble Jesus, I was not yet humble enough. I did not know what his weakness was meant to teach.
>
> Your Word, eternal truth, higher than the superior parts of your creation, raises those submissive to him to himself. In the inferior parts he built for himself a humble house of our clay. By this he detaches from themselves those who are willing to be made his subjects, and carries them across to himself, healing their swelling and nourishing their love. They are no longer to place confidence in themselves, but rather to become weak. They see at their feet divinity become weak by his sharing in our "coat of skin" (Gen. 3.21). In their weariness they fall prostrate before this divine weakness, which rises and lifts them up.[23]

This moving, densely constructed passage, doubtless familiar to anyone who has spent time with the *Confessions*, is written with such poetic power, such emotive force, that we can easily miss its programmatic theological content. In fact, it may be taken as a summary of most of the central themes in Augustine's mature understanding of the person and work of Christ: Christ's role as *Mediator*; his central identity as the Word and Wisdom of God; his work of salvation as the *healing* of humanity's central illness, which is the "swelling" of deluded *pride*; the *form* of human transformation in Christ: *humility*, expressed primarily through *faith*, and *love*, given by God as a gift—as *"grace"*—in the present life of the Church; the goal of that transformation: a *share in the Wisdom of God*, which makes us sharers in God's own inner life. To see what is distinctive about Augustine's Christology, let us consider a few of the themes in this passage more closely.

---

[23] *Conf.* VII, 18.24 [397–401] (trans. Henry Chadwick [Oxford: Oxford University Press, 1991], 152). For a study of the Christological importance of this and related passages in *Confessions* VII, see David V. Meconi, S.J., "The Incarnation and the Role of Participation in St. Augustine's *Confessions*," *Augustinian Studies* 29 (1998), 61–75.

One of Augustine's favorite terms for Christ was "*Mediator*," probably because
it was both biblical and philosophical, and echoed the self-understanding of
much ancient religious practice. It carried both the familiar warrant of I Tim.
2.5, which identified "the man Christ Jesus" as the "one mediator between God
and humanity," and the overtones of a Neoplatonic conception of the universe,
in which the single, unknowable fount of all that is, the One (τὸ Ἕν), remains in
touch with the world of multiple, limited beings through the successive mediation of the universal Mind (Νοῦς) and the life-giving Soul (Ψυχή) that issue
serially from it. Ancient conceptions of religion, too, saw human priesthood as a
form of mediation between unknown forces and the community, and ritual as
a human strategy of repairing damaged communication between the human
race and God.[24] For Augustine, it was clear that only Christ was the real, divinely
appointed mediator to bring God into contact with humanity, and that he
could only be such a mediator in the full sense because he was himself at once
both divine and human. So he argues, in a sermon from the first decade of the
fifth century:

> Therefore he is the "mediator between God and human beings" because he is God
> with the Father and because he is human among humans....Divinity without
> humanity is not a mediator, humanity without divinity is not a mediator; rather,
> between divinity by itself and humanity by itself the mediator is the human
> divinity and the divine humanity of Christ.[25]

To be a mediator between God and humanity, to offer to God the kind of
sacrifice that makes humanity acceptable to him once again, the Son must be
human as well as divine.

Put in these terms, Christ's mediatorship has a rather abstract, formal
sound. But Augustine often also emphasizes that Christ freely *became* such a
mediator *for us* within human history, and worked his mediation not simply
by being who he was, but by speaking and acting in ways that would set our
own salvation in motion—freeing us from delusion and the dominance of
demonic powers, and leading us on a uniquely challenging new path to God.
Near the beginning of Book XI of *The City of God*, for instance—probably
written in 417, as a new start on that great apologetic project, after work on it
had been interrupted for several years—Augustine writes that the human
mind, made in God's image, was meant to know God directly, and to live in
God's "unchangeable light"; but because it had been weakened and darkened
by sin

> it first had to be dipped and soaked in faith (*fide inbuenda*), and so cleansed. In
> order that in this faith it might make progress with greater confidence towards the

[24] See Augustine's reflections on this in *De civ. Dei* 9–10 [415–17]; *De Trin.* 44; 18–22
[400–5].
[25] Sermon 47.12.21 [401–11] (PL 38.310).

goal of truth, Truth itself, God the Son of God, put on humanity without putting off godhead, and established and founded this same faith, so that humanity might find a path to the God of human beings through the God-man. Here, then, is the 'Mediator between God and human beings, the man Christ Jesus'. For inasmuch as he is human, he is the Mediator, and as a human being he is the way. If there is a connecting way between the striver and the goal towards which one is striving, one has hope of reaching it; but if there is none, or if one has no knowledge of what way to take, of what avail is it to know the goal that one is to reach? Now the only way that is completely proof against mistakes is the way created when the same person is both God and human, God being the goal of our journey and the human being the way (*quō itur Deus, quā itur homo*).[26]

The purpose of the mediating role of the incarnate Word is precisely to mark out for us a secure way to God, and by traveling it ahead of us, even to make it accessible in his person. Christ *is* "the road to that blessed country," Augustine writes in *Confessions* VII, "which is meant to be no mere vision but our home."[27]

Augustine devotes the fourth book of his *De Trinitate*, in fact, to a lengthy reflection on the historical mediatorship of Christ, which in Augustine's view is the distinctive, revealing mark—at least, for us who live in time—of the *person* of the eternal Son within the complex Mystery of God. In books two and three of that work he argued—against many reputable authors of both East and West who identified all of God's self-revelation to created minds as the work of the divine Logos (who is, in Irenaeus's words, "the visible of the invisible God")—that in fact God's apparitions and locutions in the history of Israel must be seen as the work of the whole Trinity: of God, simply as God, operating through the created mediation of angels.[28] It is only in the Incarnation of the Word of God as Son of Man that one can first speak of a "mission" in time and space—of a historically distinctive involvement—of *one* of the divine Persons; this "mission" of the Son into creation was soon to be followed by a second Trinitarian "mission" at Pentecost, in the sending of the Holy Spirit—from the Father through the Son—on the apostles and the Church.[29] For Augustine, it is this first mission, the sending of the Son in human form to be mediator between God and created minds, that reveals to us the eternal relationship, the unity in distinction, of Father and Son: the Son is sent, *can* be sent from the heart of God and can bring God directly to us,

---

[26] *De civ. Dei* XI, 2 [415–17], (trans. David S. Wiesen; London: Heinemann; Cambridge, MA: Harvard University Press, 1968), 431 (altered).

[27] *Conf.* VII, 20.26 (trans. Chadwick 154); cf. 21.27.

[28] For a reflection on how Augustine's treatment of the Old Testament theophanies changed earlier Patristic tradition, see Kari Kloos, *Christ, Creation, and the Vision of God: Augustine's Transformation of Early Christian Theophany Interpretation* (Brill: Leiden, 2011).

[29] *De Trin.* IV, 29–30.

because he *is* God; yet, as one sent, he is also now seen to be God begotten as a "person" within the divine Mystery, the Son *distinct* from the Father.

> There is nothing at all to stop us believing that the Son is equal to the Father and consubstantial and co-eternal, and yet that the Son is sent by the Father: not because one is greater and the other less, but because one is the Father and the other is the Son; one is the begetter, the other begotten... That is, we should understand that it was not just the man who the Word became that was sent, but that the Word was sent to become human. For he was not sent in virtue of some disparity of power or substance or anything in him that was not equal to the Father, but in virtue of the Son being from the Father, not the Father being from the Son.[30]

Earlier in Book IV, Augustine devoted considerable effort to explaining the mediatorial *work* of Christ, apparently in terms deliberately chosen to contrast his unique and efficacious mediation between human creatures and God with the previous, largely vain efforts of ancient philosophy and religion to put human minds back in touch with their divine origin.[31] Augustine portrays the mediation of Christ, first of all, as a work of revelation: the revelation of both who *God* is, and of who *we* are—intelligent creatures, alienated by our own sinful self-absorption from the interlacing eternity and truth and love which is God.[32]

> First we had to be persuaded how much God loved us, in case out of sheer despair we lacked the courage to reach up to him. Also we had to be shown what sort of people we are that he loves, in case we should take pride in our own worth, and so bounce even further away from him and sink even more under our own strength. So he dealt with us in such a way that we could progress rather in his strength; he arranged it so that the power of charity would be brought to perfection in the weakness of humility.[33]

Augustine then goes on to reflect on the concrete human details of the person and work of Jesus, focusing especially on his passion and death as achieving this unique work of mediation—understood in terms of ancient religious practice—in two further respects: as restoring by religious practice ("binding up again": *re-ligare*) the fragmented unity of humans, among themselves and with their creator; and as purifying humanity from the self-centered drives and illusions that have kept us in slavery to the Evil One.

---

[30] *De Trin.* IV, 27, trans. Edmund Hill, O.P. (Brooklyn, NY: New City Press, 1991), 172 (altered). Augustine's distinction of the generation of the Son and the procession of the Spirit, within the Mystery of God, from their "missions" in history that reveal them to creatures, remained a key part of the Western understanding of God as Trinity; see, for example, Thomas Aquinas, *Summa Theologiae* I, qq. 33–43.

[31] For a thoughtful and persuasive analysis of Book IV of *De Trinitate* in terms of the Son's mediation, see Hill's introductory essay to the book, 147–51.

[32] *De Trin.* IV, 1–2; for similar phrasing, cf. *Conf.* VII, 10.16.

[33] *De Trin.* IV, 2 (trans. Hill, 153).

The religion of philosophy had tried to overcome the inner division of the human mind, which for Neoplatonism was rooted in the decline of primordial unity into multiplicity—a kind of ontic and psychological fall from grace—by analyzing the structure of experience, while pagan ritual had used sacrifice and talismans and magic incantations to purge the soul from the many external things that clung to it and weighed it down. Both were attempts to deal with what was intuitively recognized as our fundamental human fragmentation. Augustine presents the work of Jesus, as both revelation and sacrifice, as finally fulfilling this ancient need for reunification, by drawing humanity beyond the mere processes of enlightenment and purgation to faith and love:

> By wickedness and ungodliness, with a crashing discord, we had bounced away (*resilientes*), and flowed and faded away from the one supreme true God into the many, divided by the many, clinging to the many. And so it was fitting that at the beck and bidding of a compassionate God the many should themselves acclaim together the one who was to come ...; and that being dead in soul through many sins and destined to die in the flesh because of sin, we should love the one who died in the flesh for us without sin, and that believing in him raised from the dead, and rising ourselves with him in spirit through faith, we should be made one in the one just one ..., and that thus fully reconciled to God by him the mediator, we may be able to cling to the one, enjoy the one, and remain for ever one.[34]

From our "doubleness"—our divided heart, rooted in the ontological com-position, as well as the experienced polarity, of soul and body, and leading us to the "double mortality" of sin and bodily death—the Son, himself utterly simple as God, has rescued us by taking on a second nature, capable of experience in the world. By himself dying a "single death"—bodily death totally free from the "second," moral death of sin—he has become the "sac-rament" (*sacramentum*) or efficacious sign for the healing and restoration of our "inner self" from this kind of death, and the "model" (*exemplum*) of a bodily death, such as all of us face, in our "outer self." This "outer" death Jesus had endured without fear, because he knew it was the prelude to resurrection and transformation.[35]

> So, then, the one death of our savior was our salvation from our two deaths, and his one resurrection bestowed two resurrections on us, since in either instance—that is, both in death and in resurrection—his body served as the sacrament of

---

[34] *De Trin.* IV, 11 (trans. Hill, 161). For a profound reflection on the Christological grounding of Augustine's understanding of the "Trinity, which is God," in the mystery of Christ's person and work, see Lewis Ayres, *Augustine and the Trinity* (Oxford: Oxford University Press, 2009), 142–70.

[35] *De Trin.* IV, 6. See Basil Studer, "'Sacramentum et exemplum' chez saint Augustin," *Recherches Augustiniennes* 10 (1975), 87–141.

our inner self and as the model of our outer self, by a kind of curative accord or symmetry.[36]

Christ, in his innocent life and his victorious death, has reunited the whole human race with God and with itself. The result of this reunification of the human person, by the death and resurrection of Christ as mediator, is not only internal harmony within individuals, not only the reconciliation of individuals with God, but also their social unification: the formation of a community of love—the *Church* that Augustine repeatedly calls "the whole Christ"—among those who are cleansed, "fused somehow into one spirit in the furnace of charity," which is the earthly prelude to the eternal community of the saints.[37]

## PARTICIPATION IN IMMORTALITY

Building on this sense of the self-identification of the Son of God, as a human being, with all of us, in order to identify us with him as children of God, Augustine speaks of the work of Christ frequently in terms of an *exchange of roles*, a reciprocity of identities that is rooted in the compound structure of Christ's own person. In Book XIII of *De Trinitate* (where Augustine concerns himself again with the "economy of salvation," the person and work of the Son, as he had begun to do in Book IV), he reminds his readers that the goal of the Incarnation is expressed concisely by the prologue to the Fourth Gospel: Jesus "gave those who received him the power to become children of God—to those who believe in his name." He continues:

> But in case this feebleness that is humanity, which we see and carry around with us, should despair of attaining such eminence, [the Gospel] goes on to say, "And the Word became flesh and dwelt amongst us," in order to convince us of what might seem incredible [i.e. our deification] by showing us its opposite. For surely if the Son of God by nature became Son of Man by mercy for the sake of the sons

---

[36] *De Trin.* IV, 6. (trans. Hill, 157).

[37] *De Trin.* IV, 12 (trans. Hill, 161). For passages developing Augustine's notion of the Church as *totus Christus*, see especially Sermon 341; *In Jo. Ev. Tr.* 21.8 [419–22]; 108.5 [419]; *Enar. in Ps.* 30, Serm. 1.3 [392]; *Enar. in Ps.* 148.8; etc. Augustine expresses this vision of the Church simply and memorably in his tenth homily on the First Letter of John [406–7]: " 'In this we know that we love the children of God ....' It is as if he were to say: in this we know that we love the Son of God; he says 'the children of God,' although he has just spoken of the 'Son of God,' because the children of God are the body of the unique Son of God, and since he is the head and we the members, there is one Son of God. Therefore anyone who loves the children of God loves the Son of God, and anyone who loves the Son of God, loves the Father. And no one can love the Father unless he loves the Son; and anyone who loves the Son, also loves the children of God. Which children of God? The members of the Son of God. And by love one becomes himself a member, and is made by love part of the structure of the body of Christ; and there will be one Christ loving himself."

of men (and that is the meaning of "the Word became flesh and dwelt amongst us"), how much easier it is to believe that the sons of men by nature can become sons of God by grace and dwell in God. For it is in him alone and thanks to him alone that they can be fully happy, by sharing in his immortality; it was to persuade us of this that the Son of God came to share in our mortality.[38]

It is here, in this exchange of roles or "persons" initiated by a merciful God in the Incarnation of the Son, that Augustine grounds his own understanding of the *"deification"* or "divinization" of human creatures—a way of speaking about the fullness of salvation that is usually identified with the Greek Fathers, but that also is clearly present in Augustine's theology.[39] In several sermons, all of which seem to have been delivered around 413, Augustine argues strikingly that the purpose of the Incarnation, and thus of the "way" to God Christ has opened for us in his own life and actions, is to allow us to become, with him, sons and daughters of God, and so to share in God's eternal life. So he remarks in a homily on Psalm 146:

> If he himself is the same and cannot change in any respect, then by sharing in his divinity we also shall become immortal, and have eternal life. And this pledge was given to us by the Son of God, as I have already explained to you, my holy friends: before we were made sharers in his immortality, he himself first became a sharer in our mortality. As he is mortal, not from his substance but from ours, so we shall be immortal, not from our substance but from his.[40]

## GRACE AND FAITH

In the fourteenth book of *De Trinitate*, in fact, Augustine develops this idea of our participation in the life and being of God, through the grace given us in Christ, as the central feature of the human mind's eschatological perfection: the perfection that will realize fully and finally in us—although still "in an enigma, darkly"—the image of the Triune substance of God which we were created to bear. The mind "is in [God's] image insofar as it is capable of him and can participate in him; indeed it cannot achieve so great a good except by

---

[38] *De Trin.* XIII, 12 (trans. Hill, 353).

[39] See especially Gerald Bonner, "Augustine's Conception of Deification," *Journal of Theological Studies* 37 (1986), 369–86; "Deificare," in Cornelius Mayer (ed.), *Augustinus-Lexikon* 1 (Basel: Schwabe, 1986– ), 265–7; David Meconi, "St. Augustine's Early Theory of Participation," *Augustinian Studies* 27 (1996), 81–98; *The One Christ: St. Augustine's Theology of Deification* (Washington, DC: Catholic University of America Press, 2013).

[40] *Enar. in Ps.* 146.11 (PL 37.1906). Cf. Sermon 192.1, a Christmas sermon from around 412; also *Enar. in Ps.* 49.2; *Enar. in Ps.* 58.7. This phrasing found its way—perhaps as early as the fifth or sixth century—into texts of the Roman liturgy.

being his image."[41] Augustine calls this participative perfection of our mental and spiritual capacities "Wisdom," to distinguish it from the "knowledge" by which we are normally aware of ourselves and others, of things and events, and can conceptualize them and choose to respond accordingly in this present life, within the limits of time and space. Wisdom, in its most radical sense, is only fully available to the human mind in the state of eschatological fulfillment, the beatific vision, when the mind is finally aware of itself, as it remembers and understands and loves God and all things in God—in the power of the Holy Spirit, as a brother or sister of Christ, returning all love and thanks with him to the Father. Augustine describes this eschatological, triply structured Wisdom precisely as *participation*:

> The trinity of the mind is not really the image of God because the mind remembers and understands and loves itself [which it does even in this life, the realm of finite "knowledge"], but because it is also able to remember and understand and love him by whom it was made. And when it does this it becomes wise. If it does not do it, then even though it remembers and understands and loves itself, it is foolish. Let it then remember its God, to whose image it was made, and understand and love him. To put it in a word, let it worship the uncreated God, by whom it was created with a capacity for him and able to share in him. In this way it will be wise, not with its own light, but by sharing in that supreme light, and it will reign in happiness where it reigns eternal. For this is called human wisdom in such a way that it is also God's. Only then is it true wisdom.[42]

In this present life, such wisdom remains beyond the mind's reach. What the mind is called to, in this present order, is to know Christ, the incarnate Word: to know him by faith rather than by vision. This faith is a species of historically limited knowledge, which prepares us for eschatological wisdom: the faith that requires us to acknowledge God present among us in a lowly human form like our own, and in so doing to change our conception of how the mind discovers and holds on to ultimate Truth. Faith, in Augustine's vocabulary, is always the shadowy, limited way in which alone we can come to know the transcendent reality of God in time: it belongs to the realm of *knowledge*, of contingent consciousness, rather than to that of the contemplative, participative sharing in God that constitutes eschatological *wisdom*. The object of faith, as Augustine uses the word, is not simply the traces of God we can find in the natural world, but the narrative of redemption, presented to us in the Scriptures by human witnesses and institutions, and echoed sacramentally in our present ecclesial experience of *grace*: what God, in his mercy, has done for us in sending his Son to take on human flesh, and his Spirit to form us into Christ's Body. On the other hand, the object of vision, the light of wisdom by which we will participate in God, is for Augustine not simply grace, but *truth*: the truth

---

[41] *De Trin.* XIV, 11 (trans. Hill, 379).     [42] *De Trin.* XIV, 15 (trans. Hill, 383).

that God is, the transcendent foundation of all intelligibility, the unchanging basis of the real.

All these terms have their Scriptural resonances. In Colossians, for instance, we read that in Christ Jesus "are hidden all the treasures of wisdom and knowledge" (Col. 2.1); in the prologue to John's Gospel we hear that the Word made flesh was "full of grace and truth." So Augustine brings these two elements together, in an important passage of *De Trinitate* XIII, which presents a synthetic vision central to his Christology:

> Among things that have arisen in time the supreme grace is that humanity has been joined to God to form one person; among eternal things the supreme truth is rightly attributed to the Word of God. That the only-begotten from the Father is the one who is "full of grace and truth" means that it is one and the same person by whom deeds were carried out in time for us and for whom we are purified by faith in order that we may contemplate him unchangingly in eternity.[43]

The failing of the classical philosophers, Augustine goes on to suggest, was that they tried to find Truth without grace—that they "philosophized," sought wisdom, "without the mediator"[44]—and therefore fell prey to demons and to their own self-serving delusions. Given our history of sin, we can only hope to come to wisdom and life through the faith that knows the human Christ, that discovers divine grace and mercy in him, the true Mediator:

> Our knowledge therefore is Christ, and our wisdom is the same Christ. It is he who plants faith in us about temporal things, he who presents us with the truth about eternal things. Through him we go straight to him, we journey through knowledge to wisdom (*per ipsum pergimus ad ipsum, tendimus per scientiam ad sapientiam*), without ever turning aside from one and the same Christ, "in whom are hidden all the treasures of wisdom and knowledge."[45]

Faith in the meaning of the life and death of Jesus is, in fact, what purifies our minds during this life, "so that when we come to sight, and truth succeeds to faith, eternity might likewise succeed to mortality."[46]

---

[43] *De Trin.* XIII, 24 (trans. Hill, 363). For this same dialectic between "grace" and "truth," faith and contemplation, expressed in more concrete terms, cf. Ep. 137: "Now the fact that [Christ] relaxed in sleep and was nourished by food and experienced all the human emotions makes it clear to us human beings that he was human—that he did not consume humanity, but assumed it! And that is what happened; yet still some heretics, perversely admiring his power and praising it, refuse to recognize a human nature in him, where all grace is revealed—the grace by which he saves those who believe in him, the grace containing the deepest treasures of wisdom and knowledge, filling minds with faith, to lead them to the eternal contemplation of unchanging truth." For a discussion of the relation of historical faith and *scientia* to eschatological vision and *sapientia*, and of both to Augustine's Christology, as part of a long development in his use of Neoplatonic and Scriptural themes, see Lewis Ayres, "The Christological Context of Augustine's *De Trinitate* XIII: Towards Relocating Books VIII–XV," *Augustinian Studies* 29 (1998), 111–39.
[44] *De Trin.* XIII, 24.      [45] *De Trin.* XIII, 24.
[46] *De Trin.* IV, 24 (trans. Hill 170).

It is precisely this historical, inner-worldly focus of faith in Christ, in Augustine's view—its preoccupation with the words and the death of a strikingly attractive but failed Jewish prophet, its recognition of the basic fact that "This man truly was the Son of God"[47]—that underlies faith's moral demand, requiring from the believer a humility that can only be attained by a difficult, graced conversion of mind and heart. Pride, Augustine always held, was the very root of sin, the source of the "evil will" that, since the dawn of history, has led creatures to disobey their creator, and turn from their true life.[48] To accept the Christian message, the proclamation not simply of God as ultimate Truth (which Neoplatonism could also proclaim, if in different terms), but of a Word *made flesh*—a God who "emptied himself, taking the form of a servant" (Phil. 2.7), in order to free us from our own servitude to pride and sin—is to join in a process of reversal, an exchange of opposites, that for Augustine is the real basis of divinization. So he writes, in *De Trinitate* IV:

> The only thing to cleanse the wicked and the proud is the blood of the just man and the humility of God; to contemplate God, which by nature we are not, we would have to be cleansed by him who became what by nature we are and what by sin we are not. By nature we are not God; by nature we are human; by sin we are not just. So God became a just human, to intercede with God for sinful human beings. The sinner did not match the just, but a human did match humans. So he applied to us the similarity of his humanity to take away the dissimilarity of our iniquity, and becoming a partaker of our mortality, he made us partakers of his divinity.[49]

Since faith, in Augustine's view, is precisely the acceptance of the well-nigh-incredible story of a God who has humbled himself out of love—since it is not a direct and unclouded vision of Truth, so much as the readiness, with Paul, to "know nothing else but Jesus Christ, and him crucified" (I Cor. 2.2), to accept from other Christian believers the contingent, historical knowledge of Christ, which immediately overthrows our human ambitions of self-generated wisdom—faith includes *humility* as an indispensable component, and leads to our response of *charity*, the uncalculating, yearning love of God above all things, and of one's neighbor as oneself, which is the primary gift of God's Holy Spirit.

---

[47] Mark 15.39.    [48] See, e.g., *De civ. Dei* XIV [415–17].

[49] *De Trin.* IV, 4 (trans. Hill, 155). In an eloquent passage in *De catechizandis rudibus* [399], Augustine lays out, in similar paradoxes, the rhetorical pattern of argument by which one might attract a casual questioner to Christian faith. One should sum up the biblical narrative briefly, he says, emphasizing that God has created us and redeemed us out of love, so that our only reasonable response is to love God above all things and our neighbor, whom God loves, as ourselves. If one is loved first, one is all the more likely to be moved to love. And God's love is revealed, above all, in God's humility, which of itself is capable of undoing our pride. Augustine concludes: "A proud humanity is a great misfortune, but an even greater mercy is a humble God" (*De cat. Rud.* 4.8: CCL 46.129). For the theme of God's humility, cf. *De peccatorum meritis et remissione* 2.17.27 [411] (PL 44.168).

So, in the final paragraphs of Book VII of the *Confessions*—following that tightly woven, deeply Christological passage we mentioned before— Augustine points out that while the "books of the Platonists" could teach him a great deal about God's transcendence, and even about the co-inherence of simplicity and multiplicity in the divine substance in terms that were somewhat analogous to the Church's Trinitarian doctrine, philosophy could not enable him actually to draw close to God and to hold him fast.

> For I had now begun to wish to be thought wise [—to be considered a "philosopher"!]. I was full of self-esteem, which was a punishment of my own making. I ought to have deplored my state, but instead my "knowledge only bred self-conceit" (I Cor. 8.1). For was I not without charity, which builds its edifice on the firm foundation of humility, that is, on Jesus Christ?[50]

It was only when he turned from Plotinus to Paul, Augustine says, that he discovered the reality not only of the truth about God but of *grace*—of God's empowering and freeing gift of love, gratuitously revealed and released in the world by the death of God's Son and the sending of his Spirit. By reading Paul, he recognized the humbling fact that in the Incarnate Word, truth is now revealed by grace, and given freely by divine love, rather than laboriously discovered by human intelligence:

> I began to read, and discovered that whatever truth I had found in the Platonists was set down here as well, and with it there was praise for your grace bestowed. For Saint Paul teaches that he who sees ought not to boast as though what he sees—and even the power by which he sees—"had not come to him by gift" (I Cor. 4.7) ... By the gift of grace he is not only shown how to see you, who are always the same, but is also given the strength to hold you. By your grace, too, if he is far from you and cannot see you, he is enabled to walk upon the path that leads him closer to you, so that he may see you and hold you.[51]

It is striking, in fact, that in many of his mature works, Augustine repeatedly emphasizes the point he hints at here in *Confessions* VII: that the reality of grace—of God's creative, internal gift, which alone sets the human will free to do what is right, to respond to God's initiative of love—cannot be understood, let alone shared, apart from the person of the Incarnate Word. "The most shining light of predestination and grace," Augustine confidently asserts in his late treatise *On the Predestination of the Saints* [429] "is the Savior himself, the very Mediator between God and humanity, the human being Christ Jesus."[52] "Since he was the only Son of God not by grace but by nature," he writes in his

---

[50] *Conf.* VII, 20.26 (trans. Chadwick, 154).    [51] *Conf.* VII, 21.27 (trans. Chadwick, 155).
[52] *De praedestinatione sanctorum* 15.30 [428–9] (PL 44.981). For further reflections on the Trinitarian context of Augustine's understanding of grace, see my article, "The Law, the Whole Christ, and the Spirit of Love: Grace as a Trinitarian Gift in Augustine's Theology," *Augustinian Studies* 41 (2010), 123–44.

*Enchiridion*, "he became Son of Man, as well, that he [as a human being] might also be full of grace: and that very same one, who is both and comes from both, is the one Christ."[53] One obvious reason for a statement such as this is the gratuitous, human generosity of God that is revealed, above all, in Jesus' death: although he was free from sin, Jesus accepted the death that for the rest of us is punishment for sin, "in order to give life to the dead."[54]

And grace is also embodied, just as strikingly, in Jesus' incarnate identity itself—in the very entry of God's Word into history as one of us. We find God's gift of life not in a human being who had lived virtuously, and so had deserved to be singularly united to God by his good deeds and holy desires; rather, we find the gift in the coming of the Word to *form*, by his very presence, a new human being. Augustine puts it concisely: "in the very act of being assumed, he [the man Jesus] is created (*ipsa assumptione creatur*)."[55] Having argued this point at some length in his *Enchiridion*, Augustine there adds:

> Even the very manner in which Christ was born of the Holy Spirit, *not* as a son, and of the virgin Mary *as* a son, suggests to us the grace of God. Here a human being, without any previous merits, in the first moment of that nature by which he begins to exist, is joined to the Word of God in such a personal unity that the same one is Son of God and Son of Man, the same is Son of Man who is Son of God; and that in that act of his taking up human nature this grace should become, in some way, natural to that human being, so that he should never be able to fall into sin.[56]

Jesus embodies, in human terms, what God the Son is, and so shares that Sonship humanly with us. Thus the Incarnation serves for Augustine not only as the ultimate source of God's saving grace towards humanity, but also as the paradigm of what that grace really involves: God's intervention in our fallen and bound human nature, creating there, as a kind of new human nature, a freedom from sin that was not there before, and that could never have come about by human efforts or choices; a freedom from sin that is the behavioral manifestation of personal union; even a participated personal union, by grace, with God.

> By that same grace, by which that human being was made from his first moment the Christ, anyone at all is made a Christian from the first moment of his faith; the Christian is reborn from the same Spirit from whom he [Christ] was born; our

---

[53] *Enchiridion* 10.35 [421–2] (PL 40.250).

[54] *De correptione et gratia* 30 [426–7] (PL 44.954).

[55] *Contra sermonem Arianorum* 6.8 (PL 42.683).

[56] *Enchiridion* 12.40 (PL 40.252) [421–2]. For a development of Augustine's understanding of the person of Christ as a Mystery, in which "the grace of God is broadly and obviously represented to us," see *Enchiridion* 10.35–12.40 (PL 40.250–2); cf. "The Law, the Whole Christ, and the Spirit of Love" (see n. 51).

sins are forgiven by the same Spirit who brought it about that he [Christ] had no sin at all. God surely foreknew that he would do these things. This, then, is the predestination of the saints, which appeared most fully in the Saint of saints.[57]

Passages like this, I think, help us to see more clearly all that was at stake for Augustine in properly understanding the Mystery of the Person of Christ. Certainly he was ready to profess, when necessary, that Christ is a single human subject or person, existing simultaneously in two complete and utterly distant realities or natures, as Chalcedon would do twenty years after his death—even though it was only fairly late in his life, and with relative infrequency, that he made use of such technical language. Certainly, too, he remained convinced since his earliest Catholic writings that Christ, who was himself the eternal Son of God, had a fully operative human mind and will, and that this living consciousness, this mind or soul, was precisely the point at which the eternal Logos made the most intense substantial contact with the human being he "assumed" as his own.[58] But for Augustine the more important purpose in thinking about the Mystery of Christ was to discover what faith in the Son's Incarnation tells us about God and about ourselves: that God, who has created all things out of love, has loved us enough to humble himself and become as we are,[59] and that it is only through humbly accepting that narrative, in faith, as true, and through accepting its consequences for our inner struggles and our outer pattern of living, that we humans can ever hope to reach the *beatitudo*, the endless happiness in endless life, for which we naturally yearn. "We must walk by hope," Augustine observes in the penultimate Book of *The City of God*, keeping in mind Paul's assurance that "as many as are led by the Spirit of God are children of God." And this hope is grounded precisely in the Mystery of Christ's person:

We are children [of God] by grace, not by nature; for the only one who was by nature Son of God became, for our sakes, out of mercy, a son of man, so that we, who are by nature the children of men and women, might become through him children of God by grace. Remaining unchangeably as he was, he took up our nature from us, in order to take *us* up: holding on firmly to his divinity, he became a sharer in our weakness, so that we being changed for the better, might cast off what we are as sinful mortals, by sharing in him, who is immortal and righteous; and also that we might preserve, in the goodness of his nature, what he had made good in our nature by filling it with the highest good.[60]

---

[57] *De praed. sanct.* 15.31 (PL 44.982).

[58] On Augustine's treatment of the active presence of two wills in Christ, see Han-Luen Kantzer Komline, "From Division to Delight: Augustine and the Will," Ph.D. dissertation, University of Notre Dame, 2015.

[59] *De cat. rud.* 4.8.

[60] *De civ. Dei* XXI, 15 (emphasis mine); and see the similar passage in *De Trin.* XIII, 12 (quoted in n. 38).

Here and throughout Augustine's massive corpus, we see a reflection on the reality of Christ that is achieved mainly through the use of a precisely balanced rhetoric. It is important to recognize that rhetoric, for Augustine as for most of his ancient predecessors and contemporaries, was not simply a matter of decoration. It conveys what is, for him, the heart of the Gospel: the presence of God in the contrasting, contingent dependent reality of our created nature, in order to communicate powerfully with us, to change humanity itself from a state of mortal illness to health, from evil to good. The underlying dialectic of nature and grace, faith and vision, knowledge and wisdom, is never far from Augustine's reflections about the central Gospel proclamation, that the Son of God has become Son of Man; it can hardly be expressed with such power and depth by simple ontological analysis. Yet the very centrality of this paradox of Christ's person to the whole of Christian faith is why it was so important for Augustine, since the time of his earliest writings as a Catholic, to "get Christology right." In his days as a professor in Milan, he tells us in *Confessions* VII, he had learned enough about God from Neoplatonic philosophy to have a clear notion of the divine transcendence, of God's radical otherness with regard to time and matter. Yet, as an essentially philosophical "Christian fellow-traveller," he still stood aloof from the scandalous, thoroughly unphilosophical assertion that God's Logos had actually taken on time and matter—the dimensions of our existence—as his own, in the humility of love. Although he did not realize it at the time, he tells us, his conception of Christ—like that of Leporius, thirty-five years later—was closest to the Christology of Photinus, the fourth-century Latin modalist who seems to have emphasized only the substantial unity of God, along with God's "otherness," his transcendence of history; so he began his adult Christian life by thinking of Jesus as a uniquely inspired man.[61] Like modalist theology through the ages, from Sabellius to Schleiermacher, it was a philosopher's Christianity, not the fruitful but scandalous faith of the Gospels and the Church.

## CONCLUSION

To come to profess the faith that would lead him towards wisdom, the conversion Augustine finally needed was not an infusion of new ideas, but a turning in grace, a historical change in personal direction, that had its origin in his God-given discovery of the humility and love of God, and that would bring humility and love to reality in the heart of the convert, as well. In Augustine's view, faith is the only reliable knowledge of God that is accorded to us in this

---

[61] *Conf.* VII, 19.25.

life: faith deals with human reports, historical events, improbable narratives that have come to us from others, written down in books that lack rhetorical polish and preached in churches filled with saints and sinners, scholars and simple folk (*simpliciores*), thinkers like Marius Victorinus and devout, unlettered mothers like Monica.[62] Scripture and the Church's faith are not primarily for philosophers, but for humble people, and for philosophers who can find a way to become humble.

This, I think, is why one can say—even at the risk of terminological anachronism—that it is not simply *Christ*, but *Christology* that is, for Augustine, the way to salvation. It is not simply the *person* of the Word made flesh, who achieves and embodies God's victorious grace, that enables us to reach the goal of our being; it is also our *confession* of his person, in moving, scripturally anchored language which is itself the work of grace. We are drawn into the power of that grace precisely by realizing and acknowledging who Christ really is—by accepting for ourselves, in faith, the lowly narrative, the humiliating paradox, of a humble God. At the end of Book VII of the *Confessions*, Augustine tells us that it was only in time, after desperate inner struggles, that he came "to understand the difference between presumption and confession, between those who see the goal that they must reach, but cannot see the road by which they are to reach it, and those who see the road to that blessed country which is meant to be no mere vision but our home."[63] Through all the ceaseless teaching and preaching and letter-writing, all the speculation and pastoral intervention and heated controversy, that would fill Augustine's later life, the one continuous road he walked was the road of this growing, increasingly articulated vision of the Mystery of Christ, at once so lowly and so sublime.

---

[62] See Augustine's reflections on the necessity of faith, even for building up the knowledge we rely on in daily life, in *De utilitate credendi* [393] and in *De fide rerum invisibilium* [400].
[63] *Conf.* VII, 20.26.

# 7

## Antioch and Alexandria

### Christology as Reflection on God's Presence in History

#### ANTIOCHENE AND ALEXANDRIAN APPROACHES

However little else one has read about the Church Fathers, every beginning student of theology knows at least something of the opposition between "Antiochene" and "Alexandrian" approaches to Christology and to biblical interpretation, in the decades leading up to the councils of Ephesus and Chalcedon.[1] The usual way of characterizing their differences is to say, in Grillmeier's terminology, that the theologians of the "school of Antioch" who flourished in the late fourth and early fifth century—Diodore of Tarsus, Theodore of Mopsuestia, Nestorius of Constantinople, Theodoret of Cyrus—represented, with a variety of modulations, a classic "Word-human being" (*logos-anthropos*) approach to conceiving of the person of the Savior: God's eternal Logos, who shares fully in the divine Mystery, has "taken up" a full human being to be his "Temple," his dwelling place, and bestows his direction and favor on this human being to such a unique degree that the man represents him in the world, reveals the "face" (*prosopon*) or active form of the Word as his own, shares with him even in divine honor and status. Yet this indwelling of the Word in the man Jesus does not reduce, or substantially alter, the full operation of Jesus' human faculties, and never blurs the natural, substantial boundaries between the creator and the creature, God and human beings. God simply transcends created categories.

Along with this approach to Christology, it is usually said, scholars from the "school of Antioch" were known for their highly developed skills in interpreting Scripture as a narrative, and especially for their aversion to the complicated allegorical or figural style of exegesis—seeing every incident and every phrase in the Bible as a cipher for the human person's salvation in Christ, for

---

[1] An earlier, somewhat abbreviated version of this chapter appeared in Francesca Aran Murphy (ed.), *The Oxford Handbook of Christology* (Oxford: Oxford University Press, 2015).

his or her moral and spiritual growth—which had dominated ancient Scrip-ture scholarship since Origen. Antiochene exegetes are often seen by modern readers as showing a greater respect than their Alexandrian counterparts did for the "historical" or "literal" meaning of the biblical text—an interest that corresponded to their sober emphasis on the full humanity of Jesus.

The "school of Alexandria" of that same period, it is often said—the school that drew on the powerful legacy of Athanasius, and was influenced by the Origenist tradition of biblical scholarship, especially as represented by the late-fourth-century exegete Didymus the Blind, and that was sympathetic, to some degree, to the Christological thought of Apollinarius of Laodicaea and his followers—was dominated, in the fifth century, by the towering ecclesiastical, exegetical, and theological figure of Cyril of Alexandria. Alexandrian biblical interpretation, unlike that of Antioch, remained squarely in the allegorical, spiritualizing camp, and reached the heights of baroque elaboration at Didy-mus's hands; its picture of Christ was characteristically unworldly, representing him essentially as God the Word owning, transforming, and irradiating human flesh and the human mind—to such an extent that Jesus himself could no longer be called a human being in the strict sense, but formed "one nature," one living, active organism, with the eternal Word, who was the source and master of all his human acts.

Like all caricatures, this picture of biblical interpretation and theology as practiced at Antioch and Alexandria in the early Church has a good deal of truth to it, but it is not the whole story; so it can be, by its very exaggerations, misleading. Recent studies of the work of Antiochene and Alexandrian exe-getes in the period, for instance, have tended to conclude that it is hard to identify actual differences in exegetical "method," or even in hermeneutical principles, between scholars in the two "schools." Although interpreters from Antioch tended to be less ingenious in finding spiritual significance in every phrase and term of the Bible than their Alexandrian contemporaries were—and deliberately so, if Diodore of Tarsus's scathing asides against "Hellenistic allegory" are typical—they were also firmly committed to the general early Christian assumption that the Bible, as a continuous narrative of God's history with the world, finds its climactic and unifying meaning in the saving acts of Jesus Christ, and they recognized the need for *anagogia*, the quest for a "higher meaning" in a text, when such interpretation seemed warranted.[2] For Diodore

---

[2] See Diodore of Tarsus, *Commentary on the Psalms*, Prologue (CCG 6, 7.123–8.162): Diodore contrasts what he calls "higher interpretation" (ἡ ὑψηλοτέρα θεωρία) with "allegory," on the grounds that the latter pays no attention to the narrative framework or "story" of a biblical text (ἱστορία) but simply quarries it for moral or spiritual applications. For good general discussions of the character of Antiochene exegesis, and its similarities to and differences from other early Christian approaches, see Christoph Schäublin, *Untersuchungen zu Methode und Herkunft der Antiochenischen Exegese* (Cologne: Hanstein, 1974); and Frances M. Young, *Biblical Exegesis and the Formation of Christian Culture* (Cambridge: Cambridge University

and his pupils, the key to good exegesis was never to let the interpretation of individual texts slip out of their context in the Bible's whole story of salvation history, as they understood it. While they certainly did not share our modern understanding of historical investigation—of "history" as the reconstruction of a narrative of "what actually happened" in the past, the quest for "facts" and the depiction of the social conditions of past epochs, on the basis of present evidence, dispassionately analyzed—Antiochene scholars of the fourth and fifth centuries often did begin their interpretations of texts with a recognition of those texts' place in the overarching story of God's promises to humanity, in Israel and the Church.

In addition, the Antiochenes insisted that every passage of Scripture be interpreted first of all in the context of its presumed original location within that narrative. Influenced also by the strong tradition of rhetorical training at Antioch, they tended to be on the lookout for practical, moral applications of the passages they studied—a tendency most obvious in the exegesis of John Chrysostom. The story of God's history, looked at from the distance of today, touches *us* by providing models for how we should *act*, to become part of that history ourselves. Exegetes in Alexandria, on the other hand, such as Didymus and Cyril, although certainly interested in the events and institutions of Israel's past, seem to have taken greater interest in finding the ways in which a given text, in its details as well as its overall shape, might nourish the reader's spiritual and theological growth directly, or deepen his grasp of the Mystery of Christ as the central message of biblical faith. When properly understood, the story itself is less important than its details, which are usually about *us*. In that sense, Alexandrian exegetes tended to be grammarians rather than rhetoricians—seekers for the meaning of words and images, rather than for moving examples—and to read the Scripture contemplatively rather than kerygmatically.[3]

As far as their respective understandings of the person of Christ are concerned, however, it is certainly an oversimplification to suggest that the Antiochene theologians of the fourth and fifth centuries were primarily concerned with promoting a sense of the full humanity of Jesus, as a historical man, or that the Alexandrians gave that humanity only lip service; it is here,

Press, 1997), esp. 161–85. For a unique example of how Antiochene exegesis might be taught and used in practice as an approach to interpreting biblical texts, see the fifth-century handbook *Adrian's Introduction to the Divine Scriptures*, newly edited and translated by Peter W. Martens (Oxford: Oxford University Press, 2017).

[3] For a careful reconstruction of the development of tensions between Antiochene and Alexandrian approaches to both biblical interpretation and to the Church's traditional understanding of Christ, see Susan Wessel, *Cyril of Alexandria and the Nestorian Controversy: The Making of a Saint and a Heretic* (Oxford: Oxford University Press, 2004). Wessel devotes a substantial part of her book (pp. 183–252) to an analysis of the rhetoric used by the leading representatives of both sides.

perhaps, that Grillmeier's typology of "word-flesh" and "word-human being" Christology loses its usefulness and can become positively misleading, under the influence of mid-twentieth-century concerns.[4] Diodore himself, for instance, occasionally uses the traditional terminology of "the Logos and his flesh," without suggesting thereby any diminution of Jesus' humanity;[5] and Cyril is insistent, throughout his increasingly bitter controversy with Nestorius, that the "flesh," which he sometimes speaks of as forming "one nature" with the Word in the Incarnation, was a full human being, and that it included a complete and functioning rational human soul. Even if he made use, at times, of terms and formulas originally popularized by Apollinarius and his followers, Cyril was also, quite explicitly, no Apollinarian in his understanding of Christ's humanity. Neither "school," of course, was interested in seeking to recover a "historical Jesus" who was thought to be in any sense more real, more foundational to faith, more like ourselves, than the Jesus presented in the Gospel narrative; and neither "school" understood the "person" of Christ to be identified in any privileged way with his human consciousness, his freedom, his inner sense of identity.[6] Both of these are modern concerns—the latter perhaps anticipated in some aspects of Augustine's thought, but still remote from the general world of ancient philosophical and theological discourse.

Two things, I suggest, principally separated the thought-patterns of the theologians we label as "Antiochenes" and "Alexandrians" in the late fourth and early fifth century. One is a different sense of the relevance of *time* to human salvation in Christ. The Antiochenes, in general, seem to have thought of the fullness of human salvation as an *eschatological* state, mainly characterized by the gift of unchangeability and stability in the human response to grace, by freedom from sin and passion, and by the incorruptibility and immortality of the body. These graces are fully realized now only in the risen Jesus, who lives eschatologically already, in a different "state" (κατάστασις) or "world" than the world of space and time we inhabit. Theodore of Mopsuestia and Theodoret, especially, emphasize that salvation is given to us at present only as a promise, in the "pledge" of the Holy Spirit and in the "types" or anticipatory symbols of the Church's sacraments. When we move on from this present *katastasis* to the next, at the end of history, we will share—at least to the limited extent of which we are capable—in the state of transformation now revealed in the glorified human Christ.[7] Second, and rooted in this conviction

---

[4] See John McGuckin's sharp criticism of this widely accepted typology in *St. Cyril of Alexandria: The Christological Controversy* (Leiden: Brill, 1994), 205–7.

[5] See Rowan A. Greer, "The Antiochene Christology of Diodore of Tarsus," *JTS* 17 (1966), 327–41.

[6] See McGuckin, *St. Cyril*, 134, 207.

[7] For a discussion of this eschatological orientation of Antiochene thought, see especially Wilhelm de Vries, "Das eschatologische Heil bei Theodor von Mopsuestia," *Orientalia Christiana Periodica* 24 (1958), 309–38; Günter Koch, *Die Heilsverwirklichung bei Theodor von*

that the fullness of our salvation lies ahead of us, the Antiochene theologians show a strong interest in emphasizing the *boundaries* between God and creation, between God's sphere of being and activity and that of the concrete, historical world we inhabit.

> It is well known (writes Theodore in his fourth *Catechetical Homily*) that the one who is eternal and the one whose existence has a beginning are greatly separated from each other, and the gulf found between them is unbridgeable .... It is not possible to limit and define the chasm that exists between the one who is from eternity and the one who began to exist at a time when he was not. What possible resemblance and relation can exist between two beings so widely separated from each other?[8]

Unlike Athanasius, who also emphasized God's otherness with respect to creation, but who laid an equal, coordinate emphasis on the divine Logos's personal, substantial presence *within* creation as transcendent giver of order and life, the Antiochenes seem to have been mainly concerned to maintain God's *distance*—apparently, as we shall see, out of an underlying concern not to promote any idea of creation or salvation that might compromise the transcendent qualities of the three divine Persons: negative qualities, largely, such as freedom from circumscription and from suffering and mortality; qualities whose theoretical roots were at least as much in the Greek philosophical tradition as they were in the Bible. "Divinization" of the fallen human being— that category used frequently by Irenaeus, Athanasius, and the Cappadocians to sum up the central goal of Christ's saving work among us, and also vitally important to Augustine's thought—[9] is rarely mentioned by either Theodore or Theodoret, and then only in apparent connection with II Peter 1.4.[10]

In contrast to their admitted interest in biblical "history," perhaps, Antiochene theologians tend to begin their treatments of theological issues, including salvation in Christ, by discussing God's being in the more general terms of the unity of the divine substance and its common attributes, as understood from the Greek philosophical tradition, rather than in terms of

---

*Mopsuestia*, Münchener theologische Studien 31 (Munich: Max Hueber Verlag, 1965), 141–79; *Strukturen und Geschichte des Heils in der Theologie des Theodoret von Kyros: Eine dogmen- und theologiegeschichtliche Untersuchung*, Frankfurter theologische Studien 17 (Frankfurt: Knecht Verlag, 1974); Joanne McWilliam Dewart, *The Theology of Grace of Theodore of Mopsuestia* (Washington, DC: Catholic University of America Press, 1971), 30–48; and Brian E. Daley, S.J., *The Hope of the Early Church: A Handbook of Patristic Eschatology* (Cambridge: Cambridge University Press, 1991), 111–17.

[8] Theodore of Mopsuestia, *On the Nicene Creed*, Homily 4, trans. Alphonse Mingana, Woodbrooke Studies 5 (Cambridge: Heffer, 1932), 45.

[9] See especially David V. Meconi, *The One Christ: St. Augustine's Theology of Deification* (Washington, DC: Catholic University of America Press, 2013).

[10] For references, see Koch, *Heilsverwirklichung*, 150; *Strukturen und Geschichte des Heils*, 235–8.

the Scriptural narrative.[11] So in his so-called Sermon "against the Theotokos," which opened his long controversy with Cyril of Alexandria, Nestorius treats the person and saving work of Jesus within the context of God's general providence: because God, who transcends the world, never ceases to care for the world he has created—because God is "untouched by change," yet "benevolent and just"—he finally has "dignified [the world] with a gift which was furthest away and yet nearest to hand," and has taken up a human being, Jesus, to "bring about the revival of the human race."[12] These ideas were not new to Christian discourse, but the emphasis and priority the Antiochene theologians give them were heavy with implications for their understanding of the person of Christ.


## DIODORE OF TARSUS

Apart from his commentary on the Psalms, which was only identified as such in the twentieth century and has only been partially edited to date, *Diodore's* work unfortunately survives mainly in small fragments, most of them preserved by hostile sources. We know that Diodore was a prolific writer of vast learning; he is supposed to have produced commentaries on the entire Old Testament, as well as works on natural science and polemical treatises directed against the Jews, Neoplatonist philosophy, and a number of Christian sects. Many of the surviving dogmatic fragments that deal with the person of Christ are taken from his work *Against the Synousiasts*, which was apparently an anti-Apollinarian treatise, attacking the portrait of Christ as "the man from heaven," a unified organism formed by the divine Logos and his own living human flesh, which the Apollinarians had popularized.[13] In such a context, it is understandable that Diodore should have strongly emphasized the distinctness of the Logos from what he sometimes refers to as his "flesh"[14]—from the

---

[11] Koch, *Strukturen und Geschichte des Heils*, 235; see Theodoret, Ep. 145. For a corresponding preoccupation with God's unity of being and God's substantial attributes, rather than with the particular features of biblical revelation about God, in Theodoret's treatise on the Trinity, see Silke-Petra Bergjan, *Theodoret von Cyrus und der Neunizänismus* (Berlin: De Gruyter, 1993), 192–5.

[12] Nestorius, "First Sermon against the *Theotokos*," trans. Richard A. Norris, Jr, *The Christological Controversy* (Philadelphia, PA: Fortress, 1980), 126, 124; for the whole sermon, see 123–131.

[13] See above, pp. 127–135; also Rowan A. Greer, "The Man from Heaven: Paul's Last Adam and Apollinaris's Christ," in William S. Babcock (ed.), *Paul and the Legacies of Paul* (Dallas, TX: Southern Methodist University Press, 1990), 165–82.

[14] Fragment 36, in R. Abramowski, "Der theologische Nachlass des Diodor von Tarsus," *ZNTW* 42 (1949), 51–3; see also Aloys Grillmeier, *Christ in Christian Tradition*, I: *From the Apostolic Age to Chalcedon (451)*, trans. John Bowden (Oxford: Mowbray, 1975), 356.

historical human being in which he has revealed himself in our midst. What worried later critics was that Diodore, in his anti-Apollinarian works at least, seems also to have insisted on the distinction of "two Sons" in Christ: the son of Mary, who, as "temple" of God the Word, can be called "Son of God" by *grace*, and the one who is Son of God by *nature*, *homoousios* with the Father, God the Logos.

Like all the representatives of the Antiochene tradition who would come after him, Diodore seems to have been very concerned with theological precision; so he writes:

> If anyone, speaking inexactly, wants to call the Son of God, God the Word, son of David because of the temple of God the Word that was taken from David, let him call him so. And let him call the one descended from David's seed Son of God, by grace but not by nature—as long as he is not unaware of his natural ancestors and does not reverse the order, or say that the one who is incorporeal and before the ages *is* both from God and from David, both passible and impassible.[15]

Diodore is willing, in other words, to apply the title "Son of God" to Jesus as a conventional, non-literal way of pointing out that the man from Nazareth was, in God's providence, the bearer or dwelling-place of the eternal Son of God; but he insists one keep in mind the abiding distinction between what Jesus and the Word are in themselves, and what Jesus has become, by God's gracious action, in the divine economy. Still, in another fragment, he vigorously denies preaching "two sons" in any way that would be harmful to received Trinitarian or Christological doctrine:

> We urge you to find safety in being precise about doctrine. The Son, perfect before the ages, assumed a perfect descendant of David: the Son of God took the Son of David. You say to me, "Then you are proclaiming two sons?" I do not speak of two sons of David; for I did not say that God the Word is David's son, did I? Nor do I say there are two Sons of God in essence; for I do not say there are two produced from God's essence, do I? I say that God the eternal Word *dwelt* in him who is from the seed of David.[16]

The point seems almost a pedantic one, but one can see here already a strong sense of the need to draw a clear terminological boundary between the divine nature and the historical order in which God has worked salvation—the sense that God's transcendence needs to be protected from the assaults of pious imprecision—which would characterize both Diodore and his theological heirs.

---

[15] *Against the Synousiasts*, Frag. 4 (from Leontius of Byzantium, DTN).
[16] *Against the Synousiasts* Frag. 1. "Perfect" (τέλειος) here clearly refers to ontological completeness, not to moral excellence.

## THEODORE OF MOPSUESTIA

Perhaps the most gifted and the most influential of Diodore's theological heirs was his pupil Theodore of Mopsuestia. Like Diodore, Theodore spent at least ten years as a presbyter, teacher, and scriptural commentator in Antioch, in the 380s, before becoming bishop of Mopsuestia, some sixty miles north of the city, in 392. His exegesis, which has earned him the title "the Interpreter" in the tradition of the Assyrian Church of the East, follows the same analytical, sparingly figural approach Diodore had developed; it also seeks—as Diodore's interpretations did—to situate particular biblical passages in their presumed place within the longer narrative of God's people, as they are drawn towards eschatological salvation. But Theodore has also left catechetical and doctrinal works of great interest: fragments of a large treatise *On the Incarnation*, presumably directed against current Arian and Apollinarian conceptions of Christ, as Diodore's work had been; and a set of sixteen pre- and post-baptismal catecheses, which give us a precious view of how both the traditional creed and the prayer and sacraments of the Church were interpreted in late-fourth-century Antioch.

Like Diodore, Theodore is deeply concerned to draw a sharp, bright line between the transcendent, triune God—separated from creation, as we have already seen Theodore saying, by an "unbridgeable gulf" of being[17]—and the "human nature," the "form of a human being," which God the Son "put on" in order to reveal himself in the human world.[18] Theodore's usual way of speaking about the relation of the divine Son to the man Jesus is in terms of "indwelling," of presence as in a Temple (alluding to Jesus' words in John 2.19), or of the Son's "clothing" himself in the "form of a servant" (as suggested by Phil. 2.7). More important for him, however, than even these biblical images seems to have been the precise *mode* of the Son's presence in a visible, created human being. In a long and celebrated fragment of his treatise *On the Incarnation*, Theodore distinguishes between God's ways of being present "outside" himself in essence (οὐσία), in operation or activity (ἐνέργεια), and in "good pleasure" or "favor" (εὐδοκία). As the transcendent ground and source of all created being, and the provident guide of the universe in its continued functioning, God must be present to *all* creatures equally in his essence and in operation; so Theodore argues that the only way in which he can be *particularly* present or absent to individuals must be by the third way of "good pleasure," of love and grace. The Word's indwelling in Jesus, then, must be conceived along these lines, as representing a unique degree of divine

---

[17] Theodore of Mopsuestia, *On the Nicene Creed*, 45.
[18] *Cat. Hom.* 5 (trans. Mingana, 50–1); cf. *Cat. Hom.* 3 (Mingana, 36–7.): Jesus Christ is "the name of the man whom God put on ... , in whom he dwelt, and through whom he appeared and became known to humanity."

election and good pleasure: a unique identification of this man with the Word, by God's prior choice and action, which has enabled Jesus to reveal the Word uniquely to the world and to share uniquely in God's glory and work as judge and savior of human history. Theodore concludes:

> The indwelling took place in [Jesus] *as in a son*; it was in this sense that [God the Word] took pleasure in him and indwelt him. But what does it mean to say "as in a son"? It means that having indwelt him, he united the one assumed as a whole to himself and equipped him to share with himself in all the honor in which he, being Son by nature, participates, so as to be counted one person (*prosōpon*) in virtue of the union with him and share with him all his dominion, and in this way to accomplish everything in him, so that even the examination and judgment of the world shall be fulfilled through him and his advent. Of course, in all this the difference in natural characteristics is kept in mind.[19]

So Theodore is willing to accept the Church's traditional language of "Incarnation" to describe the presence of the Word in Jesus, provided one understands it as meaning simply that the Word of God actually became visible in human terms, and "assumed a complete man, who was a man not only in appearance but a man in a true human nature."[20] To take the Incarnation any more literally than this—to identify "the Son of the seed of David according to the flesh," of Romans 1.3, with the eternal Son of God—is theologically incorrect: "Indeed it is not God who became flesh, nor was it God who was formed from the seed of David, but the man who was assumed for us."[21] Theodore's favorite way of speaking about this "assumption," it seems, is in terms of *union*: it is a "close union" or "precise union" (ἄκρα ἕνωσις),[22] an "ineffable union" (ἄρρητος ἕνωσις),[23] a "perfect union (τέλεια ἕνωσις) between the one who was assumed and the one who assumed."[24] Theodore is insistent, too, that this union between Word and man is not something transitory: "the human form can never and under no circumstances be separated from the divine nature which put it on."[25] Jesus the man has been, since his conception, and will always be "precisely united" with God the Word. But Theodore is reluctant to speak of what it is that actually binds the divine Son and the man Jesus together in other than functional terms: the man was so led by the Holy Spirit that "he had the Logos of God working within him and throughout him in a perfect way, so as to be inseparable from the Logos in his every motion;"[26] and they are unified, most strikingly and most visibly, in the honor they

---

[19] *On the Incarnation* VII (Frag. 2), trans. Norris, 117.
[20] *Cat. Hom.* 5, trans. Mingana, 60; cf. Mingana, 54.
[21] *Cat. Hom.* 8, trans. Mingana, 91.
[22] e.g. *Cat. Hom.* 3, 6, 8, trans. Mingana, 36f.; 66f; 84; 91.
[23] e.g. *Cat. Hom.* 8, trans. Mingana, 86f.
[24] *Cat. Hom.* 6, trans. Mingana, 64.     [25] *Cat. Hom.* 8, trans. Mingana, 89.
[26] *On the Incarnation* VII (Frag. 3), trans. Norris, 117.

receive, both from God the Father and from the rest of creation, when the man Jesus is glorified.[27] Seizing on the biblical axiom that a husband and wife are "no longer two, but one flesh" (Gen. 2.24; Matt. 19.6), Theodore observes that a married couple clearly are not impeded from this unity by the abiding fact that they are still two people.

> In this same way here, they [i.e. the Word and Jesus] are two by nature and one by union: two by nature, because there is a great difference between the natures, and one by union because the adoration offered to the one who has been assumed is not differentiated from that to the one who assumed him, as the former is the temple from which it is not possible for the one who dwells in it to depart.[28]

Theodore's carefully constructed picture of the "perfect union" of two wholly different acting beings in Christ the Savior understandably affects his way of theologically interpreting the activities of Christ, as they are reported in the Gospels. In "assuming the fashion of a human being" and dwelling in him, the Logos "hid himself at the time in which he was in the world, and conducted himself with the human race in such a way that those who beheld him in a human way, and did not understand anything more, believed him to be simply human."[29] All the events of Jesus' life, guided by the indwelling Word, were intended by God to be saving Mysteries, Theodore goes on to suggest: events like his miraculous birth, his perfect observance of the Law, his baptism (which in Theodore's view "freed him from all the obligations of the Law"),[30] his formation of a community of disciples—all of which were models and types of the growth towards immortality in which we also hope to share.

> It was easy, not difficult, for God to have made him at once immortal, incorruptible and immutable, as he became after his resurrection, but because it was not he alone whom [God] wished to make immortal and immutable, but we also who are partakers of his nature, he rightly, and on account of this association, did not so make the first-fruits of us all, in order that, as the blessed Paul said, "He might have the pre-eminence in all things" (Col. 1.18). In this way, because of the communion that we have with him in this world, we will, with justice, be partakers with him of the future good things.[31]

---

[27] e.g. *Cat. Hom.* 6, 7, trans. Mingana, 65, 78, 80.

[28] *Cat. Hom.* 8, trans. Mingana, 90. For the analogy of marriage as uniting two individuals in "one flesh," see also *On the Incarnation* 8 (Frag. 7), trans. Norris, 120.

[29] *Cat. Hom.* 6, trans. Mingana, 65.    [30] *Cat. Hom.* 6, trans. Mingana, 70.

[31] *Cat. Hom.* 6, trans. Mingana, 69. Theodore explains this idea somewhat more fully a few paragraphs further on: "If Christ our Lord had immediately after his rising from the dead, raised also all those who had previously died, and had bestowed upon them new life fully and immediately, we should have been in no need of doing anything; as, however, he actually performed only on himself the renewal which is to come and through which he rose from the dead and his body became immortal and his soul immutable, it became necessary that this decrepit and mortal world should last further in order that humanity might believe in him and receive the hope of communion and future life" (*Cat. Hom.* 6, trans. Mingana, 70).

In reflections such as this, Theodore sounds strikingly similar to his contemporary, Gregory of Nyssa. Yet he emphasizes, too, that Jesus' growth in perfection was not simply the work of God; Jesus the man had to pursue virtue himself, even though

> it is plain that he fulfilled virtue more exactly and more easily than was possible for other people, since God the Logos, with his foreknowledge of the sort of person one will turn out to be, had united Jesus with himself in his very conception and furnished him with a fuller cooperation for the accomplishment of what was necessary.[32]

Passages like this make it easy to understand why the followers of Pelagius later found a welcome with Theodore's disciple, Nestorius, at Constantinople.

Theodore also emphasizes the reality of the sufferings and death of Jesus: a natural death whose public character served to emphasize by contrast the physical reality of his resurrection, "by which death was abolished."[33] Jesus' passion and death, of course, raise the ultimate difficulties to our accepting a literal understanding of the Word's Incarnation, and are only conceivable if we see them as taking place through a kind of temporary divine withdrawal from his human Temple. Alluding to a textual version of Hebrews 2.9, which was also known by Origen and some of his followers—"Apart from God ($\chi\omega\rho\grave{\iota}s$ $\Theta\epsilon o\hat{\upsilon}$) he [Jesus] tasted death for everyone"—Theodore emphasizes that Jesus was only able to die because the Godhead kept himself "cautiously remote" from him at that time, "yet also near enough to do the needful and necessary things for the nature he had assumed." He continues:

> He himself [i.e. the Word] was not tried with the trial of death, but he was near to him and doing to him the things that were congruous to his nature as the maker who is the cause of everything. That is, he brought him to perfection through sufferings and made him forever immortal, impassible, incorruptible, and immutable for the salvation of the multitudes who would be receiving communion ($\kappa o\iota\nu\omega\nu\acute{\iota}a$) with him.[34]

In all of his reflections in the *Catecheses* on the experiences of Jesus and their significance in the economy of salvation, at any rate, Theodore tends to speak of the Logos and the man in whom he dwelt, or even of the "natures" of divinity and humanity, as two agents, two "he's," without much further reflection on how precisely they can be thought of as one. Occasionally, however, he uses the terminology of *person (prosōpon)*—the concept of a "speaker" or dramatic "role," associated with an identifying theatrical "mask" or "face" *(prosōpon)*—to suggest that it is in their permanent association, in action and appearance,

---

[32] *On the Incarnation* VII (Frag. 5), trans. Norris, 119.
[33] *Cat. Hom.* 7, trans. Mingana, 74.     [34] *Cat. Hom.* 8, trans. Mingana, 87.

that the Word and the man Jesus find their lasting unity. So Theodore writes, in a fragment of *On the Incarnation*:

> When we try to distinguish the natures, we say that the "person" of the human being is complete and that that of the Godhead is complete. But when we consider the union, then we proclaim that both natures are one "person," since the humanity receives from the divinity honor surpassing that which belongs to a creature, and the divinity brings to perfection in the human being everything that is fitting.[35]

Clearly we must be careful not to read too much modern metaphysics, let alone Chalcedonian Christology, into Theodore's statement: "nature" usually carries for him the significance of "complete living reality," and "person"—far from suggesting a center of individual consciousness—seems to mean, for him and his contemporaries, the externally perceived, tangible form in which a given individual behaves. The Word and a human being, distinct "natures" that they are, so share their outward characteristics in Jesus—their form or "person"—in Theodore's view, that they become, for the rest of us, inseparably identified with each other in his activities as the "pioneer of our salvation" (Heb. 2.10).


## NESTORIUS OF CONSTANTINOPLE

Theodore's most famous pupil, undoubtedly, was the monk Nestorius, another native of the Cilician country north of Antioch. Having gained a reputation in the Syrian metropolis for both his eloquence as a preacher and his fierce commitment to Nicene orthodoxy, as well as for his ascetical seriousness, Nestorius was brought to Constantinople as bishop in the spring of 428, when the court and the local synod were unable to agree on a suitable local candidate. The contemporary ecclesiastical historian Socrates, usually restrained in his judgments, characterizes him as vain, quarrelsome, and utterly intolerant of other opinions,[36] and hazards the judgment that despite his reputation—and his high view of himself—Nestorius was "disgracefully illiterate" in the theological tradition.[37] In a response to a Marian sermon by Proclus, a revered local spiritual figure, which seems to have quickly provoked (at least in theological terms) the outbreak of open hostilities between himself and Cyril of Alexandria, Nestorius gives voice to a somewhat more rigid version of Theodore's conception of the person of Christ than we find in Theodore's own works. Like his Antiochene forbears, Nestorius is mainly concerned here to draw clear distinctions between the divine Logos, who has

---

[35] *On the Incarnation* VIII (Frag. 8), trans. Norris, 120–1.
[36] *Ecclesiastical History* 7.29.  [37] *Ecclesiastical History* 7. 32.

achieved human salvation in Christ, and Jesus, the Son of Mary, who was the Logos's "temple," "the instrument of his godhead."[38] *God* cannot be born, *God* cannot die, he insists: but God, who is above all change, is also active in the world, benevolent towards his creatures.[39] So God the Son, in Paul's words, "emptied himself, taking the *form* of a slave" (Phil 2.7); he "assumed a person (*prosōpon*), of the same nature [as ours]"[40] in order to pay to God the debt our created nature had incurred through sin.[41] In this human form or "person," which now *belongs* to the Son of God, Nestorius argues, our shared human nature, our common reality, was able to plead its case before God against the devil, who brought charges against it going back to Adam. Pointing to the innocence of Jesus, the new Adam, human nature as a whole calls out for release from the punishment of corruption and mortality;

> Our nature, having been put on by Christ like a garment, intervenes on our behalf, being entirely free from all sin and contending by appeal to its blameless origin ... [42] This was the opportunity which belonged to the assumed man, as a human being: to dissolve, by means of the flesh, that corruption which arose by means of the flesh.[43]

And the reason human nature can now make this claim on God is that it is not simply the claim of Adam's children, but is voiced by "the Christ, who is at once God and man."[44] The human being Jesus, who is the created instrument of the Word, is honored and worshipped and followed by the faithful because he has been united with the Word, because the Word is "within" him and has "assumed" him as his "instrument."[45] In Nestorius's rhetoric, the very *difference* between the deity and humanity that have come together in Christ is what makes possible his uniquely exalted position as Savior.

Later on in the 430s and 440s, the now-exiled Nestorius attempted laboriously to defend his own orthodoxy in a series of tracts and letters, some of which have come down to us in a collection known (for reasons that are not entirely clear) as the *Book of Heracleides*.[46] There Nestorius attempts, among

---

[38] "First Sermon against the Theotokos", trans. Norris, 125. In his translation, Norris here relies on the conjectural reconstruction of Nestorius's sermon—apparently delivered in reply to Proclus, probably early in 429—by Friedrich Loofs; this is based on the partial Latin translation by Marius Mercator (PL 48.757–65) and on other reassembled Greek and Latin fragments. See Loofs, *Nestoriana: die Fragmente des Nestorius* (Halle: Niemeyer, 1905), 249–64.

[39] "First Sermon" (Loofs 250–1), trans. Norris, 125–6.

[40] "First Sermon" (Loofs 256), trans. Norris, 127.

[41] "First Sermon" (Loofs 255–6), trans. Norris, 126–7.

[42] Nestorius here seems to be referring to Jesus' virginal conception.

[43] "First Sermon" (Loofs 259), trans. Norris, 128.

[44] "First Sermon" (Loofs 260), trans. Norris, 129.

[45] "First Sermon" (Loofs 260), trans. Norris, 129.

[46] This compilation of various polemical and apologetic treatises of Nestorius, written after 431 and including numerous interpolations by his later defenders, survives only in a somewhat cumbersome Syriac translation, edited by Paul Bedjan (Paris: Letouzey et Ané, 1910) and

other things, to develop a model of Christ's single agency based on the idea of "union by *persona* (or *prosōpon*)," in order to clear himself from the widely-accepted charge of having taught that the Word and Jesus were in reality "two Sons." The underlying conception behind Nestorius's argument seems to be based, in biblical terms, at least, on the familiar text Philippians 2.6–7, where Christ is said to have put aside the "form of God" (*morphē theou*) and have taken up the "form of a slave" (*morphē doulou*), so that he "came to be in human likeness (*homoiōmati*), and was found, in shape, as a human being (*schēmati hōs anthrōpos*)." Probably drawing on Neoplatonic theory as well as on earlier Antiochene usage,[47] Nestorius speaks of these various "forms" or "appearances" as *prosōpa*: "faces" or "personae." Every natural, individual being, he suggests in the *Book of Heracleides*, has its own *prosōpon*, its external form or self-presentation, put forth by its intrinsic natural properties, which allows it to be known by others. Since the Word of God and the historical man Jesus are irreducibly distinct in their own fundamental realities, and since any suggestion of a *blending* of the two would inevitably compromise either the transcendence of the Word or the humanity of Jesus—making him into either an Arian or an Apollinarian version of the Son of God—Nestorius argues that what the Incarnation really means is that each of the two realities in Christ has conferred its own "face" or form on the other, forming a single, externally perceptible composite whole, which in their collaboration appears and acts as one. Nestorius insists this exchange of *prosōpa* is more than a matter of simple behavior, of "acting as if"; by conferring their "faces" or "likenesses" on each other, the Word and the man actually "form" each other into something new. So he writes, alluding to Philippians 2:

> For he [the Word] exists in his hypostasis and has made it [the flesh?] the likeness of his likeness, neither by command nor by honor nor simply by the equality of grace, but he has made it his likeness in its natural likeness [= form], in such a way that it is none other than that very thing which he has taken for his own *prosōpon*, so that the one might be the other and the other the one, one and the same in the two substances: a *prosōpon* [of the Son of God] fashioned by the flesh and fashioning the flesh in the likeness of its own Sonship, in the two natures, and

---

translated originally by François Nau (Paris: Letouzey et Ané, 1910), as *Le Livre d'Héraclide de Damas*. An even more cumbersome English translation of the Syriac text, by Godfrey R. Driver and Leonard Hodgson, later appeared, under the title *The Bazaar of Heraclides* (Oxford: Clarendon Press, 1925). The title given the work by Driver and Hodgson takes literally the Syriac title in the manuscripts, *Tegurthā*, "market-place"; this seems, however, to be a mistranslation of Greek πραγματεῖα, "business" or "treatise." It is not clear whether "Heraclides" was a *nom de plume* of the exiled Nestorius, or the name of some correspondent.

[47] See Luigi Scipioni, *Ricerche sulla* cristologia *del "Libro di Eraclide" di Nestorio: la formulazione teologica e il suo contesto filosofico*, Paradosis 11 (Fribourg: Edizioni Universitarie, 1956); Grillmeier, *Christ in Christian Tradition*, I, 461–73.

one in the two natures—the one fashioned by the other and the other by the one, the same unique likeness of the *prosōpon*.[48]

The language is tangled, partly because it is filtered for us through a Syriac and then an English translation, but the idea seems clear enough: Nestorius wants to affirm a genuine and lasting unity of some kind between the eternal Word and the human Jesus—a unity that is more than mere association; yet he insists on conceiving this union simply in terms of an exchange of perceptible forms, the Word shaping the human Jesus into someone who reveals *God*, and Jesus giving the transcendent Word of God *human words* and a *human face*. Nestorius is strenuously opposed, here as in his earlier works, to any way of conceiving the unity of Christ in terms of classical ontology—whether one uses the more abstract, universal, Aristotelian term *ousia* (what a thing is), or the more concrete, less well-defined term *hypostasis* (the real individual thing). To see Christ's unity as substantial or concrete individual unity implies, for Nestorius, inevitably that either God the Word is capable of change and suffering, and therefore less than fully God, or that the humanity of Jesus is incomplete, simply a fleshly, external vehicle for the Word. It also implies that Christ's sufferings, because they occur in a human being naturally, would have been less than free when undergone by God the Son, and therefore less valuable in the sight of his Father. Nestorius writes:

> By all means, therefore, we shun those who speak of the Incarnation apart from this union: either by a change only in likeness, which is the view of the pagans, or in hallucinations, or in a form (*schēma*) without hypostasis which "suffers impassibly" [a phrase used by Cyril]; or in predicating natural sufferings of God the Word, as being either hypostatically united to the flesh, or in the flesh as [lacking] a rational or irrational soul;[49] or, finally, in asserting that the union resulted in a natural hypostasis and not a voluntary *prosōpon*. For we may not make the union of God the Word corruptible and changeable, nor call it passible and necessary, but it is a voluntary union, in *prosōpon* and not in nature.[50]

For Nestorius as for Theodore of Mopsuestia, what was most to be feared in speaking of the Incarnation as substantial or natural, or as the hypostatic or concretely realized union of the Word and an individual man, was that such a union compromised the transcendent qualities of God in the process: his impassibility, his unchangeability, his freedom. *God* reveals himself in Christ, but as God—not as being himself part of our world.

[48] *Book of Heracleides* 233, trans. Driver and Hodgson, 159 (altered).
[49] Here the text is uncertain.
[50] *Book of Heracleides* 264–5, trans. Driver and Hodgson, 181 (altered).

## THEODORET OF CYRUS

The final great representative of the Antiochene school, to whom we can only give brief treatment here, was Theodoret of Cyrus: a contemporary and measured defender of Nestorius, a bitter critic of Cyril of Alexandria; yet also the most moderate of the Antiochenes in his understanding of the unity of Christ, the most ready to profit from the controversies of the time and to work towards a conciliatory position. In his late work, the dialogue *Eranistes*,[51] Theodoret mounts an elaborate refutation of what he understands to be the weakness of the Alexandrian approach to Christ: that it so emphasizes the *identity* of God and the human in Christ—that it takes John 1.14, "The Word *became* flesh and dwelt among us," so literally—that the Word of God is seen as himself undergoing change, rather than simply being the saving agent of change in humanity. For Theodoret, such an assertion that would contradict "the incorporeal, illimitable character of the divine nature."[52]

Theodoret insists, throughout the three books of this dialogue, that an accurate theology, faithful to the Christian tradition, must always draw a clear, even an ontological distinction between the human Jesus, who underwent real change and suffering, and who received the gift of incorruptibility only in his resurrection, and the divine Word, who had made the human Jesus inseparably his own. Even though Theodoret is willing to accept conventional language which "exchanges the titles" proper to Jesus as man with those proper to the Word—a practice exhibited in a Pauline text like I Cor. 2.3, "They would not have crucified the Lord of glory"—he constantly stresses that it was the *man* and not "the divine nature" that suffered on the cross. So he insists that the two sets of properties, predicated properly of either a human being or of God, are in fact here united only in the *prosopon*, the single acting figure formed by the two utterly different individuals or *hypostases* that are the Word and Jesus, now functionally but indivisibly united in their saving actions as the Christ.[53] So Theodoret affirms, through the mouth of his "Orthodox" (i.e. Antiochene) speaker, a somewhat more moderate version of what has been argued by Thedodore and Nestorius:

> It behooves us to say that the flesh was nailed to the tree, but to hold that the divine nature even on the cross and in the tomb was inseparable from this flesh, though from it it derived no sense of suffering—since the divine nature is

---

[51] The title of the work means "the Beggar": an uncomplimentary term, suggesting a homeless person who lives on what he or she is able to scramble together. It seems to be a satirical reference to Cyril of Alexandria, against whom the treatise is directed, suggesting that his arguments are eclectic and unoriginal.

[52] See Theodoret, *Eranistes*, Dialogue I, ed. Gerard H. Ettlinger (Oxford: Oxford University Press, 1975), 66.4–68.12.

[53] *Eranistes*, Dial. III, ed. Ettlinger, 209.26–30.

naturally incapable of undergoing both suffering and death and its substance is
immortal and impassible … And when we are told of passion and of the cross,
we must recognize the nature which submitted to the passion; we must avoid
attributing it [i.e. suffering] to the impassible one, and must attribute it to that
nature which was assumed for the distinct purpose of suffering.[54]

The main task of orthodox theological language, Theodoret assumes, is to keep
this substantial distinction between the divine and the human constantly
before the Church's eyes, even while we affirm their wonderful unity of action
in the story of salvation.

## CYRIL OF ALEXANDRIA

The main contemporary opponent of Theodore, Nestorius, and Theodoret, of
course, from the late 420s until his death in 446, was Cyril of Alexandria,
undoubtedly the most thoughtful, as well as the most prolific, fifth-century
spokesman for the long, mutually interwoven Alexandrian tradition of theology and biblical exegesis. Apart from whatever political and ecclesiastical
motives may have lain behind Cyril's fierce campaign against Nestorius during
the late 420s, in the imperial capital of Constantinople and in the West—and
these doubtless played their part, as they did in most ancient theological
controversies—Cyril's opposition rested on a fundamentally different way
of conceiving and speaking about the Mystery of the person of Christ and
about human salvation: different terminology, different emphases, a different
rhetoric. As John McGuckin and others have emphasized in recent years,
Cyril's Christology becomes intelligible if one understands that its starting-
point, its non-negotiable axiom, is not so much the *otherness* of the divine
nature with respect to circumscribed, mutable, passible creatures, as the
*involvement* of God the Son, the second hypostasis of the divine Trinity, in
the historical process of salvation we call God's "management" of things—his
"economy."[55] As a result, it is crucial to Cyril to emphasize the *continuity* in
the narrative of the Scriptures and the creeds, by emphasizing the single
subject of the acts that have saved us: it is God the Word, God the Son, who
is born of a Virgin, who receives his own Holy Spirit from the Father in
baptism for our sakes, who heals the sick and raises the dead by his human
touch, who dies in his own human body on the cross, and who reunites that
body with his own human soul on the morning of the resurrection. Cyril is

[54] *Eranistes*, Dial. III, ed. Ettlinger 227.2–6; 228.23–5; trans. Blomfield Jackson, NPNF II,
3.233–4.
[55] McGuckin, *St. Cyril*, 184; see also John J. O'Keefe, "Impassible Suffering? Divine Passion
and Fifth-century Christology," *Theological Studies* 58 (1997), 39–60, esp. 58.

always careful to distinguish his understanding of the person of Christ from that of Apollinarius: the "one nature," as he sometimes refers to Christ—the one real, living agent; the Word, who has "been made flesh" in time—of course includes in his biblically named "flesh" a complete human mind, a "rational soul." Cyril remains willing to agree with his Antiochene critics that the Logos, as God, does not undergo change or limitation or suffering in his own *divine nature*, even while he insists that it is this very Logos as *agent*, as subject, who experiences precisely these things in what has become, by the "economy" of incarnation, his own passible, changeable *human flesh*. The Word became flesh, Cyril often reminds us, precisely in order that, as transcendent God, he might suffer what we suffer.

In his first statement of this Christological approach within a context of controversy—his so-called "second letter" to Nestorius, in which he takes the Constantinopolitan bishop to task for the deficiencies in his recent formulation of the Mystery—Cyril expresses his own position concisely yet completely, as he contrasts it with that of Nestorius. Citing the Nicene Creed as the guide for what must be said of Christ, and for how one must say it, he explains:

> We do not say that the Logos became flesh by having his nature changed, nor, for that matter, that he was transformed into a complete human being composed out of soul and body. On the contrary, we say that in an unspeakable and incomprehensible way, the Logos united to himself, in his hypostasis, flesh enlivened by a rational soul, and in this way became a human being and has been designated "Son of man." He did not become a human being simply by an act of will or "good pleasure" (εὐδοκία), any more than he did so by merely taking on a "person" (πρόσωπον).
>
> Furthermore, we say that while the natures which were brought together into a true unity were different, there is, nevertheless, because of the unspeakable and unutterable convergence into unity, one Christ and one Son out of the two. This is the sense in which it is said that, although he existed and was born from the Father before the ages, he was also born of a woman in his flesh ... It is not the case that first of all an ordinary human being was born of the holy Virgin and that the Logos descended upon him subsequently. On the contrary, since the union took place in the very womb, he is said to have undergone a fleshly birth by making his own the birth of the flesh which belonged to him. We assert that this is the way in which he suffered and rose from the dead. It is not that the Logos of God suffered in his own nature, being overcome by stripes or nail-piercing or any of the other injuries; for the divine, since it is incorporeal, is impassible. Since, however, the body that had become his own underwent suffering, he is—once again—said to have suffered these things for our sakes, for the impassible one was within the suffering body.[56]

---

[56] Cyril of Alexandria, *Second Letter to Nestorius*, ACO I, 1.26.25–27.18, trans. Norris, 132–3.

In reading this text, it is important to pay close attention to Cyril's language: to the nouns and pronouns he uses as subjects, to the tenses of his verbs, to the particular terms and expressions he chooses to signify the personal unity of Christ. As in the Nicene Creed, the subject of the narrative is God the Logos; *he* is the one who became a human being, experienced true birth from a human mother, and suffered in the way only humans can suffer. Christology is not about "divinity" and "humanity," first of all, but about *what the Son of God did* for our sakes. Second, the verbs reveal a real sense of the importance of time, of narrative sequence: "the natures he brought together *were* different, yet there *is* now convergence ... , one Son out of the two;" what *were* different *are* now, in a new sense altogether, "one and the same." And thirdly, Cyril speaks here and elsewhere of this new unity in Christ as "union in hypostasis" (ἕνωσις καθ᾽ ὑπόστασιν)—union in the concreteness of an individual existence—and later even as "union in nature" (ἕνωσις κατὰ φύσιν), apparently understanding "nature," too, not so much in a generic sense, but as the living actuality of an organic individual being.[57] The Word can be said to have "made his own (οἰκειοῦσθαι) a fleshly birth," so that the flesh of Jesus, its sufferings and even its death, are now "his."[58]

The implications of this picture of Christ, which can be found consistently— if with a discernible development in its terminology—in all of Cyril's controversial writings after 430, are both linguistic and substantive. Linguistically, Cyril delights in using the somewhat shocking turns of phrase that theologians refer to as "the communication of properties": predicating human experiences directly of God the Word, and divine qualities directly of the man Jesus. In his celebrated "Third Letter to Nestorius," for instance—doubtless a piece meant to stake out the boundaries between his own approach and that of the Antiochenes as clearly and as confrontationally as possible—he refers to the Eucharistic species as "the personal, truly vitalizing flesh of God the Word himself,"[59] and later goes on to anathematize those who "do not acknowledge God's Word as having suffered in flesh, been crucified in flesh, tasted death in

---

[57] For ἕνωσις κατὰ φύσιν in Cyril's usage, see, for example, his *Third Letter to Nestorius*, section 4: "he was united actually [or 'naturally': κατὰ φύσιν] with his flesh, without being changed into it, and brought about the sort of residence in it which a man's soul can be said to have in relation to its body" (ACO I, 1.1.36.11-13; trans. L. R. Wickham, *Cyril of Alexandria: Select Letters* [Oxford: Clarendon Press, 1983], 19). See also c. 5, where he speaks of the divinity and humanity of Christ as "two natures," and anathema 3: "Whoever divides the *hypostases* [individuals] in respect to the one Christ after the union, joining them together just in a conjunction (συνάφεια) involving rank—i.e. sovereignty—or authority instead of a combination involving actual union (ἕνωσις φυσική) shall be anathema" (ACO I, 1.1.40.28-30; trans. Wickham, 29). For a massive study of Cyril's use of "nature" language, see Hans Van Loon, *The Dyophysite Christology of Cyril of Alexandria* (Leiden: Brill, 2009).

[58] For this language, see also Cyril's *First Letter to Succensus* 6 (ACO I, 1.6.153.19-20).

[59] *Third Letter to Nestorius* 7 (ACO I, 1.1.37.28-29), trans. Wickham, 23; cf. anathema 11 (ACO I, 1.1.41.28-42.2).

flesh and been made first-born from the dead, because as God he is Life and life-giving."[60] Just like the title *Theotokos* for Mary, which first moved Nestorius to insist on some distinctions in the interest of Nicene orthodoxy, these phrases seem deliberately meant to be limit-cases, "hard sayings" (see John 6.60) that test the extent to which we are willing to affirm that God the Word is really the one who has saved us in the person and works of Jesus, that God the Word is really the one we encounter in Jesus' humanity—and even now in his sacramental presence in the Church. The Christological debate, for Cyril, is clearly not simply a debate over how we think and talk about the Savior; it is also a consideration of what we actually understand God to have done for us, to be doing still with us, in Christ.

For Cyril as well as for his Antiochene interlocutors, the most challenging and perhaps the most substantive aspect of the paradox of Christ's person was his suffering: must Christians affirm that God the Son is the one who suffered, in his own flesh, on the cross, or must one make a strict distinction in identity between the suffering one and the one who inspired and ultimately raised him? Cyril insists most emphatically, in many of his later works, that the first of these statements is, in fact, the central affirmation of Christian faith. So he asks, in his third *Tome against Nestorius*, "By faith in whom, then, are we justified? Is it not in him who suffered death according to the flesh for our sake? Is it not in one Lord Jesus Christ? Have we not been redeemed by proclaiming his death and confessing his resurrection?"[61] Cyril is willing to concede, by the mid 430s, that the humanity and the divinity that belong to Christ can be distinguished as two separate natures—two operative realms of being, in themselves wholly different from each other—by a kind of exercise in thought "at the merely speculative level" (*kata monēn tēn theōrian*), as long as one recognizes that in fact "they belong to one individual, so that the two are two no more, but one living being is brought to its full realization through both."[62] And it is this "one living being"—God the eternal Word, who has taken on our "flesh" in time—who therefore is the conscious, willing subject of his flesh's passion:

> The passion therefore will belong to the economy, God the Word esteeming as his own the things which pertain to his own flesh, by reason of the ineffable union,

---

[60] *Third Letter to Nestorius*, anathema 12 (ACO I, 1,1.42.3–5), trans. Wickham, 33. For discussions of the importance of an understanding of the Eucharist in Cyril's presentation of the person of Christ, see Henry Chadwick, "Eucharist and Christology in the Nestorian Controversy," *JTS* 2 (1951), 145–64; Ezra Gebremedhin, "Life-giving Blessing: An Inquiry into the Eucharistic Doctrine of Cyril of Alexandria," Ph.D. thesis, Uppsala University, 1977; Ellen Concannon, "The Eucharist as the Source of St. Cyril of Alexandria's Christology," *Pro Ecclesia* 18 (2009), 318–36.
[61] *Against Nestorius* 3.2 (ACO I, 1, 6.61.25–26), trans. Norman Russell, *Cyril of Alexandria* (London: Routledge, 2000), 165.
[62] *Second Letter to Succensus* 5 (ACO I, 1.6.162.2–9).

and remaining external to suffering as far as pertains to his own nature, for God is impassible.[63]

For this reason, Cyril even affirms, on a number of occasions, that Christ, as the Word with his "flesh," "suffered impassibly"—a paradox that excited the amazement and scorn of his Antiochene opponents, and has puzzled a number of modern scholars.[64] As J. Warren Smith has pointed out, in some of these passages Cyril suggests that the "impassible suffering" of Christ is more than simply a paradox intended to test our grasp of the Mystery of his person; Cyril also presents it as "an example (ὑποτύπωσις) for us in human fashion ... , so that we might follow in his steps."[65] If one remembers that suffering, like all human "passions" or passivities, was understood in the Hellenistic world as an experience that normally destroys the harmony and integrity of a natural organism, a sensory signal of lack of autonomy and of disintegration, Jesus' "impassible suffering"—seen as human passivity and vulnerability freely taken on and "owned" by the life-giving Word of God, in his human body and soul—becomes the means by which the Word heals *our* passions and destructive weaknesses, first of all in his own humanity, and so turns our suffering into a means of growth. So Cyril writes of the supreme significance of the death of Christ as the climax of his freely assumed sufferings, in his *Letter to the Monks*, one of the earliest documents of his controversy with Nestorius, during the summer of 431:

> As one of us, though he knew not death, he went down into death through his own flesh, in order that we might also go up with him to life. For he came to life again, having despoiled the nether world, not as a human like us but as God in flesh, among us and above us (μεθ' ἡμῶν καὶ ὑπὲρ ἡμᾶς). Our nature was greatly enriched with immortality in him first, and death was crushed when it assaulted the body of life as an enemy. For just as it conquered in Adam, so it was defeated in Christ.[66]

---

[63] *Scholia on the Incarnation* 13 (ACO I, 5.223.30–2), trans. P. E. Pusey (Oxford: Parker and Rivingtons, 1881), 225.

[64] Cyril, *To the Royal Ladies, on Right Faith* 2.164 (ACO I, 1.5.50.9); *On the Creed* 24 ("he suffered humanly, yet is seen as divinely impassible") (ACO I, 1.4.58.25–6); *That Christ is One* (SCh 97.468–76), trans. John McGuckin, *On the Unity of Christ* (Crestwood, NY: St. Vladimir's, 1995), 116–18; see Theodoret, *Eranistes* III, ed. Ettlinger, 218.29–34. For a discussion of what is involved in the Son's personal experience of human suffering in his flesh, see also Cyril's *Second Letter to Succensus* 4–5 (ACO I, 1.6.162.4–25). Cf. Joseph M. Hallman, *The Descent of God: Divine Suffering in History and Theology* (Minneapolis, MN: Fortress, 1991); "The Seeds of Fire: Divine Suffering in the Christology of Cyril of Alexandria and Nestorius of Constantinople," *Journal of Early Christian Studies* 5 (1997), 369–91; O'Keefe, "Impassible Suffering?"; Paul L. Gavrilyuk, *The Suffering of the Impassible God: The Dialectics of Patristic Thought* (Oxford: Oxford University Press, 2009).

[65] *To the Royal Ladies* 2.164. See J. Warren Smith, "'Suffering Impassibly': Christ's Passion and Divine Impassibility in Cyril of Alexandria," *Pro Ecclesia* 11 (2002), 463–83.

[66] *Letter to the Monks of Egypt* 26 (ACO I, 1.1.22.30–23.3), trans. John L. McInerny; Fathers of the Church 76 (Washington, DC: Catholic University of America Press, 1985), 32–3.

What was really at stake for Cyril, it seems, in the question of the suffering of the incarnate Word, as in all the other issues surrounding the unity of subject in Christ, was the divine economy itself: to attribute the acts and words, and even the sufferings, of Jesus to anyone but God the Son, to anything but the Word acting in his own flesh, is, for Cyril, to compromise the witness of the Gospel. Quoting John 3.16—"God so loved the world that he gave his only-begotten Son"—Cyril asks plaintively, in his late dialogue *On the Unity of Christ*:

> When God the Father so exalts his love for the world, explaining how immensely great and vast it is, then why do our opponents so belittle it, saying that it was not the true Son who was given for us? They introduce in place of the natural Son someone else who is like us, and has the sonship as a grace; but it really was the Only-begotten who was given for our sake ... What will then be left of the great and admirable love of the Father, if he only gave up a part of the world for its sake, and a small part at that? Perhaps it would not even be wrong to say that the world was redeemed without God's help, since it was served in this respect from within its own resources?[67]

If it is God who has redeemed the world, and if he has done it in Christ, who is personally God's own Son, then Cyril insists we must see the story of Christ as nothing less than a story about God himself.

## CONCLUSIONS

Much more, of course, needs to be said about the rich and sophisticated Christological reflections of Cyril and Theodoret, and even of Theodore and his less "literate" pupil, Nestorius. The point here is that one fails to do them or their long debate full justice if one sees it simply as a prolonged wrangling over concepts and terminology and formulas—over the relative value of *hypostasis* and *prosōpon*, "one nature" or "two"—let alone as a contest between more and less adequate ways of presenting the human soul of Christ and its faculties. In fact, the real issues that divided the theologians of Antioch and Alexandria in the fourth and fifth centuries could probably be expressed in broader questions such as these:

1. *What is the tradition of theological language really about?* For Nestorius and Theodoret, at least, its purpose was to prevent us from making dangerous mistakes about God: it needed to be precise, self-conscious, and technically sophisticated if it was to avoid the pitfalls of Arianism, Apollinarianism, or

---

[67] *On the Unity of Christ* (SChr. 97.482), trans. McGuckin, 120–1.

pagan myth. For Cyril, its purpose was to express and elicit reverence and wonder at the great things God has done for us; it was evocative of Christian faith's central mysteries, deliberately paradoxical, redolent of the atmosphere of liturgical prayer. The great danger to be avoided was speaking of Christ in overly secular, simply philosophical terms.

2. *How should one read the Scriptures?* Both the Antiochene and the Alexandrian traditions of theology were rooted in highly developed cultures of scholarly biblical interpretation; both "schools" recognized in the Christian biblical canon a single witness to a single story of salvation, beginning in Israel's remembered history and culminating in the person and work of Christ—a story summed up in the Churches' ancient "rule of faith," and in creeds like that of Nicaea.[68] But the Antiochenes insisted on the need for a certain degree of hermeneutical sophistication if one were to read the Bible in a way worthy of God—a hermeneutic based on the Greek philosophical tradition about what the ultimate divine reality is and is not. Cyril was aware of these philosophical traditions, too, and was willing to use them to the degree that they did not obscure the shocking originality of the biblical message; but Scripture itself, as received in the Christian liturgy and interpreted in the Christian tradition of faith—not philosophy—for him had to be the starting point of Christian theology, and the source of Christian theological terms. So on the question of the suffering of the Word in his flesh, he concludes his argument by saying: "Inspired Scripture tells us he suffered in 'flesh,' and we would do better to use those terms than to talk of his suffering 'in a human nature'."[69] Philosophical language always brought with it the subtle tendency to place human reasoning about what God must be like above the Gospel message about who and what God is.

---

[68] Susan Wessel plausibly argues, in fact, that much of the force of the rhetoric used by both the Antiochene and the Alexandrian sides in these debates was aimed at situating their own way of conceiving Christ's person squarely within the Nicene tradition. "Here we see a new idea," she writes, "about how orthodox doctrine is formed. The procedure seems to be similar to that by which legal precedent is set. Each party in the Nestorian controversy laid claim to a common orthodox legacy by using an argumentative strategy that would let them demonstrate by means of carefully chosen arguments that their Christological position remained true to a shared, inherited past" (*Cyril of Alexandria*, 268-9). By suggesting that their opponents held positions similar to those of recognized heretics like Arius or Apollinarius, and by insisting that only their own conception of Christ remained true to the now-normative narrative of the classic creeds, both sides implicitly presented their own position as the only possible expression of orthodox faith. From now on, this argumentative strategy was to remain the central rhetorical form of the ancient councils.

So the decree of the Alexandrian party gathered for the Council at Ephesus in the summer of 431—the council that, in its membership, never managed to be ecumenical—stipulates that no new formula of faith should ever take the place of the creed of Nicaea: "After having these read aloud [i.e. selections from contemporary theologians], the holy synod decreed that no one should be allowed to profess or compose another formula of faith, or to add to this one, which was decreed by the holy Fathers gathered at Nicaea, with the help of the Holy Spirit" (ACO I, 1.7.105.20-2).

[69] *Second Letter to Succensus* 5 (ACO I, 1.6.163.11-12), trans. Wickham, 93.

3. *How does God save us?* The Antiochene theologians tend to understand salvation in terms similar to Gregory of Nyssa's: as God-given human growth in moral virtue and stability, coupled with freedom from physical corruptibility—both of which are presently visible in the risen Christ, but are promised to us in their full realization only in the age to come. The Antiochenes speak a good deal of the work of grace and of the presence of the Holy Spirit in the Church, a work that begins the transformation of humanity; but they are noticeably reluctant to use the language of a presently experienced "divinization." In fact, these theologians tend to conceive of grace, to use Augustine's terminology, more in co-operative than in operative terms, more as assistance to us in carrying out of our choices than as the creation of new freedom. God clearly has begun the work of redemption among us, but—as in the young Jesus (Luke 2.52)—he expects us to "grow in grace by pursuing the virtue which is attendant upon understanding and knowledge."[70] For Cyril, on the other hand, grace is God's work, relying wholly on God's initiative, just as the story of salvation is the story of God's action, not ours. Nestorius, in fact, criticizes Cyril by saying "You take as the starting point of your narrative the maker of the natures [in Christ], and not the *prosōpon* of union":[71] Cyril begins with *God*, he suggests, not with the Christ who is a balanced union of what is divine and what is human.

Cyril, on the other hand, would probably have been ready to accept this criticism; he, too, sees union with God as the *end* of the narrative, but precisely as the goal of a transformation in grace that begins even now in the life of faith. Like the Antiochenes, he frequently draws on II Peter 1.4 to remind his readers that salvation in Christ means we are to become "sharers in the divine nature"; but he seems to see that process as already under way, less exclusively as an eschatological reality. So in his *Commentary on John*—a work from the 420s, antedating the Nestorian controversy by as much as five years—Cyril reflects on the Mystery of Christ's person as the foundation of the Church's unity:

> He came into being at once as God and a human being, so that by joining together in himself things that are widely separate in nature and have diverged from all kinship with each other, he might reveal humanity as a participant and "sharer in the divine nature" … So the Mystery of Christ has come into being as a kind of beginning, a way for us to share in the Holy Spirit and in unity with God: all of us are made holy in that Mystery.[72]

For Cyril, the transforming power of Christ that will result in divinization, for those who accept it, is already present in the Church, already communicated

---

[70] Theodore of Mopsuestia, *On the Incarnation* VII (Frag. 5), trans. Norris, 119. On Theodore's understanding of grace, see especially Dewart, *Theology of Grace*, 49–73.

[71] *Book of Heracleides* 225, trans. Driver and Hodgson, 153 (altered).

[72] *Commentary on John* 11.11, ed. P. E. Pusey, 998a–1000a.

to believers in the Gospel and in the Eucharist, which is "the life-giving flesh of the Word of God."[73] For those willing to accept it, the promise has already begun to be a reality.

4. *How is God related to this created order?* How *real* is God's presence in this world of space and time? The Antiochenes, clearly, were much concerned to emphasize God's *otherness* with regard to creation, God's freedom from all the limitations and vulnerabilities that classical philosophy saw as part of contingent existence. They feared that a Christology that one-sidedly emphasized a single subject in Christ's person and acts might lead to the "confusion" of God and the creaturely realm, might lose its sense of God's transcendence. Cyril, and the Alexandrian tradition since Athanasius, on the other hand, while also clearly aware of the otherness of God, were even more concerned to emphasize this transcendent God's intimate and active presence in creation: a paradox, clearly, but in their view the paradox on which biblical faith turned. Cyril's main fear was of losing a sense of the divine authorship of salvation, and of the living, personal presence of God the Son in the Jesus of the Gospels and the sacraments.

The Antiochenes saw God's history and that of the created order as related, for now, synchronically but also dialectically; the most interesting part of the narrative of salvation, for them, lay in the eschatological future, when the promise present in the Gospel, and in the symbolic "types" of the Church's liturgy, would come to fulfillment for humanity. Their Christology made room for a created order that possesses real autonomy, for real independence in human action; but the danger in their approach was of driving a wedge between God and creation, which would eventually make God remote from, even irrelevant to, everyday life. Cyril saw God's role in creation and redemption rather in diachronic, dramatic terms;[74] the turning-point in the history of salvation already lay in the past, in the Word's taking on our human flesh and our human experiences to be his own. The fulfillment of the promise was already available to the believer: in Jesus' gift of the Holy Spirit to the disciples, and through them to the Church;[75] in the Church's living unity, centered on the personal, substantial Eucharistic presence of Christ; in the incipient realization, even now, of our human participation in the life of God. Cyril's Christology took God's immediate reality in Christ, and so his reality in the life of the Christian disciple, with the utmost seriousness; the risk was that this

---

[73] *Third Letter to Nestorius* 7 (ACO I, 1.1.37.28–9).

[74] See, for example, his exposition of the narrative about the Son's "descent" into the world of temporal creation, in *On the Creed* 13–16 (ACO I, 1.4.53.21–55.30).

[75] On Cyril's theology of the procession and activity of the Holy Spirit, see my article, "The Fullness of the Saving God: Cyril of Alexandria on the Holy Spirit," in Thomas G. Weinandy and Daniel A. Keating (eds), *The Theology of St. Cyril of Alexandria: A Critical Appreciation* (London: T. and T. Clark, 2003), 113–48.

reality might so overshadow ordinary, mundane created reality—in Jesus and in the Christian's day-to-day religious life—that the Gospel might lose its credibility, reducing our experience of salvation to a Gnostic myth.

Christology, as we have seen repeatedly, is the always the affirmation of paradox. The theologians of both Antioch and Alexandria, in the fourth and fifth centuries, were acutely aware that both sides of the paradox of Christ, as "Emmanuel," had to be maintained if the Gospel message of his coming was to be proclaimed fully. The fact that subtle differences in their terminology, their rhetorical emphasis, their imagery and argument concerning the person of Christ, were able to grow within decades into different theological, exegetical, and spiritual traditions, and ultimately to lead to ideological ruptures within the Christian body that still exist today, ought to remind us just how deep the paradox of Christ's person runs, and how urgent it is for all believers still to engage it seriously and faithfully.

# 8

## After Chalcedon

### A Christology of Relationship

#### INTRODUCTION

Up to now, I have been suggesting that the Christological definition of the
Council of Chalcedon should not be considered the final solution of all
the early Church's questions about how to conceive of the person of Christ
the Savior, let alone the fullest summation of who and what the Church
believes him to be. If one reads what ancient authors themselves have to say
about Christ, without particularly looking for the relation of their Christology to the Chalcedonian formula, or asking how much their portrait of
Christ did or did not anticipate the Chalcedonian model, one finds a much
wider range of concerns and priorities—indeed, a sense that practically all
the questions we raise, as Christians, about God and the world, ourselves
and our future, are rooted and mirrored in the questions we raise about the
person of Christ.

Without in any way detracting from its importance to the Christian
tradition, the Chalcedonian definition itself, I think, can better be understood as a mid-fifth-century way station, a brilliant but largely unsuccessful
attempt to reconcile competing traditions of language and thinking about
the person of Christ, than as a final resolution of difficulties, or a foundation
for lasting ecumenical agreement. Despite the efforts of imperial policy, in
the second half of the fifth century and the first half of the sixth, either to set
the formula of Chalcedon quietly aside (as in the period of the "Acacian
schism," between 478 and 518) or to enforce it by decree, as settled imperial
law (as generally after 518), public argument over the structure and activity
of Christ's person, as one who is both God and human, continued unabated
after the council; fronts hardened, political and theological rivalries
grew more intense, and these differences occasionally became the foundations
of Church bodies which no longer shared communion. Imperially sponsored
efforts to recast the Council's statement of faith in language acceptable to

all the disagreeing parties never succeeded in establishing more than an empty hope of reconciliation.[1]

One reason, surely, for this mixed reception was the perceived ambiguity of the Chalcedonian formula itself. Its carefully crafted phrases exclude positions which most informed Christian thinkers of the mid-fifth century would immediately have recognized as extremes, and which few would have directly affirmed for themselves: thinking of the dual realities in Christ as "two sons," thinking the godhead itself can suffer, thinking that humanity and divinity have been mingled or "confused" in Christ into some new, hybrid entity which is neither divine nor human because it is both at once. But Chalcedon's positive formulation of how the Church *must* interpret Nicene theology and confess the person of Christ, for all its even-handedness, still seems to have struck many—probably a majority—of Greek-speaking Christians as too neatly symmetrical, too ready to affirm the full, continuous functioning of two utterly different "natures" in Christ's one acting "person," to count as an unambiguous affirmation of the heart of the Church's ancient faith: that it was truly God the Son who lived and healed, died and rose, as the fully human Jesus of the Gospels. The echoes of Antiochene terminology in the formula, the prominent place in it of carefully balanced phrases taken from Pope Leo's letter or "Tome" to Flavian of Constantinople (449), all continued to stimulate an allergic reaction in the many Eastern monks and faithful who had come, in the controversies of the mid-fifth century, to regard Cyril of Alexandria as the most reliable spokesman for Christian faith. The Chalcedonian statement, despite its explicit anchoring in both the Nicene and the Constantinopolitan creed, and its final assertion that the "one *persona* (*prosopon*) and individual (*hypostasis*)" formed by the two continuing realities in Christ *is* "one and the same only-begotten Son, God, Word, Lord Jesus Christ," apparently did not seem, in the eyes of many, to make it clear enough that it was indeed *God* who was the agent of the saving work of Jesus, *God the Son* who is the Church's actual referent when it speaks of the actions of the Son of Man.

The Christological controversies of the century that followed the Council of Chalcedon, then, within the sphere of influence of the imperial Church— controversies that often were, in language and spirit, still more intense than those of the three decades that preceded the Council—came to be centered on how to interpret the Chalcedonian statement of faith. More precisely, they focused on whether or not the Chalcedonian decree could be reconciled with

---

[1] See W. H. C. Frend, *The Rise of the Monophysite Movement: Chapters in the History of the Church in the Fifth and Sixth Centuries* (Cambridge: Cambridge University Press, 1972); Christian Lange, *Μία Ἐνέργεια: Kirchenhistorische und dogmengeschichtliche Untersuchungen zur miaenergetischen Einigungspolitik des Kaisers Heraclius und des Patriarchen Sergius von Constantinopel* (Tübingen: Mohr Siebeck, 2012).

the conception of the person of Christ held by the older, universally recognized representatives of the orthodox tradition: especially by Athanasius, Gregory of Nazianzus, and Cyril of Alexandria. In the process, a new style of theology, begun in the late-fourth century controversies between the Cappadocians and the anti-Nicene Eunomians or "neo-Arians," almost completely replaced the forms of theological discourse that had predominated in earlier centuries. Whereas previously, controversial theology had been written largely in oratorical style—in works formed by the rhetorical canons of epideictic and forensic rhetoric—Christological argument after Chalcedon came more and more to be couched in the style of the classroom, the scholastic disputation. The exact definition of terms, the analysis of traditional formulas, the development of complex chains of argument in syllogisms and theses, all played an increasing role in the development of theological ideas; philosophical concepts and strategies, drawn especially from the Neoplatonic commentators on the Hellenistic "scriptures" of Plato and Aristotle, suddenly also came to have a decisive, if often unacknowledged, place in reflection on the unity of the person of Christ. Learned monks and laypeople, rather than bishops, came to play an increasingly dominant role in theological disputation. In the process, it now became crucially important to establish one's credentials by claiming the right theological "ancestors": by showing that the orthodox "Fathers," from Athanasius to Cyril, supported one's position—a task one usually accomplished by appending a sizeable anthology of texts from classical earlier authors to support one's own attempts at argument.[2] As a result, Christological controversy, from the mid-fifth to the mid-eighth century, steadily turned into a series of technical, philosophically sophisticated debates over the logical consistency of the Chalcedonian formula, and over who now truly represented the legacy of the fourth- and fifth-century Fathers, who gradually came to be accepted as the classical voices of orthodoxy.

What I would like to argue here is that even in this new, "scholastic" style of argument current in the sixth and seventh centuries, much more was at stake than simply a quarrel over technical Christian terminology, or even over the ontology of the person. Among those who defended the orthodoxy and the indispensable importance of Chalcedon's "symmetrical" picture of Christ in this new philosophical way, the central issue at stake was not so much the full humanity of Christ, or the survival of what Grillmeier calls the "word-flesh" and "word-human being" models of conceiving his unity, as it was an

---

[2] For further details of this new "scholastic" style of theological argument, see my article, "Boethius's Theological Tracts and Early Byzantine Scholasticism," *Mediaeval Studies* 46 (1984), 158–91. On the use of florilegia of texts from Patristic authorities in later Patristic argument, see Marcel Richard, "Notes sur les florilèges dogmatiques du Ve et du VIe siècle," *Actes du VIe Congrès international d'Etudes byzantines* I (Paris, 1950), 307–18 (= *Opera Minora* I, No. 2); "Les florilèges diphysites du Ve et du VIe siècle," *Chalkedon* I, 721–48 (= *Opera Minora* I, No. 3).

increasingly dominant perspective that probably had never crossed the minds of the drafters of the formula itself: a new sense of the paradigmatic importance simply of the *person* of Christ, in its very structure, for revealing God's way of saving and transforming humanity—for attaining the goal of creation itself. For Leontius of Byzantium in the mid-sixth century, as for Maximus the Confessor in the mid-seventh and John of Damascus in the mid-eighth, the Christ of the Chalcedonian formula becomes, to an increasing degree, the concrete, living model of how God acts to save and "divinize" the human race. By establishing a relationship with the world and with each of us that—analogously to the person of Christ itself—makes us one with God in our concrete mode of being, in our hypostatic or (as we would say today) our personal existence, God saves us from self-destruction without compromising the natural distinctiveness of what *we* are as human creatures, or the transcendent, inconceivable fullness of what *God* is.

## LEONTIUS OF BYZANTIUM

Leontius of Byzantium remains a rather obscure figure in the debates of the decades just preceding the Second Council of Constantinople, in 553. If it is correct, as I have argued elsewhere,[3] to identify him with a monk of the same name mentioned by the monastic biographer Cyril of Skythopolis, Leontius was a learned, articulate, somewhat combative ascetic from a Palestinian monastery, the "Great Lavra," a skilled dialectician who played an important role in the highly academic disputes about Christology that took place in Palestine and Constantinople during the 530s and 540s. He was apparently a member of the Chalcedonian side in the commission of pro- and anti-Chalcedonian disputants whom the Emperor Justinian assembled in the capital in 532, in the hope of working out a reformulation of the Empire's officially approved language about Christ that would be acceptable to all parties, and so lead to a re-establishment of unity in the Eastern Church. Probably at some time in the 540s—after these attempts at reconciliation had foundered, and before the Council of 553—Leontius seems to have written down and circulated the six tracts that come down to us under his name.

---

[3] See especially my article, "The Origenism of Leontius of Byzantium," *JTS* 27 (1976), 334–5; in more detail, see the introduction, with bibliography, to my edition and translation of Leontius's works (Oxford: Oxford University Press, 2017). For an argument in a different direction, making again the case that Leontius of Byzantium was, in some sense, a genuine Origenist, see Daniel Hombergen, *The Second Origenist Controversy: A New Perspective on Cyril of Skythopolis's Monastic Biographies as Historical Sources for Sixth-Century Origenism* (Rome: Studia Anselmiana 132, 2001).

One of these tracts is an annotated anthology of works by Apollinarius and his disciples, assembled, Leontius tells us, in order to help unmask the other Apollinarian writings that were circulating under respectable orthodox pseudonyms.[4] This work shares a concern that had begun to surface more widely in pro-Chalcedonian treatises of that time, which saw in the most dogged defenders of Cyril's Christological language not only resistance to the Council's formula, but a re-emergence of Apollinarian Christological monism—the sense that even Jesus' humanity is energized and "ensouled" exclusively by the Word of God.[5] The other five treatises are really attempts to argue that the Chalcedonian portrait of Christ, if properly understood, is the only adequate formulation of the full Mystery of the Savior, as it is understood in the Church's faith. The first of these, usually known by the abbreviated title *Against the Nestorians and the Eutychians* (CNE),[6] presents tightly reasoned arguments against the "opposed extremes" of a substantively homogenized understanding of Christ's person, on the one hand, which Leontius identifies as the classical position of the monk Eutyches, and the overly divisive understanding of the "Nestorians," on the other. Both misconceptions rest, Leontius insists, on the same fundamental terminological and ontological mistake: confusing the hypostasis, or concrete individual reality of a thing, with its "substance" (*ousia*) or "nature" (*physis*)—the intelligible, formal, generic reality in which all the individuals of a class partake, in order to be what they are. Only if one keeps the two notions distinct—and so recognizes in the person or hypostasis of Jesus two wholly different universal realities or substances, transcendent divinity and earthly humanity, two "natures" united concretely in a single individual—can one begin to realize the greatness of the Incarnation.

Two of Leontius's other essays[7] are directed against the main objections of Severus of Antioch—Chalcedon's most articulate critic—to the Council's two-nature Christology. These continue in greater depth Leontius's analysis, in the CNE, of the implications of the dialectic between individual and universal reality for our conception of Christ's person. A fourth essay is a blistering attack, both personal and theological, on the Antiochene theologian Theodore

---

[4] *Adversus fraudes Apollinaristarum* (PG 86.1948 A–1976 A). Here I will make use of my own chapter divisions, but will give page references to the presently available, if deficient, text in PG.

[5] See, for instance, the Emperor Justinian's treatise *Contra Monophysitas*, written probably in 542–3. For Justinian's awareness that certain treatises had been produced in Apollinarian circles and ascribed falsely to Orthodox authors, see Kenneth Paul Wesche, *On the Person of Christ: The Christology of Emperor Justinian* (Crestwood, NY: St. Vladimir's, 1991), 52–5.

[6] *Contra Nestorianos et Eutychianos* [CNE]: PG 86.1273 A–1316 B.

[7] *Epilyseis* [*Epil*], or "Solutions Proposed to the Arguments of Severus" (PG 86.1916 C–1945 D); and *Epaporemata* [*Epap*], or "Proposals and Definitions Offered as Objections against Those who Deny the Double Reality of the Divine and the Human Nature in the One Christ, after the Union" (PG 86.1901 B–1916 B).

of Mopsuestia—now dead for over a century—and on his pupils.[8] Here
Leontius reveals (tellingly, perhaps for a determined Chalcedonian apologist)
that he began his own theological career as a sympathizer with the Antiochene
school, but that he has since seen the light. In the context of Justinian's
campaign, in the late 540s, to have Theodore and his colleagues posthumously
declared heretics, in order to placate the opponents of the Chalcedonian
formula and distance it from suspicions of heresy, one suspects that Leontius
himself here "doth protest too much" in attacking the Antiochenes' intellectual integrity. In any case, the argument in this treatise is less technical, more
*ad hominem*, than that in his other works defending Chalcedonian Christology. Finally, Leontius has left us a fascinating essay directed against a group
today known usually as the "Aphthartists" (whom he rather tendentiously
refers to as "Aphthartodocetists"):[9] people within the *Chalcedonian* party (as
he insists) who hold that the very humanity of Christ, although ontologically
like ours, was, from the beginning, in a unique state: morally and physically
"incorruptible," because of its union in hypostasis with the Word of God.
Leontius argues against them, as the anti-Chalcedonian Severus had himself
argued against a similar, "aphthartist" group within his own party, that unless
we understand Christ's sinless humanity as being in the same physical and
psychological condition as the fallen, weakened, post-Adamic humanity we all
share, we miss the greatness of what is being proclaimed to us in the Gospel.

For Leontius, it was the Chalcedonian formula, properly understood in all
its implications, which offered the most reliable guide for avoiding all these
misleading ways of understanding the person and work of Christ. It was not
simply a question of terminology;

> What is at issue for us is not a matter of phrasing, but the *manner* in which the
> whole mystery of Christ exists (περὶ τοῦ τρόπου τοῦ ὅλου κατὰ Χριστὸν μυστηρ-
> ίου). So we cannot make judgments or decisions here simply on the basis of this or
> that expression or of certain phrases, but on the basis of its fundamental prin-
> ciples (ἐκ τῶν πρώτων ἀρχῶν).[10]

The most fundamental of those principles behind the Chalcedonian portrait of
Christ, in Leontius's view, is the distinction between universal being and
particular being which we have mentioned already: between *ousia* or *physis*,
on the one hand, and *hypostasis* or *prosōpon*, on the other. This is a use of
terms developed by the Cappadocians for expressing the unity and distinction
of Father, Son, and Holy Spirit as "persons" or reciprocally oriented centers of

---

[8] *Deprehensio et Triumphus super Nestorianos* [DTN], "An Unmasking and a Triumphant
Defeat of the Unspeakable and Fundamental Impiety of the Nestorians, and of the Fathers of this
Heresy" (PG 86.1357 B–1396 A).
[9] *Contra Aphthartodocetas* [CAph], "A Dialogue against those of our Party who Adhere to
the Corrupt Doctrine of the Aphthartodocetists" (PG 86.1316 D–1357 A).
[10] DTN 42 (PG 86.1380 B).

activity within the one God, which curiously had not been applied with any consistency to the Mystery of Christ during the debates leading up to Chalcedon. "Substance" or "nature," in Leontius's terminology—which resonates constantly with the discourse-world of the Neoplatonic commentaries on Aristotle that were contemporary to his work—refers to the kind of *universal* reality in which many individuals participate, the kind of describable reality, like "horse," "cow," or "human being," that defines *what* any individual thing is. "Hypostasis," and in the case of human beings "person" (πρόσωπον), refers to a *concrete individual* within such a universal class—something existing uniquely "by itself" (καθ᾽ αὐτό) within space and time, something able to be counted, to be labeled with a proper name. And while, as Leontius readily admits, "there is no such thing as a non-hypostatic nature"[11]—universal natures or substances have no independent existence, either in this realm of being or in some separate, ideal world of forms—individual things or hypostases are also unintelligible, and to that degree unreal, apart from their relationship to universal realities.[12]

So the ontological structure of particular things, in Leontius's view, consists of a kind of dialectic, a reciprocal shaping, that takes place between universal substances or natures and concrete individuals, between "what" and "this":

> Nature (he explains) admits of the predication of being (εἶναι), but hypostasis also of being-by-oneself (τὸ καθ᾽ αὐτὸ εἶναι). The former presents the character of genus, the latter expresses individual identity. The one brings out what is peculiar to something universal, the other distinguishes the particular from the general. To put it concisely, things sharing the same essence and things whose structure (λόγος) of being is common are properly said to be of one nature; but we can define as a "hypostasis" either things which share a nature but differ in number, or things which are put together from different natures, but which share reciprocally in a common being.[13]

What distinguishes any being—universal or individual—from all others, Leontius and his contemporaries assume, are that being's "characteristics" or ἰδιώματα: universals or generic "natures" are marked off from other natures by "essential qualities" (οὐσιοποιοὶ ἰδιότητες), concrete individuals by individual qualities or "accidents." In each case, it is these particular qualities or characteristics that mark a thing off as what it is, and not something else.[14]

---

[11] CNE 1 (PG 86.1277 D–1280 A).

[12] For a discussion of the question of the status of universals and their relation to individual things in fifth- and sixth-century philosophy, and of the influence of these discussions on Leontius and his contemporaries, see my article, "'A Richer Union': Leontius of Byzantium and the Relationship of Human and Divine in Christ," *Studia Patristica* 24 (1993), 239–65, esp. 246–53.

[13] CNE 1 (PG 86.1280 A).

[14] Leontius, like many Platonically oriented Aristotelians of his time, seems simply to assume that the characteristics that allow us to tell universals or individuals from one another are, in

The importance of all of this for Christology is that it is precisely in this exchange of universal and individual qualities—of essential characteristics and particular accidents—that things become what they are; this makes it possible for a single individual thing to share at once in two distinct, unconfused natures. What distinguishes spirit from matter, soul from body, for instance, on the level of substance or nature—being intelligent and free, on the one hand, and being solid or colored on the other—is precisely the set of specific characteristics that unite *all* souls or all bodies with each other in the same universal class; but what distinguishes *this* soul from all other souls—its conscious relationship to a particular material frame, in a particular corner of time and space—is precisely what unites it ontologically to *this* body, enables them both to form *this* particular person: not just as a "soul" or a "body" or even a "human being" in general, but as Peter or John.

And it is this set of defining *relationships* (σχέσεις, in the technical vocabulary of Aristotle's *Categories* and Porphyry's *Eisagōgē*),[15] which in turn makes understandable the Chalcedonian portrait of the unique person of Christ, in Leontius's view. Christ, as Son of God and Son of Mary, is *naturally* set off from all other beings in heaven and on earth by the transcendent characteristics of God's essence, on the one hand, insofar as we (negatively) understand them, and by the universal characteristics of humanity (itself a composite of the generic characteristics of soul and body), on the other. What makes him God is not what makes him human, and vice versa: these characteristics, and the universal natures or substances they identify, are "unconfused." At the same time, the characteristics that mark the Son off, within the divine nature, from Father and Holy Spirit, that identify him as a divine hypostasis—his generation from the Father's being, his filial obedience, his role as receiver and sender of the Spirit— are precisely the characteristics which, when mingled with the unique human accidents of his historical existence—being a Jew from the early Roman Empire, the son of Mary, the carpenter from Nazareth, a man of determined appearance and height and weight—make him a single hypostasis who is both God and human, give him "coherence and unity with himself."[16]

The Son of God's distinctive character as an individual, in other words, is formed by a unique set of relationships: his relationship, as divine Son, with the Father and the Spirit; his relationship, as the man from Nazareth, with other historical human beings; and the intersection of both identities in the uniqueness of his person. This third relationship—the mutual interchange and completion, "the common share in being" (κοινωνία τοῦ εἶναι),[17] that exists

---

themselves, constitutive of the reality of those universal or individual entities. The epistemological and ontological levels of discourse are not carefully or consistently distinguished in these late antique philosophical texts.

[15] See esp. CNE 4 (PG 86.1288 A–1289 A); Daley, "'A Richer Union'", 252–3.

[16] *Epil* 1 (PG 86.1917 D); see also *Epap* 25 (PG 86.1909 CD).

[17] CNE 1 (PG 86.1280 A); *Epil* 1 (PG 86.1917 D).

concretely between these two natures, with God the Word forming Jesus for himself as his way of existing in the world, and the man Jesus fully expressing in human terms what it is to be Son of God—results in "mutually inherent life" (ἡ ἀλληλοῦχος ζωή).[18] Yet while his personal existence is based on these relationships, the unity at the core of his person is not simply extrinsic or accidental, not simply a matter of moral harmony between two wholly different conscious subjects, as the Antiochene theologians seemed (to their critics, at least) to suggest. It is a "substantial" union, in which the concrete individual, Jesus, is constituted in his being by the very confluence, the mutual shaping, of these two analogous, incommensurable, yet still radically personal realities—the Son of God and the son of Mary.[19]

Although all this analysis may seem to us like the driest form of metaphysical speculation, Leontius argues that comprehending its meaning is, in fact, central to a proper understanding of the orthodox tradition of faith. The Chalcedonian picture of Christ—as one hypostasis, one individual, one Christ Jesus, who exists in two unconfused and undivided natures, which continue to be fully intact and operative as what they are, while being joined inseparably with each other in a way that mutually defines both—is not only logically coherent, in Leontius's view, but theologically necessary to a Christian understanding of the world, as the place where the transcendent God is at work. "The mode of union, rather than the structure (λόγος) of nature, contains the great mystery of religion," he writes.[20] The Gospel is not simply the communication of a deeper understanding of what God is, or what humanity is—although each of those clearly comes to be understood in a new way because of it. Rather, the Gospel is the proclamation of the ontological *union* of God and humanity in a particular person: the news that God's eternal Son and a naturally finite human being now are, in fact, a single historical individual, without either of them ceasing to be what God the Son and that particular human being are in themselves.

The result of this union—what Leontius calls its ἀποτέλεσμα or *end-product*—is not a new, composite *kind* of being, a demigod from the world

---

[18] CNE 4 (PG 86.1288 D).

[19] *Epil* 4 (PG 86.1925 C); *Epil* 8 (PG 86.1940 D); *CAph* (PG 86.1353 A); DTN 42 (PG 86.1380 D). Although Aristotle and his earlier commentators had seen "relationship" (*to pros ti, schesis*)—spatial relationships, for instance, such as "near this tree," or temporal relationships such as "before the flood"—as the most extrinsic kind of accident, Plotinus and the Neoplatonist commentators of the fifth century had begun to argue that some kinds of relationship, at least, can represent a sharing of, and even a constitutive basis for, substantial being: see Plotinus, *Enn.* 6.1.6; Simplicius, *In Cat.* 7, ed. C. Kalbfleisch (Berlin, 1900), 169.1–173.32. For further discussion, see my article, "Nature and the 'Mode of Union': Late Patristic Models for the Personal Unity of Christ," in Gerald O'Collins, Daniel Kendall, and Stephen Davis (eds), *The Incarnation* (Oxford: Oxford University Press, 2002), 164–96.

[20] *Epil* 8 (PG 86.1940 C).

of myth, who is neither God nor human but a hybrid of both. Divinity and humanity as such, if one can speak accurately of the incomparable in such parallel terms, never cross their ontological or behavioral barriers. In fact, Leontius observes, everyone in the debate admits, when speaking of Christ, that "that there is something incommunicable in the union, which lies at the heart of the greatness of the divine nature—since otherwise there would be no condescension of divine love for humanity, but only a natural joining of the highest being with what is lowly."[21] Somewhere, he insists, between "the way of confusion," identified with the approach of Eutyches, and "the way of division," identified with that of Nestorius, lies the reality that the Church proclaims at Chalcedon: "the middle way of unconfused and inseparable union." He explains:

> What is properly characteristic of each [substance] is common to the whole, and what belongs to the whole is common to each, because of the unconfused character of the same [whole] in each. For there would not be an exchange of characteristics,[22] if the peculiar character of each did not remain undisturbed, even in union. This, then, is the kind of union we are speaking of: more unitive than the kind that completely divides, but richer than the kind that completely confuses, so that it neither makes the things united completely the same as each other, nor wholly other. If, then, a union of this kind shows its product to be neither wholly the same nor wholly different, we must investigate *how* it is the same, and *how* different. True belief recognizes the sameness to be in the hypostasis, the difference in the natures . . . [23]

Chalcedon, in Leontius's reading, sets before the Church this paradox that lies at the heart of the biblical message. The importance of the structure of Christ's person, he emphasizes in his dialogue against the "Aphthartists," who believed Christ's humanity had immediately become incorruptible, morally and physically, through personal union with God the Son, is not simply theoretical; the person of Christ, fully God and fully human in the functional realms where he lives and acts, reveals how God works in the created world to save and transform all of us. Using the Pseudo-Dionysius's recently coined terminology of "natural" and "supernatural,"[24] Leontius distinguishes both from the realm

---

[21] *Epil* 8 (PG 86.1940 A).

[22] References to the "exchange of characteristics" or "communication of idioms" (Greek: κοινωνία τῶν ἰδιομάτων) had become, by the sixth century, a generally accepted hallmark of orthodox language about Jesus, his person, and his acts. This is a deliberately paradoxical way of speaking that permits us to assert that the Son of God has characteristically human experiences (e.g. I Cor. 2.8: "they would not have crucified the Lord of glory") and that the son of Mary has divine authority (e.g. Mark 2.10: "that you may know that the son of man has the power on earth to forgive sins").

[23] *Epil* 8 (PG 86.1941 AB).

[24] The writings attributed to "Dionysius the Areopagite" are usually dated to around the year 500, and seem to have originated in the theological and liturgical world of Antioch. Who the author was, and what his own standpoint was with reference to the Chalcedonian definition,

of the "preternatural," which is simply activity that deviates from the normal functioning of a being's nature. Jesus' human nature does not operate preternaturally, Leontius insists; he is not Heracles, or Superman! Rather

> the natural is produced from unimpeded causal operation, relying upon nature; the supernatural leads upward and elevates...Yet the supernatural does not abrogate the natural, but leads it onward and sets it in motion, to be able both to carry out its own functions and to accept, in addition, the power to do what is above it.[25]

It is precisely because Jesus, as Son of God, struggled with normal human needs and physical weaknesses, Leontius argues here, even while he lived a life of perfect obedience to his Father and so was, as a human being, perfectly free from sin, that the process of transformation Gregory of Nyssa had pointed to, which ended physically in Jesus' resurrection, can be a model for our imitation and a sign of hope:

> And how are we to imitate him who possessed the summit of virtue, proportionate to the very difference of his [bodily] instrument, if we, in our passible and corruptible body, are required to be like one who is incorruptible? ... It is no great assertion to say that it is impossible to find a demonstration of virtue in a nature which is incorruptible and lacking nothing. For there is no struggle for a nature which cannot suffer; and if there is no struggle, there is no victory; and if no victory, there is no crown.[26]

The "union" of Word and human being in Christ, in fact, Leontius argues, does not show itself in the fact that his body or his psyche are structurally different from ours. The only really distinctive aspect of Jesus' human existence is the fact that he was born of a Virgin; and that is due, Leontius says, to the overshadowing power of the Spirit—to God's miraculous intervention at the start of his history, causing his fully natural humanity to exist as the Son's own humanity—rather than to the structure of the union itself. The union between divinity and humanity in the Incarnation, in fact, shows itself not in the kind of "natural" being Jesus is, but in the way Jesus *acts*:

---

remains contested. Leontius occasionally alludes to the Dionysian corpus, and may well have participated in the "union dialogue" Justinian sponsored in 531, between representatives of the Chalcedonian and anti-Chalcedonian parties, at which the identification of these works with the "Dionysius the Areopagite" of Acts 17.34 was first seriously questioned. He was, despite his anonymity, a new and powerful voice within Christian debate. For a persuasive recent study of this author's use of a biblical pseudonym, see Charles M. Stang, "Dionysius, Paul, and the Significance of the Pseudonym," in Sarah Coakley and Charles M. Stang (eds), *Re-thinking Dionysius the Areopagite* (Oxford: Wiley-Blackwell, 2009), 11–26; *Apophasis and Pseudonymity in Dionysius the Areopagite: "No Longer I"* (New York: Oxford University Press, 2012).

[25] *CAph* (PG 86.1333 AB).
[26] *CAph* (PG 86.1349 B-D).

His sinlessness and all his holiness, his complete union and identification with the whole of the One who assumed him, and his being and being called "one Son," and exhibiting the glorious signs of a Son's peculiar role: these things his organic union (συμφυὴς ἕνωσις) with the Word accomplished—things which are unalterably blessed, because the union is inseparable.[27]

And all of these aspects of existence—our use of our innate freedom, our implementation of choice, our actions, our relationships—are proper to hypostases or individual agents rather than to natures: to the *way* a human or divine being realizes his or her nature, rather than to that nature considered by itself. It is only this or that human being who can become holy and one with God, just as it is only this or that divine "Person" who can live out his transcendent divine reality in human terms.

This "organic union" (συμφυὴς ἕνωσις) of the Son's divine nature with a full human nature in the person of Jesus of Nazareth, the Christ, results, then, not in a kind of mythic hero, whose every act and thought is miraculous because his humanity is permanently changed by the union, but in something much more astonishing: in a God who is "with us" and makes our natural vulnerabilities his own, while remaining divine; and in a man who always acts humanly, even when he acts as the Son of God. For Leontius, as later for Maximus and John of Damascus, only the language and thought of Chalcedon can give adequate expression to this "Mystery of union."

## MAXIMUS THE CONFESSOR

A century after Leontius, the most eloquent and original defender of the Chalcedonian tradition was surely the monk and scholar known to posterity as Maximus "the Confessor." Although one ancient biography asserts he was born in Palestine—probably around 580—and received his early formation in a Judaean monastery, as Leontius had a century earlier, while other biographies present him as an upper-class Byzantine by birth, Maximus was certainly present and active in Constantinople by the early seventh century. After becoming a monk at Chrysopolis, across the Bosporus from the imperial capital, about the age of thirty, he seems to have fled to Cyzicus, some hundred miles further west on the Sea of Marmara, to escape invading Persian forces, in 614; he seems to have moved on again briefly to Cyprus and Alexandria, where he probably came under the influence of the aged monk Sophronius, and eventually—in stages that remain unclear—migrated as far west as Carthage,

---

[27] *CAph* (PG86.1353 A).

to escape those same invaders, around 626. Deeply concerned with the issues of human holiness and transformation in Christ, which were so important for the practice of asceticism, Maximus seems to have devoted a good deal of his early life, as monk and scholar, to the study of the mainstream tradition of late Greek Christian Platonism: of Clement and Origen (of whom he understandably says little, after Origen's condemnation at the Council of 553), Gregory of Nazianzus, Gregory of Nyssa, Evagrius, and Dionysius the Areopagite.[28]

[28]   The main Greek source for Maximus's life, still not critically edited, is in PG 90.67–109; for a translation of another Greek version of his life, see Pauline Allen and Bronwen Neil, *The Life of Maximus the Confessor, Recension 3* (Strathfield, NSW: St. Paul's, 2003). For critical comments on this material, see R. Devreesse, "La vie de S. Maxime et ses recensions," *Anal. Boll.* 46 (1928), 5–49; W. Lackner, "Zu Quellen und Datierung der Maximus-vita," *Anal. Boll.* 85 (1967), 285–316. An early Syriac biography, by the clearly hostile author Sergius of Resh'aina, with very different details about Maximus's early life, was published by Sebastian Brock in 1973: "An Early Syriac Life of Maximus," *Anal. Boll.* 91 (1973), 299–346. For reflections on the present state of our knowledge of Maximus's life, see my article, "Making a Human Will Divine: Augustine and Maximus Confessor on Christ and Human Salvation," in Aristotle Papanikolaou and George E. Demacopoulos (eds), *Orthodox Readings of Augustine* (Crestwood, NY: St. Vladimir's, 2008), 101–26. The most recent survey of what can be reconstructed of Maximus's life is Pauline Allen, "Life and Times of Maximus the Confessor," in Pauline Allen and Bronwen Neil (eds), *The Oxford Handbook of Maximus the Confessor* (Oxford: Oxford University Press, 2015), 3–18. For an expanded date-list of his writings, grouped according to their subject, with very helpful prosopographical information, see Marek Janowiak and Phil Booth, "A New Date-List of the Works of Maximus the Confessor," in Allen and Neil, *Oxford Handbook*, 19–83.

Several accounts exist of Maximus's judicial trials, in his last years. These, along with appeals and letters by some of his pupils, have been edited in the *Corpus Christianorum, Series Graeca* 39 (Turnhout: Brepols, 1999), and have been translated into English by Pauline Allen and Bronwen Neil, *Maximus the Confessor and his Companions: Documents from Exile* (Oxford: Oxford University Press, 2002). The brief account of his first trial also appears, in English translation, in George Berthold, *Maximus the Confessor: Selected Writings* (New York: Paulist Press, 1985), 17–31.

On Maximus's intellectual formation, see especially Polycarp Sherwood, *An Annotated Date-List of the Works of Maximus the Confessor*, Studia Anselmiana 30 (Rome, 1952); *The Earlier Ambigua of St. Maximus the Confessor*, Studia Anselmiana 36 (Rome, 1955); and his introduction to *Maximus Confessor, Ascetical Writings*, Ancient Christian Writers 21 (Westminster, MD: Newman Press, 1955). Sherwood originally found signs of a spiritual and intellectual "crisis" in Maximus's work, as he distanced himself from an early infatuation with the ascetical and cosmic speculations of Origen and Evagrius. Sherwood later modified this view, seeing only a change in emphasis as Maximus focused more centrally on Christological issues. In a brief precis of his unpublished paper at the Eleventh International Byzantine Conference, in 1958, for instance, he remarks: "The mystery of Christ forms the core of the controversy between Origen and Maximus. Maximus eliminates the Origenist doctrine of the *henas* [the original, pre-corporeal unity of created intellects with the Logos], and proposes the theory of anthropological-dialectical movement: the theory of a movement from a starting point (nature), through action, to a final goal (Christ, God). Along with this, there is a concrete historical movement from Paradise to heaven, into which the results of the things known by the concrete human person and revelation are also drawn. In explaining this, Maximus continues the understanding of the patristic tradition he has inherited, in a genuine way, even if it is also not without some incoherence" ("Maximus and Origenism," *Diskussionsbeiträge zum XI. internationalen Byzantinisten-Kongress* (Munich: Beck, 1958), 37–8 [trans. mine]). See also Hans Urs von Balthasar, *Cosmic Liturgy*, trans. Brian E. Daley (San Francisco: Ignatius Press, 2003); Demetrios Bathrellos, *The*

Maximus's understanding of human transformation, of ascetical holiness and human "divinization," is thoroughly centered on the Mystery of the person of Christ, just as Gregory of Nyssa's and Augustine's had been: now, however, it is focused explicitly on the understanding of Christ that had been formulated at Chalcedon and then re-formulated, under Justinian's influence, at the Second Council of Constantinople (553). Drawing liberally, at times, on the language and argument of Leontius of Byzantium (though without attribution),[29] Maximus develops a vision of the "one composite hypostasis (μία σύνθετος ὑπόστασις)"[30] of Christ, which draws out in new ways the implications of this ontological analysis of Christ's person for a basic Christian understanding of the human vocation.

Central to Maximus's Chalcedonian understanding of Christ, as a single hypostasis uniting two complete, distinct, and functioning natures, is his use of a conceptual and linguistic tradition, reaching back at least to the Cappadocians, which gives further precision to the terminology so thoroughly defended by Leontius: the "hypostasis," or concrete individual, is defined not so much in terms of "what" that individual is and can do—its "substance" or "nature" or even its "existence in itself (*kath' heauto*)"—but rather in terms of its distinctive *origin of existence*, of *how* and *from what source* it has come to be precisely what it is.[31] Maximus seems to find the grounds for this way of speaking in the Cappadocian practice of distinguishing between the three hypostases of Father, Son and Holy Spirit primarily in terms of *how* each of them possesses the single, transcendent reality of God. So he writes (in typically dense language) in his *Mystagogia*, that God is

> one substance (οὐσία), three hypostases; a tri-hypostatic singleness of substance and a consubstantial triad of hypostases; a monad in a triad and a triad in a monad; ... a monad by its structure of substance (κατὰ τὸν τῆς οὐσίας λόγον) or being, but not by synthesis or conflation or confusion of any kind; a triad by the

---

*Byzantine Christ: Person, Nature, and Will in the Christology of St. Maximus the Confessor* (Oxford: Oxford University Press, 2003).

[29] This influence is especially clear in Maximus's Epistle 15 to Cosmas, deacon of Alexandria, from the "middle" period of his literary activity (634–40): an essay on the constitution of the person of Christ that is, in places, little more than a paraphrase of passages in Leontius's CNE, *Epilyseis* and *Epaporemata*. On the development of Maximus's mature Christology in the 630s, under the clear influence of Leontius of Byzantium and other sixth-century discussions of Chalcedon, see my article, "Maximus Confessor, Leontius of Byzantium, and the Late Aristotelian Metaphysics of the Person," in Bishop Maxim (Vasiljević) (ed.), *Knowing the Purpose of Creation through the Resurrection: Proceedings of the Symposium on St. Maximus the Confessor, Belgrade, October 18–21, 2012* (Alhambra, CA: Sebastian Press, 2013), 55–70. See now also Cyril Hovorun, "Maximus: A Cautious Neo-Chalcedonian," in Allen and Neil, *Oxford Handbook*, 106–24.

[30] See, e.g., Epist. 15 to Cosmas [634–40] (PG 91.553D, 556D, 557D).

[31] See, for example, Gregory of Nyssa, *Contra Eunomium* 1.496–7 (GNO 1.169-20–170-12); *Contra Eunomium* 3.36 (GNO 2.198-16-17); and for a more general treatment of this distinction, see my article, "Nature and the 'Mode of Union'."

structure of *how* it exists and concretely comes to be (κατὰ τὸν τοῦ πῶς ὑπάρχειν καὶ ὑφεστᾶναι λόγον), but not by separation or alienation or any kind of division. For the monad is not divided up by the hypostases ... ; rather, it is identical with itself, yet in different ways (ἄλλως καὶ ἄλλως).[32]

Building on Chalcedon's definition that the personal unity of Christ is conceived of hypostatically, in terms of his concrete origins and relationships, rather than as a combination of the divine and the human in a new, compound substance or nature, Maximus speaks of the "new communion" of God with humanity, in the Incarnation—a "second" communion, replacing the first communion in grace that had been lost in the fall—and presents this in distinctively *modal* terms:

Formerly [created] nature possessed no union with God in any mode or structure (τρόπον ἢ λόγον) of substance or hypostasis, those categories in which all beings are generally understood; but now [i.e. in the person of Christ] it has received a union in hypostasis with him, through the ineffable union, preserving unchanged its own different structure of substance in relation to the divine substance, towards which it is hypostatically one and yet different, through the union. As a result, in the structure of its being (τῷ τοῦ εἶναι λόγῳ), according to which it has come into existence and continues to be, it [i.e. Christ's humanity] remains in unquestioned possession of its own being, preserving it undiminished in every way; but in the structure of *how* it is (τῷ τοῦ πῶς εἶναι λόγῳ), it receives existence in a divine way, and neither knows nor accepts at all the urge towards movement centered on any other thing. In this fashion, then, the Logos has brought into being a communion with human nature that is much more wonderful than the first one was, uniting this very nature to himself hypostatically, in a substantial way.[33]

The union of God with humanity in Jesus is "substantial" (*ousiōdēs*), Maximus will say (along with Leontius),[34] in that it affects the *way* the substances of both divinity and humanity—as utterly different, essentially incomparable realities—now concretely exist in Jesus in relationship with each other, and present themselves to us in history. Yet the locus of that union is not in some change in the fundamental identity of what is divine or what is human—in the substances themselves—but in the concrete, unique, unrepeatable historical being of the individual Jesus of Nazareth, who *is* himself Son of God. To put it differently: because Jesus, as Maximus says on numerous occasions, was

---

[32] *Mystagogia* 25 [628–30] (ed. C. Sotiropoulos, 239.57–240.72). Maximus's last phrase here seems to be a deliberate variation on Gregory of Nazianzus's famous dictum in his Epistle 101, to Cledonius, that in speaking of the Trinity we refer to "one [subject] and another and another" (ἄλλος καὶ ἄλλος καὶ ἄλλος) but not to "one [thing] and another" (ἄλλο καὶ ἄλλο). For Maximus the difference in subject among Father and Son and Holy Spirit is grounded in the *way* in which each of them possesses the one transcendent, divine reality or substance.

[33] *Difficulty* (= *Ambiguum*) *to John* 36 [628–30] (PG 91.1289 C3–D5).

[34] See, for example, Leontius, CNE 7 (PG 86.1301 BC).

"divine in a human way, and human in a divine way,"[35] he has established a communion between the divine reality and the human that serves as both the model and empowering source for a similar—although incomplete and non-substantial—communion of the divine and the human in ourselves. The "manner" of our being human, like that of Jesus, has been made new by the "second birth" of our baptism into living union with him.[36]

Maximus writes, for instance, in Letter 15 to the Alexandrian deacon Cosmas, of this interchange between divine and human, realized precisely in the "manner" in which Christ's two natures exist, as the foundation of the Son of God's ability to save us:

> We say that both the miracles and the sufferings [of Jesus] belong to the same subject, since Christ, who does divine and human things, is clearly one. [He performs] divine actions in a fleshly way, because he revealed the power of his miracles through flesh that is not deprived of its natural operation; and he performed human acts in a divine way, because he willingly accepted the trials of human sufferings, apart from any physical force and in his full freedom to act. The cross and death and burial and resurrection and ascension into heaven all belong to the same subject ... For he [= God the Son] exists, free of all circumscription; but he was manifested through flesh, as one naturally benevolent towards humanity,[37] circumscribed by being truly born of a woman, as he willed to be, and coming to exist in our way of life. Therefore we offer him worship along with Father and Spirit, even in his flesh.[38]

Maximus presents this identification of two natures in the modality of a single hypostasis, in fact, as the heart of the Logos's revelatory work, the manifestation of his transcendent being in a visible and audible form. In that sense, Jesus himself becomes a symbol: as God in flesh, he reveals his divine glory in his own human body as in an icon—an earthly reality charged with the energy and beauty of God. So in *Ambigua to John* 10, the longest of his earlier series of comments on puzzling passages in the classical Fathers, Maximus reflects on the Transfiguration scene in the Synoptic Gospels. He writes:

---

[35] See, for example, *Ambiguum to Thomas* 5.24 (ed. B. Janssens: CCG 48 [Turnhout: Brepols 2002], 33–4; Eng. trans. Joshua Lollar, Corpus Christianorum in Translation [Turnhout: Brepols, 2009], 73; Epistle 19 [633–4] (PG 91.589–97); *Opusc.* 4, to the Higumen George (PG 91.61 B10–C11) [634–40]; *Opusc.* 7, to the deacon Marinus (PG 91.84 B11–D3) [642]; *Dialogue with Pyrrhus* (PG 91 297 D13–298 A4) [July, 645].

[36] For a thorough and thoughtful discussion of the unique hypostatic character of the incarnate Word, and of its implications for human transformation, see Christoph Schönborn, *God's Human Face: The Christ-Icon* (San Francisco: Ignatius, 1994) 102–33.

[37] Following a long tradition of Greek philosophical theology, Maximus sees the Son's *philanthrōpia* as proper to his divine nature. See discussion in my article, "Building the New City: the Cappadocian Fathers and the Rhetoric of Philanthropy," *Journal of Early Christian Studies* 7 (1999), 431–61.

[38] Epist. 15, to Cosmas [634–40] (PG 91.573 BC).

Let us consider whether or not the symbol exists, safe and sound, in each of the ways (τρόποι) of knowing God that we have mentioned, in the divine Transfiguration of the Lord. For through his unmeasured love for humanity he came to be created like us in form, without himself undergoing change. He agreed to become a type and symbol of himself, and [chose] to show himself symbolically, by his own initiative, and so through his self-manifestation to lead all creation towards himself—he who remains completely hidden, and never shows himself. He offered to human beings, out of sheer benevolence, revelatory miracles through his flesh: hints of his constantly mysterious infinity, far beyond all things, although he is incapable of being known or spoken of at all, in any way, by any being.[39]

As Maximus's career went on, the test case for understanding the now-classical Christology of Chalcedon came to be the controversy in the 630s and 640s over how to understand the relationship of the two natures or substances of Christ, in terms of their "operations" (ἐνεργείαι), and more concretely in terms of the psychological operation of Christ's *will*. In the second decade of the seventh century, as the enterprising Emperor Heraclius conducted a series of bold military campaigns to reunify the Eastern Empire and secure its borders against the Persians and Avars in Syria, Mesopotamia, and eastern Anatolia, his Patriarch in the capital, Sergius of Arsinoe, again began experimenting with terminological adjustments and explanations of the official, Chalcedonian picture of Christ, which, it was hoped, might make it easier for the anti-Chalcedonian communities of the Eastern Empire to be reconciled with the imperial Church.[40] The object, as in the mid-sixth century under Justinian, was to dispel any lingering suspicion among the now-schismatic opponents of Chalcedon that the Council's portrait of Christ was fundamentally a divisive, crypto-Nestorian one, suggesting that Christ was not personally God but only God's chosen human instrument.

In an exchange of letters with a learned bishop from the Sinai peninsula, Theodore of Pharan, Patriarch Sergius discussed the suitability of a phrase coined by the Pseudo-Dionysius more than a century earlier, describing the functioning, the natural "operation," of what has come together in the person of the Savior as "some new, theandric activity (καινή τις θεανδρικὴ ἐνέργεια)"—a single combined and inseparable mode of self-manifestation that expresses, in Jesus' actions, both what is divine and what is human in him. Theodore wrote back approvingly:

Anything at all that the Lord is reported to have said or done, he said and did through his mind and senses and sense-organs; so all these things are spoken of as

---

[39] *Ambiguum to John* 10 [628–30] (PG 91.1165 D–1168 A).

[40] For a detailed account of the Byzantine Empire's attempts to reformulate the Chalcedonian Christology in the 620s and 630s, see Walter E. Kaegi, *Heraclius, Emperor of Byzantium* (Cambridge: Cambridge University Press, 2003); and Lange, Μία Ἐνέργεια, 577–672.

one activity (μία ἐνέργεια) of a whole, single individual: the Word, his mind, and the perceptible body which he used as his instrument.[41]

The result, argued Theodore, is that all the actions of Christ, even though we see them as "theandric," or as "jointly" expressing two united, functioning substances, really "have their beginning and their wellspring, as it were, in the wisdom and goodness and power of the Word":[42]

> From this we see clearly that all the things that we understand or believe about Christ, whether they are proper to his divine or his human nature, are the work of God; therefore we reverently call "one activity" both what belongs to his divinity and what belongs to his humanity.[43]

The terminology of nature and hypostasis, applied to Christ, still remained here within the range of Chalcedonian orthodoxy; Sergius and Theodore still speak of Christ as "one hypostasis in two natures." Yet this new approach to parsing the Chalcedonian formula subtly but clearly shifts the Christological emphasis: not only is the Logos the ultimate *subject* of Christ's human acts, but those acts themselves are all really *divine acts*—acts realizing and expressing the transcendent nature of God—filtered through a human instrument. As Maximus would soon come to recognize, the result is, in effect, a new and more subtle version of Apollinarianism: God the Word serves here as the sole source of life, freedom, and energy for a humanity organically united to him.

In 633, the new Patriarch of Alexandria, Cyrus of Phasis, attempted to make this version of Chalcedonian Christology the basis of a short-lived reunion with the non-Chalcedonian Church in Egypt;[44] Sergius, in the imperial capital, quickly reciprocated with a decree (*Psēphos*) proclaiming this same Christology to be now part of the official position of the Church of Constantinople. Despite strenuous attempts by the aged Sophronius, Maximus's former spiritual father (who had been elected Patriarch of Jerusalem in 634, at the age of 80), to convince Cyrus and the other Eastern bishops that this formula, when fully understood, implied a serious abandonment of the central insight of Chalcedonian Christology, Sergius's campaign flourished for several years.[45] Attempting to convince Pope Honorius of Rome that this line of interpretation was a faithful interpretation of Chalcedon, Sergius added the point that confessing "one activity" of the two natures in Christ implies that all that he

---

[41] Theodore of Pharan, *Letter to Sergius of Arsinoe,* quoted in the Acts of the Lateran Synod of 649, Excerpt 1.

[42] *Letter to Sergius,* Excerpt 3.   [43] *Letter to Sergius,* Excerpt 4.

[44] Lange, Μία Ἐνέργεια, 550–3.

[45] Lange, Μία Ἐνέργεια, 592–6, 601–6; see also Christoph von Schönborn, *Sophrone de Jérusalem: Vie monastique et confession dogmatique* (Paris: Beauchesne, 1972). For a wide-ranging account of this controversy, see Werner Elert, *Der Ausgang der altkirchlichen Christologie: Eine Untersuchung über Theodor von Pharan und seine Zeit als Einführung in die alte Dogmengeschichte* (Berlin: Lutherisches Verlagshaus, 1957).

does, as God or as a human, is under the control of the divine *will*. In this somewhat later form of his argument, after 636, Sergius attempts to rule out the internal conflict that was thought to result, if Jesus were to be conceived of in the way Athanasius, Gregory of Nyssa, and Augustine had thought of him, as having two analogous, naturally distinct wills.[46] By 638, this emphasis on the one will of Christ had become the central part of a new summary Sergius promulgated of official Christological doctrine, known as the *Ekthesis*. Pope Honorius, somewhat bewildered by the technicalities, approved the idea of a single will in Christ, probably because it seemed to reflect the portrayal of Christ in the Gospels; but he suggested that discussion of his "activities" be left to the "grammarians"![47] Maximus, now living in far-off Carthage, began to realize by the late 630s, if not before, that this new approach to reconceiving Chalcedon in fact undermined the Council's central vision, and prevented the full soteriological implications of Chalcedonian Christology from being seen.

Maximus's point, in the campaign of letters and personal interventions he waged over the next decade against the Christology of "one activity and one will,"[48] was that it is precisely in the preservation of all that belongs to the human nature of Christ—of all his human "operations" or "activities," including the central psychological activity of conscious self-determination—that his human nature is able to be fully conformed, in a human way, to the will and action of God, and so to be transformed and divinized precisely *as humanity*.[49] For Maximus, it is only if that nature remains fully and operatively human in

---

[46] Lange, Μία Ἐνέργεια, 606–10.

[47] See Honorius, *Epistula ad Sergium Episcopum Constantinopolitanum*, in *Acta* of the Lateran Synod of 649 (ed. R. Riedinger, ACO II/2.2, 548–58); Lange, Μία Ἐνέργεια, 597–601.

[48] Maximus's main letters and papers dealing with the question of the energies and wills of Christ begin, it seems, around 634, and include (in chronological order) at least the following works:

- Ep. 19, to Pyrrhus [633–4], accepting the *Psēphos* of Patriarch Sergius as orthodox (PG 91.589–97);
- *Opusc.* 4, to the priest and archimandrite George [634–40] (PG 91.56–61);
- *Opusc.* 20, to the priest Marinus [*c.*640] (PG 91.228–245);
- *Opusc.* 8, to Bishop Nicander [*c.*640] (PG 91.89–112);
- *Opusc.* 24, addressee unknown [*c.*640] (PG 91.268);
- *Opusc.* 25, addressee unknown [*c.*640] (PG 91.269–273);
- *Opusc.* 6, addressee unknown [640–2] (PG 91.65–69);
- *Opusc.* 7, to the deacon Marinus, in Cyprus [*c.*642] (PG 91.69–89);
- *Opusc.*16, addressee unknown [after 643] (PG 91.184–212);
- *Disputation with Pyrrhus* (= *Opusc.* 28) [July, 645] (PG 91.288–363);
- *Opusc.* 9, to the Monks and Faithful of the Church in Sicily [646–8] (PG 91.112–32).

[49] The existence of two wills in Christ—one belonging to God the Word and one to the "flesh," in which Christ experienced the terror of death—is recognized already by Athanasius, CA 3.57. However, the importance of the full integrity and continuing operation of the two "natural wills" possessed by the incarnate Word as a single subject only came to be seen fully in these seventh-century debates, in light of thinking out the implications of the Chalcedonian formula.

everything it does as a spiritual and material being, even while being shaped by obedience and submission to the divine, that the "ownership" of Jesus' humanity by the Word has revelatory and saving significance for other human beings.

Maximus's argument for two wills and two natural operations in Christ, as he develops it in a number of treatises and letters from the 640s, is first of all simply a matter of ontology: if every hypostasis or individual substance, by its very structure, has a *natural* way of operating—does what it does, in other words, simply because it is what it is—then confessing *two* substances or natures in the *one* hypostasis, Christ, necessarily implies recognizing in him two distinct, abiding, and undiminished (although constantly united) ways of operating: two spheres of "doing," rooted in two spheres of "being." If self-determination or willing is a central aspect of consciousness or mind, something every mind naturally does, and if both God and the human creature are understood to be—analogously—conscious and free, then the co-existence of these two isomorphic natures in Christ implies the existence in him of two natural wills: the will of God and the will of a human being.[50]

> We must not, then damage the existence of his parts by taking away their natural capacity to will ($\theta \acute{\epsilon} \lambda \eta \mu a$) and their essential activity ($\acute{\epsilon} \nu \acute{\epsilon} \rho \gamma \epsilon \iota a$), on the pretext of keeping the union undamaged and letting it bind the elements into a hypostatic unit. For if we melt down two essentially distinct faculties of will, and two natural ranges of activity, and pour them together, as a whole from parts, into one synthetic will and one activity, it will clearly be a mythical creation, wholly strange and foreign to any fellowship with the Father or ourselves.[51]

The implication is clear. If Jesus truly shared all the needs and weaknesses of human nature, as well as all our natural human capacities for

---

[50] On the logical necessity of ascribing all human operations, including that of a self-determining individual, first of all to the human *nature* of that individual, and not to his or her hypostatic "mode" of realizing that nature, see, for example, *Opusc.* 10, to the presbyter Marinus, which seems to be a set of excerpts from a longer letter [*c*.645–6] (PG 91.136 D–137 B). For a brief but useful discussion of Maximus's understanding of Christ's two wills, and his sources in earlier Patristic writing, see Andrew Louth, *Maximus the Confessor* (London: Routledge, 1996), 59–62. See also José Julián Prado, *Voluntad y Naturaleza: La antropología filosófica de Máximo el Confessor* (Rio Cuarto: Ediciones de la Universidad Nacional de Rio Cuarto, 1974); F.-M. Lethel, *Théologie de l'agonie du Christ: La Liberté du Fils de Dieu et son importance sotériologique mises en lumière par saint Maxime Confesseur*, Théologie Historique 52 (Paris: Beauchesne, 1979); Bathrellos, *The Byzantine Christ*, 99–174; David Bradshaw, "St. Maximus Confessor on the Will," in Vasiljević, *Purpose of Creation*, 143–58; John P. Manoussakis, "The Dialectic of Communion and Otherness in St. Maximus' Understanding of the Will," in Vasiljević, *Purpose of Creation*, 159–80.

[51] *Opusc.* 7, to the Deacon Marinus [*c*.642] (PG 91.73 D–76 A). It is uncertain whether this Marinus is the same person as the presbyter Marinus, addressed in *Opusculum* 20, which seems to come from about the same period. If so, it would require a revision of the chronology suggested in n. 48.

self-determination and action, he had to choose to do the human things he did in a human way:

> For if he willed these things only as God and not also as a human being, either his body was naturally divine, or he changed his essence and became flesh by casting off his own divinity; or else, quite logically, his flesh was not enlivened by a soul but was completely soulless, lacking in reason.[52] On the other hand, if it *was* endowed with a rational soul, it also had a *natural will* (θέλημα φυσικόν); for every being that is rational by nature is clearly also able, by nature, to will. And if he had, as a human being, a natural will, surely he willed those things, in accordance with his essence, that he himself—as God the creator—had placed within that nature for its own continued existence [i.e. he *naturally willed* his own self-preservation]. He did not come to do violence to the nature that he, as God and Word, had made. He came, rather, to divinize completely that nature, which he willed to have as his own, with the approval of the Father and the aid of the Spirit; he united it to himself in one and the same hypostasis, with all that naturally belongs to it, but without sin.[53]

But Maximus's concern to emphasize Christ's two "natural wills"—two very different innate capacities for self-determination, corresponding to his being as God and his human being—is not simply metaphysical speculation; it grows also out of his sense of *how* Christ saves us. For the saving Mystery of Christ's person, which he, like Leontius, holds to be centered in the "mode of union" in which Christ's two natures concretely exist, gives also a distinctive modality—that of concrete, personal union with the divine—to his human will. This prevents Jesus from living and acting amidst constant internal conflict. Maximus explains how Christ, as Son of God, might have and exercise a complete human will by distinguishing the "natural will"—the inborn ability of the creature to determine how it shapes its actions; the innate tendency of every intelligent being to seek its own well-being and continuity in being—from the "gnomic will": literally, the will formed by opinion; the will struggling to choose among concrete limited options, without full certainty of what is in its best interest; the will as we presently experience it, darkened as we are by the effects of sin. This "gnomic" or deliberative will, Maximus argues in several of his later works, is thus not the same as the *natural* human capacity for self-determination, but is rather the *mode* in which humans now realize that natural capacity in their fallen state. It is not will in its *natural* state, as it had been intended by God to function, but the will of a particular human *hypostasis*, whose concretely realized nature is presently hampered by the inherited effects of sin.[54]

---

[52] This third position—and presumably also the first—is the Apollinarian conception of Christ's inner life, put in simple terms.

[53] *Opusc.* 7 (PG 91.77 BC).

[54] See especially Maximus's late essay, *Opusc.* 3, to the priest Marinus [645–6] (PG 91.45–56; trans. Louth, 193–4).

In *Opusculum* 16, a lengthy discussion of the implications of affirming two wills in the incarnate Word, which seems to have been written after 643 and which is addressed to an unidentified superior, Maximus rejects the notion that having two natural wills would lead to destructive inner conflict in Christ. Referring to an unnamed monastic teacher (Sophronius perhaps?), from whom he claims to have learned the distinction of a natural and a gnomic will, he argues:

> And so that the aforementioned work might also define precisely the perfection of nature in God-made-flesh, and exclude opposition, he made it clear that there is a natural will in [Christ], but distinguished a deliberative (i.e. gnomic) will from it, and left no room for division by internal conflict, nor any opportunity for [a Christology of] fantasy by saying [the natural will] does not exist. But if anyone should argue, perhaps, against this, by saying that it is impossible for this to happen in him in any other way than that the two wills should be said to exist in opposition, I accept this if this means they are different in substance; but if they are understood to be actually opposite to each other, that argument is false. For surely something that is *different* is not thereby also *in opposition*. For opposition is proper to opinion (γνώμη) that is moved irrationally; but *difference* reveals that a [human] nature controlled by reason is operative. The first sets nature at variance with itself, while the latter supports nature. For surely difference in substance contributes to the cohesion of the things that nature contains; but opposition does not work this way—it leads to nature's dissolution.[55]

So Maximus insists, in his *Dialogue with Pyrrhus*, the exiled Patriarch who had succeeded Sergius of Constantinople, on the wills of Christ—an imperially-sponsored public debate held in Carthage in July, 645—that the incarnate Word had the two natural wills that must be understood as proper to God in possession of a complete human being, but that that human being, Jesus, had no "gnomic" will—no will torn by the conflicting attractions to which our wills are normally subject, because of sin. Since his humanity "existed not simply as ours does, but divinely"—since its hypostatic "mode" of being *was* in fact divine, as a result of the divine hypostasis which possessed it—he would have made all his decisions about acting in the world through the conscious, historical activity of his human mind, but under the complete guidance of divine grace, and without the uncertainty that inheres in our willing because of our alienation from God.[56]

So in Gethsemane, for example, while deeply burdened by human anxiety and by his revulsion at death, Jesus says to the Father, "Not my will, but yours be done!"—clearly showing, in Maximus's view, both the distinction between his legitimate, natural human instinct for self-preservation, and the divine will,

---

[55] *Opusc.* 16 [after 543] (PG 97.192 D–193 A). The attribution of this work to Maximus is not certain; see Sherwood, *Annotated Date-List*, 51.

[56] See especially *Dialogue with Pyrrhus* [July, 645] (PG 91.308 CD).

which he, as Son, eternally receives from and shares with the Father: his will to redeem humanity by the sacrificial self-emptying enacted on the Cross. Jesus expresses here the complete conformity of his human will to that divine will, even though the divine purpose overrules his natural human desire for life. In this way, he reveals in his own human consciousness the harmony with God which in fact is the perfection of human nature rather than a deficiency in it. So Maximus writes to Marinus the deacon:

> No natural quality, nor nature itself as a whole, can ever conflict with the cause of nature; not even our deliberation (γνώμη) and all that belongs to it, can contradict God, so long as it is in harmony with nature according to nature's innate structure ... The Logos himself showed with perfect clarity that he had a human will by nature, just as he also had by essence a divine one, in that very human prayer of his, uttered as part of his incarnate existence for us, to be spared from death. He cried out, "Father, if it is possible, let this cup pass from me," to show that the onlookers had not perceived his flesh in some mirage that deceived the senses, but that he was, truly and properly, a human being. His natural will, to which this prayer belonged as part of his incarnate existence, bore witness to this. On the other hand, that his will was completely deified and agreed with the divine will, that it was always moved and formed by it and remained in accord with it, is clear from the fact that he always carried out perfectly the decision of his Father's will, and that alone. So, as a human being, he said, "Not my will, but your will be done!" In this he offered himself to us as a model and norm for putting away our own wills to fulfill God's will perfectly, even if we should see death threatening us as a result.[57]

It is by acting divinely, even willing divinely, at great cost to his normal human interests, in other words—by being "divine in a human way, and human in a divine way," in Maximus's characteristic phrase[58]—that Jesus' natural humanity becomes most fully itself. The divinity of Christ's human nature, one might say, is adverbial rather than substantial. Such union with the will of God, with the dynamic activity of God's transcendent being, is, in Maximus's view, "the great and hidden Mystery, the preconceived end for whose sake all things exist."[59] The harmony of human and divine wills in Christ, which flows from the concrete, unique structure of his person—of his composite hypostasis—is, in Maximus's understanding, a sign of the transformation of the modalities of our own existence that will constitute our salvation, as well as the key to understanding and practicing the ascetic life in an authentic way. This is the revelation to humanity of the way of holiness, first realized by Christ himself:

> For if he himself has allowed his mysterious action of becoming part of humanity to reach its term, being made like us in every way except sin alone, and even

---

[57] *Opusc.* 7, to the Deacon Marinus (PG 91.80A, 80 CD).
[58] See n. 35 for some instances of this phrase.
[59] *Quaestiones ad Thalassium* 60 (CCG 22.75.32–4).

descending to the lower parts of the earth, where the tyranny of sin had driven the human race, then surely he will also bring to term his mysterious action of letting humanity be made divine, by making us like himself—except only (of course) for essential identity with him—and by elevating the human person above the heavens, where the fullness of love exists by nature, and where, in its limitless goodness, it invites humanity from below.[60]

It is in the union of finite and infinite natures in Christ, by the grace of God's economy, that the "exchange of qualities" in him begins: the transformation of God's mode of being and ours, not only in linguistic predication but in an ontological embrace. This is the Christian story of salvation.

## JOHN OF DAMASCUS

A century after Maximus, the Syrian monk John of Damascus continued this same line of reflection on the implications of the Chalcedonian picture of Christ, adding—with his characteristic clarity and his synthetic vision—new fullness and cohesion to the long Greek tradition that had groped, haltingly but perceptively and at times eloquently, to express the Mystery. Like most of the influential Christian writers since Chalcedon, John was not a bishop but a scholar, a monk and priest who devoted most of his energies, it seems, to study and writing. A member of the Palestinian monastic community of Mar Saba for almost fifty years, John was a prolific poet, an accomplished and profound preacher, and above all a theologian who saw his work as one of synthesis within a longer tradition: "I will say nothing of my own," he insists in the preface to his ambitious compendium of philosophical and theological learning, the *Spring of Knowledge* (Πηγὴ γνώσεως), "but will collect into one place the labors of the most respected of our teachers, ... and keep my language as brief as possible."[61] Like the Western scholastics of the thirteenth century and later, who admired and imitated him, John saw his work as chiefly one of systematization and integration.

The Damascene begins his monumental treatise on human and ecclesial wisdom with a section usually called the *Dialectica*: a summary of the key concepts and logical rules of late antique reasoning and analysis, largely drawn from Aristotle's *Categories* and Porphyry's *Eisagōgē*, here conveniently presented in 68 terse chapters.[62] He then offers us, in Part II, 101 chapters

---

[60] *Quaestiones ad Thalassium* 22 (CCG 7.139.36–46).

[61] *Spring of Knowledge*, Prooemium, ed. Bonifatius Kotter, *Die Schriften des Johannes von Damaskos*, I (Berlin: De Gruyter, 1969), 53.

[62] Since the second and third parts of the *Spring of Knowledge* consist each of 100 chapters, it is possible that John planned to offer 100 preparatory philosophical chapters, as well. The project

outlining the key "heresies" or sects of the early Christian centuries, each focused on what John sees as a particular misconstrual of the Church's tradition of understanding faith. Significantly, the final, "bonus" chapter of the work is a description of Islam—the dominant religious system at the time in John's native Damascus, and which he took to be the most recent Judaeo-Christian heresy. Part III—with the title, *An Accurate Exposition of the Orthodox Faith*—contains a further 100 chapters, outlining what John understands to be the chief recognized teachings of mainstream Christianity. These are expressed in terms that often draw on Hellenistic philosophy, but that are directly based on the Christian Scriptures and their traditional interpretation within the Church.[63]

The guiding theme of the whole, tripartite *Spring of Knowledge* is the unsurpassable importance of knowledge, as our access to the truth; this is grounded in God's creation, and revealed to us both in Scripture and in the operation of human reason.

> Nothing is more precious (John begins the first chapter of the *Dialectica*) than knowledge (γνῶσις). For if knowledge is the light of the rational soul, ignorance, on the other hand, must be darkness. And as the deprivation of light is darkness, so the deprivation of knowledge is a darkness of our reason. But ignorance is proper to irrational beings, knowledge to rational ones. If someone does not possess knowledge, then, when he is naturally able to know and to give reasons for things, this person—being rational by nature—is, because of indifference and laziness of soul, worse than irrational beasts![64]

Knowledge is the intellectual creature's contact with reality; but it is always endangered for the human mind, because the mind is "covered, as it were, with the veil of the flesh,"[65] and so can choose to embrace ignorance or half-truth rather than real knowledge. As a result, the mind needs to be purified from its passionate attachments, and patient in its search. More important still, John points out, it needs a Teacher.

> Let us draw near to the Truth [he continues], the Teacher who does not deceive. But Christ is Wisdom and Truth personified; in him "all the treasures of

---

may not have been finished—a possibility suggested by the somewhat disorganized and repetitive character of the last three chapters of the longer version of the *Dialectica*—or John may simply have run out of suitable material.

[63] This final section of the *Spring of Knowledge* was translated several times into Latin in the early Middle Ages, most famously by Burgundio of Pisa in the second half of the twelfth century, and was known in the West as *De fide orthodoxa*. This Latin translation, in which the numbering of chapters is altered to turn the treatise into four "books," corresponding to the four parts of Peter Lombard's *Sentences*, was the vehicle through which St. Thomas Aquinas came to know it and to use it so widely as a guide for his own arguments. We will refer to this theological compendium here as the *Expositio Fidei*.

[64] *Dialectica* 1 (ed. Kotter, I, 53; translation mine).

[65] *Dialectica* 1 (ed. Kotter, I, 53; translation mine).

knowledge are hidden,"[66] and he is "the Wisdom and Power of God" the Father.[67] Let us listen to his voice speaking through the divine Scriptures, and let us learn the true knowledge of all things that are.[68]

In order to know Christ, who is divine Wisdom in person, and through contact with him to be able to use human reason as a reliable instrument for discovering Truth, John is convinced—as Origen and Augustine were before him—that we need to undertake the laborious task of "knocking at the door" of *Scripture*, since it points to Christ's person and work in figures, and discloses his historical presence in our midst.

> And as we move forward, let us not be satisfied with simply arriving at the gate, but let us knock vigorously, so that the door to the bridal chamber might be opened to us and we might see the beauties within it. The gate, after all, is the letter; but the bridal chamber within the gate is the beauty of the thoughts which it hides, or the spirit of truth. Let us knock vigorously; let us read the Scriptural text once, twice, many times, and so—by opening the treasury of knowledge—we shall find it and feast on its riches.[69]

Knowledge of the truth of things, in other words, engages the human mind in the hard labor of analysis and argument and critical thought—in what we have come to call philosophy—as well as in the equally hard labor of seeking for the real meaning of Scriptural revelation, within the continuing story of God's unpredictable actions in human history. In the end, all knowledge of the Truth is an encounter with Christ, the Wisdom of God and the foundation of the truth of everything else that is; so to know the Truth depends both on human shrewdness and effort, and on God's gratuitous self-disclosure in the history. "If we love to learn," John writes, "we shall learn much! All things can naturally be grasped by concentration and labor, and before and after all else by the grace of God, who has given them all to us."[70]

With this as his presupposition, John then goes on to sketch an outline of what reason can achieve by engaging the world around us. He gives brief definitions of what the Greek world has come to understand by being, substance and accident, genus and species and differentiating characteristic, what an individual is and how it is related to universals—essentially the kind of philosophical terminology one would need to know, in order to understand classic Christian discussions of the Trinity and the person of Christ. Yet the focus, even in this essentially philosophical treatise, is on what the mind can do with *revelation*. So in chapter 3 of the *Dialectica*, where he offers several definitions of philosophy itself, John begins with what one can also find in

---

[66] Col. 2.3.  [67] I Cor. 1.24.
[68] *Dialectica* 1 (ed. Kotter, I, 53; translation mine).
[69] *Dialectica* 1 (ed. Kotter, I, 54; translation mine).
[70] *Dialectica* 1 (ed. Kotter, I, 54; translation mine).

Porphyry's *Eisagogē* and in the Neoplatonic commentators on Aristotle: "Philosophy is knowledge of the things that are, insofar as they are—that is, knowledge of the nature of what is."[71] But he concludes the same chapter, six definitions later, with a characterization of philosophy that is not found in the commentators, but seems to grow from the Church's wisdom, and from his own experience of monastic study: "Philosophy, once again, is love of Wisdom. But true Wisdom is God. Therefore the love of God is true philosophy."[72]

Like Maximus, John also drew on the conceptual distinctions worked out by Leontius of Byzantium and his sixth-century contemporaries, especially on Leontius's analysis of the metaphysics of substance and individual, to explain, with new clarity, the coherence and central importance of the earlier councils' picture of Christ.[73] In the *Exposition of the Orthodox Faith*, for instance, he begins the long section on the person of Christ with a summary of what is proposed by Chalcedon and Constantinople II:

> The natures were united with each other without change or alteration, without the divine nature departing from its proper simplicity, nor the human either being turned into the nature of divinity, nor losing its own existence, also without a single, composite nature coming into being out of the two—for a composite nature cannot be of the same substance as either of the natures from which it is formed, having been produced as something different, out of different things ... But we do *not* teach that Christ comes from a single, composite nature, *nor* that he is something different, produced from different things, as a human being comes from soul and body or as the body comes from the four elements, but [we teach] that the same things remain, which come from different sources: for we confess that from divinity and humanity a perfect God and a perfect man exist, and are said to be one and the same—from and in two natures.[74]

This ontological unity of two wholly disparate kinds of being in the life and activity of a single subject leads, as John reaffirms, to the traditional Christian theological practice of shared predication:

> In the case of our Lord Jesus Christ, since we recognize his natures as two but [recognize him as] a single hypostasis, put together from both, when we contemplate his natures we call them divinity and humanity, but when we look at the hypostasis composed from both natures, sometimes we name the Christ formed out of both of them "God and a human being at once," or "God in the flesh"; but

---

[71] *Dialectica* 3 (ed. Kotter, I, 56; translation mine).

[72] *Dialectica* 3 (ed. Kotter, I, 56; translation mine).

[73] See, for instance, *Dialectica* 30, 43–5, 67; *Exp. Fid.* 47–55, 57, 91; *Contra Jacobitas* 52; *De duabus in Christo voluntatibus* 7. For an excellent survey of John's Christology in these works, see Andrew Louth, *Saint John Damascene: Tradition and Originality in Byzantine Theology* (Oxford: Oxford University Press, 2002), 144–79.

[74] *Exp. Fid.* 47 (= III, 3; ed. Kotter, *Die Schriften des Johannes von Damaskos*, II [Berlin: De Gruyter, 1973] 111.1–7, 17–21).

sometimes we speak of him on the basis of one of the parts, calling him simply "God" and "Son of God," or simply "a human being" and "son of man," and at other times simply by higher titles or more humble ones. For he who exists as the one or the other reality is still a single subject: being the one as he eternally exists, without cause, from the Father, and becoming the other in time, out of love for humanity.[75]

A few chapters later on, John adds, in what seems deliberately provocative language:

He is wholly, on the one hand, God in God's fullness, but God is not the whole of him—for he is not only God, but human; and he is wholly, on the other hand, a human in human fullness, but a human being is not the whole of him—for he is not only human, but also God. The term "the whole (ὅλον)" refers to his nature, but "wholly (ὅλως)" refers to his hypostasis—just as "one thing (ἄλλο)" refers to nature, "one subject (ἄλλος)" refers to hypostasis.[76]

The Chalcedonian portrait of Christ, as a single hypostasis existing in and from two complete, interwoven, yet utterly diverse natures, is expressed here with new clarity.

John also took up Maximus's argument for the presence of two complete natural "operations" and wills in Christ, as a result of his two unconfused but inseparable natures.

In every human being, freedom to determine one's actions in accord with reason and appetite is part of our natural constitution; we are free by nature, in other words, even though the particular way each of us realizes that freedom in action is an expression of our "mode of being" what we are—of our hypostatic existence as particular human beings in history. So he explains, in his treatise *On the Two Wills in Christ*:

One must realize, too, that every human hypostasis receives his or her existence and the fact that he or she is from nothing, as a gift from the Creator: in other words, being a creature who is alive and active, able to perceive and know and calculate, and endowed with sensible and intellectual appetites—that is, able to will on one's own—and also the fact that he or she is composed of substance and accidents. All of this is part of the human substance and is natural. But the particular, chosen way these are put into action constitutes our hypostatic

---

[75] *Exp. Fid.* 48 (= III, 4; ed. Kotter, II 116.14–117.23). For further articulations of John's understanding of the union of two natures in one hypostasis, see *Dialectica* 50 (ed. Kotter, I, 139–40); *De Duabus in Christo Voluntatibus* 1–29 (ed. Kotter, *Die Schriften des Johannes von Damaskos*, IV [Berlin: De Gruyter, 1981], 173–215); *Contra Jacobitas* 50–4 (ed. Kotter IV, 124–8). (The full title of John's treatise on the two wills in Christ, in fact, is given in the manuscripts as: "Concerning the characteristics of the two natures in the one Christ, our Lord, and, in a summary way, also concerning his two wills and activities and his one hypostasis.")

[76] *Exp. Fid.* 51 (= III, 7; Kotter, II 126, 52–5). At the end of this passage, John is of course alluding to the celebrated passage in Gregory of Nazianzus's *First Letter to Cledonius* 20–1 (SChr. 208.44–6).

difference. For to share in these characteristics is what makes our nature one, but the *manner* of our existing (ὁ δὲ τρόπος τῆς ὑπάρξεως) introduces the difference in hypostases, and the distinctive existence and constitution, and the particular way and motion and varying use of natural abilities, shapes our hypostases and allows us to speak of many human beings. So, too, in the case of the Father and the Son and the Holy Spirit, since the existence of each of them is distinct, they are three hypostases; but since the nature of each and its characteristics is seen to be the same in each of the hypostases, they are of one substance and nature. And since each hypostasis does not will or act independently or in its own way or by its own choice, but as one, the three are—and are spoken of—not as three gods, but one God with each other and in each other.[77]

In the Trinity and in the human world, the Damascene insists here and elsewhere, the concrete, existing individual—the hypostasis, in the now-classical terminology of the Cappadocians and Chalcedon—is defined by its origin and expressed in its particular, freely chosen behavior: in how and from where the individual has its being—its "place in the family," one might say—and in the manner in which it lives out its natural characteristics, makes use of its natural potential. John shows, in fact, a greater awareness than his predecessors seem to have had that we use the word "hypostasis" or "person," like all other words, only "improperly" (καταχρηστικῶς)—or as Western medieval theologians would say, analogically—in speaking of Father, Son, and Holy Spirit. Unlike human hypostases, the "Persons" of the Trinity have no beginning in time to define their individuality, no personal accidents or differences of particular activity outside the divine being to mark them off from each other, in the way human individuals have such characteristics. Their differences lie simply in their internal relationships of origin or cause, and in their way of giving themselves to one another: "the mode of their existence."[78] But it is precisely the hypostasis of the Son, the one who receives his divine being filially from the Father for all eternity, who expresses that filial way of being in terms of a human nature as well in his shared divinity; otherwise, we would have to say that all three persons in the Trinity could have taken on human flesh in the Incarnation, which would be a repudiation of the very basis for our knowing and speaking of the divine Trinity at all. As John strikingly puts it, later in the same paragraph:

> It is not possible, then, to say that one of the divine hypostases has anything that all the hypostases do not have, except for the manner of their existing. And the incarnation is a manner of the second way of existing, befitting only the only Son and Word, so that his particularity might remain unshaken.[79]

---

[77] *De Duabus in Christo Voluntatibus* 7 (Kotter, IV, 183–4).
[78] *Contra Jacobitas* 52 (Kotter, IV 126.25–7).
[79] *Contra Jacobitas* 52 (Kotter, IV 127.55–8).

So the distinctive mark of Jesus, who combines in a single hypostasis the utterly different—yet, causally speaking, utterly interwoven—realities of God and a human being, is that he reveals both of these realities in their natural, infinitely differentiated operations; yet in him, each is always conditioned by the other, each always reveals the other translated into its own terms. So, borrowing language from the Pseudo-Denys, in the *Expositio Fidei* John discusses the miracles of Christ as signs of both humanity and divinity:

> Just as Christ received, in his birth from a Virgin, "super-substantial substance,"[80] so also he revealed his human way of acting in a superhuman way, walking with earthly feet on unstable water: not by turning the water into earth but by causing it, in the superabundant power of his divinity, not to flow away nor yield beneath the weight of material feet. For not in a merely human way did he do human things: he was not only human, after all, but also God, and so even his sufferings brought life and salvation. Nor yet, as God, was he active simply in God's manner: for he was not only God, but also human, and so it was by touch and words, and things such as this, that he worked miracles.[81]

Even now in glory, John goes on to suggest, the incarnate Word still remembers his past as past, still knows and loves, all in a human way—even as he governs the universe with the transcendent "mind" of God. In the sense that both these distantly analogous forms of consciousness mold and express each other—because both belong to a single subject, work towards the same saving ends, relate to the same created or uncreated "other"—one can even speak of Christ's work, John suggests, by using the Dionysian phrase, "a new theandric activity," in an orthodox, not a monenergist, way.

> This is what the phrase "theandric activity" expresses: that when God became human—that is, when he became incarnate—both his human activity came to be divine or deified, and not without a part (οὐκ ἄμοιρος) in his divine activity, and his divine activity was not without a part in his human activity, but each of them was now observed in conjunction with the other.[82]

---

[80] See Dionysius, *De Divinis nominibus* 2.4 (ed. Beate M. Suchla, *Corpus Dionysiacum* 1 [Berlin: De Gruyter, 1990] 126.14–15); Epist. 4 (PG 3.1072 C). As John interprets this phrase, it seems to point to the divine *way* in which Jesus' authentically human substance or nature is generated and born. Natural, created objects, when drawn into the saving work of God, behave in ways that point beyond their own natural limits to God's presence, without losing their own natural identities.

[81] *Exp. Fid.* 59 (= III, 15; Kotter, II 151.188–96), echoing also Dionysius, *De divinis nominibus* 2.9 (Suchla, 133). See also Maximus Confessor, *Ambiguum to Thomas* 5.8 (CCG 48.23 23; trans. Lollar, 65).

[82] *Exp. Fid.* 63 (= III, 19; ed. Kotter, II 161.40–44). John is referring here to the "mia-energetic" controversy (discussed earlier in this chapter), which took its inspiration from the final phrase of Dionysius, Epist. 4 (PG 3.1072 C): reflecting on the humanity and actions of Christ, Ps-Dionysius asserts that the Word "truly became human in a manner above any human, and from then on did not do divine things in the way God does, nor human things in the way a human does, but as God become a man, he lived among us and revealed a new, theandric way of

As Maximus had so memorably emphasized, Christ must always be under-stood as "humanly divine, and divinely human." In those adverbs, those modalities of his natural levels of being, lies the saving mystery of Christ's person—of "God with us." And that very sharing, that mutual shaping of each other by God and a human being, is also itself the promise of our own transformation to be with God, our own share in the Mystery of Christ.


# CONCLUSION

In the work of these three late representatives of Greek Patristic Christology, the dense, technical style of argument and the use of consistently philosophical language may mask the continuities between their thought and the longer theological tradition on which they drew. Clearly all three of them, as defend-ers of Chalcedon's decree, regard the Council's formulation of the Mystery of Christ's person as a starting-point, a norm for remaining within the field of Orthodox conversation. Yet for all three of them, as for many of those whose work preceded the Chalcedonian crisis, theological reflection on Christ was important precisely because it concerned far more than simply the relation-ship of the various elements of his own particular personality: the Logos, a human mind, a human body. Rather, it was important because that relation-ship of the "parts" in Christ includes, in a way, the whole of what Christian faith has to say about God and the world and human salvation. In the person of Christ, these post-Chalcedonian writers emphasized, two wholly incom-mensurable realities—the transcendent, unknowable, yet omnipresent Creator and a complete, naturally defined, finite human being—are joined as one subject, become one acting individual. The two realities exist and function in perfect harmony with each other and reveal each other; indeed, the Word brings to graced perfection the human Jesus' naturally characteristic way of being. Yet although the long-term effect of the union, from our perspective, is to communicate divine qualities to the human Jesus—a virtue, a holiness, an integrity and beauty beyond human capacity, life and indestructible energy beyond the mortal—still God the Word does not utterly swallow up or obliterate all traces of the man who is "his own." The union of divine and human in Christ remains that of a *substantial relationship* of a unique sort: not simply the moral guidance or inspiration of Jesus the man, or the Word's symbolic self-representation in his words and actions, but also not a hom-ogenization of these two realities that swallows up their differences. What Leontius of Byzantium recognized as unique in Christ, what reveals Jesus of

---

acting (καινήν τινα τὴν θεανδρικὴν ἐνέργειαν)." Dionysius here seems to be referring to the way Christ behaves in the Gospels, rather than speculating on the ontological structure of his person.

Nazareth to be the Word made flesh, is the way he *acts* with relationship to Israel's God: "his sinlessness and all his holiness, his complete union and identification with the whole of the one who assumed him, and his being and being called one Son, showing the signs of a Son's peculiar character."[83] It is by being completely, even primordially, human, yet freely acting as, and knowing himself literally to be, the *Son of God*, that Jesus most fully reveals to us who he is, and what we are called to become with him, in his Spirit.

---

[83] *CAph* (PG 86.1353 A).

# 9

## The Iconoclastic Controversy

### Christology and Images

The last, and in some ways the most bitterly remembered, of the great doctrinal controversies that engulfed the early Church was the controversy over the veneration of Christian images, which raged, mainly in parts of the Eastern Roman Empire and for a time also in the West, in the eighth and ninth centuries—the controversy that was the context for the last of the great councils that the Churches of both East and West accept as ecumenical.[1] This was not strictly, as a modern person might suppose, a controversy over the value or the appropriate forms of Christian art. Nor does the skepticism of some contemporary French and Anglo-Saxon scholars about the reliability of our sources[2]—mainly ninth-century chroniclers, monastic hagiographers, and theologians with a clearly pro-icon agenda—justify our making light either of

---

[1] The controversy over the veneration of images, which had begun in the Byzantine Empire, became acute in the Latin West in the decades after the Second Council of Nicaea (787), and continued until the mid-ninth century, beginning with a rather hasty and inaccurate reading of the decrees of the Council of 787, and spurred on especially by the anti-icon campaign of Bishop Claudius of Turin (d. 827). Theodulf of Orléans's massive treatise against the cult of images, in four books, called the *Libri Carolini* or *Opus Caroli Regis*, rejected the decree of the Second Council of Nicaea (787) that affirmed image-veneration, and dealt with the theological and political issues involved, from the perspective of the newly confident Frankish court. It soon lost its relevance, however, as the theological questions at stake became better known in the Latin world. Since our concern here is with the controversy in the context of the longer flow of the Christological tradition, we will confine our discussion to the two stages of the dispute in the Eastern Roman Empire. For a thorough, original and subtle examination of the Western controversy, see Thomas F. X. Noble, *Icons, Iconoclasm, and the Carolingians* (Philadelphia, PA: University of Pennsylvania Press, 2009).

[2] See Noble, *Icons*, 47–61, and the sources cited there. For a thorough, more classic exposition of the controversy over images in the Greek Patristic Church, especially its theological aspects, see Christoph Schönborn, *God's Human Face* (San Francisco: Ignatius Press, 1994). Jaroslav Pelikan has also provided a readable and engaging, but much less comprehensive survey of the controversy: *Imago Dei: The Byzantine Apologia for Icons* (Princeton, NJ: Princeton University Press, 1990). For a recent collection of relevant texts on the controversy see Stéphane Bigham, *Les images chrétiennes: Textes historiques de Constantin le Grand jusqu'à la période posticono-claste (313–900)* (Montreal: Médiaspaul, 2010).

the basic facts, as we know them, or of the intensity of the controversy in its own time. There is abundant archaeological and art-historical evidence from the Byzantine world to confirm the story of conflict and destruction to which surviving textual polemics point.[3] The Greek controversy over devotion to images was real, whatever judgment we make about its causes and its relative magnitude; contemporary authors saw it as a serious and urgent debate involving much of the Eastern Empire. And as it developed, it became ever more clearly a controversy not simply about images, but about the Incarnation of the Word, and about the proper human response to what Christians believe the Incarnation achieved in history.

The early Jewish, Christian, and Islamic traditions of faith all took generally negative positions about the use and role of religious images in community life, although actual practice, in Jewish and Christian circles, was more ambivalent. The Torah and the prophetic books of ancient Israel forbade the making and veneration of idols of all kinds, and expressed contempt for the other nations' foolishness in thinking that "the works of human hands" could have divine power.[4] The human person, however, in the creation narrative in Genesis, is said to have been made in "God's image ($\epsilon\grave{\iota}\kappa\grave{\omega}\nu$) and likeness;"[5] and in the New Testament this language is applied primordially to Christ as God's eternal Son,[6] and through him to all human beings, who, in the process of redemption, are "called to be conformed to his image."[7] Yet in both ancient Israel and in early Christianity, images made by human effort and craft were also not entirely rejected; the elaborate wall paintings, representing biblical events, in both the third-century Christian church and the contemporary synagogue at Dura-Europos, in eastern Syria, uncovered as recently as the 1930s, show that visual images did decorate Jewish and Christian places of worship in at least some parts of the Mediterranean world, in the early centuries of our era.

The most sharply expressed Jewish critique of religious images was really the philosophical one offered in the works of Philo, the Middle Platonist biblical commentator, who—like Plato—considered any attempt to depict the spiritual

---

[3] For a summary of this evidence, see, for example, Robin Cormack, *Byzantine Art* (Oxford: Oxford University Press, 2000), 92–102. For a detailed description of the archaeological evidence of widespread Islamic-sponsored iconoclasm in Christian Churches in Palestine in the early eighth century, I am especially indebted to Christian Sahner's yet-unpublished paper, "'Angels Do Not Enter a House containing an Image:' Reconsidering the Iconoclastic Edict of Yazīd II, A.D. 723/A.H. 105." See also A. A. Vasiliev, "The Iconoclastic Edict of the Caliph Yazīd, A.D. 721," *Dumbarton Oaks Papers* 9/10 (1956), 23–47, 120–59.

[4] See, for example, Exod. 20.4–5; Lev. 19.4; 26.1; Deut. 29.17–18; Ps. 31.6. Idols are the quintessential expression of religious frivolity: Isa. 44.9–11; Jer. 10.5; Pss. 96.5, 115.4–8, and 135.15–18. Israel's God will destroy their cult, along with those who worship them: Hos. 8.4; Mic. 1.7.

[5] Gen. 1.26–7.     [6] See Col. 1.15; cf. Phil. 2.6; Heb. 1.3.

[7] Rom. 8.29; cf. I John 3.3.

realm artistically as deceptive.[8] In the writings of the rabbis in the first five centuries of our era, on the other hand, Jewish artisans were allowed to make images for non-Jewish consumers, and Jews might even possess images in their houses, as long as they did not worship them. Early Christian burial sites, too, especially in the Roman catacombs or underground cemeteries, often were decorated with murals that made use of the representative conventions of their non-Christian contemporaries to depict favorite biblical themes, such as Christ the Good Shepherd, or Christ the Judge, in culturally recognizable forms.[9] But attitudes began to harden after the beginning of imperial religious tolerance, as boundaries between Jewish and Christian communities sharpened, in the second half of the fourth century.[10] By the time of the fixing of the Talmudic corpus in the eighth century, rabbinic Judaism had come to ban all representative images from places of worship, and the new Islamic movement, rooted in the tradition of Jewish and Christian Scripture and biblical interpretation, took an equally strong stand against human and animal images, as a thinly disguised form of idolatry.

Second-century Christian apologists, of course, like Justin and Athenagoras,[11] drew on the Old Testament to heap what soon became standard contempt on "pagan" devotional practices, centered on statues and paintings made by human hands. Clement of Alexandria, generally affirming towards the cosmopolitan culture of his day, nevertheless insisted that well-formed Christians worshipped a totally transcendent God without the aid of images;[12] the north African Tertullian, two decades later, contrasted the abstract purity of Christian worship with the visual luxuriance of pagan idolatry.[13] Origen insisted that only the incarnation of the Word genuinely succeeded in making the transcendent God visible;[14] otherwise, God's image in the world was achieved most fully in the creation and the virtuous life of the human person.[15]

---

[8] See, for instance, *De Vita Contemplativa* 1.7; *De Gigantibus* 13.58–9.

[9] See Paul Corby Finney, *The Invisible God: The Earliest Christians on Art* (New York: Oxford University Press, 1994); Robin M. Jensen, *Face to Face: Portraits of the Divine in Early Christianity* (Minneapolis, MN: Fortress, 2005). See also Ernst Kitzinger, "Christian Imagery: Growth and Impact," in Kurt Weitzmann (ed.), *The Age of Spirituality: A Symposium* (Princeton, NJ: Princeton University Press, 1980), 141–63.

[10] See Daniel Boyarin, *Dying for God* (Stanford, CA: Stanford University Press, 1999), 1–19; *Border Lines* (Philadelphia, PA: University of Pennsylvania Press, 2004), esp. 6–13.

[11] See Justin, *Apol.* 1.9, 24; Athenagoras, *Plea for the Christians* 17–18; *Letter to Diognetus* 2; Theophilus, *To Autolycus* 2.2. On the evidence for the theme of disapproval of images in early Christian literature, see Paul Corby Finney, "Antecedents of Byzantine Iconoclasm: Christian Evidence before Constantine," in Joseph Gutmann (ed.), *The Image and the Word* (Missoula, MT: Scholars Press, 1977) 27–47.

[12] Clement, *Protreptikos* 4.1; *Paedagogos* 3.59.2; *Stromateis* 5.1, 11–14.

[13] *De Idololatria* 3–4, 6, 18, 20. Tertullian does later admit, however, that Christians in Carthage used religious pictures of some kind: *De Pudicitia* 7.1–3.

[14] So *De Principiis* 1.6.4; 2.4.3.     [15] *Homilies on Genesis* 1.13; 4; 13.4.

## EUSEBIUS

The first extended Christian polemic against the use of visual images for Christian devotion, however, was the celebrated letter later attributed to the fourth-century church historian and Origenist theologian, Eusebius of Caesaraea, supposedly written to the Empress Constantia, the sister of Constantine and wife of his rival Licinius. The authenticity of this letter, which survives only in large fragments quoted by the protagonists in the eighth-century iconoclastic controversy,[16] has frequently been questioned, because it is otherwise unattested in fourth-century sources and because its argument seems so conveniently to fit into eighth-century polemics; its language and its theology, however, seem to resonate remarkably well with the rest of Eusebius's spiritualizing, Platonically inspired thought.[17] In these fragments, Eusebius responds to the Empress's request for a painted image of Christ—the kind of portrait he elsewhere says he himself has seen of both Paul and of the Savior[18]—by a detailed but forceful refusal. Assuming that she cannot be asking for a picture of the Son of God in his true, eternal identity, which transcends imagining, Eusebius concludes that she is looking for a depiction of "that image, which he took up for our sakes, when he put on 'the form of a servant'."[19] But even this form, the bishop argues, cannot be drawn by an artist, since the transfigured human body of Christ, now in heaven as once on Mount Tabor, radiates heavenly splendor.

> Who, then, would be able to draw, with dead and lifeless colors and lines, the flashes of splendor and glory that shine forth and burst out of him, since even the holy disciples could not endure gazing on him when he appeared in this way, but fell on their faces, confessing that the sight was beyond their endurance?[20]

To attempt this would be to try to limit the transcendent, to grasp the ungraspable; even the pagans—if they are philosophically sophisticated—know such a project is impossible. Eusebius continues:

> If even among unbelieving Gentiles no one would, in this way, try to depict what has no resemblance to anything else—as for example an artist, attempting to draw

---

[16] Parts of this letter are cited at the Second Council of Nicaea (787) [Mansi 13.313 A–D], and later by the ninth-century iconophile Patriarch Nicephorus, in his *Contra Eusebium et Epiphanium* (*Spic.Sol.* 1.383–6). The Greek text of many of these fragments is conveniently reproduced in Herman Hennephof, *Textus Byzantini ad Iconomachiam Pertinentes* (Leiden: Brill, 1969), 42–4.

[17] For a measured argument in favor of the likelihood that the letter is indeed a work of the bishop of Caesaraea, see Stephen Gero, "The True Image of Christ: Eusebius' Letter to Constantia Reconsidered," *JTS* 32 (1981), 460–70. Gero argues that if it is not by Eusebius, its forger knew Eusebius's way of thinking and writing intimately. If the letter is genuine, its date remains unknown; Constantia died about 330, which would offer a *terminus ante quem*.

[18] Eusebius, *Church History* 7.18.

[19] Eusebius, *Letter to Constantia*, sec. I (Hennephof, *Textus Byzantini*, 42).

[20] *Letter to Constantia*, sec. IV (Hennephof, *Textus Byzantini*, 43).

what has nothing like it, ends up sketching and sculpting shapes that look like humans, yet are wholly different [from the gods] (for such are those who form idols, either of what they think is divine, or of what they call heroes, or of something of this sort, and want to make images of them, but are unable to draw them or even anything close to them)—then you will conclude yourself that it is wrong for us, too, to do such things.[21]

Pictorial representation, as Eusebius understands it, always attempts to show a link between two different realities—the original and the attempted copy—that in some respect share the same *form*. With the divine, no such visual comparison is possible.

Eusebius goes on to remind the Empress of the biblical prohibition of venerating "graven images," which he insists has also been the universal practice of the Christian Church up to his time. He tells the story of meeting "a certain woman," who casually mentioned that she had pictures of St. Paul and of the Savior, as if they belonged among the sages (ὡς ἂν φιλοσόφους); he confiscated them, he says, to avoid scandalizing people by seeming to condone idolatry.[22] The practice resembles what Gnostics have done, in making portraits of their own leaders.

> For us, such practices are forbidden. When we confess the Lord our Savior as divine, after all, we are preparing ourselves to see God, purifying our hearts with all seriousness, so that—in purity—we may gaze on him; for "Blessed are the pure in heart, for they shall see God." And if you think images are really important, besides this, before the face-to-face vision and sight of our Savior that is to come, what greater portrait could a person have than the very word of God?[23]

Like his hero Origen, Eusebius seems to assume that the Word of God became "flesh" in the word of the Bible, before becoming flesh in the Virgin's womb. Study the Scriptures, he is urging the Empress, and you have the only representation of the Lord you will ever need!

## EPIPHANIUS

During the last two decades of the fourth century, another busy author who was later claimed as a spiritual ancestor by the opponents of sacred images was Epiphanius, a Palestinian who later became bishop of Salamis in Cyprus. Learned, but less intellectually subtle than Eusebius, Epiphanius was essentially

---

[21] *Letter to Constantia*, sec. V (Hennephof, *Textus Byzantini*, 43).
[22] *Letter to Constantia*, sec. VII (Hennephof, *Textus Byzantini*, 44). Are these the same portraits he refers to in CH 7.18?
[23] *Letter to Constantia*, sec. VIII (Hennephof, *Textus Byzantini*, 44).

a theological polemicist, who served the later Christian tradition mainly by his careful and detailed descriptions of ancient Christian heresies. He also seems to have been opposed to the public erection and veneration of sacred images, on the traditional philosophical grounds of the essential deceptiveness of artistic representation.[24] A passage from his letter to the Emperor Theodosius I, probably from around 394, gives a representative example of Epiphanius's position:

> I beg you, O devout Emperor, enemy of the wicked: challenge all deviance by the zeal for God that is truly in you, through your firm legislation—sanctioned by fines, if possible. And I trust that you can accomplish, by God's grace, whatever you will. Wherever tapestries are found, with false pictures on them that nonetheless claim to represent the Apostles or the prophets or even the Lord Christ himself, they should all be stripped from the Churches or baptisteries or residences or martyrs' shrines where they are hanging, and you should provide them with a poor man's burial! What is painted on walls should be whitewashed. And since it will be difficult to remove what is planned for depiction in mosaics, your God-given wisdom will know what orders to give; if it is possible to remove them, that would be best, but if that is impossible, one should imitate the efforts of our forebears, and never have figures represented in this way again. Our ancestors, after all, painted nothing but the sign of Christ, the cross, on their doors and everywhere.[25]

Epiphanius's main objection to images, in the anti-iconic passages of his works that survive, also seems to be their lack of authenticity: they falsify the realities they claim to represent, by relying simply on the painter's imagination.[26] In contrast, he argues, the only representation of Christ and the saints that can lay claim to adequacy is the image offered in the lives of the people who imitate them.[27] Beyond this, the simple sign of the cross should be enough to satisfy both the need for decoration and the demand for religious symbolism. As Son of God, Jesus is, in his very person, "beyond our grasp" (ἀκατάληπτον); so it is strictly impossible to form an adequate image of him, in words or by any other human art.[28] A lifeless portrait cannot take the place of the living God; so to offer genuinely religious veneration to such an image is idolatry.[29]

---

[24] John of Damascus, *On the Divine Images* 1.25; 2.18, rejects the anti-iconic passages attributed to Epiphanius as spurious. Some modern scholars have also questioned the authenticity of these fragments, which—like those of Eusebius's letter—are mainly preserved in the *acta* of the Second Council of Nicaea (787), or in the treatises of Patriarch Nicephorus in defense of icons. Besides an a priori unwillingness on the part of some to think of this venerable enemy of heresies condemning the use of images, however, there seems to be little reason to doubt that this was Epiphanius's position.

[25] This passage is cited by Nicephorus, in his *Challenge and Refutation* 202 (ed. J. M. Featherstone; CCG 33 [Turnhout: Brepols, 1997] 323.7–27).

[26] Epiphanius, *Letter to Theodosius* (Hennephof, *Textus Byzantini*, 46–7).

[27] *Letter to Theodosius* (Hennephof, *Textus Byzantini*, 47–8).

[28] *Letter to Theodosius* (Hennephof, *Textus Byzantini*, 49).

[29] *Letter to Theodosius* (Hennephof, *Textus Byzantini*, 50). For a discussion of fourth-century Christian reflection on the problems of depicting the divine, see Jensen, *Face to Face*, 101–9.

## AFTER CHALCEDON

Assuming these passages are genuine (and there seems to be no strong reason to reject them), Eusebius and Epiphanius represented at least one strand in Patristic thought, which showed the influence of Jewish and earlier Christian concerns about pagan idol-worship, as well as that of the Platonic critique that all artistic representation falsifies what it depicts.[30] Yet the late fifth and early sixth centuries were undoubtedly an age of widespread artistic creativity and innovation in the decoration of places of worship, and probably even of private homes. Mosaics and frescoes of biblical scenes and personalities, and of the saints, begin to appear in churches;[31] iconic tapestries were produced— especially in Egypt, where the art of weaving flourished;[32] smaller painted images of Jesus and the saints were executed, often with the high degree of artistic accomplishment that testifies to a wider general practice.[33] Significantly, this increased interest in representing Christ and the saints, doubtless for devotional as well as decorative purposes, coincided in time with the heated debates over Christological language that followed the Council of Chalcedon in the Eastern part of the Roman Empire during the late fifth and sixth centuries, as Christians struggled to find adequate categories to describe the human reality embodying Christ's personal identity as Savior and Son of God. To pay homage to a mosaic or tapestry that depicted his human form was doubtless, for many, the most personally engaging way to recognize the real effect of the Incarnation.[34]

The writings of the Pseudo-Dionysius, probably dating from the end of the fifth or the beginning of the sixth century, witness to a renewed sense of the

---

[30] See, for example, Plato, *Republic* 10 (595 B–596 E; 607 B–608 B).

[31] As examples, one might point to the mosaic of Mary as Mother of God in the church of Santa Maria Maggiore in Rome, from 432; to the great Ravenna mosaics in fifth- and sixth-century Christian structures, both Nicene and "Arian," beginning with the image of Jesus as the Good Shepherd in the so-called "mausoleum" of the Empress Galla Placidia, built around 430; or to the monumental apse-mosaic of the Transfiguration in the Church of the monastery of St. Catherine on Mount Sinai, which bears the date of 565–6. Frescoes, which are less easily preserved, survive from as early the fifth century in Rome, in the funerary chapel of Sts. Felix and Adauctus, in the catacombs of Commodilla: see Kurt Weitzmann, *The Icon: Holy Images, Sixth to Fourteenth Century* (New York: Braziller, 1978), 48–9.

[32] For example, the monumental wool tapestry icon of the Mother of God surrounded by angels and the twelve Apostles, now in the Cleveland Museum, which was woven in Egypt sometime in the sixth century; on it, see Weitzmann, *The Icon*, 46–7; Pelikan, *Imago Dei*.

[33] For example, the sixth-century encaustic icons of Christ in majesty, or of Mary with St. George, discovered in St. Catherine's monastery of Sinai and published by Kurt Weitzmann. For plates and brief commentary, see Weitzmann, *The Icon*, 40–3; 50–1; 54–5.

[34] For the abundant evidence for an increased interest in icons, relics, and other material foci for devotional practices in the sixth century, and for reflections on their roots in post-Chalcedonian piety, see especially Ernst Kitzinger, "The Cult of Images before Iconoclasm," *Dumbarton Oaks Papers* 8 (1954), 85–150, and further literature cited there.

need for spiritual, physical, and liturgical mediation to connect the conscious-ness of human believers with the transcendent Mystery at the source of all reality.[35] Hypatius of Ephesus, too, a pro-Chalcedonian bishop active in the 530s and an early advisor of Justinian, argues in a partially preserved letter that material images are necessary to guide the minds of the less educated faithful to an awareness of the ineffable divine beauty and light.[36] Yet, as often happens with religious devotion, abuses and excesses suggesting fairly wide-spread superstition in image-veneration were occasionally reported, as well, especially during the "second" iconoclastic period in the ninth century. An icon of the Virgin in a church in Constantinople, in the 830s, was said to have real milk miraculously flowing from her painted breasts, but the discharge was soon shown to be a trick.[37] Theodore of Stoudios, in the early ninth century, praises the strong faith of the courtier John the Spatharios, for choosing an icon of the martyr St. Demetrios as his son Demetrios's baptismal sponsor, but warns John not to let this become widely known, for fear of scandalizing the skeptical.[38] A letter addressed to the Frankish King Louis the Pious, purport-edly from the iconoclast Emperor Michael II, which is included in the *acta* of the Western synod of Paris of 825, repeats this same accusation, and charges that pious people in Constantinople had abandoned their earlier devotion to "the life-giving cross" and were honoring images as if they could work miracles. The Emperor also alleges here that priests in the East were using boards painted with icons as Eucharistic altars, and flaking chips of paint from icons into the Eucharistic chalice.[39] Gestures of veneration could seem very close to adoration, and could suggest the inability of many of the faithful to distinguish what was a creature from what was divine.[40]

---

[35] See, for instance, *De Ecclesiastica Hierarchia* 1.2.

[36] See his *Letter to Julian of Atramyttion* in Franz Diekamp, *Analecta Patristica* (= Orientalia Christiana Analecta 117; Rome, 1938), 127–9. Interestingly, Hypatius also challenged the purported date and authorship of the writings attributed to Paul's convert, Dionysius, which had become known only recently. See Innocent of Maroneia, *Epistula ad Thomam de Collatione cum Severianis Habita* (ACO IV/2, 172.1–8; 173.12–18). See also Jean Gouillard, "Hypatios d'Éphèse, ou du Pseudo-Denys à Théodore Studite," in *La Vie religieuse à Byzance* (London: Variorum, 1981), VII.

[37] See the Arabic chronicle of bishop Eutychius of Alexandria (PG 111.1136 D–1137 B). A century before this, however, Germanus of Constantinople wrote to Thomas of Claudiopolis, attesting to an inexplicable flow of myrrh from the palm of an icon of the Theotokos: Ep. 1.17 (PG 98.185 AB).

[38] PG 99.961–2.

[39] In Latin translation, this letter appears in MGH, Conc. 2.2, 475–80; Mansi 14.420 BC. For a discussion of the letter, see Noble, *Icons*, 260–2; for the Colloquy of Paris of 825, see Noble, *Icons*, 263–86.

[40] See the remark of the early seventh-century monk and Patriarch, Sophronius of Jerusalem, *Miracles of Cyrus and John* 36 (PG 87.3553 C); also Theodore of Stoudios, Ep 2.167 (PG 99.1529 C–1531 A).

The first formal attempt by the imperial government to control, even to repress altogether the veneration of sacred images is identified in Byzantine sources with the Emperor Leo III (717–41). A native of Isauria, in southeastern Asia Minor north of Antioch, Leo was above all a military leader who struggled to defend the empire against increasingly successful Muslim incursions into Byzantine territory. In the early years of Leo's reign, the Muslim caliph Yazīd II (720–4) is recorded to have begun a policy of actively forcing Christian communities in his territory to destroy mosaics and other religious images in their Churches.[41] Shortly after this campaign by the caliph, the Emperor Leo himself seems to have allowed his soldiers and bureaucrats to impose similar restrictions on the veneration of icons by Christians throughout Asia Minor. According to the ninth-century iconophile historian Theophanes, Leo and his advisors were frightened by the eruption of a volcano on the Aegean island of Thera in the summer of 726, seeing it as possibly a sign of divine anger towards the Christian Empire; drawing a connection between this disaster and the recent successes of the anti-iconic Muslim forces, Leo is said to have allowed his officials to remove a celebrated sixth-century image of Christ from the Chalkē Gate to the royal palace in Constantinople—a domed and vaulted vestibule, built by Justinian I, which served as the main entrance to the royal palace—and to replace the picture with a plain cross, the traditional Christian sign of life-giving blessing.[42] Modern scholars continue to debate how much this gesture, recorded in historical and hagiographic narratives written a century later, represented a major campaign by the imperial government against images, or the start of organized persecution directed against those who venerated them. On the basis both of surviving documents and of archaeological evidence from the period it seems undeniable, however, that Leo and his advisors *were* convinced of the need for some sort of reform in religious practice within the Empire—for a simplification and rationalization of ordinary people's piety, to make it conform better with the Bible and earlier Christian tradition. Like their "iconoclastic" successors, they also seem to have been determined to keep the religious beliefs and practices of the people firmly under the civil control of the "Christ-loving emperors," rather than being guided by the clergy. A century-long struggle between imperial

---

[41] See Theophanes, *Chronography* for 723 (text: Hennephof, *Textus Byzantini*, 1). For the archaeological evidence abundantly confirming the effects of this edict in Syria and Palestine, see A. A. Vasiliev, "The Iconoclastic Edict of the Caliph Yazid II, A.D. 721" *Dumbarton Oaks Papers* 9/10 (1956), 23–47; and the unpublished paper of Christian Sahner (see n. 2).

[42] Theophanes, for the year 726 (Hennephof, *Textus Byzantini*, 2). For further details, see André Grabar, *L'Iconoclasme byzantin* (Paris: Collège de France, 1957), 130–42; Hans Belting, *Das echte Bild: Bildfragen als Glaubensfragen* (Munich: C. H. Beck, 2005), 136–40. Grabar suggests (135) that "the cross, which the two emperors [Leo III and Constantine V] substituted for the icon of Christ was above all a sign of triumph, the instrument of imperial victory since Constantine." An image of Christ, on the other hand, might be interpreted as competition for the Emperor's image on coins and public buildings.

policy and popular spirituality had begun, which would remarkably anticipate some of the ideological conflicts of the Western Reformation.

As early as the reign of Leo III, too, serious attempts to offer an apologia for the veneration of religious images were made by several Orthodox theologians, who sensed that more than simply excessive forms of popular practice were at stake. Germanus (*c.650–c.732*), Patriarch of Constantinople from 715 to 730 and a respected preacher and liturgical commentator, was removed from office in 730, apparently for his unwillingness to cooperate with the Emperor's reform program.[43] In a letter to Metropolitan John of Synada in Phrygia, Germanus complains of the new hostility of the imperial government to traditional piety focused on icons, and names a bishop of John's own province, Constantine of Nacoleia, as at least partly responsible for the program. Constantine had apparently argued, on the basis of the biblical prohibition of image-making in Exodus 20.4, that no human artifact—nothing "made by hands"—could be the object of veneration, in any genuinely monotheistic tradition.[44] Germanus insists, in response, that the real issue in all religious activity is not the physical object or objects it uses, but the one who is the intended *object* of veneration. The Incarnation, in fact, has changed humanity's relationship to God, revealing God to us personally and visibly, in flesh like ours. Idolatry is no longer a temptation for the Christian believer, because he can now see God in human form.[45]

## JOHN OF DAMASCUS

From about the same time come three treatises on the veneration of images by the Palestinian monk, preacher and theologian, John of Damascus (*c.650–c.750*). The first, seemingly written in the late 720s, is apparently intended as a systematic response to the new anti-iconic religious policies of both the Muslim caliphate, which ruled John's native Syria and Palestine, and the

---

[43] According to the ninth-century chronographer Theophanes, Pope Gregory II protested to the Emperor Leo III that he had no right to interfere in this way in the government of the Byzantine Church (Theophanes, *Chronographia*, ed. C. de Boor [Leipzig: Teubner, 1883], 1.408); cf. *Liber Pontificalis* 1.432–3.

[44] Germanus, Letter to John of Synada (PG 98.157 B–D; Mansi 13.100 B–101C). See also Germanus's letter to Constantine of Nacoleia, where he tells the bishop he is aware that he has ordered that "nothing be said or done to dishonor the Lord or his saints by means of an image of them, but has instead only proposed the Scriptural teaching that one should not consider any creature worthy of divine honor." Germanus insists that he himself firmly believes this, and has always acted accordingly. (PG 98.161 D–164 A) He is not, in other words, advocating a careless attitude towards idolatry!

[45] PG 98.157 B–D; see also Germanus, Letter to Thomas of Claudiopolis (PG 98.168 D–169 A; 173 C–175 C; 181 D–84 C).

Byzantine Empire under Leo III, with which John's Church still identified itself religiously. The second and third of these treatises, written apparently after the deposition of Germanus in 730,[46] simply repeat the arguments of the earlier treatise more concisely, but in a more noticeably polemical style.

In his typically well-organized, academic way, John begins his first treatise by acknowledging the divine prohibition, in the Hebrew Bible, against making human or animal images, and observes that the purpose is clearly to prevent our "venerating creation instead of the Creator," the image rather than the original it represents.[47] He even offers a definition: an image "is a likeness depicting an archetype, but having some difference from it."[48] John distinguishes then between various kinds of images important to the life of faith. First of all, the Son is "a living, natural, and undeviating image of the Father" within the Mystery of God, "bearing in himself the whole Father, equal to him in every respect, differing only in being caused."[49] The created realm, in turn, contains a variety of images that reflect, in their otherness, some divine original: God's own ideas of creatures, which are "images and paradigms of what he is going to bring about" within time;[50] the mental images we form for ourselves of immaterial things, of angels, and even of God;[51] biblical types of future events in the history of salvation;[52] memories of God's works of the past, recorded in words and even depicted in visible artifacts.[53] All of these, different as they are, play a central role in the living practice of faith.

Veneration ($\pi\rho o\sigma\kappa\dot{\upsilon}\nu\eta\sigma\iota\varsigma$), too, which essentially means bowing down before a thing or a person as "a sign of submission and honor," takes different legitimate forms and degrees, John observes.

> The first is a form of worship, which we offer to God, who is alone by nature worthy of veneration. Then there is the veneration offered, on account of God who is naturally venerated, to his friends and servants..., or to the places associated with God..., or to things sacred to him..., or to those rulers who have been ordained by him... Either, therefore, reject all veneration, or accept all of these forms in their proper measure and manner.[54]

The key to genuinely religious veneration, in the biblical tradition, is to offer it in a graduated way to persons and images and objects bearing some significance in the community of faith because of their relationship to *God*, who

---

[46] See John of Damascus, *On Divine Images* 2.12.
[47] *On Divine Images* 1.6 (trans. Andrew Louth [Crestwood, NY: St. Vladimir's, 2003], 23).
[48] *On Divine Images* 1.9 (trans. Louth, 25).
[49] *On Divine Images* 1.9 (trans. Louth, 25).
[50] *On Divine Images* 1.9 (trans. Louth, 25).
[51] *On Divine Images* 1.11 (trans. Louth, 26).
[52] *On Divine Images* 1.12 (trans. Louth, 27).
[53] *On Divine Images* 1.13 (trans. Louth, 27).
[54] *On Divine Images* 1.14 (trans. Louth 27–8).

alone deserves our acts of real worship. To show them proportionate honor is, in effect, to worship *him*.

To venerate not simply holy places and persons, but material objects which represent and recall them, is also an outcome of the Incarnation of God the Son. John writes:

> I do not venerate matter; I venerate the fashioner of matter, who became matter for my sake and accepted to dwell in matter, and through matter worked my salvation...I do not reverence it as God—far from it! How can that which has come to be from nothing be God? Even if the body of God has become God unchangeably through the hypostatic union, what gives anointing remains distinct, and what was by nature flesh animated with a rational soul is something formed, not uncreated. Therefore I reverence the rest of matter, and hold in respect that through which my salvation came: because it is filled with divine energy and grace.[55]

So a genuine recognition of God's continuing work in the material world as creator and savior leads to a deep respect for the words, sights, objects, and persons that lead the creature's heart and mind to him, as part of a sacramental sense of reality. The wood of the cross, the holy places in Jerusalem, the book of the Gospels, the Eucharistic vessels and species, holy people and institutions, all share to varying degrees in the same status of being—at least potentially—vehicles for God's action in the world, and occasions for our reverent response. John concludes:

> Either do away with reverence and veneration for all these, or submit to the tradition of the Church and allow the veneration of images of God and friends of God, sanctified by name and therefore overshadowed by the grace of the divine Spirit.[56]

## CONSTANTINE V

With the accession of Leo III's son, Constantine V (*c*.720–775), to full imperial power in 741, official opposition to the veneration of religious images in the Byzantine Empire became more organized and more intense. A well-educated administrator, as well as a courageous and successful military leader, Constantine seems to have constructed an elaborate theological and philosophical rationale for continuing his father's policy of trying to turn popular piety away

---

[55] *On Divine Images* 1.16 (trans. Louth, 29 [altered]).

[56] *On Divine Images* 1.16 (trans. Louth, 30). John appears to be referring here to the already-established practice of *labeling* the images of Christ, the saints, or sacred events that are represented iconographically.

from the veneration of pictorial representations of Christ and the saints, notably in a long treatise entitled *Inquiries* (Πεύσεις); the Patriarch Nicephorus preserved fragments of this work in his *Antirrhetikoi* (*Refutations*), written some seventy years later. Constantine here seems to have argued, through an interpretation of what was now the accepted post-Chalcedonian understanding of the person of Christ, that the Savior's *face* (πρόσωπον)—his individual, external *form*—cannot be depicted, because it is the single face, the "one *hypostasis* or *prosōpon*," that has been formed inseparably "*from* the two unmingled natures of divinity and humanity." The form, the "person," of Christ, he insisted, is neither simply human nor simply divine, but a single composite (σύνθετος) character or "face" produced from both. It is the form of divinized humanity, or humanized divinity; as such, it shares in the uncircumscribable, transcendent characteristics of God, as well as in limited human attributes. To picture Jesus is either to try to form a material image of a divine person, or else to assume that his human "face" can be separated from his divine nature, as simply a human "person." The first of these alternatives is the heresy of Eutyches, the second that of Nestorius. Even to attempt to portray Mary or the saints, as they now exist, is to overlook the fact that they have been transformed by the divinizing power of God, as made present in the incarnate Word.

As this theological justification for the imperial policy emerges, in the fragments later quoted by the Patriarch Nicephorus, it seems, predictably enough, to rest on a somewhat over-simplified reading of the understanding of Christ formed at Chalcedon and interpreted at Constantinople II. In the first book, for instance, the Emperor offers this argument:

> Since [Christ] possesses another, immaterial nature united to the flesh, and exists as a single subject (εἷς), along with the two natures, and since his *persona* (πρόσωπον—literally "face") or individuality (ὑπόστασις) is inseparable from those two natures, we do not suppose that it is possible for him to be limited by visible form;[57] in fact, what is to be represented is one *persona*, and anyone representing that *persona* obviously represents also the divine nature, which is uncircumscribable.[58]

In the second book of the *Inquiries*, as quoted by Nicephorus, the Emperor suggests that what the venerators of icons are striving for, in their devotion to

[57] Lit. "to be circumscribed."
[58] Cited in Nicephorus, *Antirrhetikos* (PG 100.236 C; see Hennephof, *Textus Byzantini*, 53). A little further on, Nicephorus quotes another sentence from Constantine's work, which repeats one of the charges frequently made against Antiochene conceptions of Christ in the fifth and sixth centuries: "After this union, the whole business (πραγματεία) [i.e. the composite hypostasis of Christ] is incapable of being separated. And if one makes an image simply of his flesh, it follows that one is attributing a proper *persona* (πρόσωπον) to the flesh, and a quaternity is thus imposed on the whole Godhead: that is, three Persons in the Godhead, and the one [person] of the humanity—and that is a mistake!" (PG 100.248 D–249 A; Hennephof, *Textus Byzantini*, 53).

images of Christ and the saints, is really to share in the divine presence and power: a communion through earthly signs that is truly available, by the Lord's own institution, only in the Eucharist. Constantine writes:

> Knowing, in his divine mind, of his death and resurrection and ascension into heaven, and in order that we believers might constantly have a memorial of his Incarnation, night and day, with us,...he commanded his holy disciples and apostles to hand on, as a concrete act of love, a type of his body: so that through this sacred symbolism (ἀναγωγή), which takes place in fact by participation and by divine arrangement, we might share, literally and truly, in his body.[59]

The Eucharist, then, is itself a kind of participatory image or icon of Christ in his sacrifice, but has been made legitimate by the Lord's own act of institution; "and if we wish to consider it an image of his body coming directly from him, we do have it, in order to give his body concrete form."[60] But in order to become this real image of Christ, the Bread of the Eucharist must be changed: transformed by God's action from being simply a human artifact:

> Not every loaf of bread is his Body, nor is every cup of wine his Blood, but only if it is offered up by the priestly act of sacrifice, [transformed] from being a human product into what is not made by hands.[61]

The underlying reason, it seems, for Constantine's reservations about depicting Christ in paint or mosaic is not simply his understanding of the Incarnation, as the assumption of an individual human nature into the unity of the divine person of the Son, but also the present transformation of that human nature through Christ's resurrection:

> You want to circumscribe Christ before Christ's passion and resurrection. But what would you say after his resurrection? The situation, after all, is no longer the same; for the body of Christ, from that point on, has become incorruptible, and has received a share in immortality. What room is left for you now to circumscribe him? How can he be circumscribed, who entered through closed doors into the midst of the disciples, and could not be shut out by any barrier?[62]

The body of Christ, as the Emperor here presents it, is now, in its risen state, clearly redolent with a divine presence and power that makes human attempts at depicting him both irreverent and futile.

But Constantine V's opposition to the use and veneration of religious images, as far as we can reconstruct it from the sources, was not simply

---

[59] PG 100.332 D–333 B; Hennephof, *Textus Byzantini*, 54.

[60] PG 100.336 A; Hennephof, *Textus Byzantini*, 55. Constantine may be alluding in this last phrase to the effect of the Eucharist on believers, as shaping them more perfectly into Christ's Body, the Church.

[61] PG 100.337 C; Hennephof, *Textus Byzantini*, 55.

[62] PG 100.437 B; Hennephof, *Textus Byzantini*, 56. This passage may come from a third book of Constantine's *Inquiries*.

based on a strongly theocentric, if still orthodox, understanding of Christ and his work; it also seems to have had political implications and motivations. A society less dominated by public expressions of devotion to Christ and the saints could be more confidently engaged in the secular business of social reconstruction and military organization, free from what seemed to be the excessive influence of clergy and monks. One must, of course, be careful not simply to read Western, post-Enlightenment categories of sacred and secular, Church and state, or modern Western tendencies to see all religious activities as crypto-political, back into the culture of early Byzantium. Yet clues for such an interpretation are clearly there, in some degree; as the struggles of the eighth and ninth centuries continued, opposition to images came chiefly from civil officials, military leaders, and army veterans, interested in the simplification and rationalization—although clearly not the total abandonment—of public Christian expressions of faith; while the traditional honoring of relics, holy sites, and images, as operative signs of the divine in our midst, was passionately defended by many monks and bishops, as well as by the more pious among the ordinary faithful.

In the end, the defenders of icon-veneration won the day, and much of the narrative literature—hagiographical and chronographic—is written from the perspective of the ninth-century Church establishment, which saw in the emperors' policy of opposition to images a violent campaign of persecution directed against orthodox Christianity. The story of a monk from Bithynia named Stephen, for instance, who was allegedly clubbed to death around 764 for his stubborn and outspoken opposition to the official anti-image policy, became a paradigm for what later became the Church's narration of the conflict.[63] Three characteristic treatises, too, in defense of the cult of icons, dating from around 752, are attributed to a monk from Cyprus named Gregory, who was then head of a monastery called "the Mount of Olives" in southern Asia Minor; Gregory vigorously defended the right of Christians to pay honor to representations of Christ and the saints, as well as to other holy objects and places, despite the Old Testament prohibition against "graven images." Gregory of Cyprus's polemics are not works of particular theological refinement. He simply insists, over and over, that what Christians do in venerating images, relics, and other holy things is vastly different from the pagan idolatry prohibited by the law of Moses.

In his dialogue with Cosmas, for instance—a bishop sent by the imperial court to reprimand him—the abbot writes:

---

[63] See the *Life of St. Stephen the Younger* by Stephen, deacon of the Hagia Sophia, written about 810: (*La Vie d'Étienne le Jeune par Étienne le Diacre*, ed. and trans. Marie-France Auzépy [Aldershot: Variorum, 1997]).

Far be it from us to venerate idols, nor do we worship icons as gods—never!—but in reverence we venerate the image of [Christ's] immaculate form, which has been given by the holy Apostles to the Church.[64]

After all, tradition tells us, Jesus sent a portrait of himself to the Syrian King Abgar,[65] and Luke the Evangelist was also "a wise and respected painter (χρωματουργός), the first to produce for us the immaculate image of the holy and glorious Mother of God, in paint and on a board."[66] For Gregory, the analogy between the written Gospel and the painted image is the main point of emphasis; so, thinking presumably of pictures of Christ crucified, he writes:

> Just as the person who venerates the sacred words in the Gospel is not honoring parchment pages, but the holy teachings, so in the pictures of the Church we are not venerating the color or the material surface, but a kind of holy explanation and a concise description of his sufferings. For just as we read it aloud, so we see it here, and these things enkindle the love of God in us all the more.[67]

Sacred images are, for Gregory of Cyprus, an extension of the Scriptural narrative, a kind of visual homily.

Constantine V was determined, however, to put his program of reform into effect. In the late winter of 754, he summoned bishops to what he apparently intended to be an ecumenical council, which met from February 10 to August 8 in the imperial palace of Hieria, on the Asian side of the Bosporus just north of Chalcedon. Three hundred and thirty-eight bishops attended, but none of the five Patriarchs of the ancient Apostolic Churches were among them; the bishop of Rome had not been invited, the see of Constantinople was vacant, and Antioch, Jerusalem, and Alexandria were all at that time under strict Muslim control. A lengthy "definition" (ὅρος)—more accurately, a treatise—produced by the council has come down to us, preserved in the *Acta* of the Second Council of Nicaea (787), which follows the general Christological line of argument of Constantine's own *Inquiries* without reaffirming all of that work's technical details.[68] Doubtless in order to adopt what was by now a standard feature of the decrees of previous councils, the statement summarizes the main doctrinal features of the six received ecumenical councils since

---

[64] Gregory of Cyprus, *Dialogue with Cosmas*: ed. Boris M. Melioranski (St. Petersburg: Theological-Historical Faculty, 1901) 14.

[65] *Dialogue with Cosmas*, ed. Melioranski, 21–2.

[66] *Dialogue with Cosmas*, ed. Melioranski, 28–9.

[67] *Dialogue with Cosmas*, ed. Melioranski, 30.

[68] On the arguments of this Council, see especially Milton V. Anastos, "The Argument for Iconoclasm as Presented by the Iconoclastic Council of 754," in Kurt Weitzmann (ed.), *Late Classical and Medieval Studies in Honor of Prof. Albert M. Friend, Jr.* (Princeton, NJ: Princeton University Press, 1954), 177–88; "The Ethical Theory of Images Formulated by the Iconoclasts in 754 and 815," *Dumbarton Oaks Papers* 8 (1954), 151–60.

Nicaea,[69] rightly presenting them as developing, in sequence, a coherent portrait of Christ the Savior. Christ himself, the document insists, is the true "image of God and humanity," in his very person; so he is, in principle, both circumscribed and uncircumscribed. Yet the very union of these two utterly different natures—God and the human—in one hypostasis or individual has endowed his humanity with transcendence, as well as making his divinity present and knowable among us.

> We must, therefore, consider this: if, according to the orthodox Fathers, this [humanity] is at once both flesh and the flesh of God the Word, and can never admit of any notion of separation [from God], but is completely taken up, whole and entire, and is utterly deified, how can it be separated or seen as independently existing by those who impiously attempt to do such things? And the same thing is true for his holy soul. For when the divinity of the Son takes on the nature of the flesh in his own hypostasis, the soul plays the mediating role between his divinity and the coarseness of his flesh; and just as this [latter] is at once flesh and the flesh of God the Word, so it is at once soul and the soul of God the Word, and is in fact both at once: because the soul is divinized just as the body is, and exists inseparably from the divinity, even at the moment when the soul is separated from the body in his willing act of suffering. Wherever Christ's soul is, there his divinity is also, and wherever the body of Christ is, there his divinity is too.[70]

The synod then goes on to apply this synthetic model of Christ's person, now standard, to humanly made images of him: they present the would-be devotee with the same unacceptable Christological dilemma—monophysitism or Nestorianism—that Constantine had identified:

> We shall compare, then, those who intend to draw an image of Christ either to those who treat the divine as circumscribed, mingled with flesh, or to those who consider Christ's body to be undivinized and separated, and make an independently existing *persona* of his flesh, resembling on this point the Nestorians' rebellion against God. Having fallen into this kind of blasphemy and godlessness, let those who do this—who desire and honor what is falsely made and called by them an image of Christ—be ashamed of themselves, and let them experience a change of heart, and stop what they are doing. Far from us, equally, be Nestorian division, and the confusion of Arius, Dioscorus, Eutyches and Severus: opposite evils that are equally branded as impiety.[71]

Here and throughout the Synod's long document, the divinizing influence of the Word in the humanity of Jesus, and so also the union with Christ that is brought about in the saints by the gift of the Spirit, is taken as distancing both Jesus and the sanctified disciple from ordinary human qualities and interactions. Even their visible appearance has become mysterious and divine.

[69] Mansi 13.233 B–237 D.      [70] Mansi 13.256 E–257 B.      [71] Mansi 13.260 AB.

The reign of Constantine V was perhaps the time of the most intense official repression of image-veneration in the history of the Byzantine Church. Ninth-century sources, at any rate, which largely show strongly pro-iconic sympathies, witness to intense persecution, at that time, of those who continued to show devotion to pictorial representations of Christ and the saints. Mosaics were certainly removed from walls, and frescoes painted over, in the patriarchal palace in Constantinople during the patriarchate of Nicetas (766–80); the newly built church of St. Irene in Constantinople, as well as that of the Hagia Sophia in Thessalonike, were ornamented simply with a gold mosaic cross in the apse.[72] Constantine V's government was apparently determined to bring about a reorientation, a sobering and spiritualization, of popular Christian piety.

## THE SECOND COUNCIL OF NICAEA

Constantine was succeeded, at his death in 775, by his son Leo IV, who at first enforced his father's anti-iconic policies in a more conciliatory way, allowing monks who had been exiled for advocating religious images to return to the capital. Shortly after he began moving towards stricter measures of repression, however, Leo died, aged 30—probably of a fever—in September of 780. Since his son, Constantine VI, was still only nine years old, Leo's widow Irene (752–803), an autocratic Athenian who herself favored the cult of images, became regent;[73] she remained in power until 802, ruling as sole Empress after Constantine VI's death—at the hands of her followers—in 797. During the twenty-two years of Irene's reign, the tide again turned in favor of permitting devotion to images. With the support of Tarasius, her former secretary, who was elected patriarch in 784, Irene had a new council summoned, with the clear intention of reversing the decisions of the synod of 754. After an abortive attempt to start proceedings in the capital on August 1, 786, when the gathering was interrupted by soldiers loyal to the memory and policies of Constantine V, Irene's Council finally met—significantly—in Nicaea, from Sept 24 to Oct 13, 787, moving to Constantinople for its final session. It was attended by some 263 bishops, many of whom had also attended the anti-icon synod of 754, whose position was now to be reversed; this time, the gathering

---

[72] See Cormack, *Byzantine Art*, 92–5.

[73] Confusingly, Leo IV's mother—a Khazar princess who had married Constantine V—also had the baptismal name Irene. On the unprecedented role of the younger Empress Irene as regent and then sole ruler for a total of some twenty-two years, see Judith Herrin, *Unrivalled Influence: Women and Empire in Byzantium* (Princeton, NJ: Princeton University Press, 2013), 194–207.

also included two legates of the bishop of Rome, who were intentionally given a prominent role in presiding over the sessions.

The Council's main definition follows the form now familiar from earlier ecumenical gatherings. After an introductory section, acknowledging imperial patronage and pointing to a contemporary crisis of faith in the Church, it affirms that it intends to follow the faith of the "six holy synods" that have gone before—the six councils since Nicaea (clearly *not* including the Synod of Hieria) that were by now received as normative. After quoting the creed of Nicaea in full, and summarizing the decrees of the others, which had come to be understood as filling out and contextualizing Nicaea's teaching, the definition then declares its intention to reaffirm "the production of representational images" squarely within this Christological tradition, as "supportive of the proclamation of the Gospel in narrative form, reaffirming the truth of the Incarnation of God the Word."[74] The definition then comes to its main content:

> Since this is so—holding, as it were, to the royal road, and following the inspired teaching of our holy Fathers and the tradition of the Catholic Church (for we recognize that this come from the Holy Spirit, who dwells in her)—we define, with all precision and care, that, just like the form of the precious and life-giving cross, revered and holy images may be set up, whether painted or of mosaic or other suitable material, in the holy churches of God, on sacred vessels and vestments, on walls and boards, in houses and along the roads: images of our Lord and God and Savior Jesus Christ, and of our immaculate Lady the holy Mother of God, of the honorable angels, and of all the saints and holy people. For the more frequently they are seen in representational form, the more those who gaze on them are stirred up to remember and long for the original persons, and to offer them acknowledgement and respectful veneration. According to our faith, this is not real adoration, which befits only the divine nature, but resembles the honor we show to the form of the precious and life-giving cross, and the holy Gospels, and the other sacred objects we set up for devotion. The use of incense and candles to pay honor to them is also allowed, as was reverently practiced from ancient times. For "honor shown to an image passes over to the model" (Basil, *On the Holy Spirit* 18.45), and the person who reverences an image reverences in it the concrete individual (*hypostasis*) who is depicted by it.[75]

This definition is followed by four brief canons, excommunicating—declaring as anathema—those who refuse to admit that Christ is "circumscribed in his humanity," who refuse to honor pictorial representations of the Gospel stories, who refuse to salute images in the name of the Lord and his saints, or who

---

[74] Second Council of Nicaea, *Horos*: Alberigo/Tanner 1.135.25–9 (trans. mine). For an annotated translation of the *acta* of the entire sixth session of the Council of 787, with historical introduction, see Daniel J. Sahas, *Icon and Logos: Sources in Eighth-Century Iconoclasm* (Toronto: University of Toronto Press, 1986).

[75] Second Council of Nicaea, *Horos*, Alberigo/Tanner 1.135.36–136.30 (trans. mine).

reject Church tradition, whether written or unwritten.[76] What is at issue for the Council, above all, is clearly the reaffirmation of what it regards as traditional popular devotion, and the connection between such practices and the proclamation of the Gospel. The decree is surely not breaking new doctrinal ground, or attempting to sketch out a profound theological link between the veneration of images and faith in the Incarnation. It is, however, clearly insisting that the cult of images is an ancient practice in the Church— reaching back, it is understood, well before the anti-iconic policies of recent emperors—and it characterizes this cult, as John of Damascus had done, not as worship, but in sacramental terms: as a concrete way to pay honor to the persons—Christ and the saints—who are represented in them.

## THE SECOND ICONOCLASTIC PERIOD

The Council of 787, which has subsequently been received, in the canonical lists of the Churches of both East and West, as the Church's seventh ecumenical council,[77] introduced a lull, but not an end, to the imperial policy banning devotion to religious images. Irene, who exercised surrogate imperial power with increasing violence, during and after the reign of Constantine VI, was finally forced to abdicate in 802, and retired to the island of Lesbos, where she died in obscurity the following year. Her former finance minister, the Byzantine patrician Nikephoros, succeeded her as Emperor, and resumed an official government policy of moderate opposition to the public cult of icons. During his reign, however, and presumably at the Emperor's behest, another Nikephoros, who had been a cautious promoter of the veneration of images, was elected Patriarch of Constantinople in 806. The Patriarch Nikephoros was eventually to become one of the most thoughtful apologists for the icon-cult after his forced resignation in 815, strongly influencing the later course of Byzantine theology in the direction of this popular devotion.

The Emperor Nikephoros was killed in battle by the Bulgars in 811; his successor, the aristocratic general Michael I Rangabe, worked for political reconciliation, but seemed to lack the motivation to play the brutal games of court politics. After some military setbacks, Michael resigned—apparently under pressure—and entered a monastery in 813, and was succeeded by a general of Armenian descent, Leo V. Leo began his reign promising moderation in his relations with the various parties of Church and state, including

---

[76] Second Council of Nicaea, *Horos*, Alberigo/Tanner 1.137.28–138.3.
[77] See Hermann-Josef Sieben, "Das zweite Nizänum und die Probleme der Rezeption," *Die Konzilsidee der alten Kirche (Konziliengeschichte, Series B: Untersuchungen)* (Paderborn: Schöningh, 1979), 306–43.

the Patriarch Nikephoros. By 815, however, the Empire's security from outside attack had been bolstered by military success against the Bulgars and Islamic forces. Leo was persuaded by his advisors—especially by John, known as "the Grammarian," a learned scholar and an admirer of the spiritual and theological legacy of Origen and Evagrius—that the military weaknesses of the previous decade had been due, at least in part, to an official permissiveness towards those who favored devotion to images, as well as to the growing dominance of monks in the capital; too much outward piety was seen as weakening public resolve! So Leo deposed the Patriarch Nikephoros in the early spring of 815, appointed an obscure bureaucrat named Theodotos in his place, and summoned a new gathering of bishops—probably simply a local synod—to meet in the Hagia Sophia at Constantinople during Easter Week of that year. Aided by a florilegium of anti-iconic patristic authorities that had been prepared for the Emperor by John the Grammarian, this synod apparently declared the decree of the Council of 787 to be null and void, and recognized again as binding the earlier decree of the Council of the Hierea of 754, banning religious images as a form of idolatry because of the uncircumscribable divine nature of Christ.[78] Official policy had been reversed once again, and what is often called the "second iconoclastic period" had begun.

In general, this renewed campaign to remove religious images from public Christian life is not portrayed by the extant sources in the same dramatic

---

[78] No official *acta* or *horos* have come down to us directly from the Synod of 815. In 1903, however, D. Serruys reconstructed this declaration from Nicephorus's then still-unpublished treatise, *Refutatio et Eversio*, and published it in *Mélanges d'archéologie et d'histoire* 23, 345–51; the treatise was finally published by J. M. Featherstone in 1997, as CCG 33 (see n. 25). See also Paul Alexander, "The Iconoclastic Council of Sancta Sophia (815) and its Definition (Horos)," *Dumbarton Oaks Papers* 7 (1953), 35–66; Hennephof, *Textus Byzantini*, 79–82. From quotations in Nicephorus's treatise, the main points decreed by that synod seem to have been:

(a) to recognize the anti-iconic policies of emperors Leo III and Constantine V as still normative for the Church's life;

(b) to characterize the devotional veneration of images, with gestures, candles and incense, as pointless and misleading;

(c) to brand the representation of Christ, Mary, and the saints in "lifeless images" as a form of idolatry, and as such forbidden by the Ten Commandments;

(d) to ground this prohibition of images also in orthodox Christology, with the argument that if one tries to represent Christ pictorially, one is either trying to depict the uncircumscribable God, as he has revealed himself in divinized flesh—which is impossible—or else one is assuming that his humanity is separable from his divinity.

In one phrase that seems to come from the Synod's decree, the continuing veneration of images is attributed to bad leadership in Empire and Church, "in a period when royal power passed from men to women, and God's Church was shepherded in feminine softness" (Hennephof, *Textus Byzantini*, 81, no. 272). The Empress Irene was clearly beginning to be demonized by the (male) opponents of icons. On the role of women, and hostility towards women, in the controversy, see Herrin, *Unrivalled Influence*, 38–79, esp. 66–7.

terms as are the actions of Constantine V, perhaps because the emperors themselves, during the time of "the second iconoclasm," were more cautious in enforcing their policies. Archaeological evidence still exists, however, showing that mosaics were in fact removed from the apses of churches in Thessaloniki and Nicaea, as well as in the capital itself, during the early decades of the ninth century, and were replaced with plain crosses.[79] Theologically, too, the argument continued: now in an apparently more leisurely way, and on a more theoretical plane. The main source for the reasoning behind the renewed imperial policy against icons was certainly John the Grammarian, who was himself finally appointed Patriarch, as John VII, by his former pupil, the Emperor Theophilus, in 837.[80] The main defenders of image-veneration, both of them prolific and subtle writers, were the former Patriarch Nicephorus, who remained active as a controversialist during his years of retirement in a monastery in the capital until his death in 828, and the monastic leader and prolific activist Theodore of Stoudios (759–826).

## NICEPHORUS

Much of Nicephorus's written work is aimed at refuting the now-hoary arguments of Constantine V against the propriety of venerating religious images, since the late Emperor's treatise *Inquiries* remained the theoretical foundation of the Empire's anti-icon policy; he also argued that the Council of 754, and the Synod of 815 that rehabilitated it, were illegitimate as Church councils on formal grounds.[81] Nicephorus criticizes Constantine's understanding of *circumscription*, for instance, as being based on the assumption that material limitation is always a kind of imperfection, linked with mortality and corruptibility. Drawing on the Aristotelian *Categories*, he points out that circumscription is simply another name for finitude, which always implies logical and formal, as well as spatial, limitation; only God is infinite by nature, and so completely uncircumscribed. Thus all creatures—even angels, which do not possess material bodies—are circumscribed in both time and space, and so

---

[79] Cormack, *Byzantine Art*, 93–8.

[80] John is said to have been a devotee and even a painter of icons as a young adult, but was converted into a fierce critic of them by his Origenist studies. No written works of his survive.

[81] For a full list of Nicephorus's works, along with a description of their content and details of their publication (up to 1972), see Patrick J. O'Connell, S.J., *The Ecclesiology of St. Nicephorus I, Patriarch of Constantinople: Pentarchy and Primacy*, Orientalia Christiana Analecta 194 (Rome: Pontificio Istituto Orientale, 1972), 54–66. O'Connell emphasizes Nicphorus's concern that neither the Council of Hieria nor the Synod of 815 had involved the Patriarchs of the Pentarchy, and so lacked ecclesial authority (29–35).

can, in principle, be imagined, described, and even drawn.[82] Against Constantine's argument that the risen Christ, who could pass through locked doors, was therefore no longer bound by spatial limits, Nicephorus observes that while the qualities of his risen body, as described in the Gospels, certainly had changed from its pre-resurrection state, it could still be seen and even touched, because it was still a human body.[83] To exist as a body, which is inescapably part of human nature, is surely not a result of the fall, but is simply part of being a finite creature.[84] The nature of each thing is rooted in the divine idea of it, the *logos* that exists in God's eternal plan; as the Christological tradition had long emphasized, in Christ, the natures of God and man are arranged in a new way (καινοτομοῦνται)—they are not transformed into different natures altogether![85]

Nicephorus concentrates his refutation of Constantine's critique of images on attacking the idea that every image in some way is meant to offer the viewer participatory access to the original. Rather, he insists, every image is a reality *distinct* from its original, which only *resembles* it in a more or less adequate way. To draw or paint a picture of a person is not, in itself, to circumscribe the *person*, even though only finite beings—beings that are by nature circumscribed, which means all beings but God—can, in principle, be represented pictorially.[86] A *natural* image, like a son or daughter, certainly differs from an *artificial* image in the way it resembles its original, but both—as images—are by definition distinct from their originals. As such, an image is connected to its original by the Aristotelian category of *relationship* (σχέσις, πρός τι);[87] it *points to* the original, directs the observer's attention to it by the similarity in form both possess, but it is understood to be different in nature, purpose, and location.

> Likeness is a mediating relationship standing between extremes: that which is represented, namely, and that which represents. It joins them in form and brings them together, although they differ in nature.[88]

So a religious icon, too, is always understood to be distinct in nature from what it represents; it is not honored as if it really *were* Christ or Mary or a saint, let alone God, nor can it make any of them present by itself. To show it reverence is simply to show reverence to what it points to.

---

[82] Nicephorus, *Antirrheticus adversus Constantinum* 1.23 (PG 100.257 D–260 A; *Antirrh. adv. Const.* 2.7 (PG 100.345 B–D); *Antirrh. adv. Const.* 2.13 (PG 100.357 C–360 D).

[83] *Antirrh. adv. Const.* 1.39 (PG 100.296 C–297 C; 1.41 (PG 100.301 C–304 A); 2.38 (PG 100.437 B–440 C). See also *Antirrheticus contra Eusebium et Epiphanium* 1.26 (*Spic.Sol.* 1.415–16); 1.34 (*Spic.Sol.* 1.424–5).

[84] *Antirrh. adv. Const.*2.39 (PG 100.440 C–445 C).

[85] *Ctr. Eus. et Epiph.* 1.37 (*Spic.Sol.* 1.429–30); cf. Leontius of Byzantium, *Epil* (PG 86.1921 B); Maximus Confessor, Ep. 19 (PG 91.592 D); etc.

[86] Cormack, *Byzantine Art*, 93–8.

[87] *Antirrh. adv. Const.* 1.30 (PG 100.277 D–280 A); 2.15 (361 D–364 A).

[88] *Antirrh. adv. Const.* 1.30 (PG 100.280 A).

Nicephorus then takes up Constantine's strategy, and criticizes the Emperor's understanding of Christ, as implying an essentially monophysite understanding of the Incarnation, by assuming that the hypostatic union in Christ has in fact compounded his *natures* into one—has, in Paul's phrases, hybridized the "form of a servant" with "the form of God." Emphasizing, in contrast, the Chalcedonian definition of the reality of the Incarnate Word as one hypostasis, one concrete individual, existing *in* two abiding and unconfused natures, the ex-Patriarch stresses that these united natures must retain their essential characteristics to continue to be what they are, even though some accidental characteristics may change in the state of union. To remain human, Christ must remain circumscribed, and in some way perceptible—must retain his human form. Some qualities of that form may be divinized, as one recognizes in the Gospel story of Jesus' Transfiguration, when Jesus' face "shone like the sun, and his garments became white as snow" (see Matt. 17.1–9; Mk. 9.2–9; Lk. 9.28–36); but his natural form remained the form of a creature, limited and visible; for that reason it could—and can still—be represented by creaturely means.[89]

Nicephorus's exposition of the Christological grounds for image-veneration, then, takes up the approach of sixth- and seventh-century orthodoxy, of Leontius of Byzantium and John of Damascus, by relying heavily on the Aristotelian distinction of categories to explain the Chalcedonian definition. Christ's two abiding natures or substances are the reason we can depict him as a divinely endowed man, and venerate the human nature that belongs to him as both visible and holy. The Logos, the personal subject and center of these two natures, who in himself remains uncircumscribed because he is divine, is "called to mind" and venerated as God, when we venerate his humanity through its bodily image.[90]

## THEODORE OF STOUDIOS

Nicephorus's articulate and combative contemporary, Theodore of Stoudios (759–826), offers many similar theological arguments in defense of the practice of venerating sacred images, although with a somewhat broader range of terms. Born to a family of important imperial financial administrators in the reign of

---

[89] This point is explicitly made by Nicephorus's contemporary Theodore of Stoudios, *Antirrhetikos* 3.1.543 (PG 99.413 C; Roth 97).

[90] So *Antirrh. adv. Const.* 1.23 (PG 100.256 AB): "For [the icon-painter] does not simply reproduce Christ's visible human form, through recalling it and through relating it to its archetype. The Logos himself—even if he is not circumscribed or depicted as far as his own nature is concerned (for he is invisible, and totally inconceivable)—still, since he is one and indivisible in hypostasis, is also called to our memories, for that reason, in a unified way." Cf. 1.20 (237 CD).

Constantine V, Theodore might not have been expected, in his early life, to sympathize with the pro-icon monastic party in the Church. In the year of his birth, however, his maternal uncle Platon left public life to become a monk in Bithynia, southeast of the capital; in 780, Platon persuaded the whole family to join him, and to turn their estate there, a place called Sakkoudion, into a new, pastorally active monastic community, following the monastic rules of St. Basil. Theodore, who had already acquired a thorough humanistic and theological education, was Platon's main assistant in shaping the daily life of the community, which remained committed to the service of the local Church; both he and his uncle played an important part in formulating the decision in favor of images at the Council of Nicaea 787. He was ordained a priest by Patriarch Tarasius shortly after that Council, and took over the leadership of the Sakkoudion community fully in 794, when his uncle retired from office.

In 795, however, Theodore became involved in controversy with high imperial and church officials, when he protested vigorously against the divorce of the Emperor, Constantine VI, from the Empress Maria, and his subsequent marriage to her lady-in-waiting, Theodore's own cousin Theodote. He and the rest of the community at Sakkoudion were eventually dispersed, and exiled to Thessalonike by Constantine VI's order; but after the Empress Irene overthrew and blinded her son Constantine, Theodore was brought home to Constantinople and put in charge of the long-established monastery of Stoudios in the city. There he put his prodigious energy and self-confidence to work, reorganizing the life of the community and establishing a whole system of affiliated houses in the surrounding countryside, building up a new conception of monastic life through community catecheses, letters, and even verse inscriptions that described the duties of community officials. In this period of his life, Theodore—probably with the encouragement of Irene—continued to promote the veneration of images.

When Patriarch Tarasius died in 806, Theodore's name was apparently suggested as a candidate to replace him, but the Emperor Nicephorus instead chose a civil servant by the same name, who became, as we have seen, the Patriarch Nicephorus I. Theodore, and the whole Stoudite community, protested the appointment of a lay bureaucrat to this office, and his relations with the new Patriarch grew more and more strained, especially over the continuing question of how to treat those who had been involved in blessing Constantine VI's uncanonical marriage a decade earlier. Theodore, his brother Joseph—who was now archbishop of Thessalonike—and their uncle Platon were all declared schismatics by a local synod in 809, and were exiled to the Princes' Islands in the Sea of Marmara. While in exile, Theodore continued an active worldwide correspondence,[91] wrote further catecheses and instructional epigrams for his monks, and continued to play a lively role in public life.

---

[91] Jean Gouillard, "L'église d'Orient et la primauté romaine au temps de l'iconoclasme," *La Vie religieuse à Byzance*, V, argues (49) that while the Patriarchs Tarasius and Nicephorus were

When the new Emperor, Michael I Rangabe, took office in 811, Theodore and his family were recalled from exile, and began to engage directly in public life. But when Michael abdicated two years later, amid general signs of failure, his successor, Leo V ("the Armenian"), dreamed of reviving the strong, anti-iconic policies of the previous century, as part of what was now widely accepted as the recipe for a successful imperial government.[92] Theodore and the Patriarch Nicephorus now found themselves on the same side of the public debate, and were gradually reconciled, especially after Nicephorus's forced resignation in the winter of 815. Both were sent into exile in 815; Theodore, who continued to be outspoken in letters and apologetic essays, was frequently moved from place to place, and was even flogged by imperial order in 817. After Leo V's brutal murder at Vespers on Christmas Day, 820, Theodore again returned to Constantinople, but was disappointed when the new Emperor, Michael II ("the Amorian"), refused to reverse imperial policy against the veneration of images, preferring not to impose the policy forcefully but to leave it officially in place, permitting some deviation as long as public devotion was not carried on in an overly demonstrative way.[93] Theodore returned to monastic retirement, where he continued a vigorous correspondence in support of icons, and died in November of 826.

Theodore left three apologetic treatises (*Antirrhetikoi*) in defense of the veneration of images,[94] as well as numerous letters, homilies, and epigrams. His treatises show a wider range of argument than Nicephorus's works, but generally make similar points. Much of his apologetic centers on the question of whether Christ, as both God and human, is now personally uncircumscribable in virtue of his divinity. Theodore insists, like Nicephorus, that only God,

---

eager to involve the other patriarchs of the Pentarchy in the Byzantine Church's resistance to imperial pressure against image-veneration, Theodore of Stoudios went further in appealing directly to the Pope, as successor of Peter, to exercise his authority in the universal Church. See also O'Connell, *The Ecclesiology of St. Nicephorus I*, 196–204, 218–26.

[92] Paul Alexander, *The Patriarch Nicephorus of Constantinople: Ecclesiastical Policy and Image Worship in the Byzantine Empire* (Oxford: Oxford University Press, 1958), 111–25, argues at length that poor and disaffected ex-soldiers in the capital played an active role in the opposition to the veneration of images, particularly in the "second" period of iconoclasm after 815. Discouraged at the Empire's lack of military success against the Bulgars, and probably feeling themselves marginalized by civilians and the better-educated clergy during the reign of the Empress Irene, they seem to have readily joined in the efforts of some court officials to control and rationalize popular devotion, especially under Leo V.

[93] Some sources tell us that religious images in churches and other public places were now tolerated, as long as they were placed high enough to be out of reach for those who wanted to touch or kiss them. For Michael II's continuing concern about exaggerated devotion to icons, see his letter to Louis the Pious (n. 39).

[94] See PG 99.327 B–436 A. These apologetic treatises, of uncertain date, have been translated by Catherine Roth: *St. Theodore the Studite, On the Holy Icons* (Crestwood, NY: St. Vladimir's, 1981). For a study of Theodore's life and influence, including a biography and a full listing of his works, see Roman Cholij, *Theodore the Stoudite: The Ordering of Holiness* (Oxford: Oxford University Press, 2002).

as God, is beyond circumscription, beyond form and concept, because God is infinite, omnipresent, and simple; Christ, as the Word incarnate, is confessed by the faith of Chalcedon not simply to be God, but God and man existing as a single individual:

> That which is uncircumscribable is simple and not composite, because it is exempt from any kind of position or composition. But Christ, who is double and composite, if he were not circumscribed, would lose the form and fact of doubleness and composition. But we confess that he is double and composite, and therefore that he is circumscribed.[95]

Further, in the Incarnation God the Son has taken on the particular characteristics (ἰδιώματα) both of human nature in general, as distinguished from other created natures, and of a concrete, historical human being: he is a male Jew from first-century Galilee, the son of Mary of Nazareth. To be a concrete hypostasis that is both human and divine, he must be "marked off" (as Leontius of Byzantium had insisted three centuries before) both from the other divine hypostases—from his Father and from the Spirit—by the characteristics of his origin within the divine Mystery, and from all other humans, by his human origins and particularity of accidents. Otherwise he would not share in human nature at all:

> General substances have their existence *in* particular individuals: for example, humanity in Peter and Paul and the others of the same species. If particular individuals did not exist, man in general would be eliminated. Therefore humanity is not in Christ, if it does not subsist in him as in an individual; otherwise we would have to say that he became incarnate in fantasy, and so could not be touched, or portrayed with various colors. But this is the Manichaeans' idea.

This concrete, fully circumscribed human individuality, in fact, is precisely how the Gospels present Jesus to us; so Theodore continues:

> Generalities are seen with the mind and thought; particular individuals are seen with the eyes, which look at perceptible things. If, therefore, Christ assumed our nature in general, not as contemplated in an individual manner, he can be contemplated only by the mind and touched only by thought. But he says to Thomas, "Because you have seen me, you have believed; blessed are those who have not seen and yet believe" (John 20.29). And he also says, "Put your finger here, and see my hands; and put out your hand, and place it in my side" (John 20.27). Thus he associates perceptible things with the means of perception, and visible things with bodily eyes. And therefore he is circumscribed.[96]

Circumscription, or limitation in time, space, and form, is an indispensable part of creaturely existence, and is fundamental to bodiliness; if the Incarnation

---

[95] *Refutation* 3.1.44 (PG 99.411 C), trans. Roth, 94 (altered).
[96] *Refutation* 3.1.15–16 (PG 99.396 D–397 A), trans. Roth, 83 (altered).

means the Son is embodied, then the Son can also be seen and depicted. This is implied, Theodore argues, by the classic Christology of Chalcedon:

> If uncircumscribability is characteristic of God's essence, and circumscription is characteristic of man's essence, but Christ is from both, then he is made known *in* two sets of properties, as in two natures. How would it not be blasphemous to say that he is uncircumscribed in body as well as in spirit, since if his circumscription were removed, his human nature would be removed also?[97]

The clear implication is: Christ can be represented in pictures, as well as seen in the flesh.

Although his terminology is sometimes obscure, Theodore bases his discussion of the appropriateness of venerating religious pictures on what one might call a metaphysics of form. An image, he argues in a number of places, resembles what it depicts by in some way capturing its "form" ($\epsilon\hat{\iota}\delta os$) or "shape" ($\mu o\rho\phi\acute{\eta}$, $\sigma\chi\hat{\eta}\mu a$); a *natural* image, such as a child's resemblance of his or her parent, captures something of the parent's form in a similar nature ($\phi\acute{\upsilon}\sigma\iota s$), while an *artificial* image, such as a sculpture or a painting, captures it in a materially different medium, a different nature.[98]

> Thus no one could say that Christ is imageless, if indeed he has a body with its characteristic form; rather, we can see in Christ his image, existing by implication, and in the image Christ, plainly visible as its prototype. From the simultaneous existence of both, it follows that when Christ is seen, then his image is also potentially seen, and consequently is transferred by imprint into any material whatever.[99]

In Christ, God has a human face: a face embodying a particular form, one that can be drawn or painted. If he were in the world today, he could be photographed, his fingerprints taken, his voice recorded. He has all the sensible qualities of human particularity.

The implication for religious practice is clear for Theodore: when a disciple of Jesus venerates an image of him, he is venerating not a mosaic of stone fragments or a painted board but Jesus himself, through the common form that represents him. This is the reason, too, that religious icons must be properly *labeled* with the name of Christ—usually "He who is" ($\acute{o}$ $\acute{\omega}\nu$)—or of the saint or Gospel event being represented: to remind the viewer that he or she is not simply gazing on a beautiful picture, but contemplating an aspect of the Mystery of our redemption in Christ.[100] So Theodore writes:

---

[97] *Refutation* 3.1.3 (PG 99.392 B), trans. Roth, 79 (altered); see also *Refutation* 3.1.12–13 (PG 99.393 D–394 A), trans. Roth, 81–2, where Theodore reflects on the inescapable paradoxes that result from the Incarnation of the uncircumscribed God in the concreteness of a human existence.

[98] *Refutation* 3.2.2 (PG 99.417 BC), trans. Roth, 100.

[99] *Refutation* 3.4.2 (PG 99.429 A), trans. Roth, 109.

[100] On this point, see *Antirrh*.3.3.5 (PG 99.421 CD; Ep. 2.21 (1184 C)).

The image of Christ is nothing else but Christ, except obviously for the difference of essence, as we have repeatedly shown. It follows that the veneration of the image is veneration of Christ. The material of the image is not venerated at all, but only Christ, who has his likeness in it. Those things which have a single likeness obviously receive a single veneration. Therefore Christ does not give his glory to another in his own image, but rather obtains through it glory for himself, since the material is something other than the likeness. Doubtless the same form is in all the representations, though they are made with different materials. The form would not remain unchanged in the different materials if it were not for the fact that it shares nothing with them, but is conceptually distinguished from the materials in which it occurs.[101]

The religious image, for Theodore, is essentially an aid to contemplating Christ, in all the richness of his activity and presence in the world. It connects the person of faith with Christ, by purifying and focusing the imagination, enabling the viewer to grasp again—not conceptually, but in a visual, conscious way—some part of the full meaning of his Incarnation. Reproduced many times in many places, the image—like the sign of the cross and the Gospel book—makes present to the individual believer the paradoxical proclamation that the transcendent God has become one of us, and shares our human weakness and beauty.[102]

In a letter to Naucratius, one of his deputies in the monastic community of Stoudios, who has been imprisoned and flogged for civil disobedience, expressed in his stubborn devotion to images, Theodore writes eloquent words of encouragement:

> Depict Christ wherever necessary. Have him dwelling in your heart, so that you hear him read aloud in the Scriptures and so that you see him in painted form. As he is perceived by these two senses, let him enlighten your mind; so, what you have learned through the words of religious instruction, you will see with your eyes. For then, surely, when he is heard and seen this way, our nature can only glorify God, and the devout person will be converted and reformed. What could be more conducive than this to salvation? What else could give us such access to God?[103]

To honor an icon expresses and builds on faith; it shows that one knows Christ, recognizes Christlike holiness. The visual representation of the Mystery of salvation and transformation in Christ is understood by Theodore and his monks as the core of a lived, pastorally active spirituality.

---

[101] *Refutation* 3.3.14 (PG 99.425 D–428 A; Roth 107–8).
[102] See *Antirrh.* 1.7 (PG 99.336 D); 1.13 (PG 99.344 C); 1.19 (PG 99.349 A); 3.2–6 (PG 99.392 AD); Ep. 2.36 (1213 AB); Ep. 3.171 (1537 C).
[103] Ep. 2.36 (PG 99.1213 CD).

## THE REINSTATEMENT OF ICONS

In 829, Michael II's son, Theophilus, succeeded him as Emperor, at the age of 16. A well-educated young man, who had been tutored by the learned opponent of icons, John "the Grammarian,"[104] Theophilus set out to reinforce, in a consistent but non-violent way, the prohibition of images that his father had upheld, and issued a new edict to that effect in 832. But apart from the higher civil and military bureaucracy and some army veterans, there seems to have been less official enthusiasm now for continuing a policy that obviously had found little resonance in the Christian population of the Empire as a whole. At Theophilus's death in 842, after a long illness, his wife Theodora took over as regent for their two-year-old son, Michael III. Theodora, who seems to have come from an Armenian family, was herself devoted to religious images, and quietly set about reversing official policy on them.[105] With the help of a long-influential court minister, the eunuch Theoktistos, she deposed John "the Grammarian," whom Theophilus had named Patriarch (as John VII) in 837, and replaced him with Methodius, who was also known to be favorably disposed to icons. Theodora was apparently concerned not to appear to condemn her late husband posthumously, and chose to reverse the official ban on images not by decree, but with a solemn and symbolic act that signaled the end of more than a century of intermittent repression. On Sunday, March 11, 843, the new Patriarch, accompanied by Theoktistos, the regent Empress Theodora, and the young Emperor Michael III, processed with religious icons from the Church of the Blachernae, in Constantinople, to Hagia Sophia, where they solemnly enthroned them. This *oikonomia*, or gesture of accommodation, is still celebrated each year in the Orthodox Churches on what is known as the "Sunday of Orthodoxy," a commemoration of the survival of a tradition of popular piety that had its intellectual roots in the Christological tradition, and witnessed to the fullness of that tradition's deep affective and liturgical associations within Orthodox cultures. What had been rescued for posterity was not simply an artistic idiom, but a spirituality—a way of letting the Christological center of the Church's faith be expressed and visually proclaimed in daily life.

An echo of the whole controversy over icons—now virtually at an end—can be heard in Constantinople a quarter-century later, during the heated dispute over the Patriarch Photius. A learned and highly successful lay civil servant, Photius—an iconophile—was appointed patriarch in 858 by the Emperor Michael III, to take the place of his deposed predecessor Ignatios, who had

---

[104] For fragments of a text promoting a mystical, imageless conception of God, which may be by John, see Jean Gouillard, "Fragments inédits d'un antirrhétique de Jean le Grammairien," *La Vie religieuse à Byzance*, VIII.

[105] On Theodora and icon-veneration, see Herrin, *Unrivalled Influence*, 62–3.

been a protégé of Theodora, but a moderate in his treatment of the former opponents of images.[106] In 867, a new emperor, the Macedonian usurper Basil I, removed Photius from office, with the encouragement of Pope Nicholas I of Rome, on the grounds that he had been elevated to the bishop's office from the lay state, without a suitable period of clerical formation; in 869, Basil summoned a synod to confirm the reinstatement of Ignatios. This synod—received as an ecumenical council in most Western collections from the eleventh century on—has, however, never been received as such by the Eastern Churches, and its status was also considered questionable by a number of Western medieval canonists, including Ivo of Chartres. In any case, its decree and canons are formulated in a way clearly intended to evoke those of earlier ecumenical gatherings, and include a number of disciplinary regulations that go beyond the affair of Ignatios's return to office and Photius's patriarchal legitimacy. Canon 3 of this council—perhaps as a gesture of reassurance to Photius's iconophile supporters—gives solemn, final legal form to the reinstatement of the veneration of sacred images, which, as we have just seen, had been accomplished less formally in the time of the Empress Theodora twenty-six years before. In its rather literal, somewhat longer Latin version, by Anastasius Bibliothecarius, this text reads as follows:

> We decree that the sacred image of our Lord Jesus Christ, the redeemer and savior of all, be venerated with same honor as the book of the holy Gospels. For just as through the written words that are contained in the book we all will attain to salvation, so through the effect of colored images all of us, educated and uneducated alike, will enjoy the benefits of what is before us; for what language proclaims and urges in syllables, painted figures also do. So it is only right that, as befits reason and ancient tradition, icons should be honored—even if in a derivative way—because of the honor that is paid to their originals, and that they should be venerated to the same degree as the holy book of the Gospels, and the form of the sacred cross.
>
> If anyone, then, does not venerate the image of Christ the savior, may he not see his form when he comes in the glory of the Father, "to be glorified and to glorify his saints" (II Thess. 1.10), but let him be cut off from a share in his splendor.[107]

Like a Bible in pictorial form, sacred images proclaim the news of Christ without using words or communicating ideas; so their significance, as a communication of the Gospel, calls forth the same faithful reverence in the contemplative beholder as the words ought to do, and inspires believers with the same hope.

---

[106] Noble (*Icons*, 366–7) suggests that Photius had been promoted in Ignatios's place by those—Stoudite monks, for instance—who may have wanted revenge on former iconoclasts.

[107] Council of Constantinople, 869–70, can. 3 (Alberigo/Tanner, 168 [trans. altered]).

## CONCLUSION

The controversy of the eighth and ninth centuries over the legitimacy of venerating sacred images was a complicated one, as it unrolled, with a number of changes in direction of the arguments that drove it. Modern scholarship is divided over the seriousness with which the public use of images, and public devotion shown to them, was actually repressed by violent action, especially in the beginning stages of the conflict, and also over what may have led Byzantine emperors and their staff, from Leo III in the 720s through Theophilus in the 840s, to take an almost unanimously negative attitude to the objects of Christian devotion, including pictorial representations. Yet the evidence, archaeological and narrative, is clearly that some kind of official anti-iconic policy was largely in force, from the early eighth century to the middle of the ninth.

After a certain ambivalence toward religious images, which one detects in early Patristic writing, based on a strong sense of the mysterious transcendence of God and the seductive danger of idolatry, the Christian community, from the early fourth century, began to cultivate a more concrete piety, centered on holy places, the tombs and relics of martyrs, pilgrimage, and the use of the imagination. By the end of that century, Christian themes and figures began to be depicted on household objects as well as sacred vessels and hangings, and the fifth and sixth centuries witnessed a real explosion of Christian iconic creativity. Personal and paraliturgical devotion, focused on sacred pictures, places, and things and expressed in gestures of reverence, lamps, and incense, seems to have grown, as well, and was said to have occasionally led to disedifying excess. Then suddenly, with the rise of the Isaurian dynasty in the 720s, things began to change.

Just why the Byzantine court began to oppose the cult of sacred objects, places, and images in the time of Leo III, after encouraging it fairly consistently since the time of Constantine, remains something of a riddle. Perhaps the strict anti-iconic policy of Caliph Yazīd II in Syria and Palestine in the 720s, coupled with Muslim military success against the Byzantines in that same decade, did actually lead Leo III and his advisors to wonder if the apparent materialism of much Christian devotion was not provoking divine displeasure, as some later chroniclers suggest. Perhaps popular veneration of religious images had come to be felt as presenting a kind of competition to the status and public face of the Emperor, who had traditionally been regarded, in Hellenistic royal ideology, as the personal image of the divine power on earth. Perhaps the new anti-image policy represented the practical rationalism of a new breed of bureaucrats and generals who, though Christian, themselves had little time for dramatic acts of popular piety; perhaps it was an early form of pragmatic secularism or anti-clericalism that had taken root, or a way for the leaders of the army and the state to take back control of a deeply Christian

populace from the perceived influence of the charismatic monks and hermits
who encouraged their devotions. Perhaps it was simply part of a larger central
project of reform by the state, in a society that had not begun to imagine
Church and Empire as separate, or separable, realms. Whatever the reason, it
is striking that over the next century and a quarter, the Byzantine state
discouraged the public display of religious images, and public acts of devotion
centered on them, with varying levels of intensity, and that this official policy
was strongly resisted by many leading bishops and monastic leaders, as well as
by a number of politically powerful women.

It is also striking that the controversy quickly became a theological one,
however practical or political its origins, and that the reasons advanced both
for and against the practice of venerating holy things and holy images were
generally rooted, from the 730s on, in the Church's classical understanding of
the Incarnation. The Patriarch Germanus and the Palestinian monk-
theologian John of Damascus both pointed out clearly, in the first stage of
the controversy, that the coming of God the Son to be enfleshed in our world
meant that matter, and even the visible human form, were now a vehicle for
God's self-revelation; while created manifestations of God's power and presence were clearly not meant to be *adored* in the literal sense—not to be
acknowledged as strictly divine—they still deserved religious veneration,
affection and respect, because of their religious meaning. The Emperor Constantine V, who mounted what was certainly the most elaborate Christological
argument *against* images, based his reasoning on the now-classical Chalcedonian understanding of Christ as a single divine person possessing two
unmixed natures; to attempt to depict Christ, who as Son of God transcends
all imagining, implies either the "monophysite" assumption that his appearance has literally made the transcendent God imaginable, his divine person or
"face" visible, or else the "Nestorian" assumption that his human nature is a
separate individual from God the Son, capable of being portrayed in images
even if God is not. And bishops took up the theological arguments: the anti-
iconic Council of Hiereia in 754 accepted at least Constantine's conclusions,
while the Second Council of Nicaea, in 787, in promoting the cult of images
once again, returned to the distinctions made by John of Damascus, as the
more logical outcome of the long Christological tradition. Struggles over
practical reform had become fused with the development of doctrine.

In the ninth century, the official prohibition of image-making and image-
cult continued, usually in a less violent way than had been the practice under
Constantine V, and the council of 754 was again recognized as normative—
and as an ecumenical council—by the Synod of the Hagia Sophia in 815. Now
the counter-arguments in favor of icon veneration received a more philosophical and technical turn, however, in the polemical works of the former
Patriarch Nicephorus and the abbot Theodore of Stoudios. Their emphasis
was focused on the image as a *pointer*, as representing by likeness an original

prototype that could not simply be made present whole. So an image of Christ, or of one of the saints or a sacred event, was, in a sense, truly an image of the unimaginable: in Christ's case, a sign of what is hypostatically one with the Son of God's transcendent, super-personal reality, and which finds its meaning in the *relationship* of an always-imperfect likeness to what it signifies. In becoming one hypostasis, one *prosōpon*, with Jesus, Theodore reminds his readers, God the Son now has a human form for his divine "face."

Images, in this late stage of the iconoclastic controversy, had come to be seen more fully in what Western theology would later call *sacramental* terms; they make present what they signify, without actually losing their earthly character—bring the divine before our eyes by signifying it in creaturely form. God, in a new way, had become *visible*, and that visibility engaged the heart as well as the senses. The roots of this kind of thinking, surely, lay in the personal reality of Christ, "who is the image of the invisible God" (Col. 1.15). The Christological tradition had now taken its place concretely, even pictorially, as the center of the Christian life of contemplation and prayer, and so at the heart of ordinary people's daily life of faith. A new sense of the meaning of the Church and its practices, and of the potential meaning of all created and circumscribed reality, had begun.

# 10

Epilogue

## Christology and the Councils

Christian faith, it is often remarked, rests on a paradox: the conviction that the transcendent, ineffable divine being who is the source and heart of all reality has become human, has "spoken to us" not simply in prophets and revelatory events, but "in a Son" (Heb. 1.1). This underlying paradox—that the unknowable one has become immediately and humanly knowable, that the infinite one has become circumscribed in time and space while remaining who he is, the sublimely distant one present and ordinary—gives rise, of course, to other paradoxes and enigmas: that his suffering is the cause of human well-being and joy, his voluntary subjection the source of radical human freedom, his death at a distant point of history the cause of life for people of every generation. The message of the disciples of Jesus, since the earliest years of the Christian community, has been, in fact, to emphasize this astonishing conviction about him; so we read in the beginning of the First Letter of John: "That which was from the beginning, which we have heard, which we have seen with our eyes, which we have looked upon and touched with our hands, concerning the word of life...we proclaim to you, so that you may have fellowship with us" (I John 1.1–3). Jesus, the Galilean prophet and teacher, a follower of John the Baptist and herald of the coming Kingdom of God, a dangerous radical in the eyes of the religious and political leaders of his day, is recognized by disciples, from the writings of the New Testament on, as the victor over death, the bearer and the personal embodiment of that eternal "word of life," the Word who has "become flesh, and dwelt among us" (John 1.14).

It is Jesus in his person, then, even more than simply his teaching or his practice, his relation to the faith and piety of his own Jewish people, who constitutes the challenging distinctiveness of Christian theology. What theologians since the seventeenth century have called "Christology" is the effort of faith-filled Christian thinkers to reflect on *how* the paradox of the person of Jesus might be analyzed and parsed by the religious mind. For many, as we have seen, it is the terse formulation of Christian bishops, at the Council of Chalcedon in 451, that expresses that paradox most clearly:

> Following therefore the holy Fathers, we unanimously teach [Christians] to confess one and the same Son, our Lord Jesus Christ, the same perfect in divinity and perfect in humanity, the same truly God and truly human, composed of rational soul and body... We confess that one and the same Lord Jesus Christ, the only-begotten Son, must be acknowledged in two natures, without confusion or change, without division or separation. The distinction between the natures has not been abolished by their union, but rather the character proper to each of the two natures has been preserved as they have come together in one *persona* and one hypostasis. He is not split into two *personas*, but he is one and the same only-begotten, God the Word, the Lord Jesus Christ.[1]

For the bishops and theologians gathered at Chalcedon, representatives of different schools and terminological traditions with different concerns about what needed to be emphasized, the clearest way to capture the paradox of Christ was to speak of him as a single concrete individual or *hypostasis*, a single *persona* or character on the stage of history, who claimed as his own way of being two utterly different realities, two defining identities that underlie his ability to act and to express himself: two undiminished and unmixed "substances" or "natures" that define his limits and possibilities for action, spell out the "what," of his single personal subjectivity. Using the terms that centuries of Greek philosophical reflection, and decades of intense theological controversy within the Christian community, had put at their disposal by October of 451, they laid out the boundaries, at least, for further thought on who and what Jesus the Savior really is.

Chalcedon's definition remains crucially important for later Christian thought, if this thought hopes to remain within the boundaries of tradition. For modern Western theologians, in particular, it has been particularly appealing: in its metaphysical precision, rooted in antique philosophy, which was crucially important to medieval and early modern scholastic theologians, Catholic and Protestant; and more recently in its very emphasis on the Christian paradox itself, which has captivated theologians steeped in the dialectical strategies of German idealism. Clearly Chalcedon cannot be ignored or underestimated by theological reflection on Jesus that aims to represent Christian orthodoxy.

The argument of this book, however, has been that Chalcedon's formula must also not be isolated from still earlier reflections on the person of Jesus or from the wider and longer discussions that immediately prompted its formulation, let alone seen as a "final settlement" of early Christian questioning

---

[1] Dogmatic Definition of Chalcedon: trans. J. Neuner and J. Dupuis, *The Christian Faith in the Doctrinal Documents of the Catholic Church* 614–15 (New York: Alba House, 1982), 154–5, nos 614–15 (adapted).

about the meaning of the person of Christ, if one is to grasp the continuing value for faith of that ancient orthodoxy. To grasp the full weight of reflection on Christ's person during the crucial first millennium of Christian theological development, I have argued, it is important to look beyond Chalcedon, at what the most articulate voices among those we call "Fathers of the Church" were saying about Christ: what they considered most important to emphasize about him, as well as what they were eager to reject. It is essential, too, to see the definition of Chalcedon as itself part of something slightly different from this ongoing theological discussion: to see it within the context of a longer, self-consciously continuous tradition of early *conciliar statements* that began at Nicaea in 325: a tradition of attempts by varyingly representative gatherings of the worldwide Christian leadership to enunciate a commonly agreed framework—derived from the Christian Bible—in which particular statements of the Bible, and particular Christian practices of worship and piety, could be contextualized and interpreted. To put it simply, Chalcedon needs Nicaea, Constantinople, and Ephesus to be correctly understood, and points ahead, in the Church's continuing tradition of faith, to Constantinople II, Constantinople III, and Nicaea II. The common concern in all of these dogmatic statements, when one looks at their central significance, is to articulate an understanding of the person and meaning of Christ. The phenomenon of what many Christians have come to recognize as the "seven ecumenical councils" of early Christianity has been, in fact, one of the guiding threads in our narrative, as will be obvious to any reader; the decisions of these extraordinary, highly occasional meetings of bishops in the first eight centuries of our era together shaped, in cumulative fashion, the basic structure of what medieval and modern "orthodox" Christianity considers fundamental, even non-negotiable in its understanding of who and what Jesus is.

What constitutes this doctrinal orthodoxy, of course, is always subject to question and debate. But while for many modern Christians only the canonical Bible can be considered normative for Christian faith and practice, most of the older ecclesial bodies that profess their reception also of the long Christian tradition in which the Bible is recognized and interpreted—the Eastern Orthodox, Catholic, Anglican, Methodist, Lutheran, and Reformed families of churches, at the very least—see in the creedal formulations of these seven early councils a continuing, authoritative guide to how the Gospel is to be understood and applied, even today. They express the core of the normative tradition.

In one sense, the early "ecumenical councils" were only a small part of a larger phenomenon. Local bishops, as the leaders of Christian communities in the ancient cities of the Mediterranean, had gathered, on provincial and wider regional levels, to discuss common problems of discipline and pastoral practice within the community since the earliest days of Christianity. The meeting of the Apostles and their co-workers recounted in Acts 15 probably served as a model, and Eusebius of Caesaraea records a number of decisive episcopal meetings in the first three centuries of Christian history.[2] But with the new freedom of the Church that began in the Roman imperial world during the reign of the Emperor Constantine (312–37), a new dimension of this phenomenon of Christian synods also began, and with it new questions of Church leadership and structure, as well as of the best way to clarify and formulate the Christian tradition of faith. Alongside these regular local and regional meetings, more occasional attempts now also came to be made to bring together Christian bishops and leaders, of varying rank, from widely distant parts of the Greco-Roman Empire—from what was thought of as the *oikoumenē*, the whole "civilized world"—to deal with larger, more urgent disputes over faith and practice that were thought to be posing radical challenges to the unity of the Christian movement.

Our narrative in the preceding chapters has largely been centered on the disputes that occasioned these extraordinary meetings, on their very different forms of procedure and criteria for membership, and on the informal, somewhat unpredictable process of their "reception" or general recognition among the Churches of the wider *oikoumenē*, as gatherings whose formulations should be considered binding. A few general observations should be made here about the significance of such early conciliar statements.

(a) Doctrinally, all of these early councils were convened to reflect on the tradition of *faith in Christ* as savior, and cumulatively articulated an understanding of him that remains—despite internal oscillations—the indispensable core of what later theological reflection on the person of Jesus (in modern terms: Christology) affirms of him.

(b) In each of the councils after Nicaea I, one sees clear efforts being made by the bishops present to underline the *continuity* of their decisions and doctrine with the *"faith of Nicaea"*: to see their own formulations as embellishments and footnotes, one might even say, to the Nicene Creed. Their role, as they presented it, was not to innovate, but to reaffirm Apostolic tradition—distilled from Scripture and the long history of its interpretation—in the context of current challenges and controversies. Nicaea affirmed clearly and challengingly that Jesus, as Son of God,

---

[2] See, for example, his references to bishops' synods in Thrace and Asia Minor during the 160s, to decide on how to receive the "new prophecy" proclaimed by Montanus and his followers, in CH 5.16, 19, and the synods held to legislate a common date for the Paschal celebration in the 190s (CH 5.23–25). Cyprian's correspondence witnesses to frequent synods of bishops in North Africa and Rome, in the 240s and 250s, to deal with the question of reconciling Christians who had voluntarily "lapsed" from their faith during outbreaks of persecution. See my article, "Structures of Charity: Bishops' Gatherings and the See of Rome in the Early Church," in Thomas J. Reese (ed.), *Episcopal Conferences; Historical, Canonical, and Theological Studies* (Washington, DC: Georgetown University Press, 1989), 25–58; also "Christian Councils" in the *Encyclopedia of Religion* (2nd edn; New York: Macmillan, 2005), 2039–46.

shares fully in God's "substance"—his transcendent and creative reality. The subsequent "received" councils of the early Church clearly saw themselves as articulating the implications of Nicaea's faith for the Church's understanding of his and our humanity, and of the life, practices, and piety of the Christian community. So, as I have argued, Chalcedon's formulation of the Mystery of Christ—like those of Constantinople II and Constantinople III in its wake—are simply meant as steps in this unfolding of Nicaea, guides for its correct interpretation.

(c) In addition to doctrinal formulation, however, most of these councils (all of them except Constantinople II and III) enacted *canons*, which were meant to regulate *Church order*. Most of these canons legislate about the authority and territorial responsibility of bishops: calling them to hold regular synods, defining the role of metropolitans in their provinces, etc. Some also seek to protect the authority of bishops from political intrusion; so Canon 3 of Nicaea II declares: "Any election of a bishop, priest, or deacon brought about by rulers (ἄρχοντες) remains invalid."[3] Securing the independence and healthy institutional functioning of the Christian religious sphere is also one of the purposes of councils, closely connected to the continuity of the faith that holds believers together.

(d) Clearly, the *interdependence of the imperial, or civic, and ecclesial worlds* is one of the main phenomena to which the early councils also bear witness. All seven of the early ecumenical councils were summoned by *emperors*; at some of them (Nicaea, Chalcedon, Constantinople III, Nicaea II), the Emperor attended one or more sessions; and at all of them, in a variety of ways, they let their concerns and demands be known—as part of the accepted self-understanding of Christian emperors that part of their role was to oversee the healthy functioning of the Church. At all of these councils, too, some attempt seems to have been made to attract a wider attendance than simply local bishops. Not all of them, however, were actually characterized by heavy involvement by the bishops of the ancient "Apostolic" sees of Jerusalem, Alexandria, Antioch, Rome, and Constantinople (in Justinian's terminology, the Patriarchs of the "Pentarchy"), or their representatives. During the sessions of Constantinople II, in fact, Pope Vigilius of Rome was being held in house arrest by order of the Emperor, and protested against the proceedings during the Council sessions; the Patriarchates of Antioch, Alexandria, and Jerusalem were not personally represented at any councils after Chalcedon. Imperial sponsorship, on the other

---

[3] Alberigo/Tanner, 140 (my trans.).

hand, was indispensable for all the early councils—the one external element of continuity among them. The Empire, as the civil context of early Christianity, forced the community of faith to stay together.

(e) Nevertheless, it seems justified to see in the actual histories and texts of these seven early councils also a growing sense of the Church's need to affirm its integrity and its *independence from political pressure* in the proclamation of the tradition of faith, as well as its need to develop practical structures that might protect that independence. In the appeals of various leading theologians (Theodoret of Cyrus in 449, Maximus Confessor in the 640s, Theodore of Stoudios in the years after 815) to the bishops of Rome to adjudicate disputes, to affirm previously settled conciliar decisions, and to be a court of appeal, one sees the early growth of a sense of need, among many believers, for a genuine, if practically limited, universal religious primacy—to engage in a kind of dialectic of mutual definition with civil society.

(f) What holds these seven councils together for Christian posterity as "ecumenical"—as normative for the "universal" body of Christians—is simply the fact that they have been *received* as such by the Churches. Sometimes (Chalcedon, among the Churches not then in schism; Constantinople III) the reception seems to have been immediate and almost unquestioned; more often, it took time and painful argument—in the cases of Nicaea I, Constantinople II, and Nicaea II, more than fifty years. But there were many other gatherings of bishops, called by emperors, attended by bishops from many regions, and aspiring to be considered "ecumenical" themselves—many councils of the mid-fourth century; the council led by Dioscorus of Alexandria at Ephesus in 449; the iconomachic councils of the Hiereia in 754 and of the Hagia Sophia in 815, to name a few—which have *not been received* as universally normative by most Churches through the years. The reason is not some flaw in their formal constitution; it seems simply to be that the Church, by some Spirit-led intuition, has not recognized its faith to have been expressed there. The only clue to the fact of reception is what has been received!

(g) Nevertheless, the sense that all of the seven "ecumenical" councils, even those whose membership was far from universally inclusive, were dealing with *issues of universal import* for Christians rather than simply of local or ephemeral concern, seems to have been a prime motive for their ultimate reception. In a somewhat obscure publication of early Byzantine canonical texts from 1905, the great Russian historian of Orthodoxy and twentieth-century martyr, Vladimir Nikolaevich Beneševič, included a brief, anonymous list that he had found in manuscript of some thirteen local and ecumenical councils, apparently composed in the second half of the sixth century, sometime shortly after Constantinople II. The catalogue ends with this general reflection:

> Since, then, when we recall these many synods, we have named only five of them as ecumenical—namely, the one in Nicaea; and the one in Constantinople; and the one in Ephesus; and the one in Chalcedon; and the one which met again in Constantinople to condemn Origen and Theodore [of Mopsuestia]—readers should know that the other synods we have mentioned are, like these five, received by the Church. Everything decided at them the Church declares to be apostolic law. But only these five are called "ecumenical" for this reason: because at the command of Emperors, archbishops[4] were summoned from all over the Roman Empire, and either attended themselves or sent delegates; and because at each of these five synods, an investigation of the faith took place, and a vote or dogmatic definition was produced. The synod of Nicaea brought out the holy Creed or summary of teaching (μάθημα). The synod of Constantinople, likewise, broadened and clarified that same holy Creed. The first synod at Ephesus received the chapters of the blessed Cyril;[5] these expressed judgment by correct teaching. The synod at Chalcedon uttered a dogmatic statement against Eutyches and his aberrant heresy. And the fifth synod, at Constantinople, proclaimed the teachings of orthodoxy in fourteen chapters.
>
> But the rest of the synods were partial (μερικαί), since not all the bishops of the world were invited; they did not set out any dogmatic teaching, but either attempted to reinforce things that had been defined dogmatically at preceding synods, or to purge away what some had impiously dared to argue against them, or to specify what seemed right to say about the Church's rules, and about questions raised with the good ordering of the Church in view.[6]

Already, it seems, in the years shortly after 553, theologians reflecting on the normative teaching of the Church had begun to distinguish two very different kinds of synod or council: those summoned (in principle, at least) from the whole Christian world, which had to do primarily with the clarification and teaching of the Christian faith, with the tradition going back to the Scriptures and the preaching of the Apostles—put simply, with the Mystery of Christ; and gatherings of more limited scope and membership, called to reinforce and implement these basic teachings, and to enable the Church to live by them more consistently. Both kinds of council were essential to Church life, both were authoritative; yet the issues dealt with, and the lists of those called to

---

[4] This term may refer, in the sixth century, only to the five "great bishops" or Patriarchs of the Apostolic sees—what Justinian called the Pentarchy.

[5] This apparently refers to the twelve anathemas that Cyril of Alexandria—or a synod under his chairmanship—appended to his so-called "Third Letter to Nestorius," written in 430. This letter, with the anathemas, came to be seen as the classic exposition of Cyril's view of Christ.

[6] Vladimir N. Beneševič, *Kanoničeskij Sbornik XIV Titulov so Vtoroj Četverti VII Věka do 883 G* (repr. Leipzig: Zentrantiquariat der DDR, 1974), 78–9. See also Hermann-Josef Sieben, *Die Konzilsidee der alten Kirche (Konziliengeschichte, Series B: Untersuchungen)* (Paderborn: Schöningh, 1979), 356–61.

make decisions, varied unmistakably. It was the difference between faith and order, catechesis and canon law. It was the difference between issues at the lasting center of Christian faith, and the necessarily narrower issues of their application.

*

It might be helpful, at the conclusion of this narrative of early Christian understandings of Christ, to offer a few general reflections on what I have called the "long tradition" of Christology.

1. *Christology is about God.* The developing early Christian tradition articulating an understanding of Christ is really a way of understanding the distinctively Christian understanding of God. God, for Christian theology, is not simply the utterly transcendent First Cause of Greek philosophy, or Aristotle's "unmoved Mover,"[7] although philosophical reflection is clearly in use by Jewish and Christian theologians from the first century on, to interpret the biblical portrait of the God who has acted in history. For Christian tradition, the Hebrew Bible's portrait of the nameless God who spoke to Moses on Sinai, the God who sent the prophets, the cosmic creator and guide of the Wisdom books, is now further understood to mean the one whom Jesus calls "Father," who identifies Jesus at the Jordan and on the mount of transfiguration as his "beloved Son," who sends the Holy Spirit on Jesus and his disciples. So the gradual identification of Jesus, through the early centuries, as personally divine, although also a real human being, lies at the root of the new, distinctively Christian understanding of the transcendent divine Mystery as a Trinity of related persons, a God who is *beyond* time in his own being, yet intimately— even personally—*involved* in time since the start of creation. As we have seen, the Christian doctrine of the Trinity, classically understood as three distinct hypostases or individuals sharing and constituting a single divine substance (*ousia*) or reality, begins in the efforts of the Cappadocian Fathers to make sense of the Nicene conception of Jesus. God's personal nearness and involvement in our history—as source, companion, and animator—as well as God's enduring radical otherness, is expressed in the Christian doctrine of God as Trinity, and this has its origin in the conception that Jesus is himself "of the same substance" as God.

2. *It is about the World in its Relationship to God.* In conceiving Christ as a single divine person, living out in the two utterly distinct natures of divinity and humanity the creative, saving will of God, Patristic theology gradually came to understand more deeply the way in which God is present to creation: present as other, as perfect, as in no way lessening or compromising his own

---

[7] See *Physics* 8.4 (255b29–31); 8.10 (267b18–26); *Metaphysics* 12.7 (1072a23–26, b8–9). A better translation might be "uncaused cause."

transcendent power and holiness; yet present also completely, personifying what it is to be Son of God in a complete human body and mind, and a full human life. The real underlying issue in theological reflection on the person of Christ since the Cappadocians' debate with Apollinarius in the 370s, after all, was how it could be possible for Jesus to possess a complete and normal humanity while still being truly the Son of God, "of one substance with the Father." From the Cappadocian Fathers on, those who articulated the main-stream tradition of orthodoxy insisted on the completeness of both the realities or "natures" of the incarnate Word; as a result, the "zero-sum" understanding of Jesus' twofold identity—the assumption that the more divine he is, the less he can be fully human, and vice versa—gradually began to disappear.

In fact, the recognition begins to emerge in the centuries after Chalcedon that Jesus' personal divine identity actually frees him to realize in himself, more fully than the rest of the race, the natural human identity God had intended and formed at creation. So Maximus writes to the Cypriot deacon Marinus, in the midst of the controversy over Christ's two natural wills, around the year 642:

> Nothing that is natural, and certainly not nature itself, would ever resist the cause of nature, nor would our faculty of deliberation (γνώμη) or anything that belongs to deliberation [do this], as long as it agrees with the structure (λόγος) of nature. For if anyone said that something natural resisted God, this would rather be a charge against God than against nature... That nothing natural is opposed to God is clear from the fact that these things were originally fashioned by him through the process of generation.[8]

The fact that Jesus' entire human nature belongs to God the Son as his own humanity frees that individual humanity, in Maximus's view, to be fully natural, completely what it was intended to be—to be completely human in ways that our own versions of that same human nature, since Adam and Eve, may never fully realize. Freedom and virtue are natural; sin and our inherited inclination to sin are unnatural, destructive of human integrity. As one free from sin and fully oriented to God as his Father, Jesus realizes in himself the λόγος or plan God had in mind for all humanity at the start of creation.[9]

---

[8] *Opusc.* 7 (PG 90.80A; trans. Andrew Louth, *Maximus the Confessor* [London: Routledge, 1996] 185 [altered]).

[9] See also, for instance, *Quaestiones ad Thalassium* 21: "In his love for humanity, the only-begotten Son and Logos of God became perfect man, with a view to redeeming human nature from this helplessness in evil. Taking on the original condition of Adam as he was in the very beginning (γένεσις), he was sinless but not incorruptible, and he assumed, from the procreative process (γέννησις) introduced into human nature as a consequence, only the liability to passions, not the sin itself" (CCG 7, 129.36–42; trans. Paul M. Blowers and Robert Louis Wilken, *On the Cosmic Mystery of Jesus Christ* [Crestwood, NY: St. Vladimir's, 2003], 110–11). The *Quaestiones ad Thalassium*, a set of responses to questions about various Scripture passages, are an early work

3. *Metaphysical Categories are Always Used Analogously of God and Humanity.* Another, perhaps deeper reason for the gradual disappearance of the "zero-sum" conception of the two realities in Christ among later Patristic authors is their apparently growing realization—never fully articulated—that the characteristics we ascribe to God's nature are not such as to compete with similar characteristics ascribed to ourselves. In speaking about our knowledge of God, for instance, John of Damascus—echoing Pseudo-Dionysius's *Mystical Theology*—insists that "we can know that God exists, but what he is in essence and nature is beyond all understanding."[10] Somewhat farther on, he explains this more fully:

> Since the divinity is incomprehensible, he must remain absolutely nameless. Accordingly, since we do not know his essence, let us not look for a name for his essence, for names are indicative of what things are. However, although God is good and has brought us from nothing into being to share his goodness and has given us knowledge, yet, since he did not communicate his essence to us, so neither did he communicate the knowledge of his essence. . . . Therefore, insofar as he is incomprehensible, he is also unnameable. But since he is the *cause* of all things and possesses beforehand in himself the reasons and causes of all, so he can be named after all—even things which are opposites, such as light and darkness, water and fire—so that we may know that he is not these things in essence, but is superessential and unnameable. Thus, since he is the cause of all beings, he is *named after* all things that are caused.[11]

John is presumably thinking here, in Dionysian terms, of the qualities and attributes we ascribe to God, such as power, wisdom, goodness, justice, and so on. We identify these qualities with his being, because, as creatures who strive for these qualities ourselves as goods that perfect us, we assume that the basis for all that is good in creation is its dependence on, and thus its causal relationship with, the Creator. This relationship is the epistemological basis for what Aquinas and the medieval Western scholastics would call "the analogy of proportion."[12]

Although neither Maximus nor John of Damascus explicitly apply this hermeneutical procedure to their discussions of the two natures of Christ, it

---

of Maximus, apparently written between 630 and 633, just before the controversy about Christ's two operations or wills became a serious dispute in the Greek-speaking Church.

[10] *Exp. Fid.* 4 (= 1.4; (ed. B. Kotter, *Die Schriften des Johannes von Damaskos*, II [Berlin: De Gruyter, 1973], 12; trans. Frederic H. Chase, Jr; Fathers of the Church 37 [Washington, DC: Catholic University of America Press, 1958], 170).

[11] *Exp. Fid.* 12 (= 1.12; ed. Kotter, II 35; trans. Chase, 194). This section is not attested in all the Greek manuscripts, but appears in four early medieval codices and seems likely to be the work of John.

[12] See ST I, q. 13, a. 5. Thomas insists, however, in the next article that names signifying perfection are predicated primarily of God and secondarily of creatures, precisely because God is their cause.

seems reasonable to suppose that the Orthodox tradition, by the seventh century, had at least begun to grasp the idea that language about will and intelligence in God are also used analogously: that whatever mental and personal processes we ascribe to God, or to the divine Son who became human in Christ, are not to be understood in a way that would conflict with Christ's human consciousness or human will. However God knows and thinks and wills, it is not the same activity as human knowing and thinking and willing, and so cannot be understood to replace or duplicate them; we attribute these actions to God because they are central to our own life as free and conscious creatures. Even the language of "substance" and "individual," "nature" and "person," when applied to God, must be understood to be free of the limitations and subjective exclusiveness that we necessarily identify with them in the world of human experience. To be a divine hypostasis, to have a divine nature as one's proper identity, is not to be understood as keeping God the Son from having a complete, functioning human identity that humanly "personifies" his subjective existence as Son of God.

4. *The Incarnation is a Mode of the Son of God's Divine Being.* As we have mentioned, Maximus Confessor several times resorts to adverbs to denote the "exchange of properties" brought about by the Incarnation of the Word: in Jesus, the Word made flesh, we encounter God living "in a human way," as well as a man existing "in a divine way."[13] The point of such expressions is not simply rhetorical effect. Rather, given the relationship of distant similarity-in-distinction between God and ourselves that is implied in the biblical and theological understanding of creation and redemption, the act of taking on a human nature implies, for the divine and living Word of God, that without ceasing to be a constitutive agent within the divine Mystery—without ceasing to be God's Beloved Son—he now expresses that personal existence in the created world in a way other creatures can perceive, acts out his selfhood now fully within the confines and the possibilities of a human individual: in this case, of a Jewish man from Galilee, a carpenter who lived two millennia ago, Jesus, the Son of Mary.

This way of understanding the Incarnation seems to move the Church's reflection beyond simply focusing on the ontological categories of universal substance and individual thing, beyond hypostasis and nature and the other terms that have been used since the fourth century to clarify discussion of the paradox of Christ's person. God the creator and the world of his creating, bound though it is in the categories of time and space, of what Augustine called "extension," are understood to be intrinsically related as well as infinitely distinct: God is not a "piece of the world," but the world, in all its intelligible reality, finds its source and its goal in God, depends on him for

---

[13] See chap. 8.

its being and its perceptible form. So while Jews and Christians take as fundamental to faith God's word to Moses on Sinai, "You cannot see my face; for a human being cannot see me and live" (Exod. 33.20), both traditions rest on the assumption that God reveals himself to created eyes and minds in historical words and events, encounters with historical persons, and that these worldly appearances make God accessible to us, despite the enduring hidden-ness of his being. The central conviction of Jesus' disciples, summed up in the episode of his transfiguration as narrated in the Synoptic Gospels, is that Jesus himself—human in form, yet radiating divine glory as God's "beloved Son"—is the summit of God's revelation in history.

5. *Christ Himself is the Beginning of Salvation.* Like the history of Israel as God's people, the Christian story is a story of salvation. God, the creator and sovereign of history, has reached into a world of his creating, where the human race has grown increasingly isolated within its own interests and enmities, to save them from themselves, to form them into a new people, a new humanity, living for him and eventually drawing "all nations" to faith and peace. Christian faith begins within the longer Jewish tradition, in that it sees that hope fulfilled in the person of Jesus, and in the community of faith that was gathered around him, after his resurrection from the dead, by his Holy Spirit. What we call Christology begins in the recognition of Jesus—specifically of the risen Jesus—as the divine Savior.

Classical histories of early Christology have repeatedly pointed to the centrality of this conviction in the development of our ontological categories for identifying who and what Jesus is. If God is the giver and restorer of life. then the one who brings the work of restoration to fulfilment must be able to act and speak as God in the midst of humanity. So Athanasius writes, in the *Third Oration against the Arians*:

> When the Son is beheld, so is the Father, for he is the Father's radiance; and thus the Father and the Son are one. But one cannot say that this is so with things originate and with creatures. For when the Father works, it is not any angel that works, or any other creature; for none of these is an efficient cause; but they belong to the class of things which come to be; and moreover, being separate and divided from the only God, and other in nature—and being, in fact, creatures—they can neither effect what God does, nor, as I said before, when God gives grace, can they give grace along with him.[14]

To rescue and restore creation, Athanasius assumes, is the work of none but the creator. If Christ is indeed the savior of humanity, the source of the renewal of the grace of God that has been lost through the history of sin, then Christ must himself be a divine agent.

---

[14] *Oration 3 against the Arians* 13–14 (PG 26.349 BC), trans. John Henry Newman; NPNF, Second Series 4 (repr. Peabody, MA: Hendrickson, 1994), 401 (altered).

And if the full expression of Jesus' saving mission was his suffering and death on the cross, in obedience to his Father's will, then that human death—as memorialized and made present within the community in the celebration of the Eucharist—requires that even his flesh, his sacrifice, if it is life-giving, must be the real human flesh of the Son of God. So Cyril of Alexandria and his synod wrote to Nestorius, almost a century after Athanasius:

> For being by nature life, as God, when he became one with his own flesh he rendered it vitalizing; and so, though he tells us "truly I say to you, unless you eat the flesh of the Son of Man and drink his blood" (John 6.53), we must not suppose it [= this flesh and blood] belongs to one of us humans—for how could a man's flesh be vitalizing by its own nature? But we must recognize that it was made the truly personal possession of him who, for us, has become and was called "Son of Man."[15]

The classical formulation of the Church's understanding of who Jesus is, in other words, as that was first suggested in the Nicene Creed and then refined and developed by later early theologians and councils, is a formulation of what faith understands to be required if Jesus is to be our Savior. The ontological terms used at Chalcedon, Constantinople II, and Constantinople III, in their terse formulations of orthodox faith, were seen as necessary to bring out as clearly as possible, in the learned language of the times, the dimensions of this paradox of the Savior's person. Philosophy, as Athanasius observed in his later reflections on Nicaea, and its continually developing technical terminology, while not itself part of the original Christian kerygma, was eventually necessary as a tool, to clarify and reinforce the Church's considered, authentic understanding of the apostolic tradition.[16]

Christian thinkers have struggled for centuries to give some kind of explanation for how it is that Jesus, the Galilean prophet who was crucified, can be the central agent in the drama of human salvation. Many—especially in the West, since Anselm of Canterbury in the late eleventh century—conceive of Christ's work of redemption in predominantly transactional terms, as repaying an unpayable debt of honor to God on behalf of an alienated humanity. Others, like Peter Abelard, have emphasized the revelatory or exemplary character of Christ's death, as an act of "faithful witness" (see Rev. 1.5) and obedience. Still others, like Harnack and the nineteenth-century liberal Protestants, stress the centrality of Jesus' life and teaching: the simplicity and humility of his behavior, his stress on forgiveness and love of enemies, his refusal to allow his disciples to become the core of a Messianic political movement.

---

When one reads the works of early Christian writers, however, as debates over the person and the significance of Christ developed during the first millennium of the Christian era, one notices rather a reluctance to identify his central achievement as humanity's savior with any particular aspect or activity of his life, or even his death, as if it were in itself the focal point of his role as Savior. Surely the death of Jesus, in humility and obedience to the Father's will, is of crucial importance to his significance for humanity, but so also is his miraculous birth, as told by Matthew and Luke, and his baptism and transfiguration as key points in his developing public career, and above all his resurrection.[17]

In fact, it seems more accurate to say that for most early Christian theologians who wrote about the person of Christ, it is his very *person* itself that constitutes his saving meaning for the human race—it is Christology itself, one might say (to use a more modern term), that forms the core of Christian soteriology. Jesus Christ, the Son of God in his full, historical humanity, is for the early theologians and recognized ecumenical councils what he is in the letters of Paul: the beginning of a new creation (II Cor. 5.17; see Eph. 4.24; Rev. 3.14). To be part not only of the descendants of Adam, not only even of the people Israel, but to belong to the community of Jesus' disciples—what Augustine would repeatedly call the "whole Christ"—is to share already in divine redemption.

6. *Christ the Mystery.* This vision of Christ as humanity's new beginning stands out clearly in the first chapter of the Letter to the Colossians, in the New Testament. There Paul—or one of his close co-workers and intellectual heirs—begins, as he often does, by praising and thanking God for the faith and fruitful lives of a community he seems not yet to have met in person (1.3–8), and solemnly prays for their progress in spiritual gifts (1.9–12), as people whom God "has delivered from the dominion of darkness and transferred ... to the kingdom of his beloved Son, in whom we have redemption, the forgiveness of sins." Christ is this for the community of believers, because he is both the personal reflection of what God is, and the promise of a new form of the humanity made in God's image. It is Christ, as God and man, whom Paul then powerfully describes:

> He is the image of the invisible God, the first-born of all creation; for in him all things were created, in heaven and on earth, visible and invisible ... He is the head of his body, the Church; he is the beginning, the first-born from the dead, that in

---

[17] See my article "'He Himself is our Peace' (Eph. 2.14): Early Christian Views of Redemption in Christ," in Stephen T. Davis, Daniel Kendall, S.J., and Gerald O'Collins, S.J., *The Redemption: An Interdisciplinary Symposium on Christ as Redeemer* (Oxford: Oxford University Press, 2004), 149–76.

everything he might be pre-eminent. For in him all the fullness of God was pleased to dwell.   (1.15–19)

Because he makes that "fullness" present, even Jesus' death takes on reconciling value as his work of mediation between God and creation, "making peace by the blood of his cross" (1.20).

So Paul, a few verses farther on, can speak boldly of "the mystery hidden for ages and generations, but now made manifest to the saints . . . , which is Christ in you, your hope of glory" (Col. 1.26–7). Jesus Christ, in his own person, is the realization of God's plan for a straying humanity since the beginning. And the point of that plan is the inclusion of humanity, the reciprocal placement of humanity "in" Christ and Christ "in" humanity, through and in the community of disciples, in the assumed shape of Christ's own life: a life darkened now also by suffering, as his was, but pointed towards resurrection, towards what the Fathers of East and West call divinization, and so towards a growing participation in the same Mystery. The saving reality of Christ is God made present in our midst: "God with us." It is God visible—our brother.

# Bibliography

Abramowski, R., "Der theologische Nachlass des Diodor von Tarsus," *Zeitschrift für die neutestamentliche Wissenschaft* 42 (1949), 51–3.

Alberigo, Giuseppe et al. (eds), *Decrees of the Ecumenical Councils*, I, trans. Norman Tanner et al. (London: Sheed and Ward; Washington, DC: Georgetown University Press, 1990).

Alexander, Paul, *The Patriarch Nicephorus of Constantinople: Ecclesiastical Policy and Image Worship in the Byzantine Empire* (Oxford: Oxford University Press, 1958/2001).

Allen, Pauline and Bronwen Neil, *Maximus the Confessor and his Companions: Documents from Exile* (Oxford: Oxford University Press, 2002).

Allen, Pauline and Bronwen Neil, *The Life of Maximus the Confessor, Recension 3* (Strathfield, NSW: St. Paul's, 2003).

Allen, Pauline and Bronwen Neil (eds), *The Oxford Handbook of Maximus the Confessor* (Oxford: Oxford University Press, 2015).

Anastos, Milton V., "The Argument for Iconoclasm as Presented by the Iconoclastic Council of 754," in Kurt Weitzmann (ed.), *Late Classical and Medieval Studies in Honor of Prof. Albert M. Friend, Jr.* (Princeton: Princeton University Press, 1954) 177–88.

Anastos, Milton V., "The Ethical Theory of Images Formulated by the Iconoclasts in 754 and 815," *Dumbarton Oaks Papers* 8 (1954), 151–60.

Anatolios, Khaled, "The Influence of Irenaeus on Athanasius," *Studia Patristica* 36 (2001), 463–76.

Anatolios, Khaled, *Retrieving Nicaea: The Development and Meaning of Trinitarian Doctrine* (Grand Rapids, MI: Baker Academic, 2011).

Andia, Ysabel De, *Homo Vivens: incorruptibilité et divinisation de l'homme selon Irénée de Lyon* (Paris: Études Augustiniennes, 1986).

Arnold, Duane W. H., *The Early Episcopal Career of Athanasius of Alexandria* (Notre Dame, IN: Notre Dame University Press, 1991).

Ayres, Lewis, "The Christological Context of Augustine's *De Trinitate* XIII: Towards Relocating Books VIII–XV," *Augustinian Studies* 29 (1998), 111–39.

Ayres, Lewis, *Nicaea and its Legacy: An Approach to Fourth-Century Trinitarian Controversy* (Oxford: Oxford University Press, 2004).

Ayres, Lewis, *Augustine and the Trinity* (Oxford: Oxford University Press, 2009).

Ayres, Lewis and Gareth Jones (eds), *Christian Origins: Theology, Rhetoric and Community* (London: Routledge, 1998).

Balthasar, Hans Urs von, *Cosmic Liturgy*, trans. Brian E. Daley (San Francisco, CA: Ignatius Press, 2003).

Barnes, Michel, *The Power of God: Dynamis in Gregory of Nyssa's Trinitarian Theology* (Washington, DC: Catholic University of America Press, 2001).

Bathrellos, Demetrios, *The Byzantine Christ: Person, Nature, and Will in the Christology of St. Maximus the Confessor* (Oxford: Oxford University Press, 2003).

Baumstark, Anton (rev. Bernard Botte), *Comparative Liturgy* (Westminster, MD: Newman, 1958).

Beeley, Christopher A., *The Unity of Christ: Continuity and Conflict in Patristic Tradition* (New Haven, CT: Yale University Press, 2012).

Behr, John, *The Nicene Faith* (Crestwood, NY: St. Vladimir's, 2004).

Belting, Hans, *Das echte Bild: Bildfragen als Glaubensfragen* (Munich: C. H. Beck, 2005).

Bergjan, Silke-Petra, *Theodoret von Cyrus und der Neunizänismus* (Berlin: De Gruyter, 1993), 192–5.

Berthold, George, *Maximus the Confessor: Selected Writings* (New York: Paulist Press, 1985).

Bertrand, Frédéric, *Le Mystère de Jésus chez Origène* (Paris: Aubier, 1951).

Bienert, Wolfgang, "Zur Logos-Christologie des Athanasius von Alexandrien in *Contra Gentes* und *De Incarnatione*," *Studia Patristica* 21 (1989), 402–19.

Bigham, Stéphane, *Les images chrétiennes: Textes historiques de Constantin le Grand jusqu'à la période posticonoclaste (313–900)* (Montreal: Médiaspaul, 2010).

Bonner, Campbell, *The Homily on the Passion by Melito Bishop of Sardis and some Fragments of the Apocryphal Ezekiel*, Studies and Documents 12 (London: Christophers; Philadelphia, PA: University of Pennsylvania Press, 1941).

Bonner, Gerald, "Augustine's Conception of Deification," *Journal of Theological Studies* NS 37 (1986), 369–86.

Bonner, Gerald, "Deificare," in Cornelius Mayer (ed.), *Augustinus-Lexikon* 1 (Basel: Schwabe, 1986– ), 265–7.

Boyarin, Daniel, *Dying for God* (Stanford, CA: Stanford University Press, 1999).

Boyarin, Daniel, *Border Lines* (Philadelphia, PA: University of Pennsylvania Press, 2004).

Brent, Allen, *Ignatius of Antioch: A Martyr Bishop and the Origin of Episcopacy* (London: Continuum, 2007).

Chadwick, Henry, "Eucharist and Christology in the Nestorian Controversy," *Journal of Theological Studies* NS 2 (1951), 145–64.

Charlesworth, James H., "Les Odes de Salomon et les manuscrits de la mer morte," *Revue Biblique* 77 (1970), 522–49.

Charlesworth, James H., *The Odes of Solomon* (Oxford: Oxford University Press, 1973).

Charlesworth, James H., *The Old Testament Pseudepigrapha* 2 (New York: Doubleday, 1985).

Chenu, "Position de Théologie," *Revue des sciences philosophiques et théologiques* 25 (1935), 232–57 (trans. Denis Hickey, "What is Theology?" *Faith and Theology* [New York: Macmillan, 1968]. 15–35).

Cholij, Roman, *Theodore the Stoudite: The Ordering of Holiness* (Oxford: Oxford University Press, 2002).

Concannon, Ellen, "The Eucharist as the Source of St. Cyril of Alexandria's Christology," *Pro Ecclesia* 18 (2009), 318–36.

Corby Finney, Paul, "Antecedents of Byzantine Iconoclasm: Christian Evidence before Constantine," in Joseph Gutmann (ed.), *The Image and the Word* (Missoula, MT: Scholars Press, 1977), 27–47.

Corby Finney, Paul, *The Invisible God: The Earliest Christians on Art* (New York: Oxford University Press, 1994).

Cormack, Robin, *Byzantine Art* (Oxford: Oxford University Press, 2000).

Corwin, Virginia, *St. Ignatius and Christianity in Antioch* (New Haven, CT: Yale University Press, 1960).

Crouzel, Henri, *La Théologie de l'image de Dieu chez Origène* (Paris: Aubier, 1956).

Crouzel, Henri, *Origène et la " connaissance mystique"* (Paris: Desclée de Brouwer, 1961).

Daley, S.J., Brian E., "Structures of Charity: Bishops' Gatherings and the See of Rome in the Early Church," in Thomas J. Reese (ed.), *Episcopal Conferences; Historical, Canonical, and Theological Studies* (Washington, DC: Georgetown University Press, 1989), 25–58.

Daley, S.J., Brian E., *The Hope of the Early Church: A Handbook of Patristic Eschatology* (Cambridge: Cambridge University Press, 1991).

Daley, S.J., Brian E., 'A Richer Union': Leontius of Byzantium and the Relationship of Human and Divine in Christ," *Studia Patristica* 24 (1993), 239–65.

Daley, S.J., Brian E., "The Giant's Twin Substances: Ambrose and the Christology of Augustine's *Contra sermonem Arianorum*," *Collectanea Augustiniana* (1994).

Daley, S.J., Brian E., "Divine Transcendence and Human Transformation: Gregory of Nyssa's Anti-Apollinarian Christology," *Studia Patristica* 32 (1997), 87–95.

Daley, S.J., Brian E., "Origen's *De Principiis*: A Guide to the 'Principles' of Christian Scriptural Interpretation," in John Petruccione (ed.), *Nova et Vetera: Patristic Studies in Honor of Thomas Patrick Halton* (Washington, DC: Catholic University of America Press, 1998), 3–21.

Daley, S.J., Brian E., "Building the New City: the Cappadocian Fathers and the Rhetoric of Philanthropy," *Journal of Early Christian Studies* 7 (1999), 431–61.

Daley, S.J., Brian E., 'Heavenly Man' and 'Eternal Christ': Apollinarius and Gregory of Nyssa on the Personal Identity of the Savior," *Journal of Early Christian Studies* 10 (2002), 469–88.

Daley, S.J., Brian E., "Nature and the 'Mode of Union': Late Patristic Models for the Personal Unity of Christ," in Gerald O'Collins, Daniel Kendall, and Stephen Davis (eds), *The Incarnation* (Oxford: Oxford University Press, 2002), 164–96.

Daley, S.J., Brian E., "The Fullness of the Saving God: Cyril of Alexandria on the Holy Spirit," in Thomas G. Weinandy and Daniel A. Keating (eds), *The Theology of St. Cyril of Alexandria: a Critical Appreciation* (London: T. and T. Clark, 2003), 113–48.

Daley, S.J., Brian E., "'He Himself is our Peace' (Eph 2.14): Early Christian Views of Redemption in Christ," in Stephen T. Davis, Daniel Kendall, S.J., and Gerald O'Collins, S.J., *The Redemption: An Interdisciplinary Symposium on Christ as Redeemer* (Oxford: Oxford University Press, 2004) 149.

Daley, S.J., Brian E., "Christian Councils," in the *Encyclopedia of Religion* (2nd edn; New York: Macmillan, 2005), 2039–46.

Daley, S.J., Brian E., "*La nouvelle théologie* and the Patristic Revival: Sources, Symbols, and the Science of Theology," *International Journal of Systematic Theology* 7 (2005), 362–82.

Daley, S.J., Brian E., "Making a Human Will Divine: Augustine and Maximus Confessor on Christ and Human Salvation," in Aristotle Papanikolaou and George E. Demacopoulos (eds), *Orthodox Readings of Augustine* (Crestwood, NY: St. Vladimir's, 2008), 101–26.

Daley, S.J., Brian E., "The Enigma of Meletius of Antioch," in Ronnie J. Rombs and Alexander Y. Hwang (eds), *Tradition and the Rule of Faith in the Early Church* (Washington, DC: Catholic University of America Press, 2010), 128–50.

Daley, S.J., Brian E., "Maximus Confessor, Leontius of Byzantium, and the Late Aristotelian Metaphysics of the Person," in Bishop Maxim (Vasiljević) (ed.), *Knowing the Purpose of Creation through Resurrection: Proceedings of the Symposium on St. Maximus the Confessor* (Alhambra, CA: Sebastian Press, 2012), 55–70.

Daley, S.J., Brian E., *Leontius of Byzantium: The Complete Works* (Oxford: Oxford University Press, 2017).

Daniélou, Jean, "Le comble du mal et l'eschatologie de S. Grégoire de Nysse," in E. Iserloh and P. Manns (eds), *Festgabe Joseph Lortz* 2 (Baden-Baden: Bruno Grimm, 1958), 27–45.

Daniélou, Jean, *L'Être et le temps chez Grégoire de Nysse* (Leiden: Brill, 1970), 95–115.

Dempf, Alois, "Der Platonismus des Eusebius, Victorinus, und Pseudo-Dionysius," *Sitzungsberichte der Bayrischen Akademie der Wissenschaften, phil.—hist. Klasse* 3 (Munich, 1962).

Devreesse, R., "La vie de S. Maxime et ses recensions," *Analecta Bollandiana* 46 (1928), 5–49.

Drobner, Hubertus, *Person-exegese und Christologie bei Augustinus: zur Herkunft der Formel "Una Persona"* (Leiden: Brill, 1986).

Droge, Arthur J., "Justin Martyr and the Restoration of Philosophy," *Church History* 56 (1987), 304.

Edwards, Mark, *Catholicity and Heresy in the Early Church* (Farnham: Ashgate, 2009), 79–108.

Elert, Werner, *Der Ausgang der altkirchlichen Christologie: Eine Untersuchung über Theodor von Pharan und seine Zeit als Einführung in die alte Dogmengeschichte* (Berlin: Lutherisches Verlagshaus, 1957).

Fiedrowicz, Michael, *Psalmus Vox Totius Christi: Studien zu Augustins "Enarrationes in Psalmos"* (Freiburg: Herder, 1997).

Filoramo, Giovanni, *A History of Gnosticism*, trans. Anthony Alcock (Oxford: Basil Blackwell, 1990).

Fitzgerald, Allan, (ed.), *Augustine through the Ages: An Encyclopedia* (Grand Rapids, MI: Eerdmans, 1999).

Florovsky, George, "Origen, Eusebius and the Iconoclastic Controversy," *Church History* 19 (1950), 77–96.

Fortin, Ernest, *Christianisme et culture philosophique au cinquième siècle: La querelle de l'âme en Occident* (Paris: Études Augustiniennes, 1959).

Frend, W. H. C., *The Rise of the Monophysite Movement* (Cambridge: Cambridge University Press, 1972).

Galtier, Paul, *L'unité du Christ: Être . . . Personne . . . Conscience* (Paris: Beauchesne, 1939).

Galtier, Paul, "Un monument au concile de Chalcédoine—Nestorius mal compris, mal traduit," *Gregorianum* 34 (1953), 427–33.

Gavrilyuk, Paul L., *The Suffering of the Impassible God: The Dialectics of Patristic Thought* (Oxford: Oxford University Press, 2006).

Gebremedhin, Ezra, "Life-giving Blessing: An Inquiry into the Eucharistic Doctrine of Cyril of Alexandria," Ph.D. thesis, Uppsala University, 1977.

Gero, Stephan, "The True Image of Christ: Eusebius's Letter to Constantia Reconsidered" *Journal of Theological Studies* NS 32 (1981), 460–70.

Gero, Stephan, *Ascensio Isaiae: Textus*, CCSA 7 (Turnhout: Brepols, 1995).

Grabar, André, *L'Iconoclasme byzantin* (Paris: Collège de France, 1957).

Greenspahn, F. E., E. Hilgert, and B. L. Mack, *Nourished with Peace: Studies in Hellenistic Judaism in Memory of Samuel Sandmel* (Chico, CA: Scholars' Press, 1984).

Greer, Rowan A., "The Antiochene Christology of Diodore of Tarsus," *Journal of Theological Studies* NS 17 (1966), 327–41.

Greer, Rowan A., "The Man from Heaven: Paul's Last Adam and Apollinaris's Christ," in William S. Babcock (ed.), *Paul and the Legacies of Paul* (Dallas, TX: Southern Methodist University Press, 1990) 165–82.

Grillmeier, Aloys, "*Kyriakos anthropos*: Eine Studie zu einer christologischen Bezeichnung der Väterzeit," *Traditio* 33 (1979), 1–63 [= *Fragmente zur Christologie* (Freiburg: Herder, 1997), 152–214].

Grillmeier, S.J., Aloys, "Der Neu-Chalkedonismus: um die Berechtigung eines neuen Kapitels in der Dogmengeschichte," in *Festschrift B. Altaner: HJ* 77 (1957), 151–66 (= *Mit Ihm un in Ihm*, 371–85).

Grillmeier, S.J., Aloys, *Christ in Christian Tradition* (2nd edn; Oxford: Mowbrays, 1965).

Grillmeier, S.J., Aloys, and Heinrich Bacht, S.J., (eds), *Das Konzil von Chalkedon: Geschichte und Gegenwart* I (Würzburg: Echter Verlag, 1951 [1952]); II (1952); III (1954).

Hadot, Pierre, *What is Ancient Philosophy?*, trans. Michael Chase (Cambridge, MA: Harvard University Press, 2002).

Hall, S. G., *Melito of Sardis: On Pascha and Fragments* (Oxford: Oxford University Press, 1979; rev. edn, 2012).

Hanson, R. P. C., *The Search for the Christian Doctrine of God: The Arian Controversy, 318–381* (Edinburgh: T. and T. Clark, 1988).

Harl, Marguerite, *Origène et la fonction révélatrice du Verbe incarné* (Paris: Éditions du Seuil, 1958).

Helmer, Siegfried, "Der Neuchalkedonismus: Geschichte, Berechtigung und Bedeutung eines dogmengeschichtlichen Begriffes," dissertation, University of Bonn, 1962.

Hennecke, Edgar and Wilhelm Schneemelcher (eds), *New Testament Apocrypha* 2 (London: Lutterworth, 1963–5).

Herrin, Judith, *Unrivalled Influence: Women and Empire in Byzantium* (Princeton, NJ: Princeton University Press, 2013), 194–207.

Hill, Charles E., *Regnum Caelorum* (Oxford: Oxford University Press, 1992; Grand Rapids, MI: Eerdmans, 2001).

Himes, Michael J., "The Ecclesiological Significance of the Reception of Doctrine," *Heythrop Journal* 33 (1992), 146–60.

Hofer, O. P., Andrew, *Christ in the Life and Teachings of Gregory of Nazianzus* (Oxford: Oxford University Press, 2013).

Hombergen, Daniel, *The Second Origenist Controversy: A New Perspective on Cyril of Skythopolis's Monastic Biographies as Historical Sources for Sixth-Century Origenism* (Rome: Studia Anselmiana 132, 2001).

Hurtado, Larry W., *Lord Jesus Christ. Devotion to Jesus in Early Christianity* (Grand Rapids, MI: Eerdmans, 2003).

Jensen, Robin M., *Face to Face: Portraits of the Divine in Early Christianity* (Minneapolis, MN: Fortress, 2005).

Kaegi, Walter E., *Heraclius, Emperor of Byzantium* (Cambridge: Cambridge University Press, 2003).

Kantzer Komline, Han-Luen, "From Division to Delight: Augustine and the Will," Ph.D. dissertation, University of Notre Dame, 2015.

Koch, Günter, *Die Heilsverwirklichung bei Theodor von Mopsuestia*, Münchener theologische Studien 31 (Munich: Max Hueber Verlag, 1965), 141–79.

Koch, Günter, *Strukturen und Geschichte des Heils in der Theologie des Theodoret von Kyros. Eine dogmen- und theologiegeschichtliche Untersuchung*, Frankfurter theologische Studien 17 (Frankfurt: Knecht Verlag, 1974).

Kloos, Kari, *Christ, Creation, and the Vision of God: Augustine's Transformation of Early Christian Theophany Interpretation* (Leiden: Brill, 2011).

Lackner, W., "Zu Quellen und Datierung der Maximus-vita," *Analecta Bollandiana* 85 (1967), 285–316.

Lange, Christian, *Mia Energeia: Kirchenhistorische und dogmengeschichtliche Untersuchungen zur Einigungspolitik des Kaisers Heraclius und des Patriarchen Sergius von Constantinopel* (Tübingen: Mohr Siebeck, 2012).

Lattke, Michael, "Die Messias-Stellen der Oden Salomos," in Cilliers Breytenbach and Henning Paulsen (eds), *Anfänge der Christologie: Festschrift für Ferdinand Hahn* (Göttingen: Vandenhoeck & Ruprecht, 1991), 429–45.

Layton, Bentley, *The Gnostic Scriptures* (Garden City, NY: Doubleday, 1987).

Lethel, F.-M., *Théologie de l'agonie du Christ: La Liberté du Fils de Dieu et son importance sotériologique mises en lumière par saint Maxime Confesseur*, Théologie Historique 52 (Paris: Beauchesne, 1979).

Lienhard, Joseph T., "The 'Arian' Controversy: Some Categories Reconsidered," *Theological Studies* 48 (1987), 415–37.

Lienhard, Joseph T., *Contra Marcellum: Marcellus of Ancyra and Fourth-Century Theology* (Washington, DC: Catholic University of America Press, 1999).

Lightfoot, J. B., *The Apostolic Fathers: Ignatius and Polycarp* 1.31–3; 2.377–91.

Lohse, Bernhard, *Das Passahfest der Quartodecimaner* (Gütersloh: Bertelsman, 1953).

Loon, Hans Van, *The Dyophysite Christology of Cyril of Alexandria* (Leiden: Brill, 2009).

Lorenz, Rudolf, *Arius Judaizans? Untersuchungen zur dogmengeschichtlichen Einordnung des Arius?* (Göttingen: Vandenhoeck & Ruprecht, 1979).

Louth, Andrew, *Maximus the Confessor* (London: Routledge, 1996).

Louth, Andrew, *Saint John Damascene: Tradition and Originality in Byzantine Theology* (Oxford: Oxford University Press, 2002).

Luibhéid, Colm, *Eusebius of Caesaraea and the Arian Crisis* (Dublin: Irish Academic Press, 1981).

Markschies, Christoph, "Was bedeutet οὐσία? Zwei Antworten bei Origenes und Ambrosius und deren Bedeutung für Bibelerklärung und Theologie," in *Origenes und sein Erbe: Gesammelte Studien* (Berlin: De Gruyter, 2007), 173–93.

Martens, Peter W., *Origen and Scripture: The Contours of the Exegetical Life* (Oxford: Oxford University Press, 2012).

Martens, Peter W., *Adrian's Introduction to the Divine Scriptures: An Antiochene Handbook for Scriptural Interpretation* (Oxford: Oxford University Press, 2017).

McCarthy Spoerl, Kelly, "Apollinarius and the Response to Early Arian Christology," *Studia Patristica* 26 (1993), 421–7.

McCarthy Spoerl, Kelly, "Apollinarian Christology and the Anti-Marcellan Tradition," *Journal of Theological Studies* NS 43 (1994), 545–68.

McCarthy Spoerl, Kelly, "The Liturgical Argument in Apollinarius: Help and Hindrance on the Way to Orthodoxy," *Harvard Theological Review* 91 (1998), 127–52.

McGuckin, John, *St. Cyril of Alexandria: The Christological Controversy* (Leiden: Brill, 1994).

McGuckin, John, *St. Gregory of Nazianzus: an Intellectual Biography* (Crestwood, NY: St. Vladimir's, 2001).

McWilliam Dewart, Joanne, *The Theology of Grace of Theodore of Mopsuestia* (Washington, DC: Catholic University of America Press, 1971).

Malingrey, Anne-Marie, *Philosophia: Étude d'un groupe des mots dans la literature grecque, des présocratiques au IVe siècle après J-C.* (Paris: Klincksieck, 1961).

Maraval, Pierre, "Chronology of Works," in L. F. Mateo-Seco and G. Maspero, *The Brill Dictionary of Gregory of Nyssa* (Leiden: Brill, 2010), 152–69.

May, G., "Die Chronologie des Lebens und der Werke des Gregor von Nyssa," in M. Harl (ed.), *Écriture et culture philosophique dans la pensée de Grégoire de Nysse* (Leiden: Brill, 1971) 51–66.

Mead, G. R. S., *Pistis Sophia: A Gnostic Miscellany* (London: Watkins, 1921).

Meconi, David V., "St. Augustine's Early Theory of Participation," *Augustinian Studies* 27 (1996), 81–98.

Meconi, David V., *The One Christ: St. Augustine's Theology of Deification* (Washington, DC: Catholic University of America Press, 2013).

Moeller, Charles, "Le chalcédonisme et le néo-chalcédonisme en orient de 451 à la fin du Vie Siècle," in Grillmeier, S.J., Aloys, and Heinrich Bacht, S.J., (eds), *Das Konzil von Chalkedon: Geschichte und Gegenwart* I (Würzburg: Echter Verlag, 1951), 637–720.

Murphy, Francesca (ed.), *The Oxford Handbook of Christology* (Oxford: Oxford University Press, 2015).

Murray, Charles, "Art and the Early Church," *Journal of Theological Studies* NS 28 (1977), 303–45.

Noble, Thomas F. X., *Images, Iconoclasm, and the Carolingians* (Philadelphia, PA: University of Pennsylvania Press, 2009).

Norelli, Enrico, *Ascensio Isaiae: Commentarius*, CCSA 8 (Turnhout: Brepols, 1995).

O'Connell, S.J., Patrick J., *The Ecclesiology of St. Nicephorus I*, Orientalia Christiana Analecta 194 (Rome: Pontificio Istituto Orientale, 1972), 54–66.

O'Keefe, John J., "Impassible Suffering? Divine Passion and Fifth-century Christology," *Theological Studies* 58 (1997), 39–60.

Opitz, H. G., *Athanasius' Werke* 3/1 (Berlin: De Gruyter, 1934), 14–15 [=Urkunde 7].

Pelikan, Jaroslav, *Imago Dei: The Byzantine Apologia for Icons* (Princeton, NJ: Princeton University Press, 1990).

Prado, José Julián, *Voluntad y Naturaleza: La antropología filosófica de Máximo el Confessor* (Rio Cuarto, Argentina: Ediciones de la Universidad Nacional de Rio Cuarto, 1974).

Prestige, G. L., *St. Basil the Great and Apollinarius of Laodicaea*, ed. Henry Chadwick (London: SPCK, 1956).

Richard, Marcel, "Notes sur les florilèges dogmatiques du Ve et du VIe siècle," *Actes du VIe Congrès international d'Etudes byzantines* I (Paris, 1950), 307–18.

Richardson, Cyril C., "The Quartodecimans and the Synoptic Chronology," *Harvard Theological Review* 33 (1940), 177–90.

Richardson, Cyril R. (ed.), *Early Christian Fathers*, Library of Christian Classics (Philadelphia, PA: Westminster, 1953).

Ricken, Friedo, "Der Logoslehre des Eusebios von Caesaraea und der Mittelplatonismus," *Theologie und Philosophie* 42 (1967), 341–58.

Ricken, Friedo, "Nikaia als Krisis des altchristlichen Platonismus," *Theologie und Philosophie* 44 (1969), 321–41.

Ricken, Friedo, "Zur Rezeption der platonischen Ontologie bei Eusebios von Kaisareia, Areios und Athanasios," *Theologie und Philosophie* 53 (1973), 321–52.

Riedinger, Richard, *Kleine Schriften zu den Konzilsakten des 7. Jahrhunderts* (Turnhout: Brepols, 1998).

Ritter, Adolf Martin (ed.), *Kerygma und Logos*, Festschrift for Carl Andresen (Göttingen: Vandenhoeck & Ruprecht, 1979).

Robertson, Jon M., *Christ as Mediator: A Study of the Theologies of Eusebius of Caesarea, Marcellus of Ancyra and Athanasius of Alexandria* (Oxford: Oxford University Press 2007), 163–4.

Roldanus, Johannes, *Le christ et l'homme dans la théologie d'Athanase d'Alexandrie: Etude de la conjonction de sa conception de l'homme avec sa christologie* (Leiden: Brill, 1968).

Roldanus, Johannes, "Die Vita Antonii als Spiegel der Theologie des Athanasius und ihr Weiterwerken bis ins 5. Jahrhundert," *Theologie und Philosophie* 58 (1983), 194–216.

Rowe, J. Nigel, *Origen's Doctrine of Subordination* (Bern: Peter Lang, 1987).

Rudolph, Kurt, *Gnosis: the Nature and History of Gnosticism*, trans. Robert McLaren Wilson (San Francisco, CA: Harper and Row, 1983).

Sahas, Daniel J., *Icon and Logos: Sources in Eighth-Century Iconoclasm* (Toronto: University of Toronto Press, 1986).

Schäferdieck, Klaus, "Zur Verfasserfrage und Situation der Epistula ad Constantiam de Imagine Christi," *Zeitschrift für Kirchengeschichte* 91 (1980), 177–86.

Schäublin, Christoph, *Untersuchungen zu Methode und Herkunft der Antiochenischen Exegese* (Cologne: Hanstein, 1974).

Schönborn, Christoph, *Sophrone de Jérusalem: Vie monastique et confession dogmatique* (Paris: Beauchesne, 1972).

Schönborn, Christoph, *God's Human Face: The Christ-Icon* (San Francisco, CA: Ignatius, 1994), 102–33.

Schmidt, Carl, *Koptisch-Gnostische Schriften* (Leipzig: Hinrichs, 1905).

Scipioni, Luigi, *Ricerche sulla* cristologia *del "Libro di Eraclide" di Nestorio: la formulazione teologica e il suo contesto filosofico*, Paradosis 11 (Fribourg: Edizioni Universitarie, 1956.

Seibt, Klaus, *Die Theologie des Markell von Ankyra* (Berlin: De Gruyter, 1994).

Sherwood, Polycarp, *An Annotated Date-List of the Works of Maximus the Confessor*, Studia Anselmiana 30 (Rome, 1952).

Sherwood, Polycarp, *The Earlier Ambigua of St. Maximus the Confessor*, Studia Anselmiana 36 (Rome, 1955).

Sieben, Hermann-Josef, "Das zweite Nizänum und die Probleme der Rezeption," *Konziliengeschichte I: Die Konzilsidee der alten Kirche* (Paderborn: Schöningh, 1978), 306–43.

Smith, J. Warren, "'Suffering Impassibly': Christ's Passion and Divine Impassibility in Cyril of Alexandria," *Pro Ecclesia* 11 (2002), 463–83.

Stang, Charles M., "Dionysius, Paul, and the Significance of the Pseudonym," in Sarah Coakley and Charles M. Stang (eds), *Re-thinking Dionysius the Areopagite* (Oxford: Wiley-Blackwell, 2009), 11–26.

Stang, Charles M., *Apophasis and Personality in Dionysius the Areopagite: "No Longer I"* (New York: Oxford University Press, 2012).

Stewart Sykes, Alistair, *The Lamb's High Feast: Melito, Peri Pascha, and the Quartodeciman Paschal Liturgy at Sardis* (Leiden: Brill, 1998).

Studer, Basil, *Trinity and Incarnation: The Faith of the Early Church* (Edinburgh: T. and T. Clark, 1993).

Strutwolf, Holger, *Gnosis als System: Zur Rezeption der Valentinianischen Gnosis* (Göttingen: Vandenhoeck & Ruprecht, 1993).

Strutwolf, Holger, *Die Trinitätstheologie und Christologie des Euseb von Caesaraea* (Göttingen: Vandenhoeck & Ruprecht, 1999).

Testuz, M., *Papyrus Bodmer X–XII* (Cologny-Genève: Bibliothèque Bodmer, 1959).

Testuz, Michel, *Papyrus Bodmer XIII: Méliton de Sardes, Homélie sur la Pâque* (Geneva: Biblioteca Bodmeriana, 1960).

Trevett, Christine, *A Study of Ignatius of Antioch in Syria and Asia* (Lewiston, NY: Edwin Mellen Press, 1992).

Vasiliev, A. A., "The Iconoclastic Edict of the Caliph Yazid II, A.D. 721," *Dumbarton Oaks Papers* 9/10 (1956), 23–47.

Vinzent, Markus, *Markell von Ankyra: Die Fragmente* (Leiden: Brill, 1997).

Vries, Wilhelm de, "Das eschatologische Heil bei Theodor von Mopsuestia," *Orientalia Christiana Periodica* 24 (1958), 309–38.

Weitzmann, Kurt, *The Icon: Holy Images, Sixth to Fourteenth Century* (New York: Braziller, 1978).

Weitzmann, Kurt, (ed.), *The Age of Spirituality: A Symposium* (Princeton, NJ: Princeton University Press, 1980), 141–63.

Wesche, Kenneth Paul, *On the Person of Christ: The Christology of Emperor Justinian* (Crestwood, NY: St. Vladimir's, 1991), 52–5.

Wessel, Susan, *Cyril of Alexandria and the Nestorian Controversy: The Making of a Saint and a Heretic* (Oxford: Oxford University Press, 2004).

Williams, Michael Allen, *Rethinking "Gnosticism": An Argument for Dismantling a Dubious Category* (Princeton, NJ: Princeton University Press, 1996).

Williams, Rowan, *Arius: Heresy and Tradition* (2nd edn; Grand Rapids, MI: Eerdmans, 2002).

Young, Frances M., *Biblical Exegesis and the Formation of Christian Culture* (Cambridge: Cambridge University Press, 1997).

# Index

Alexander of Alexandria 98
Alexandria, "school" of 175-9
  contemplative emphasis 176
  grace as divinization 197
  presence of God 198
  salvation realized in present 177
Antioch, "school" of 174-9, 195-6
  human agency stressed 197
  otherness of God 198
  philosophical basis 178-9
  salvation eschatological 177-8, 197
  Scripture, interpretation of 196
"Aphthartist" conception of Christ's
  humanity 205
*Apocryphon of John* 95
Apollinarius of Laodicaea 126-33
  career and influence 128, 130
  Christ as "lordly human" 131
  flesh of Christ from heaven, eternal 132-3,
    145-6
  intellectual soul of Christ 127, 131
  literary gifts 129
  *Logos—sarx* model of Christ 127-8
  "new Adam" Christology 130
  Nicene orthodoxy 129
  sensitive soul of Christ 132
  Son as "heavenly man" 130
  Word and body have one essence, one
    operation 131
Arius of Alexandria 97-100
  Son of God as created mediator 98-100
  Son of God as limited 99
*Ascension of Isaiah* 43-9
  Christ as "the Beloved" 45-6
  Church, seen as corrupt 46
  Christ, story of 47
  Christology docetic? 44, 48-9
  cosmic setting 46, 48
  persons of Trinity 48
Asterius the "Sophist" 105
Athanasius of Alexandria 115-25
  "active faith," effect of 120
  *Against the Pagans* and *On the*
    *Incarnation* 116-17
  body as instrument of mind, Logos 121-2
  emphasis on cross of Christ 117
  Incarnation of Word 118
  influences on his thought 115
  *Life of Antony* 119

  pattern of his thought 116
  psychology of human Jesus not
    emphasized 124
  rationality as "second gift" 117-18
  soul of Christ 121
  salvation of humanity 117
Augustine of Hippo 150-79
  Arian propaganda, response to 155
  balance of divine and human
    emphasized 152
  Christ, central to Augustine's thought 150
  Christ as mediator 159-61, 163
  Christ reveals grace 169-71
  Christ reveals humility of God 159, 168-9
  humility as key to knowledge of Christ 168,
    171, 173
  Incarnation as mission of Son 161-2
  Incarnation as revelation of God 162
  knowledge of Christ in history by faith
    167, 173
  language of "substance" and "person" 154
  Leporius, case of 156
  mind of Christ as contact between God and
    humanity 153
  philosophical mediation 163
  reunification of divided humanity in
    Christ 163
  rhetorical approach to speaking of
    Christ 151, 172
  salvation as exchange of roles 164, 168
  salvation as deification 165
  union of unequal elements in Christ 157-8
  wisdom as participative contemplation 166

Bacht, Heinrich, SJ 1-2
Basil I, Emperor 262

Chalcedon, Council of (451) vii, 12-15
  definition of faith viii, 12-15, 200, 267
  historical setting 10-12
  hypostasis of Christ not identified
    further 201
  implications for salvation 203
  importance 22-3, 267
  reception 16-19, 201
Chalke gate, Constantinople 240
Christology, developing emphases 25-6
  implications for theology 273-8
  Incarnate Word like us in humanity 127

Christology, developing emphases (*cont.*)
    mediation 94–6
    paradoxical 266
    second-century 28–30
    self-manifestation of Word 66
Constantine V, Emperor 243–9
    Christological argument against images of
        Christ 244–5
    Eucharist as only permissible image of
        Christ 245
    *Peuseis* (= *Inquiries*) 244–5
Constantine VI, Emperor 249
Constantine of Nacoleia, bishop 241
Constantinople I, creed 12
Constantinople II, Council of (553) 19–20
Constantinople III, Council of (680–1) 20–1
Councils, Seven "Ecumenical" x, 268–73
Cross, early Christian interpretations of 29
Cross, Frank Leslie 1–2, 27
Cyril of Alexandria 11, 190–5
    "communication of properties" 192
    distinction of natures "in theory" 193
    emphasizes continuity of Scriptural
        narrative 190
    Eucharist as "God's flesh" 192–3
    human nature of Christ complete 191
    human nature of Christ belongs to
        Word 191–2
    normative role of his writings 13–14
    suffering of God the Son 193–5
    union of hypostasis in Christ 192
    union of natures in Christ 192
Cyrus of Phasis 217

Diodore of Tarsus 179–80
Dionysius the Areopagite 216–17, 239
    mediation 239
    "new theandric operation" in Christ
        216, 229
Dioscorus of Alexandria 11–12

Ephesus, Synod (449) 11–12
Epiphanius of Salamis, attitude to images 237
Eusebius of Caesaraea 102, 106–15
    accepts Nicene definition 102, 107
    emphasizes divine transcendence 107–8
    generation of Word as image,
        mediator 108–10, 114
    Incarnation of Word heals creation 112–13
    originally sympathetic to Arius 106
    Son and Spirit God by participation 111, 112
    Son as preserver of creation 112
    Son rules other creatures 111
Eusebius of Caesaraea (?), *Letter to
    Constantia* 113–14, 236
Eusebius of Dorylaeum 11

Eusebius of Nicomedia 98–9
Eutyches 11

Germanus, Patriarch of Constantinople:
    defends veneration of images 241
Gnostic Christianity 67–9
Gregory of Cyprus, defense of images 246
Gregory of Nazianzus 133–7
    communion between God and
        humanity 137
    *First Letter to Cledonius* 134
    "mixture" of God and human in
        Christ 135–7
    non-technical language about
        Incarnation 134, 136
    personal engagement with doctrine 136
    rhetorical style 135
    titles of Christ 137
Gregory of Nyssa 138–47
    baptism 143
    Eucharist 144
    full human being taken up, transformed by
        God 139, 142
    God as absolute virtue 140, 145
    God as ineffable 146–7
    Incarnation as revelation of God 138, 143
    "mixture" language 138
    perfection as growth 140, 145
    salvation of humans 143–5
    substance as formed of qualities 140
    transformation of human being by the
        Word 139–42
    universalism 145
Grillmeier, Aloys, SJ vii, 1–3, 5–8
    interpretation of Chalcedonian
        Christology 6–9

Hagia Sophia, Council of (815) 262
Heraclius, Emperor 20
Hiereia, Council of (754) 247–8
Honorius, Pope 217
Hypatius of Ephesus, on images 239

iconoclasm, archaeological evidence 233
iconoclastic controversy in the East: political
    influences 246
    possible cultural and religious
        causes 263–4
    struggle between bureaucrats and
        clergy 240
    theological issues 264–5
iconoclastic controversy in the West 232
Ignatius of Antioch 37–43
    Christ as revealer 40–1
    death of Christ 41–2
    setting of letters 38–9

Ignatius, Patriarch 261–2
images, defense: analogous to Scripture 237
images, early Christian Apologists 234
images, sacred, in fifth and sixth centuries;
    reported miracles; reported abuses 238f.
images in early Christian burial sites 234
images in early Islam 234
images in Jewish tradition 233
images, official opposition 240
images, reinstatement by *oikonomia*
    (843) 261
Irenaeus of Lyons 66–83
    Christology 79
    final form of human person 82
    glory of God 73, 76
    growth, change as positive processes 77–8
    Holy Spirit descends on Jesus,
        Church 73–4
    Holy Spirit constitutive of human
        person 80
    life 69
    millenarian hope 81–2
    revelation of God by Word 74, 75–6
    salvation as restored relationship with
        God 72
    theologian of unities 69–70
    vision of God 76, 78
Irene, Empress and regent 249–50

Jewish character of early Christology 28–9
John of Damascus 223–30, 241–3
    Christ as source of Wisdom 225
    Christology 226–30
    defense of images 241–3
    definitions of "image" 242
    different kinds of veneration 242
    hypostasis as "manner of existence" 228
    philosophy, use of 223, 226
    *Spring of Knowledge* 223
    tradition, use of 223
    works 223
John "the Grammarian" (= Patriarch John
    VII) 252–3, 261
Justin 55–62
    Christ as Logos 59
    Christ as revealer of God 62
    classical philosopher 55–7
    Hebrew Bible, understanding 57–8, 60
Justinian I, Emperor 18–20

Lateran synod (649) 20
Leo I, Pope 12, 14
Leo III, Emperor 240
Leo IV, Emperor 249
Leo V, Emperor 251–2, 257
Leontius of Byzantium vii, 203–11

Chalcedonian terminology 208
    Christology 206–8, 210
    "characteristics" of a being 206, 209
    life and works 203–5
    philosophy, use of 207
    relationship, category of 207
    terminology 204, 206
    union of natures in Christ 209–11

Manichaeism 116
Marcellus of Ancyra 104–6
Marcian, Emperor 12
Maximus the Confessor 211–23
    Gethsemane a key scene in Gospels 222
    "gnomic will" 220
    hypostasis, conception of 213, 215
    Letter 15, to Cosmas 215
    life 211–12
    "manner" of Christ's human
        existence 214–15
    "natural will" 220, 222
    "one composite hypostasis" in Christ 213
    operations of Christ 216, 218
    transfiguration of Jesus 216
    union of natures in Christ 214
    wills of Christ 216, 219–22
Meletius of Antioch 129
Melito of Sardis 49–55
    death of Christ, value 53–4
    fall of humanity 53
    passion of Christ foreordained 51
    setting of *On Pascha* 49–51
    typological interpretation of Pasch 52–5
Methodius, Patriarch 261
Michael I Rangabe, Emperor 251, 257
Michael II, Emperor 257
Michael III, Emperor 261
Monenergist controversy 20
Monothelite controversy 20

"Neo-Chalcedonian" Christology 19
Nestorius of Constantinople 185–8
    affirms Nicene theology 185
    "assumed man" Christology 186
    *Book of Heracleides* 186–8
    humanity of Christ sinless 186
    "prosopic" union of Word and human
        being 187–8
    Word assumes human form and role 186,
        187–8
Nicaea I, Council of (325) 100–4
    creed 12
    "hypostasis" language 103
    "substance" language 102–3
Nicaea II, Council of 21–2, 249–51
    Christology 250

Nicephorus I, Emperor 251
Nicephorus, Patriarch 251, 253–5
　circumscription of creatures 253–4
　image, relation to original 254
　relationship, logical category 254
　representation of Son's humanity 255
Numenius of Apamaea 95

*Odes of Solomon* 30–7
　death of Christ 34–6
　historical setting 31
　understanding of Christ 31–4
Origen of Alexandria 83–93
　biblical scholarship 83
　Christ as "himself the Kingdom" 87
　Christ in Scriptures 86, 92–3
　Christ one with Church 90
　devotion to Jesus 91
　growth towards knowledge of God 89
　origin and fall of souls 87
　person of Christ a paradox 91–2
　revelation by Word 88
　"rule of piety" 84
　Son of God: multiple in being 85

Photius, Patriarch 261–2
Pius XII, Pope 2
Platon, uncle of Theodore of Stoudios 256
post-Chalcedonian theology, academic style
　of 202
Pyrrhus of Constantinople, Patriarch 221

Rahner, Karl 4
reception of conciliar decisions 271
*ressourcement* 3–4
Richard, Marcel vii

Sakkoudion monastery 256
"second" iconoclastic period (815–43) 252–3

Sergius, Patriarch of Constantinople 217–18
Severus of Antioch 204
Sophronius, Patriarch of Jerusalem 217
Stephen the Younger, monk 246
Stoudios monastery 256
Synod (Council) of 869, Constantinople 262
　links icons with Scripture 262

Tarasius, Patriarch 249
Theodora, Empress and Regent 261
Theodore of Mopsuestia 181–5
　"assumed man" Christology 182
　*Catecheses* 181–4
　Christology of "indwelling" 181
　death of Jesus does not affect Word 184
　divine favor singles Jesus out 181
　Word uniquely guides Jesus 183–4
Theodore of Pharan 216–17
Theodore of Stoudios 255–60
　Christology 258–9
　contemplation aided by images 260
　defense of images 257–60
　early life 256
　labelling of figures in icons 259
　literary activity 256
Theodoret of Cyrus 189–90
　distinctions between man Jesus and
　　Word 189
　"prosopic" union 189
Theodosius II, Emperor 12
Theodotus Cassiteras, Patriarch 252
Theophilus, Emperor 253

"What has not been assumed, has not been
　healed" 127

Yazid II, Caliph, and images 240

Zeno, Emperor 17–18